The Adobe® Illustrator® CS3

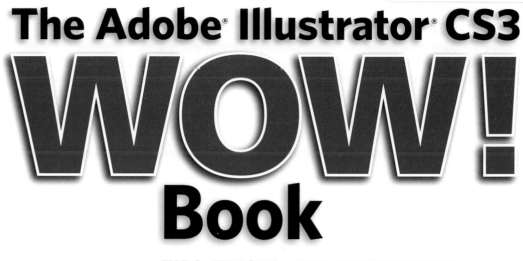

WOW!

Book

TIPS, TRICKS, AND TECHNIQUES
FROM 100 TOP ILLUSTRATOR ARTISTS

SHARON STEUER

Peachpit
Press

The Adobe Illustrator CS3 Wow! Book

Sharon Steuer

Peachpit Press

1249 Eighth Street

Berkeley, CA 94710

510/524-2178, 510/524-2221 (fax)

Find us on the Web at: www.peachpit.com

To report errors, please send a note to errata@peachpit.com

Peachpit Press is a division of Pearson Education

Real World Adobe Illustrator CS3 excerpted content is ©2008 Mordy Golding

Used with permission of Pearson Education, Inc. and Peachpit Press.

Contributing Writers & Consultants to this Edition:
Cristen Gillespie, Randy Livingston, Dave Awl, Andrew Dashwood, Lisa Jackmore, Steven H. Gordon, Conrad Chavez, Mordy Golding

Technical Editor: *Jean-Claude Tremblay*
Line Editor: *Elizabeth Rogalin*
Cover Designer: *Mimi Heft*
Cover Illustrator: *Christiane Beauregard*
Indexer: *Rebecca Plunkett*
First edition *Illustrator Wow! Book* designer: *Barbara Sudick*
***Wow!* Series Editor:** *Linnea Dayton*

ISBN 13: 978-0-321-51842-2

ISBN 10: 0-321-51842-X

9 8 7 6 5 4 3 2

Printed and bound in the United States of America.

The Adobe® Illustrator® CS3

WOW!

Book

The Adobe Illustrator CS3 Wow! Book
Team of Contributing Writers and Editors

Sharon Steuer is the originator of *The Illustrator Wow! Book,* and author of *Creative Thinking in Photoshop: A New Approach to Digital Art.* Sharon has been involved with the digital art world since 1983, teaching, exhibiting, and writing. In between *Wow!* books, Sharon is a full-time artist working in traditional and digital media (www.ssteuer. com). She lives with her cats, Puma and Bear, and her professor husband, Jeff Jacoby (jeffjacoby.net), who teaches audio and radio at San Francisco State University. As always, she is extremely grateful to her co-authors, editors, testers, *Wow!* team members (past and present), Peachpit, Adobe and of course the *Wow!* artists for making this book possible.

Cristen Gillespie has contributed to other *Wow!* books, and is the co-author of the recent *Photoshop CS/CS2 Wow! Book.* She has also co-authored articles for *Photoshop User* magazine. Unhindered by her dialup modem connection (rural Southern California, along with the majority of the world's population, does not have access to broadband), Cristen is a wonderful writer and a fabulous collaborator, and we hope that she'll stay with *Illustrator Wow!* for many years to come.

Randy Livingston has been a contributor to *Illustrator Wow!* books since the mid-1990s. For this edition, he was a wordsmith of several chapter introductions (among other things). Randy is Assistant Professor of Media Design at Middle Tennessee State University. When he's not teaching and writing, he's racing motocross. Nurses and doctors know him well at many hospitals near the various racetracks where he competes.

Dave Awl is a Chicago-based writer and editor. Returning to the *Wow!* team, he revised many of the chapter introductions. Dave is also a poet, performer, and alumnus of Chicago's Neo-Futurists theater company. His work is collected in the book *What the Sea Means: Poems, Stories & Mono-logues 1987–2002.* You can find out more about his various projects at his website: Ocelot Factory (www.ocelotfactory.com).

Andrew Dashwood (www.adashwood.com) is a Swiss illustrator and first-time contributing writer with this edition of the *Wow!* book. Andrew has been working with Illustrator and Adobe's other products throughout Europe since the release of the original *Illustrator Wow!* book over a decade ago. He is currently working in Amsterdam providing technical support and training for Adobe Illustrator. He thanks his brother and dad for their lifetimes of help and support.

Lisa Jackmore has returned as a contributing writer for Galleries, as well as the *Illustrator Wow! Course Outline*. She is a wonderful artist both on and off the computer, creating miniatures to murals. Lisa continues to share her talent as a writer and a digital fine artist, evident throughout this book. She would like to thank the sources of distraction—her family and friends—as they are so often the inspiration for her artwork.

Conrad Chavez has had a long and fruitful relationship with the Pen tool that began during his days as the support lead for Aldus (later Macromedia) FreeHand 1.0–4.0, continuing in the 1990s when he was a technical writer for print, Web, and video products at Adobe Systems Inc. Now a Seattle-based writer, editor, and trainer, Conrad also works the bitmap side as a fine-art photographer (www.conradchavez.com), and is co-author of *Real World Adobe Photoshop CS3*.

Steven H. Gordon is a returning co-author for Step-by-Steps and Galleries. Steven has been an ace member of the team since the *Illustrator 9 Wow! Book*. He has too many boys to stay sane. If only they wouldn't fall off cliffs in Bryce—the National Park, not the software. Steven runs Cartagram (www.cartagram.com), a custom mapmaking company located in Madison, Alabama. He thanks Monette and his mom for their encouragement, and the boys for their cessation of hostilities.

Jean-Claude Tremblay has nearly 20 years of experience using Illustrator. He works full-time at Quadriscan Inc. (a printing company in Montreal) as senior prepress technician and "Illustrator guru." After serving as a magnificent *Wow!* Tester, Jean-Claude returns as the *Wow!* technical editor, chief advisor, software collector, and resident magician—our rescuer of corrupt files. He lives in Candiac, Quebec, with his wife Suzanne and his wonderful four-year-old daughter Judith.

Mordy Golding has been a contributor to the *Illustrator Wow! Books* from the beginning, and was the primary co-author on the second edition of the *Wow!* book. Since then, Mordy has been busy writing his own books and working for a while as product manager for Adobe Illustrator. Mordy is author of *Real World Adobe Illustrator CS3*. In addition to continuing as a *Wow!* technical consultant, he's author of the popular *Real World Illustrator* Blog (http://rwillustrator.blogspot.com).

Additional contributing writers and editors: **Elizabeth Rogalin** edited *The Illustrator 7 Wow!* book, and she now returns to this edition as line editor. She is a writer and freelance editor living in New Jersey with her two sons. **Laurie Grace** is an artist, illustrator and university professor who teaches Illustrator, as well as all things digital. Laurie is one of the original artists featured in the book, and returns periodically to help us update screenshots. **Peg Maskell Korn** is a woman of many hats, functioning as Sharon's savior in the last hours of the first edition, and the master proofer of the visuals and writing in the book. Please see the Acknowledgments for a thorough listing of the *Wow!* team contributors.

Contents

Important: Read me first!

Where's the AICS3 User Guide?

Once upon a time, buying software meant getting a big, thick, printed user guide. Now all that content (and more) is available via Help > Illustrator Help. From here you can search for topics and key words, or link to Adobe's online help—which is where you can find the most up-to-date information. If you prefer a traditional book format, you can find the User Guide in PDF form (the PDF is named Help) along with other reference materials that came with your copy of AICS3. (In the Design Suite, the "References" folder is on the "Resources and extras" DVD). You can purchase a printed copy of the guide from adobe.com.

Plug-ins & software on the CD

Wow! tech editor Jean-Claude Tremblay and *Design Tools Monthly*'s Jay Nelson teamed up to collect and summarize for you their favorite Illustrator-related plug-ins and software on the *Wow! CD*. Find this listing, along with bonus Illustrator tips compiled from *Design Tools Monthly* by Jay Nelson, in a *Wow! Appendix*. Find this appendix in PDF (with clickable links to the products' websites) on the *Wow! CD*, along with back issues of *Design Tools Monthly*.

Back in 1994 when I embarked on the creation of the original *Illustrator Wow! Book* (with no version number!), Adobe Illustrator was still a fairly simple program. Even though the first edition was only 224 pages, it was packed with almost every detail found in the longer "bible" type books at the time.

First, I want readers to know that this ninth edition of *The Illustrator Wow! Book* is no longer a solo project. In order to provide you with the most thoroughly updated information as possible, in a timely manner (as close as possible to the shipping of the new version of the program), this book now requires a large team of experts working simultaneously. Our technical editor, Jean-Claude Tremblay, and I are involved with every page of the book, all along the way. Writers work on sections based on their expertise in Illustrator, and then the rest of the writers (and our stellar team of *Wow!* testers) test and critique that section. This book is the result of this amazing group of experts scattered around the globe, coming together by email, iChat, and PDF to deliver the best book possible to you, the reader. I'm immensely proud of and grateful to everyone who works with me on this project.

With the skyrocketing price of printing in full-color, we can no longer increase the page count without considerably raising the price of the book. As a result of keeping the book to the current page count, we realized that we can no longer address all aspects of Illustrator. Instead, *The Adobe Illustrator CS3 Wow! Book* should be thought of as a reference by and for artists that focuses on creating art and design with Adobe Illustrator. We'll leave the most technical aspects of the program to more comprehensive books, such as *Real World Adobe Illustrator CS3*, by Mordy Golding. Mordy continues to consult on this book (he advised us a lot with Live Color!), and both of us feel strongly that our books should be considered companion books, as there is very little overlap in content.

In order to provide you with lots of new work in this fully updated, reworked, and expanded edition of *Illustrator Wow!*, we have replaced many wonderful artworks that have been in this book for a number of editions. In their place are new gorgeous examples of art generously shared by *Illustrator Wow!* artists worldwide, as well as many new essential production techniques and timesaving tips. In addition to the wonderful contributing artists and contributing writers, our amazing team of *Wow! testers* sets this book apart from all others. This team thoroughly tests every lesson and gallery to make sure everything actually works. We deliberately keep all lessons short to allow you to squeeze in a lesson or two between clients, and to encourage the use of this book within the confines of supervised classrooms.

In order to keep the content in this book relevant to everyone, I've assumed the reader has a reasonable level of competence with basic Mac and Windows concepts, such as opening and saving files, launching applications, copying objects to the Clipboard, and performing mouse operations. I've also assumed that you understand the basic functionality of most of the tools.

Unfortunately, you can't learn Adobe Illustrator simply by flipping through the pages of this book; there really is no substitute for practice. The good news is that the more you work with Illustrator, the more techniques you'll be able to integrate into your creative process.

Use this book as a reference, a guide for specific techniques, or simply as a source of inspiration. After you've read this book, I encourage you to read it again—you'll undoubtedly learn something you missed the first time. The more experienced you become with Adobe Illustrator, the easier it will be to assimilate all the new information and inspiration you'll find in this book. Happy Illustrating!

Sharon Steuer

Where's Live Color?

There are two lessons using basic features of Live Color in the *Drawing & Coloring* chapter. Find the other more advanced Live Color lessons in the *Live Color* chapter.

Additional Illustrator training

You'll find additional lessons in the "Ch02-zen_lessons" folder on the *Wow! CD*. Included in that folder are the *Zen Lessons* (which supplement *The Zen of Illustrator* chapter). These lessons walk you through some basics of working with the Pen tool, Bézier curves, layers, and stacking order. And also starting in this edition, you'll find the "Zen of the Pen" commercial edition (by Sharon Steuer and Pattie Belle Hastings) in the Ch02-zen_lessons folder; these lessons include QuickTime movies to help you learn to work with the Pen tool and Bézier curves in Illustrator, Photoshop and InDesign. If you're new to Illustrator, you may even want to begin by taking a class. If you're teaching a class in Illustrator, download the *Illustrator CS3 Wow! Course Outline* from: www.ssteuer.com/edu (by Sharon Steuer and Lisa Jackmore). Finally, don't miss the terrific Illustrator training videos on Adobe's website: http://www.adobe.com/designcenter/video_workshop/: scroll to click on AI from the application list, and choose a topic!

How to use this book...

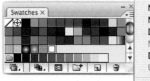

With the All Swatches icon selected, choose "Sort by Name" then "List View" from the pop-up menu

The Swatches panel viewed with "Sort by Name" and "List View" selected

Before you do anything else, read the *Wow! Glossary* on the pull-out quick reference card at the back of the book. The Glossary provides definitions for the terms used throughout *The Illustrator CS3 Wow! Book* (for example, ⌘ is the Command, or Apple, key for Mac).

WELCOME TO *WOW!* FOR WINDOWS AND MAC
If you already use Adobe Photoshop or InDesign you'll see many interface similarities to Illustrator CS3. The similarities should make the time you spend learning each program much shorter. Your productivity should also increase across the board once you adjust to the new shortcuts and methodologies (see "Shortcuts and keystrokes" following, and the *Illustrator Basics* chapter).

Shortcuts and keystrokes
Because you can now customize keyboard shortcuts, we're restricting the keystrokes references in the book to those instances when it's so standard that we assume you'll keep the default, or when there is no other way to achieve that function (such as Lock All Unselected Objects). We'll always give you Macintosh shortcuts first, then the Windows equivalent (⌘-Z/Ctrl-Z). For help with customization of keyboard shortcuts, and tool and menu navigation (such as single key tool access and Tab to hide panels), see the *Illustrator Basics* chapter.

Setting up your panels (previously called palettes!)
In terms of following along with the lessons in this book, you'll probably want to enable the "Type Object Selection by Path Only" option (see Tip "Selecting type by accident" in the *Type* chapter). Next, if you want your panels to look like our panels, you'll need to sort swatches by name. Choose "Sort by Name" and "List View" from the Swatches pop-up menu. (Hold Option/Alt when you choose a view to set this as the default for all swatches.)

Illustrator CS3 sets an application default that could inhibit the way Illustrator experts work. In order for your currently selected object to set all the styling attributes for the next object you draw (including brush strokes, live effects, transparency, etc.), you must open the Appearance panel (Window menu) and disable New Art Has Basic Appearance. You can disable (and re-enable) this default by either: 1) clicking on the bottom-left icon in the Appearance panel (dark shows that it's enabled; see Tip at right), or 2) choosing New Art Has Basic Appearance from the Appearance panel pop-up menu (✓ shows it's enabled). Your new setting sticks even after you've quit.

HOW THIS BOOK IS ORGANIZED...

You'll find six kinds of information woven throughout this book—all of it up to date for Illustrator CS3: **Basics, Tips, Exercises, Techniques, Galleries,** and **References.** The book progresses in difficulty from chapter to chapter.

1 Basics. *Illustrator Basics* and *The Zen of Illustrator* qualify as full-blown chapters on basics and are packed with information that distills and supplements your Adobe Illustrator manual and disk. Every chapter starts with a general overview of the basics. These sections are designed so advanced Illustrator users can move quickly through them, but I strongly suggest that novices and intermediate users read them very carefully.

2 Tips. When you see this icon (⊙), you'll find related artwork on the *Adobe Illustrator CS3 Wow! CD* (referred to hereafter as the *Wow! CD*) within that chapter's folder. Look to the information in the gray and red boxes for hands-on Tips that can help you work more efficiently. Usually you can find tips alongside related text, but if you're in an impatient mood, you might just want to flip through, looking for interesting or relevant tips. The red arrows ——▶, red outlines and **red text** found in tips (and sometimes with artwork) have been added to emphasize or further explain a concept or technique.

1

1

Illustrator Basics

2 (⊙) The CD icon indicates that related artwork is on the *Adobe Illustrator CS3 Wow! CD*

Tip boxes

Look for these gray boxes to find Tips about Adobe Illustrator.

Red Tip boxes

Red Tip boxes contain warnings or other essential information.

3

A Finger Dance

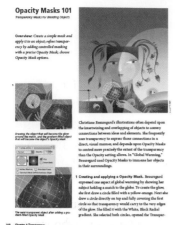

4

5

6

3 Exercises. (Not for the faint of heart.) We have included step-by-step exercises to help you make the transition to Illustrator technician extraordinaire. *The Zen of Illustrator* chapter and the *Zen Lessons* on the *Wow! CD* are dedicated to helping you master the mechanics (and the soul) of Illustrator. Take these lessons in small doses, in order, and at a relaxed pace. All of the Finger Dances are customized for Mac and Windows.

4 Techniques. In these sections, you'll find step-by-step techniques gathered from almost one hundred *Illustrator Wow!* artists. Most *Wow!* techniques focus on one aspect of how an image was created, though we'll often refer you to different *Wow!* chapters (or to a specific step-by-step technique, Tip, or Gallery where a technique is introduced) to give you the opportunity to explore a briefly-covered feature more thoroughly. Feel free to start with almost any chapter, but each technique builds on those previously explained, so you should try to follow the techniques within each chapter sequentially. Some chapters include **Advanced Technique** lessons, which assume that you have assimilated all of the techniques found throughout the chapter. *Advanced Techniques* is an entire chapter dedicated to advanced tips, tricks, and techniques.

5 Galleries. The Gallery pages consist of images related to techniques demonstrated nearby. Each Gallery piece is accompanied by a description of how the artist created that image, and may include steps showing the progression of a technique detailed elsewhere. *Illustrator & Other Programs* consists almost entirely of Gallery pages to give you a sense of Illustrator's flexibility.

6 References. *Resources* and *Artists* appendixes, *Glossaries*, and *General Index* can be found in the back of this book and on the pull-out card. In addition, we will occasionally direct you to *Illustrator Help* when referring to specific information that's well-documented in the Adobe Help Viewer. To access this choose Help > Illustrator Help.

Acknowledgments

As always, my most heartfelt gratitude goes to the more than 100 artists and Illustrator experts who generously allowed us to include their work and divulge their techniques.

Special thanks must also go to Mordy Golding, who, as author of *Real World Adobe Illustrator CS3,* continues to champion this book, and to share his expertise with the *Wow!* team. Jean-Claude Tremblay is our amazing technical editor, and we are so lucky to have JC advising us on every technical detail of this project. And thanks to all at Adobe, including Philip Guindi, Lon Lorenz, John Nack, Brenda Sutherland, Ian Giblin, and Teri Pettit. Thank you Terri Stone for continuing to foster the alliance between creativepro.com and the *Wow!* book.

This revision required a major team effort, and would not have happened without an amazing group of people. Thankfully joining the team for the first time is Cristen Gillespie, who was fortunately between *Photoshop Wow!* editions. Cristen immediately became an invaluable new addition to the team, creating the vast majority of the new lessons and galleries, updating our book's style guide, and even updating a chapter introduction. Randy Livingston also joined the writing team this edition, taking on the daunting task of updating many of the chapter intros, including the new intro for Live Color. Our final new writer was Andrew Dashwood. Sending in files, critiques and comments from Amsterdam, Andrew has become our resident Flash expert, as well as our Live Color "pinch-hitter." We are grateful that veteran *Wow!* writer Dave Awl returned to his post to update a huge batch of the intro sections. Lisa Jackmore again did a great job with Galleries and the *Illustrator CS3 Wow! Course Outline* (from ssteuer.com/edu). Luckily for the team, Steven Gordon agreed to return and tackle much-needed reworking to important Step-by-Steps and Galleries—Steven always adds a dose of humor to his incredible resourcefulness. Conrad Chavez returned for just one lesson this time, but that's because he's now a famous author (with *Real World Photoshop CS3*). Thank you Elizabeth Rogalin for working so hard to get back up to speed with *Wow!* lingo (Elizabeth edited *The Illustrator 7 Wow! Book*). I am endlessly grateful to Peg Maskell Korn for being involved since the beginning, and putting up with me on a moment to moment basis. As always, thanks also go to our stellar team of testers and consultants, especially Vicki Loader, Federico Platón, Bob Geib, Nini Tjäder, and Mike Schwabauer. A special thank you to Adam Z Lein for helping us set up and back up the fabulous updated online database so we can track who's doing what. Thanks to Sandee Cohen who continues as our official kibbitzer. And thank you Rebecca Plunkett for being so flexible with your scheduling so you could do the index! Thank you to Jay Nelson for the partnership between *Wow!* and *Design Tools Monthly.*

Thank you to CDS for the fabulous printing job. And thanks to everyone at Peachpit Press for all the things you do to make sure this book happens. Thanks *especially* to Nancy Davis, Lupe Edgar, Connie Jeung-Mills, Nancy Ruenzel, Rebecca Ross, Mimi Heft (for the gorgous cover design using Christiane Beauregard's lovely illustration, and for the emergency redesign). and our patient media producer Eric Geoffroy. Thank you Linnea Dayton for being the *Wow!* series editor. And lastly, heartfelt thanks to all my wonderful family and friends.

Wow!
Contents
at a
Glance...

Illustrator Basics

Start here!

Make sure to read both "How to Use This Book" earlier in the book, and the pullout *Glossary*.

Minimum system requirements

Macintosh:

- PowerPC® G4 or G5 or multi-core Intel processor
- Mac OS X v.10.4.8

Windows:

- Intel® Pentium® 4, Intel Centrino®, Intel Xeon®, or Intel Core™ Duo (or compatible) processor
- Microsoft® Windows® XP with Service Pack 2 or Windows Vista™ Home Premium, Business, Ultimate, or Enterprise (certified for 32-bit editions)

Both systems:

- 512MB of RAM (1GB suggested)
- 2.5GB of available hard-disk space (additional free space required during installation)
- 1,024 x 768 monitor resolution with 16-bit video card
- DVD-ROM drive for installation
- QuickTime 7 software required for multimedia features
- Internet or phone connection required for product activation
- Broadband Internet for Adobe Stock Photos, kuler, etc.

This chapter contains a multitude of tips and techniques carefully chosen to help you use Adobe Illustrator with optimal ease and efficiency. Whether you're a veteran user of Illustrator or a relative newcomer, you'll find information here that will greatly increase your speed and efficiency using the latest features. Make sure you read the "Start here!" Tip at the left.

COMPUTER & SYSTEM REQUIREMENTS

The software world has seen significant improvement in the past few years, and Adobe Illustrator is no exception. Minimum system requirements have drastically risen to accommodate the demands of faster and more powerful applications. It is very likely that Adobe Illustrator CS3 will not run well (if at all) on older computer systems. For example, Illustrator CS3's minimum RAM requirement is 512MB (that's doubled from CS2). You'll also need more hard disk space than ever before: at least 2.5GB (also doubled). Another consideration: the Adobe Illustrator CS3 DVDs contain lots of bonus content (templates, libraries, and fonts) that you may wish to store on your hard disk. Your monitor should accommodate a resolution of at least 1024 x 768 pixels so your work area won't be cramped. Even so, major improvements have been made that help minimize panels while maximizing your document working area. It's now possible to customize your workspace better than ever before.

SETTING UP YOUR PAGE
New Document Profiles

When you first launch Illustrator, and whenever all document windows are closed, you'll see a Welcome screen that offers two primary routes for getting started with your new session: Open a Recent Item and Create New. Just as you'd expect, Open a Recent Item lists the nine most recent documents you've had open in Illustrator.

The list is chronological, with the most recent document at the top. At the bottom of the list, there is a folder icon labeled "Open" which will bring up the Open dialog that lets you navigate to and open any pre-existing file.

In the Create New list you will see six default document profiles; Print, Web, Mobile and Devices, Video and Film, Basic CMYK, and Basic RGB. These each have pre-configured settings on which to base your new document. Of course, you can override or change all the settings in the New Document dialog that comes up when you click any document profile in the list. Keep in mind that you can create and save your own document profiles (see the Tip "Create document profiles" to the right).

New, New from Template, Open, and Open Recent Files are accessible from the File menu. In the New Document dialog, you can name your new file and confirm the New Document Profile type, as well as confirm the Size, Color Mode (CMYK or RGB), and other parameters you want for a particular project.

If you don't see it, the Welcome screen is always available from the Help menu.

Using Templates

Under Create New on the Welcome screen is the From Template folder icon. Clicking this icon opens the New from Template dialog, which takes you to Illustrator's collection of stock templates. You can also open template files by selecting File > New from Template. To save any of your own work as a template, choose File > Save as Template. Template files make it easy for you to create a new document based on finished designs. This comes in handy when you need to create a number of documents or pages with common design elements or transposable content.

Illustrator's templates are actually a special file format (ending in .ait). When you choose New from Template (from the File menu or from Template on the Welcome screen), a new Illustrator document (name ending in .ai) is created based on the template. The original .ait template

The Welcome screen offers you a number of useful options for starting your session, as well as convenient access to information and extras

Adobe training

In addition to Help > Illustrator Help, get some great resources at www.adobe.com/designcenter.

Create document profiles

Find the folder New Document Profiles on your hard disk. Duplicate one of the existing profiles inside, open it in Illustrator, customize (e.g., change content, change color mode, and so on), and then save it in the same location. It will appear in the Welcome screen. It is very important to start from one of the existing six basic document profiles (Print, Web, Video, etc...) when creating your own custom profile. If you want to have your own custom profile for print use, start by duplicating the Print Document profile (⌘-D/Ctrl-D and then renaming it). In this way, you'll maintain the metadata encoding Illustrator uses to identify the document profile type (such as Print or Web).

One of the free templates that ships with Illustrator CS3—this one is a DVD menu (Document Profile: Video and Film)

file remains unchanged and ready to use again. No matter what changes you make to your new document, the original template file will not be affected.

When you create a new file from a template, Illustrator automatically loads the various settings from the template file such as dimensions, swatches, type styles, symbols, or guides, as well as any content the template contains.

You can create as many original templates as you need or want. You can also take advantage of the more than 200 professionally designed templates included with Illustrator—everything from business cards to Web pages to restaurant menus.

The Artboard

In the document wndow, the box with a solid black outline defines the Artboard dimensions, i.e., the final document size. Double-click the Hand tool to fit your image to the current window (or ⌘-0/Ctrl-0). You can use View > Show Page Tiling to display the dotted lines that represent the printable area of your document page. Use the Page tool to click-drag the dotted-line page parameters around the Artboard.

With Illustrator's sophisticated print controls (File > Print), you can make very precise choices about what to print. From Print > Setup > Crop to Artboard pop-up, you can choose Artboard, Artwork Bounding Box, or Crop. Artboard uses the dimensions of your Illustrator page size to determine what gets printed. Artwork Bounding Box uses the artwork bounding box. And Crop uses the crop area you've defined on the Artboard. (For Web and video documents you should use only the Crop area as the printing size; the Artboards for these document profiles are very large. See the *Web & Animation* chapter for more about this.)

The One-Stop Print Dialog

Illustrator's full-service Print dialog lets you control all print functions from one interface. It's not necessary to use a Page Setup dialog to change things like page size and orientation. (In fact, it's recommended that you set all options from within Illustrator's Print dialog.)

As previously mentioned, the preview area in the Print dialog shows you the page's printable area. The Print dialog lets you scale artwork and see a preview before you print. By dragging the print preview image, you can choose exactly what part of your Artboard you want to print (you can also include parts of the scratch area—sections of art that lie outside Artboard boundaries). As a result, you don't have to change the size of the Artboard itself or move and scale objects in order to print a certain area with different scaling.

What's more, Illustrator lets you save your Print settings as time-saving presets. For example, if you frequently work with very large media sizes, you can set the appropriate printing scale and then save it as a Print preset for easy access. Using a Print preset eliminates having to check and set all the various parameters each time before you print.

MAKING YOUR MOVES EASIER

Take time to study this section in order to learn the many ways to select tools and access Illustrator features. These simple navigation techniques will free you from having to mouse to the Tools panel, or to rely solely on pull-down menus.

Keyboard shortcuts for tools and navigation

Save time and use a key instead of going to the Tools panel. Press "T" to choose the Type tool, "P" for the Pen tool, and so on. Choose any tool in the Tools panel by pressing its keyboard shortcut. To learn the default keyboard shortcuts for your tools, hold the cursor over any tool in the Tools panel (Show Tool Tips must be enabled, which is the default) and its keyboard shortcut will appear in parentheses next to the tool name (toggle the Tool Tips option in General Preferences).

Note: *Keyboard shortcuts won't work while you're in text editing mode. Press Escape to leave text editing mode and*

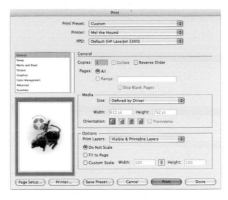

Illustrator's one-stop Print dialog—note the preview area in the lower left corner, which shows you the printable area of the page, and lets you adjust and scale your artwork to print

Mac users: It's recommended that you set all your options in Illustrator's Print dialog, rather than through the OS-provided Page Setup dialog. If you forget, Illustrator will remind you with the message shown here.

Custom keyboard shortcuts

To assign a shortcut to a menu item or tool, select Edit > Keyboard Shortcuts. Making any changes will rename the set "Custom." If you choose a shortcut already in use, you will get a warning that it is currently being used and that reassigning it will remove it from the item to which it is currently assigned. When you exit the dialog you will be asked to save your custom set. You can't overwrite a *preset*.

Resizing and stroke weight

Double-click the Scale tool to resize your selection with or without altering line weights:

- To scale a selection while also scaling line weights, enable the Scale Strokes & Effects checkbox.
- To scale a selection while maintaining your line weights, disable Scale Strokes & Effects.
- To decrease line weights (50%) without scaling objects, first scale the selection (200%) with Scale Strokes & Effects disabled. Then scale (50%) with it enabled. Reverse these steps to increase line weights.

PAPCIAK-ROSE

Various options displayed in the Control panel when a (non-text) vector object is selected

Various options displayed in the Control panel when a Type object is selected

Various options displayed in the Control panel when a Live Paint group is selected (Live Paint is discussed in the Beyond the Basics *chapter)*

use a keyboard shortcut. Your text will remain unchanged, with edits preserved.

Changing keyboard shortcuts

To change a shortcut for a tool or menu item, open the Keyboard Shortcut dialog (Edit > Keyboard Shortcuts). Making a change to a shortcut will change the set name to "Custom." When you're finished making changes and want to exit the dialog, you will be asked to save your shortcuts to a new file. This custom file will be saved in Preferences > Adobe Illustrator CS3 Settings and will end in ".kys." In addition, every time you make any changes to a saved set (not a default preset), you'll be asked if you want to overwrite that set. You can also use the Save button to create a new keyboard shortcut file. Click the Export Text button if you need a text file as a reference for a specific set of shortcuts, or if you need to print them. **Note:** *You can't change most panel items, but the few you can change are found at the bottom of the menu commands list in the Edit > Keyboard Shortcuts dialog.*

The Control panel

The Control panel is one of Illustrator's handiest features and, by default, it's docked at the top of the working area. It is a contextual panel in that it displays different tools and controls depending on the type of object currently selected. For example, if you select a text object, the panel will display text-formatting controls; on the other hand, selecting an art object will display options such as Stroke, Brush, Style, or perhaps Expand and Release buttons, depending on the kind of object. If you have multiple kinds of objects selected, the Control panel displays alignment controls in addition to other options for all the selected objects.

You can customize the Control panel by clicking on its menu button. From that menu, you can choose to dock the Control panel to the bottom of your working area rather than the top, and select or deselect various types of controls for display in the panel. The Control panel can also be repositioned as a floating panel by simply grabbing the panel's handle and dragging it where you want it. When you drag the Control panel to the top or bottom of the work area, at a certain point you'll see a blue bar indicator appear. When you see this, simply stop dragging and let go to redock the panel.

When you see underlined words in the Control panel, you can click them to display relevant options. For instance, clicking on the word Stroke will display Stroke options as a kind of pop-up panel. Clicking on the word Opacity opens a pop-up Transparency panel. Clicking on the arrows will reveal mini pop-ups, such as the arrow to the right of Opacity, which reveals a handy pop-up Opacity slider!

Context-sensitive menus

If you're not already familiar with Context-sensitive menus, you might find them to be a great time saver. Windows users merely click the right mouse button. If you're on a Mac with a single-button mouse, press the Control key while you click and hold the mouse button. In both cases a menu will pop up (specific to the tool or item you are working with), providing you with an alternative method to choose options.

Tear off panels

The Illustrator Toolbox lets you *tear off* subsets of tools so you can move the entire set to another location. Click on a tool with a pop-up menu, drag the cursor to the arrow end of the pop-up, and release the mouse.

WORKING WITH OBJECTS
Anchor points, lines, and Bézier curves

Instead of using pixels to draw shapes, Illustrator creates objects made up of points, called "anchor points." They are connected by curved or straight outlines called "paths" and are visible if you work in Outline mode. (Choose View > Outline to enter Outline mode, and View > Preview to change back.) Illustrator describes

An example of a clickable underlined word in the Control panel; if you click on the word Stroke, a drop-down version of the Stroke panel will open

Flotation device

You can "float" the Control panel and position it anywhere you like just by dragging its gripper bar (at the left edge of the panel). To redock the panel, just drag it back to the top or bottom of your working area. When you see the blue bar, let go and it will snap back into place.

As you move a panel, a bluish bar appears, to indicate where the panel can be docked

Tearoff tool panels

Changing measurement units

To set units of measurement for rulers, panels, and some dialogs or filters, as well as units for measuring strokes and text, use the Units & Display Performance area of Preferences.

Note: *Control-click (Mac)/right-click (Mac or Win) on the rulers to select different units or cycle through ruler units with ⌘-Option-Shift-U/Ctrl-Alt-Shift-U.*

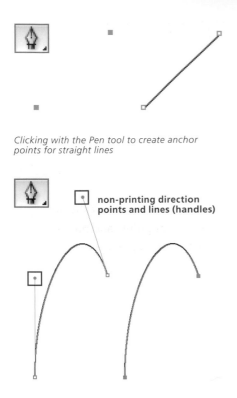

Clicking with the Pen tool to create anchor points for straight lines

non-printing direction points and lines (handles)

Click-dragging with the Pen tool to create anchor points and pulling out direction lines for curves

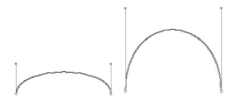

When direction handles are short, curves are shallow; when handles are long, curves are deep

The length and angle of the handles determine the "gesture" of the curves

information about the location and size of each path, as well as its dozen or so attributes, such as its fill color and stroke weight and color. Because you are creating objects, you'll be able to change the order in which they stack. You'll also be able to group objects together so you can select them as if they were one object. You can even ungroup them later, if you wish.

If you took geometry in your school days, you probably remember that the shortest distance between two points is a straight line. In Illustrator, this rule translates into each line being defined by two anchor points that you create by either clicking with the Pen tool or drawing with the Line Segment tool.

In mathematically describing rectangles and ellipses, Illustrator computes the center, the length of the sides, or the radius, based on the total width and height that you specify.

For more complex shapes involving free-form curves, Adobe Illustrator allows you to use the Pen tool to create Bézier curves, defined by non-printing anchor points (which literally anchor the path at those points), and direction points (which define the angle and depth of the curve). To make these direction points easier to see and manipulate, each one is connected to its anchor point with a non-printing direction line, also called a "handle." The direction points and handles are visible when you're creating a path with the Pen tool or editing the path with either the Direct Selection tool, or one of the path editing tools accessed from the Pen tool (see figures opposite). While all of this might sound complicated, manipulating Bézier curves can become intuitive. Mastering these curves, though initially awkward, is the heart and soul of using Illustrator. And being comfortable with Illustrator's Pen tool can help you immensely when you're working working in Photoshop and InDesign as well.

More about Bézier curves

If you're new to using Bézier curves, take some time to go through the Adobe training materials. Also, the "Ch02-

zen_lessons" folder on the *Wow! CD* includes several "Zen" practice lessons that will help you fine-tune your Bézier capabilities (such as the "Zen of the Pen" Bézier lessons, which include QuickTime demonstrations on drawing and editing paths and curves).

Many graphics programs include Béziers, so mastering the Pen tool, though challenging at first, is very important. Friskets in Corel Painter, paths in Photoshop and InDesign, and the outline and extrusion curves of many 3D programs all use the Bézier curve.

The key to learning Béziers is to take your initial lessons in short doses and to stop if you get frustrated. Designer Kathleen Tinkel describes Bézier direction lines as "following the gesture of the curve." This artistic view should help you to create fluid Bézier curves.

Some final rules about Bézier curves

- The length and angle of the handles "anticipate" the curves that will follow.
- To ensure that the curve is smooth, place anchor points on either side of an arc, not in between.
- The fewer the anchor points, the smoother the curve will look and the faster it will print.
- Adjust a curve's height and angle by dragging the direction points, or grab the curve itself to adjust its height.

WATCH YOUR CURSOR!

Illustrator's cursors change to indicate not only what tool you have selected, but also which function you are about to perform. If you watch your cursor, you will avoid the most common Illustrator mistakes.

If you choose the Pen tool:

- **Before you start**, your cursor displays as the Pen tool with "×" indicating that you're starting a new object.

- **Once you've begun your object,** your cursor changes to a regular Pen. This indicates that you're about to add to an existing object.

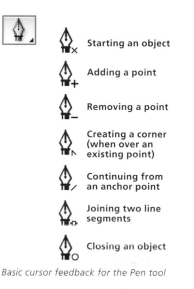

Starting an object

Adding a point

Removing a point

Creating a corner (when over an existing point)

Continuing from an anchor point

Joining two line segments

Closing an object

Basic cursor feedback for the Pen tool

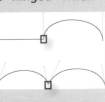

- **If your cursor gets close to an existing anchor point,** it will change to a Pen with "–" indicating that you're about to delete the anchor point! If you click-drag on top of that anchor point, you'll redraw that curve. If you hold the Option (Mac)/Alt (Win) key while you click-drag on top of the point, you'll pull out a new direction line, creating a corner (as in the petals of a flower). If you click on top of the point, you'll collapse the outgoing direction line, allowing you to attach a straight line to the curve.

- **If your cursor gets close to an end anchor point of an object,** it will change to a Pen with "o" to indicate that you're about to "close" the path. If you do close the path, then your cursor will change back to a Pen with "×" to indicate that you're beginning a new object.

- **If you use the Direct Selection tool to adjust the object as you go,** be sure to look at your cursor when you're ready to continue your object. If it's still a regular Pen, then continue to place the next point, adding to your object. If the Pen tool has "×" (indicating that you are about to start a new object), then you must redraw your last point. As you approach this last anchor point, your cursor will change to a Pen with "/"; click and drag over this last point to redraw the last curve.

  To form a hinged corner on a point *as you draw*, hold down Option (Mac)/Alt (Win) as you click-drag out a new direction line.

BÉZIER-EDITING TOOLS

Bézier-editing tools are the group of tools you can use to edit Illustrator paths. To access them, click and hold the Pen, Pencil, or Scissors tool and drag to select one of the other tools. You can also tear off this panel. (To learn how to combine paths into new objects, read about the Path-finder panel in the *Beyond the Basics* chapter.)

- **The Pen tool** and **Auto Add/Delete** can perform a variety of functions. Auto Add/Delete (which is on by default, but can be disabled in General Preferences) allows the Pen tool to change automatically to the Add Anchor Point tool when the tool is over a selected path segment, or to the Delete Anchor Point tool when over an anchor point. To temporarily disable the Auto Add/Delete function of the Pen tool, hold down the Shift key. If you don't want the path to constrain to an angle, release the Shift key prior to releasing the mouse.

- **The Convert Anchor Point tool,** hidden within the Pen tool (default is Shift-C), converts an anchor point from a smooth curve to a corner point when you click on it. To convert a corner point to a smooth curve, click-drag on the anchor point counterclockwise to pull out a new direction handle (or twirl the point until it straightens out the curve). To convert a smooth curve to a hinged curve (two curves hinged at a point), grab the direction point and hold Option/Alt as you drag out to the new position. With the Pen tool selected, you can temporarily access the Convert Anchor Point tool by pressing Option/Alt.

- **The Add Anchor Point tool,** accessible from the Pen pop-up menu or by pressing the + (plus) key, adds an anchor point to a path at the location where you click.

- **The Delete Anchor Point tool,** accessible from the Pen pop-up menu or by pressing – (minus), deletes an anchor point when you click directly on the point.
  Note: *If you select the Add/Delete Anchor Point tools by pressing + or –, press P to get back to the Pen tool.*

- **The Pencil tool** reshapes a selected path when Edit selected paths is checked in the tools preferences. Select a path and draw on or near the path to reshape it.

- **The Smooth tool** smooths the points on already-drawn paths by smoothing corners and deleting points. As you move the Smooth tool over your path, it attempts to keep the original shape of the path as intact as possible.

The Ellipse, Polygon, Star, and Spiral are great tools when used with the following key combinations:

- **Spacebar-drag** allows you to reposition your object.
- **Shift** constrains the object's proportions.
- **Up-arrow (↑)** increases points on a star, sides on a polygon, and coils on a spiral.
- **Down-arrow (↓)** removes points from a star, sides from a polygon, and coils from a spiral.
- **Option (Mac)/Alt (Win)** increases the angle of a star's points.
- **⌘-drag/Ctrl-drag** fixes the position of the inner radius for a star, or increases or decreases the decay in a spiral.
- **~-drag (tilde-drag) on US keyboards** creates multiple objects based on the speed and length of your drag.

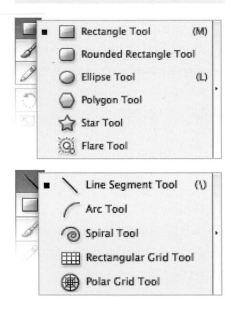

- **The Path Eraser tool** will remove parts of a selected path (use any Selection tool to select the path). See the *Drawing & Coloring* chapter for more about the Path Eraser tool.

- **The Eraser Tool**
The Eraser tool removes a swath from vector objects as you "slice through" them. If a vector object is selected, the Eraser tool will affect only that selected object. If there is nothing selected, all vector objects that are touched by the Eraser tool will be affected (through all unlocked and visible layers). See the *Drawing & Coloring* chapter for more about the Eraser tool.

- **The Scissors tool** cuts a path where you click by adding two disconnected, selected anchor points exactly on top of each other. To select just one of the points, deselect the object, then click with the Direct Selection tool on the spot where you cut. This will allow you to select the upper anchor point and drag it to the side in order to see the two points better.

- **The Knife tool** slices through all unlocked visible objects and closed paths. Simply drag the Knife tool across the object you want to slice, then select the object(s) you want to move or delete. Hold down the Option (Mac)/Alt (Win) key to constrain the cut to a straight line.

GEOMETRIC OBJECTS

The Ellipse, Rounded Rectangle, Polygon, and Star tools create objects called "geometric primitives." These objects are mathematically described symmetrical paths grouped with a non-printing anchor point, which indicates the center. (In order for the center of a star or polygon to be visible, you'll need to choose Window > Attributes and then click the Show Center icon.) Use the centers of the geometric objects to snap-align them with each other, or with other objects and guides. You can create these geometric objects numerically or manually (see the section following for directions on how to do this). Access the hidden tools in the pop-up panel from the Rectangle tool in the Toolbox. (See the *Zen of Illustrator* chapter for exercises in creating and manipulating geometric objects, and Tip top right.)

- **To create a geometric shape manually,** select the desired geometric tool, and click-drag to form the object from one corner to the other. To create the object from the center, hold down the Option (Mac)/Alt (Win) key and drag from the center outward (keep the Option/Alt key down until you release the mouse button to ensure that it draws from the center). Once you have drawn the geometric objects, you can edit them exactly as you do other paths.

- **To create a geometric object with numeric input,** select a geometric tool and click on the Artboard to establish the upper left corner of your object. Enter the desired dimensions in the dialog and click OK. To create the object numerically from the object's center, Option-click (Mac)/Alt-click (Win) on the Artboard.

  To draw an arc, select the Arc tool and then click and drag to start drawing the arc. Press the "F" key to flip the arc from convex to concave, and use the up and down Arrow keys to adjust the radius of the arc. Pressing the "C" key will "close" the arc by drawing the perpendicular lines that form the axes, and pressing the "X" key will flip the arc without moving these axes ("F" flips both the arc and the axes). Release the mouse to finish the arc.

  To draw a grid, select either the Rectangular Grid tool or the Polar Grid tool and click-drag to start drawing the grid. You can control the shape of the grid by pressing various keys as you draw (see *Illustrator Help* for details). Release the mouse to finish the grid.

SELECTING & GROUPING OBJECTS
Selecting
The Select menu gives you easy access to basic selection commands, including the ability to select specific types

Tool tolerance options

Drawing freehand while holding a mouse, or even a digital pen, can be less than elegant. The Pencil, Smooth, and Brush tools contain options that can help you to create more types of paths, ranging from very realistic to more shapely and graceful, without the constant need to adjust anchor points. Double-click on the tool to view the options.

- **Fidelity** increases or decreases the distance between anchor points on the path created or edited. The smaller the number, the more points that will make up the path, and vice versa.
- **Smoothness** varies the percentage of smoothness you'll see as you create and edit paths. Use a lower percentage of smoothness for more realistic lines and brush strokes, and a higher percentage for less realistic but more elegant lines.

Note: *Closing Pencil and Brush tool paths is a bit awkward. If you hold down the Option/Alt key when you are ready to close a path, a straight line segment will be drawn between the first and last anchor points. If you hold down the Option/Alt key and extend slightly past the first anchor point, the path will close automatically. Set the tool preferences to low numbers to make closing easier.* — Sandee Cohen

Selection tool	Direct Selection tool	Group Selection tool

of objects and attributes. You can use the Selection tools to select individual or multiple objects. You can use the target indicators in the Layers panel to select and target objects, groups, and layers. Targeting a group or layer selects everything contained within it, and makes the group or layer the focus of the Appearance and Graphic Styles panels. (For detailed instructions explaining targeting and selecting via the Layers panel, see the *Layers & Appearances* chapter.)

Use the Lasso tool to select an entire path or multiple paths by encircling them. Combining Option/Alt with the Lasso tool subtracts entire paths from a selection (though this may require a certain amount of finesse). Combining Shift with the Lasso tool adds entire paths to a selection.

You can also use the Direct Selection tool or the Lasso tool to select individual anchor points or path segments. Click with the Direct Selection tool to select points, or click-drag to draw a marquee around the area you wish to select. With the Lasso encircle the points or path segments that you wish to select. Combining Option/Alt with the Direct Selection or Lasso tool subtracts anchor points from a selection; Shift with the Lasso tool adds anchor points to a selection.

Grouping and selecting

Many programs provide you with a grouping function so you can treat multiple objects as one unit. In Illustrator, grouping objects places all the objects on the same layer and creates a "<Group>" container in the Layers panel; remember, don't choose Group if you want your objects on different layers. (For more on layers and objects, see the *Layers & Appearances* chapter.) So, when *do* you want to group objects? Group objects when you need to select them *repeatedly* as a unit or when you want to apply an appearance to the entire group. Take an illustration of a bicycle as an example. Use the Group function to group the spokes of a wheel. Next, group the two wheels of the bicycle, then group the wheels with the frame. We will continue to refer to this hypothetical bicycle below.

- **With the Direct Selection tool.** Click on a point or path with the Direct Selection tool to select that point or portion of the path. If you click on a spoke of a wheel, you'll select the portion of the spoke's path you clicked.

- **With the Selection tool.** Click on an object with the Selection tool to select the largest group containing that object. In our example, this would be the entire bicycle.

- **With the Group Selection tool.** Use the Group Selection tool to select sub-groupings progressively. The first click with the Group Selection tool selects a single spoke. The next click selects all of the spokes. The third click selects the entire wheel; the fourth selects both wheels, and the fifth, the entire bicycle. (Or, marquee part of the objects to select all of them.) To move objects selected with the Group Selection tool, drag without releasing the mouse. If you continually click with the Group Selection tool, you're always selecting additional groups.

- **See the "Finger Dance" lessons in the *Zen* chapter.** This section includes a variety of selection exercises.

USING THE ALIGN PANEL

The Align panel (Window > Align) contains a highly useful set of tools that allow you to control how selected objects, or selected anchor points, are aligned or distributed. If you select objects with the Selection or Group Selection tool, then these functions will align and distribute the selected objects. However, if your selection includes any anchor points selected with the Direct Selection or Lasso tools, then these functions will align *all of the points in the selected objects*, as if you used the Average function (see the section below on Joining & Averaging). Even though most Align and Distribute controls also appear in the Control panel, there are a few very powerful controls that only show up in the Align panel itself. So if you're aligning or distributing objects via the Control panel, you might need to open the Align panel to

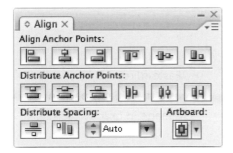

The Align panel with all of its options displayed

Align warning

Once you specify a value in the Align panel Options section for Distribute, you have to choose a key object every time. If you get this dialog warning, reset the value to Auto. —*Mordy Golding*

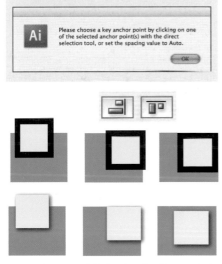

Use Preview Bounds helps visually align stroked objects, but yields mysterious results with live graphic effects such as drop shadows: The left rectangles are unaligned; at center are the same rectangles, each pair having been aligned top and right; at right the pairs are aligned top/right with "Use Preview Bounds" enabled

To use the current unit of measurement, type the number, then Tab to the next text field or press Return/Enter. To use another unit of measurement, *follow* the number with "in" or " (for inch), "pt" (point), "p" (pica), or "mm" (millimeter) and press Return/Enter. To resume typing into an image text block, press Shift-Return. You can also enter *calculations* in panels. For example, if you were specifying the size of a rectangle, you could type 72 pt + 2 mm for the height. Illustrator would then perform the calculation and apply the result. Partial calculations work as well; if you type + 2, Illustrator will add two of whatever unit you're currently using. Try it!

If you get an error message that you can't join points, do the following—in addition to the conditions in the warning:

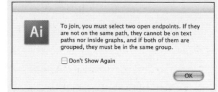

- Make sure you've selected only two points (and no third stray point selected by mistake).
- Make sure you've selected *endpoints*, not midpoints.

access some of its advanced functions, such as Cancel Key Object or the Distribute Spacing controls.

To make sure all of the Align panel's options are showing, click the double triangle on the Align panel tab or choose Show Options from the panel's menu.

The Align panel lets you align objects along a specified axis, according to either the edges or the anchor points of objects. Begin by selecting the objects that you want to align or distribute. If you want to align or distribute relative to the bounding box of all the objects you have selected, just click whichever button on the Align panel reflects the arrangement you want.

If you want to align or distribute relative to a specific object, click that object first and then click the appropriate button on the Align panel. (Choose Cancel Key Object from the panel menu at any time while the original set is still selected to "reset" the controls so they no longer align or distribute relative to the object you previously clicked.)

You can also align objects relative to the Artboard or Crop Area by choosing Align to Artboard or Align to Crop Area commands from the panel menu, and then clicking the appropriate button on the panel itself. You'll also find this feature in the Control panel.

Note that by default, Illustrator uses the paths of objects to determine how the objects will be aligned and distributed. But you can also use the edge of the stroke to determine alignment and distribution, by choosing Use Preview Bounds from the panel menu. (This is useful for objects with differing stroke weights.) But keep in mind that "the edge of the stroke" includes any effects applied to that object, including things that extend well beyond the visible edge of the stroke, such as drop shadows.

The Align panel even lets you specify exact distances by which objects should be distributed. First, select the objects you want to distribute; then, in the Distribute Spacing field of the Align panel, enter the amount of space by which the objects should be separated. (Remember, you may need to choose Show Options in order for the Distribute Spacing field to be visible in the Align panel; these controls don't appear in the Control panel.) Using the Selection tool, click on the path of the object you want to remain fixed, while the other objects distribute themselves relative to it. Then click either the Vertical or Horizontal Distribute Space button. (Choose Auto from the pop-up menu to cancel this option.)

JOINING & AVERAGING

Two of Illustrator's most useful functions are Average and Join. (Both are found under the Object >Path menu or in the Context-sensitive menu. There is also now a "Connect selected end points" button in the Control panel.)

To average, use the Direct Selection tool or Lasso tool to marquee-select or Shift-select any number of points belonging to any number of objects. Then use the Context-sensitive menu (Control-click for Mac/right button-click for Mac/Windows) to Average, aligning the selected points horizontally, vertically, or along both axes.

You can also use the Average function (or the Align buttons) to stack two selected endpoints on top of each other. The Join function will connect two endpoints; Join operates differently depending on the objects.

- **If the two open endpoints are exactly on top of each other,** then Join opens a dialog asking if the join should be a smooth point or a corner. A smooth point is a curved Bézier anchor that smoothly joins two curves, with direction handles that always move together; a corner point is any other point connecting two paths. Once you've clicked OK, both points will fuse into a single point. However, keep in mind that a true smooth point will only result if the proper conditions exist: namely, that the two curves that you are trying to join have the potential to join together into a smooth curve. Otherwise, you'll get a corner point, even if you chose Smooth in the dialog.

- **If the two open endpoints are not exactly on top of each other,** then Join will connect the two points with a line. If you try to Join two points to fuse as one but don't

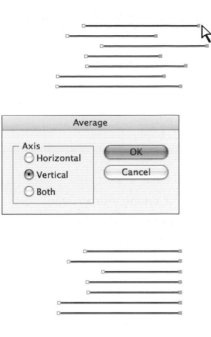

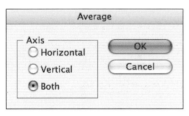

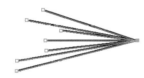

Using the Average command to align selected endpoints vertically, then choosing Both

Copying stroke and fill

It's easy to copy your stroke and fill settings from one object to the next. Select an object with the stroke and fill you want for your next object. Illustrator automatically picks up those attributes, so the next drawn object will have the same stroke and fill as the last one selected.

Note: *This doesn't work for type.*

Panel docking is totally customizable

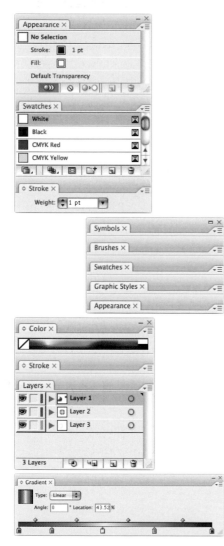

A small sampling of arrangements of panels and tabbed panel groupings, in various states of expansion and collapse

get a dialog, then you've merely connected your points with a line! Undo (⌘-Z for Mac/Ctrl-Z for Windows) and see "To Average & Join in one step" below.

- **If you select an open path** (in this case, you don't need to select the endpoints), then Join closes the path.

- **If the two open endpoints are on different objects,** then Join connects the two paths into one.

- **To Average & Join in one step,** use the following keyboard command: ⌘-Option-Shift-J (Mac)/Ctrl-Alt-Shift-J (Win); there is no menu equivalent! This command forms a corner when joining two lines, or a hinged corner when joining a line or curve to a curve.

WORKING WITH PANELS

Most of Illustrator's panels are accessible via the Window menu. By default, some panel icons appear at the right in your work area. In fact, in CS3, they're now "docked" there, and panel docking is completely configurable! You can resize the icon view of the docked panels by dragging the left edge of the panel dock left or right. You can drag left to show icons and names. As you drag right, you'll see that the column of panels can be collapsed until only the icon represenation remains.

The panel dock can be multiple columns and rows—just drag a panel alongside another and you'll see a blue bar appear (when you get close enough). This indicates that the panel can be docked there simply by letting go of your mouse button.

Clicking on a panel icon reveals the complete panel. Further, each panel will auto-collapse as you select another panel icon. Clicking the double arrow at the upper right of the panel dock will expand the entire column to reveal all the tabbed groups of panels at full size. If you need to see panels docked within a tab group at the same time, you can grab the tab for one of the panels and drag it up or down, or left or right, to dock it alone, with another panel, or with a tabbed group of panels. Look for the blue line to signal where it will attach.

Of course, you can always tear off individual panels from the dock so they'll float anywhere you wish. However, once a panel is floating, it won't auto-collapse, and closing it doesn't shrink it to its icon. You must drag floating panels back to the right side of the screen in order to redock it and have access to its icon.

If you want to save a particular arrangment of your dock set-up, go to Window > Workspace > Save Workspace. See the section below, "Workspaces: Managing Your Working Area," for more about Workspaces.

- **You can also regroup tabbed panels to save desktop space.** Reduce the space that panels require by nesting them together into smaller groups. Grab a panel's tab and drag it to another panel group to nest it. You can also drag a tab to the *bottom* of a panel to dock the panels on top of one another.

- **You can make most panels smaller or larger.** If there's a sizing icon in the lower right corner, click and drag it to shrink or expand the panel. Panels also have pop-up menus offering additional options. If a panel contains more options, it will have a double arrow to the left of the panel name. Click on the arrows to cycle through the various options. Double-click the title bar to cycle through the states, from maximum to collapsed.

- **Reset panels easily.** Certain panels (including the Character, Paragraph and OpenType panels) contain a Reset Panel command that allows you to easily restore the panel's default settings.

- **You must select your object(s) before you can make changes.** With your objects selected, you can click on the label or inside any edit box in the panel containing text and begin typing. If you're typing something that has limited choices (such as a font or type style), Illustrator

Magic peekaboo panels

Use Tab to toggle hide/show panels (Shift-Tab to hide panels but keep Tool and Control panels visible). With panels hidden, mouse over the area where panels were and they'll magically appear!

Teeny tiny panels

Double-click the name of a panel, or single-click the double arrows on the tab to cycle through expanded and collapsed views of the panel. Only panels with more options have double arrows on the panel tab.

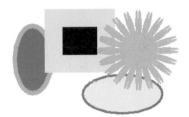

The original objects

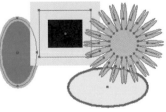

Objects selected (the bottom of the Tools panel indicates different strokes and fills are selected)

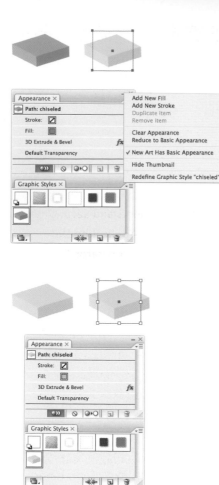

To update or replace a graphic style throughout the entire document, select an object and apply the style you want to modify and update. With the object selected, make changes to its appearance and choose Replace Graphic Style from the Appearance panel menu. The name of the style will display next to the replace command. This will globally update all objects using this named graphic style. To change the name of the style, double-click on the proxy in the Graphic Styles panel and rename it.

Window > Workspace shows default and custom workspaces

will attempt to complete your word; just keep typing until your choice is visible. If you're typing into a text field, use the Tab key to move to other text fields within the panel. **IMPORTANT:** *When you've finished typing into panel text fields, you must press Return/Enter. This action tells the application that you are ready to enter text somewhere else or to resume manipulating your artwork.*

- **There are many ways to fill or stroke an object.** Focus on a selected object's fill or stroke by clicking on the Fill or Stroke icon near the bottom of the Toolbox, or toggle between them with the "X" key. To set the stroke or fill to None, use the / (slash) key. Set your color by: 1) adjusting the sliders or sampling a color from the color ramp in the Color panel, 2) clicking on a swatch in the Swatches panel, 3) sampling colors from the color picker, or 4) using the Eyedropper to sample from other objects in your file. In addition, you can drag color swatches from panels to selected objects or to the Fill/Stroke icon in the Toolbox.

- **You can associate appearances with objects, groups of objects, or layers.** *Appearance attributes* are properties that affect the look of an object without affecting its underlying structure—such as strokes, fills, transparencies and effects. The term *appearance* is used in this book to refer to an object's collective appearance attributes. All objects have an appearance, even if that appearance is "no stroke and no fill."

- **You can apply a graphic style to an object, group of objects, or a layer.** The total sum of applied characteristics can be saved as a style in the Graphic Styles panel. *Graphic styles* are "live" (updatable) combinations of fills, strokes, blending modes, opacities, and effects. For details about working with combinations of effects and the Graphic Styles panel, see the *Live Effects & Graphic Styles* chapter, especially the chapter introduction and the "Scratchboard Art" lesson.

WORKSPACES: MANAGING YOUR WORKING AREA

Speaking of panels—once you've arranged your panels and the other features of your working area to your liking, the Workspaces feature allows you to save that arrangement as a custom workspace. If you like to have different arrangements of panels for different kinds of tasks, you can save multiple workspaces and then easily switch back and forth between them as you're working. Multiple users who share a computer setup can each create their own saved workspaces.

To save a custom workspace, once you've got everything arranged on your screen, just choose Workspace > Save Workspace from the Window menu. Enter a name for your custom workspace in the Name field, and click the OK button. Once you've created and saved a custom workspace, its name will show up in the Window > Workspace submenu, so you can easily switch between different workspaces just by clicking on their names. And you can always click on [Basic] in the Workspace submenu to restore the basic Illustrator workspace.

The Manage Workspaces dialog allows you to delete, duplicate, or rename your custom workspaces at any time. Choose Window > Workspace > Manage Workspaces, and select the name of an existing custom workspace in the dialog. Rename it by changing the text in the Name field, click the New button to create a duplicate of the current one, or click the Trash icon to delete.

TRANSFORMATIONS

Moving, scaling, rotating, reflecting, and shearing are all operations that transform selected objects. Since this chapter is devoted to Illustrator basics, this section will concentrate on the tools and panels that help you to perform transformations. (For live effects that perform transformations, see the *Live Effects & Graphic Styles* chapter.) Begin by selecting what you wish to transform. If you don't like a transformation you've just applied, use Undo before applying a new transformation—or you'll end up applying the new transformation on top of the

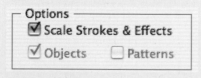
previous one. In Illustrator, you can perform most transformations manually using a dialog for numeric accuracy. Illustrator remembers the last transformation you performed, storing those numbers in the appropriate dialog until you enter a new transform value or restart the program. For example, if you previously scaled an image and disabled Scale Strokes & Effects, the next time you scale (manually or numerically), your strokes and effects won't scale. (Also see the Tip "Transform again" at left, and see the *Zen of Illustrator* chapter for exercises using transformations.)

The bounding box

The bounding box should not be confused with the Free Transform tool (which allows you to perform additional functions; see discussion of the Free Transform tool below). The bounding box appears around selected objects when you are using the Selection tool (solid arrow), and can be useful for quickly moving, scaling, rotating, or duplicating objects. With the bounding box, you can easily scale several objects at once. Select the objects, click on a corner of the bounding box, and drag. To constrain proportionally while scaling, hold down the Shift key and drag a corner. By default, the bounding box is on. Toggle it off and on via the View > Hide/Show Bounding Box, or switch to the Direct Selection tool to temporarily hide it. To reset the bounding box after performing a transformation so it's once again square to the page, choose Object > Transform > Reset Bounding Box. **Note:** *As long as one of the bounding box handles is selected, holding down the Option/Alt key when you transform with the bounding box will not create a duplicate, but will instead transform from the center.*

Moving

In addition to grabbing and dragging objects manually, you can specify a new location numerically: Double-click the Selection arrow in the Toolbox or use the Context-sensitive menu to bring up the Move dialog (select the

Preview option). For help determining the distance you wish to move, click-drag with the Measure tool the distance you wish to calculate. Then *immediately* open the Move dialog to see the measured distance loaded automatically, and click OK (or press Return/Enter).

The Free Transform tool

The Free Transform tool can be an easy way to transform objects once you learn numerous keyboard combinations to take advantage of its functions. In addition to performing simple transformations that can be performed with the bounding box (such as rotate and scale), you can also shear, and create perspective and distortions (see the Tip "Free Transform variations" at right, and the "Distorting Views" lesson in the *Drawing & Coloring* chapter). Bear in mind that the Free Transform tool bases its transformations on a fixed center point that cannot be relocated. If you need to transform from a different location, use the individual transformation tools, Transformation panel, or the Transform Each command.

The Transform panel

From this panel, you can determine numeric transformations that specify an object's width, height, and location on the document, as well as how much to rotate or shear it. You can also access a panel pop-up menu that offers options to Flip Horizontal and Vertical; Transform Object, Pattern, or Both; and to enable Scale Strokes & Effects. The current Transform panel is a bit odd: You can Transform Again once you've applied a transformation, but the information in the text fields is not always retained. To maintain your numeric input, apply transformations through the transformation tool's dialog, discussed in the next section.

Individual transformation tools

For the scaling, rotation, reflection, and shearing of objects with adjustable center points, you can click (to manually specify the center about which the transforma-

Free Transform variations

With the Free Transform tool, you can apply the following transformations to selected objects:

- **Rotate**—Click outside the bounding box and drag.
- **Scale**—Click on a corner of the bounding box and drag. Option-drag/Alt-drag to scale from the center and Shift-drag to scale proportionally.
- **Distort**—Click on a corner handle of the bounding box and ⌘-drag/Ctrl-drag.
- **Shear**—Click on a side handle of the bounding box and ⌘-drag/Ctrl-drag the handle.
- **Perspective**—Click on a corner handle of the bounding box and ⌘-Option-Shift-drag/Ctrl-Alt-Shift-drag.

Illustrator is tracking you...

| 100% | ▼ 🕐 | Toggle Direct Selection | ▶ |

The status line in the lower left corner of your image window is actually a pop-up menu that lets you choose to display Current Tool, Date and Time, Number of Undos, or Document Color Profile (and if applicable, Version Cue Status).

```
  Version Cue Status
✓ Current Tool
  Date and Time
  Number of Undos

  Document Color Profile
```

Kevan Atteberry drew one squiggle of hair with a chalk art brush, and then used the Reshape tool to reshape it, holding Option (Alt) when he dragged to make copies. He reshaped the triple strands to shape the witch's hair (he selected all of the three strands with the Selection tool, then with the Reshape tool he selected only the top anchor on each strand to reshape all three together), and then reshaped again to form the surprised witch's hair and hat.

ATTEBERRY

The Transform Each dialog
(Object >Transform >Transform Each)

tion will occur), then grab your object to transform it. For practice with manual transformations using these individual tools see the *Zen* chapter. Each transformation tool has a dialog where you can specify the parameters for the tool, whether to transform the object or make a copy with the specified transform applied, and whether to transform just the objects and/or any patterns they may be filled with. (For more on transforming patterns see the *Drawing & Coloring* chapter.)

Here are three additional methods you can use to apply the individual transformation tools to objects:

- **Double-click on a transformation tool** to access the dialog. (Or press Return/Enter with a transformation tool already selected.) This allows you to transform objects numerically, originating from an object's center.

- **Option-click/Alt-click on your image with a transformation tool** to access the dialog that allows you to transform your objects numerically, originating from where you clicked.

- **Click-drag on your image with a transformation tool** to transform the selected objects, originating from the center of the group of selected objects.

Reshape & Shear

The Reshape tool is different from the other transformation tools. Start by selecting all the points in the paths you wish to reshape (use the Group Selection or Selection tool). Next, choose the Reshape tool (hidden under the Scale tool) and marquee or Shift-select all points you wish to affect, then drag the points to reshape the path. The selected points move as a unit, but rather than move the same distance, as they would if you dragged with the Direct Selection tool, the points nearer to the cursor move more, and the ones farther away move less.

You will also find the Shear tool hidden within the Scale tool. Use the Shear tool to slant objects.

Transform Each

To perform multiple transformations at once, open the Transform Each dialog (Object > Transform > Transform Each). You can perform the transformations on one or more objects. Additions to this dialog include the ability to reflect objects over the X and Y axes, and to change the point of origin. If you want to apply a transformation, but you think you might want to change it later, try a Transformation Effect (see the *Live Effects & Graphic Styles* chapter for more about live effects).

WORKING SMART

Saving strategies

Probably the most important advice you'll ever get is to save every few minutes. Whenever you make a substantial change to your image, use File > Save As and give your image a new name.

It's much more time-efficient to save incremental versions of your image than it is to reconstruct an earlier version. Back up your work at least once a day before you shut down. Just think to yourself, "If this computer never starts up again, what will I need?" Develop a backup system using CDs, DVDs, external storage drives, DATs (digital audio tapes), or opticals so you can archive all of your work. Use a program such as Dantz's Retrospect to automatically add new and changed files to your archives.

Get in the habit of archiving virtually everything, and develop a file-naming system that actually helps you keep track of your work in progress—simplifying your recovery of a working version if necessary. Also, make sure that you keep all files in a named and dated folder that distinguishes them from other projects. (For more information about saving in other formats see "Image Formats" later in this chapter.)

Multiple Undos

Some programs give you only one chance to undo your last move. Illustrator allows "unlimited undos," which, practically speaking, means that the number of undos

Interrupting Preview

You don't have to wait for Illustrator to finish redrawing the Preview before you pull down the next menu or perform another task. You can interrupt redrawing the preview and go to Outline mode by typing ⌘-./Ctrl-. (period), or the Esc key for Windows.

Two views

Illustrator allows you to preview precise anti-aliasing in Pixel Preview mode, and allows you to preview overprints and traps in Overprint Preview mode.

Close	⌘W
Save	⌘S
Save As...	⇧⌘S
Save a Copy...	⌥⌘S

Save As allows you to keep iterations of a project by using different file names. This strategy can be very useful if you need to backtrack for any reason.

Don't forget about your edges!

Once you hide your edges in Illustrator (View > Hide Edges or ⌘-H/Ctrl-H), they stay hidden for all subsequent paths and selections. If you are trying to select a path or draw a new object, but the anchor points and path are not visible, try toggling to Show Edges.

The Navigator panel (always in Preview mode) offers many ways to zoom in and out of documents:

- Double-click the mountain icons along the bottom edge of the panel window to increase or decrease the amount of zoom in 200% increments.
- Hold the ⌘/Ctrl key and drag to marquee the area in the panel thumbnail that you want to zoom into or out from.
- Enable View Artboard Only to keep your view limited to the Artboard area. This is helpful if you are working on a document with objects on the pasteboard (outside the page margins) that are distracting your focus.

You can change the color of the border around the thumbnail in the View Options dialog (in the Navigator panel pop-up).

Note: *Navigator might slow you down if your file contains a lot of text objects. The Navigator creates a thumbnail view of the document; every time you zoom or scroll, the Navigator must redraw its thumbnail. Unless you need to view the Navigator panel, close it.*

If you have many file windows open, simply select the file you want to bring to the front from the list of files at the bottom of the Window menu.

you can perform is limited only by how much memory you have available.

Even *after* you save a file, your Undos (and Redos) will still be available (as long as you haven't closed and reopened the file), making it possible for you to save the current version, undo it to a previous stage and save it again, or as a different name, or continue working from an earlier state. But once you close your file, your undos are cleared from memory, so they won't be available the next time you open the file.

You can also revert the file to the most recently saved version by choosing File > Revert, but you can't undo a revert, so you'll want to be careful.

Note: *Not all operations are undoable. For example, changes to Preferences aren't affected by Undo, and neither are screen zooms.*

CHANGING YOUR VIEWS

From the View menu, you can show and hide several items, such as grids, guides, smart guides, transparency grids, edges, Artboards, and page tilings.

Preview and Outline

To control the speed of your screen redraw, learn to make use of the Preview mode and the Outline mode, which can be toggled in the View menu. In Preview mode, you view the document in full color; in Outline mode, you see only the wire frames of the objects.

Illustrator also offers a great way to control the speed and quality of your screen redraws when using the Hand Tool. In the Units & Display Performance area of Preferences, there's a Display Performance slider for the Hand Tool that lets you set your own preferred balance between the speed and quality of redraws.

New View

In truth, this feature hasn't work reliably since Illustrator layer structures included sublayers and objects. Theoretically, using View > New View allows you to save your current window viewpoint, remembering also your zoom level and which layers are hidden, locked, or in Preview mode. Custom views are added to the bottom of the View menu to let you recall a saved view. You can rename a view, but the views themselves are not editable. (For detailed help with with layers and sublayers, see the *Layers & Appearances* chapter.)

New Window

Illustrator gives you the ability to display different aspects of your current image simultaneously. This allows you to separately view different Proof Setups, Overprint or Pixel Previews, and zoom levels. You can resize each window separately, and for each window you can make edges hidden or visible, or hide or lock different *layers* in Preview or Outline (see the *Layers & Appearances* chapter and "Hide/Show Edges" later in this chapter). For instance, using multiple windows of the same file, you can view the full image in Preview and simultaneously work on close detail in Outline mode. This can be useful if you are using a large monitor or multiple monitors. Most window configurations are saved with with your file when you save.

Window controls

There are four choices to Change Screen Mode at the very bottom of the Tools panel. The default is Standard Screen mode (desktop showing around the edges of your file), Full Screen mode with menu bar (file window visible, but confined to the center of the screen with no desktop showing; you can access your menu bar), Full Screen mode (same as above, but you cannot access your menu bar), and Maximized Screen mode (desktop hidden around the edges of your file). You can toggle among the views by pressing the "F" key.

Zooming in & out

Illustrator provides many ways to zoom in and out:
- **From the View menu** Choose Zoom In/Out, Actual Size, or Fit in Window.

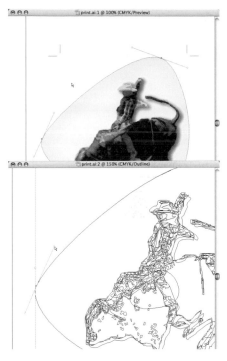

Window > New Window gives you another view of the same artwork. Each window can be sized differently, in a different viewing mode (Preview, Outline, etc.), different magnification, and with different layers visible and/or locked

Zoom shortcuts while typing

Press ⌘/Ctrl with the spacebar to zoom in or ⌘-Option/Ctrl-Alt with the spacebar to zoom out. As long as you press the ⌘/Ctrl first, this works even while you're typing in text-entry mode with the Type tool. (If you then let go of the spacebar, you'll have the Hand tool.)

Zippy zooming

Current magnification is displayed in the bottom left corner of your document. Access a list of percentages (3.13% to 6400%) or Fit on Screen from the pop-up, or simply select the text and enter any percentage within the limit.

There are a multitude of Smart Guide preferences. Here's what each one does:

- Text Label Hints provide information about an object when the cursor passes over it—helpful for identifying a specific object within complicated artwork.
- Construction Guides are the temporary guidelines that help you align between objects and anchor points.
- Transform Tools help with transformations.
- Object Highlighting enables the anchor point, center point, and path of a deselected object to appear as your cursor passes within a specified tolerance from the object. This can be very useful for aligning objects. For best alignment results, select an object's anchor point or center point.

Note: *Smart Guides will slow you down when working on very large files. Also, you can't align using Smart Guides if View > Snap to Grid is enabled.*

Adobe provides many ways to help you learn Illustrator and troubleshoot problems. Choose Help > Illustrator Help (or press F1).

- **With the Zoom tool.** Click to zoom in one level of magnification; hold down the Option/Alt key and click to zoom out one level. You can also click-drag to define an area, and Illustrator will attempt to fill the current window with the area that you defined.

- **Use the ⌘/Ctrl keys for Zoom.** With any tool selected, use ⌘-hyphen/Ctrl-hyphen (minus sign)—think "minus to zoom out"—and ⌘+/Ctrl+ (plus sign)—think "plus to zoom in." Or, you can hold ⌘-spacebar/Ctrl-spacebar and click-drag to zoom in; add Option/Alt to zoom out.

- **Use Context-sensitive menus.** With nothing selected, Control-click (Mac)/right mouse button (Win) to access a pop-up menu so you can zoom in and out, change views, undo, and show or hide guides, rulers, and grids.

- **Navigator panel.** With the Navigator panel, you can quickly zoom in or out and change the viewing area with the help of the panel thumbnail (see Tip "The Navigator panel & views" earlier).

Rulers, Guides, Smart Guides, and Grids

Toggle Illustrator's Show/Hide Rulers, or use the ⌘-R/Crtl-R shortcut, or use the Context-sensitive menu (as long as nothing in your document is selected). The per-document ruler units are set in Document Setup. If you want all new documents to use a specific unit of measurement, change your preferences for Units (Preferences > Units & Display Performance).

Even though the ruler sits in the upper left-hand corner of the page, the location of the ruler origin (0,0) is in the lower left corner of the page. To change the ruler origin, grab the upper left corner (where the vertical and horizontal rulers meet) and drag the crosshair to the desired location. The zeros of the rulers will reset to the point where you release your mouse (to reset the rulers to the default location, double-click the upper left corner). But beware—resetting your ruler origin will realign all patterns and affect alignment of Paste in Front/Back between documents (see the *Layers & Appearances* chapter for more on Paste in Front/Back).

To create simple vertical or horizontal ruler guides, click-drag from one of the rulers into your image. A guide appears where you release your mouse. You can define guide color and style in General Preferences. Guides automatically lock after you create them. To release a guide quickly, ⌘-Shift-double-click (Mac)/Ctrl-Shift-double-click (Win) on the guide. You can lock and unlock guides with the Context-sensitive menu in Preview mode. You should note that locking or unlocking guides affects *every* open document. If you have too many guides visible in your document, simply choose View > Guides > Hide Guides. To make them visible again choose View > Guides > Show Guides. If you want to delete them all permanently, choose View > Guides > Clear Guides. This only works on guides that are on visible, unlocked layers. Hiding or locking layers retains any guides you have created. To learn how to create custom guides from objects or paths, see the "Establishing Perspective" lesson in the *Layers & Appearances* chapter.

Smart Guides can be somewhat unnerving when you see them flash on and off as you work. However, with practice and understanding, you'll be able to refine how to incorporate them into your workflow (see Tip at left). Illustrator also has automatic grids. To view grids, select View > Show Grid, or use the Context-sensitive menu. You can adjust the color, style of line (dots or solid), and size of the grid's subdivisions from Preferences > Guides & Grid. You can also enable a snap-to grid function. Toggle Snap to Grid on and off by choosing View > Snap to Grid (see Tip "Glorious grids" at right).

IMPORTANT: *If you adjust the X and Y axes in Preferences > General > Constrain Angle, it will affect the drawn objects and transformations of your grid, as they will follow the adjusted angle when you create a new object. This works out well if you happen to be doing a complicated layout requiring alignment of objects at an angle.*

Glorious grids

Customize your grids in Illustrator. Select a grid style and color.

- View > Show Grid, use the Context-sensitive menu or ⌘-'(Mac)/ Ctrl -' (Win) (apostrophe).
- Toggle Snap to Grid on and off from the View menu or use the shortcut ⌘-Shift-' (Mac)/ Ctrl-Shift-' (Win) (apostrophe).
- Set the division and subdivision for your grid in Preferences > Guides & Grid and choose either dotted divisions or lines and the color of those lines.
- To toggle the grid display in front or in back of your artwork, check or uncheck the Grids In Back checkbox (Preferences > Guides & Grid).
- Tilt the grid on an angle by choosing Preferences > General and then changing the Constrain Angle value.

Note: *The Constrain Angle affects the angle at which objects are drawn and moved. (See the* Drawing & Coloring *chapter on how to adjust it for creating isometrics.)*

AICS3 images & files cropped!

Unlike pre-CS2 versions of Illustrator, when you place or open an AiCS2 or CS3 image in another application (PS, ID, or a previous version of AI), art extending beyond the paper size will be cropped. To avoid this, choose a larger paper size before saving as a CS3 file.

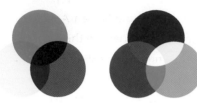

CMY Color Model   RGB Color Model

*CMY (Cyan, Magenta, Yellow) **subtractive** colors get darker when mixed; RGB (Red, Green, Blue) **additive** colors combine to make white.*

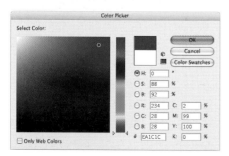

Adobe Color Picker

Transparency Grid & Simulate Color Paper

You can change the background of the Artboard to the transparency grid (to help you see transparency), or to a color. Both the transparency grid and simulated color paper are non-printable attributes.

To view the transparency grid, select View >Show Transparency Grid. Change the grid colors in the Transparency panel of the Document Setup dialog. If you change both grid colors to the same color, you can change the white background to a color (see the *Transparency* chapter).

Hide/Show Edges

If looking at all those anchor points and colored paths distracts you from figuring out what to do with selected objects in your current window, choose View >Hide/Show Edges to toggle them on or off (or use the shortcut: ⌘-H/Crtl-H). Once you hide the edges, all subsequent path edges will be hidden until you show them again. Hide/Show Edges is saved with your file.

COLOR IN ILLUSTRATOR

Consumer-level monitors, which display color in red, green, and blue lights (RGB), cannot yet match four-color CMYK (cyan, magenta, yellow, black) inks printed onto paper. Therefore, you must retrofit the current technology with partial solutions, such as calibrating your monitor.

Working in RGB or CMYK

Illustrator offers you the flexibility of working and printing in either RGB or CMYK color. This is a mixed blessing, because the printing environment cannot accurately capture vibrant RGB colors. As a result, the RGB colors are usually muddy or muted when printed. If your final artwork is going to be printed, work in CMYK!

Work in an RGB color space when creating artwork that will be displayed on-screen, or to simulate a spot color (such as a day-glo color) on your printer. (For more on working in RGB, see the *Web & Animation* chapter.)

Single color space

When you open a new document, you select a color model (or color space). Illustrator no longer allows you to work in multiple color spaces at the same time. If you work in print, always check your files to make certain they are in the appropriate color model before you output. The document's color model is always displayed next to the file name, on the title bar. You can change the document's color mode at any time by choosing File >Document Color Mode >CMYK Color or RGB Color.

Opening legacy documents (documents created with older versions of Illustrator) with objects containing mixed color spaces will invoke a warning asking you to choose a color space (RGB or CMYK). Currently, linked images are not converted to the document's color space. If you open the Document Info panel and select Linked Images, the "Type" info is misleading. For example, if you have a CMYK document with a linked RGB image, the linked image type is Transparent CMYK. The linked image has not been converted, but the image preview has been converted to CMYK.

Color systems and libraries

While your documents can be in RGB or CMYK, you can also mix colors with HSB sliders (Hue, Saturation and Brightness). You can also select colors from other color matching systems, such as the 216-color Web color palette or the color picker. You can access Focoltone, DIC Color, Toyo, Trumatch, and Pantone libraries or the Web palette by choosing Swatch Libraries from the Swatches pop-up menu, from the pop-up menus accessed from the Control panel (by clicking fill or stroke color or arrow), or from the Window menu. Keep in mind that color libraries open as separate uneditable panels, but once you use a color swatch, it will automatically load into your Swatches panel, where you can then edit it. The default for the Swatches panel is to open with swatches—not view by name. Use the panel menu to change to List View if you want your panels to match ours. If you hold

Out of Gamut Warning caution

If you plan to print in CMYK and see an Out of Gamut Warning in the Color panel, take this as a caution that the current color is out of the range of printable colors. Either switch your color mode to CMYK from the Color pop-up menu, or click on the Closest Approximation box next to the gamut warning for an RGB or HSB color approximation. Switching to CMYK mode will allow you to see the actual values of the plates.

The proof is in the Preview

Want the best on-screen preview for your art? Choose View >Overprint Preview for the best way to proof color on your screen and to see how your art will look when printed.

Exchange swatches

The Save Swatches for Exchange feature lets you share swatches between CS3 applications. So swatches you create in Illustrator can be saved for use in Photoshop or InDesign, and vice versa. See the *Drawing & Coloring* chapter for more about this new feature.

The Save Adobe PDF dialog (choose Illustrator PDF in the Format menu of the File > Save or File > Save As dialog)

Acrobat 4 (PDF 1.3)
Acrobat 5 (PDF 1.4)
✓ Acrobat 6 (PDF 1.5)
Acrobat 7 (PDF 1.6)
Acrobat 8 (PDF 1.7)

The Compatibility menu in the Save Adobe PDF dialog

Custom

✓ [Illustrator Default]

[High Quality Print]
[PDF/X–1a:2001]
[PDF/X–3:2002]
[PDF/X–4:2007]
[Press Quality]
[Smallest File Size]

The Preset menu in the Save Adobe PDF dialog

Verify PDF settings

When preparing a PDF file for a commercial printer or service provider, remember to check with the provider to find out what the final output resolution and other settings should be. It may be necessary to customize the settings for a particular provider, in which case you may find it helpful to create a custom preset.

Option/Alt when you choose a view, such as List View, then all swatches will switch to the view you chose. To access styles, brushes, or swatches in other documents, either choose Window > Graphic Style, Brush, Symbol, or Swatch Libraries > Other Library. You can also use the Open Library command in the Graphic Styles, Brushes, Symbols, or Swatches panels (and there is a new button to load them in the lower left corner of each of these panels). Then select the file that contains the item you want. This opens a new panel with that document's components. To automatically store a component from an open library in your current document, just use the graphic style, brush, symbol, or swatch—or drag the swatch from its library panel to the document's panel. (For more information about working with Swatches see the *Drawing & Coloring* chapter introduction.)

SAVING AS PDF

Although you may be used to thinking of PDFs and Illustrator files as two different animals, underneath their hides they have a lot in common. In fact, as long as you save your Illustrator file (.ai) with "Create PDF Compatible File" enabled in the Illustrator Options dialog, for all intents and purposes it *is* a PDF, and can be viewed in Adobe Reader and other PDF viewers.

However, if you want more control over the final PDF product you create, Illustrator makes it easy, letting you choose what version of PDF you'd like to save as, while providing handy PDF presets that let you quickly save PDFs with different settings for different circumstances.

To save a document as a PDF, choose File > Save or File > Save As, and choose Illustrator PDF from the Format menu. After you click Save, you'll be presented with the Save Adobe PDF dialog, where you can choose from a variety of options and settings, including compatibility (PDF version), compression, printer's marks and bleeds, security settings, and more.

The Compatibility menu lets you choose from a number of versions of PDF. Illustrator CS3's default is PDF 1.5, which is compatible with Acrobat 6. You can also choose to save in the newer PDF 1.6 and 1.7 formats, which are compatible with Acrobat 7 and 8 respectively, and which preserve advanced features, such as PDF layers. However, these files may not be compatible with earlier versions of Acrobat, so if you're going to be distributing the file widely, you may want to save as PDF 1.4 or even 1.3 to maximize compatibility. PDF 1.3 is compatible with Acrobat 4 and will be viewable and printable by the widest range of users, but it doesn't support transparency. (There are times when that may be exactly what you want—for example, when you want to flatten the file for sending to a commercial printer.)

You can quickly access frequently used preset PDF settings from the Preset menu. You can create your own custom presets by choosing Custom from the menu, adjusting your settings, and then clicking the Save Preset button at the bottom of the dialog. Additionally, Illustrator ships with a number of predefined presets for experimenting. PDF settings can also be shared among different applications within the Creative Suite.

IMAGE FORMATS

You might need to open a document created in an earlier version of Illustrator (FreeHand, CorelDraw, and some 3D programs allow you to save images in older Illustrator formats). To open any file saved in an earlier version (known as a *legacy file*), drag it onto an Illustrator alias, or open the older formatted file from within Illustrator by choosing File >Open and selecting the document you want to open. Your document will be converted to Illustrator CS3 format, and [Converted] will be added to the file name. If you want to save it in any pre-Illustrator CS3 format, you can do so by choosing File >Save As and then choosing Adobe Illustrator Document from the Format menu in the dialog. After you name your file and click Save, you'll be presented with the Illustrator Options dialog, with a pop-up Version menu that lets you choose from a number of earlier AI versions.

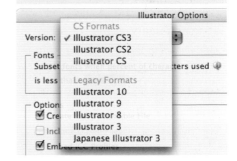

To access legacy formats, you must first choose the standard Illustrator format (.ai) from the Save or Save As dialog; in the resulting Illustrator Options dialog, then choose the desired legacy format from the Version pop-up

Opening Illustrator CS3 files...

You can open Illustrator CS3 files in an earlier version of Illustrator, as long as the file is saved with the Create PDF Compatible File option enabled. You'll get a warning message upon opening the file, and you will lose all your layers, swatches, symbols, styles, and some editable text, but the file will maintain its appearance.

New levels of PostScript

Adobe PostScript Language Level 3 (PS3) improves printing, delivers smoother gradients, and produces better results with files that contain transparency. For technical info on PS3, go to adobe.com and search for "PostScript 3," adding other terms you need info on, such as "trapping" or "printing" (without the quote marks).

Is Raster the answer?

Most printing problems in Illustrator involve transparency and flattening. The optimal setting for the Raster/Vector slider in your flattening settings is all the way to Vector, but if you're having trouble printing, you can try setting it all the way to Raster, which may help in some cases. The flattening settings can be accessed via the Print dialog and the Flattener Preview panel, among other places. See the *Transparency* chapter for details.

If you open any legacy file containing type, you'll get a dialog asking you how to handle the conversion, because Illustrator's current type engine handles type very differently from the way engines did in versions prior to CS. See the *Type* chapter (as well as *Illustrator Help*) for details on working with legacy type.

Other image formats

Illustrator supports many file formats (such as SWF, SVG, GIF, JPEG, TIFF, PICT, PCX, Pixar, and Photoshop). You can also open and edit PDF documents, and even "raw" PostScript files, directly from within Illustrator. If you place images into a document, you can choose whether these files will remain *linked* (see Tip "Links are manageable" on the previous page) or will become *embedded* image objects (see the *Illustrator & Other Programs* chapter for specifics on embedding, and the *Web & Animation* chapter for details on Web-related formats). If you use File > Open, then images become embedded. (See *Illustrator Help* and *Read Me* files for lists of supported formats that shipped with this version.) Check Adobe's Web site (www.adobe.com) for the latest information on supported formats, as well as other file format plug-ins. (For more on file format issues, see the *Other Programs* chapter.)

POSTSCRIPT PRINTING & EPS

When you're ready to print your image, you should use a PostScript printing device for most accurate results. Adobe owns and licenses the PostScript language, making PostScript printers somewhat more expensive than non-PostScript printers. You can proof your images to many non-PostScript printers. Although Illustrator images often print just fine to these printers, sometimes you can run into problems. In general, the newer the PostScript device, the faster and less problematic your printing. PostScript Level 2 and Level 3 printers provide better printing clarity and even some special effects, such as Illustrator's integration of PostScript Level 3's "smooth shading" technology (which should greatly enhance gradients and reduce banding problems). Finally, the more memory you install in your printer, the quicker your text and images will print. For crucial jobs, develop good relations with your service bureau, and get into the habit of running test prints to identify possible problems.

Save As > Illustrator EPS may be necessary if you plan to use QuarkXPress for page layout. Unlike Adobe applications, XPress sometimes does not interpret native Illustrator files sufficiently. For the most part, Encapsulated PostScript (EPS) is a dead format, but, it's still sometimes the only solution. However, saving as Adobe PDF format may work as well, so try it yourself, or ask your service bureau or client what format they prefer.

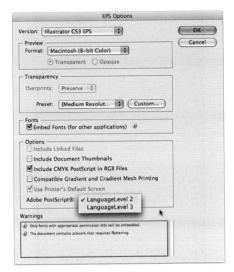

EPS may be dead, but, you can still save your Illustrator work in EPS format if needed by older applications

Correcting and avoiding printing problems

If you have trouble printing, first make sure your placed images are linked properly and the fonts needed to print the document are loaded. Second, check for any complex objects in the document (e.g., objects with many points, compound masks or shapes, or gradient meshes). (See the *Blends, Gradients & Mesh* chapter for issues regarding printing gradient mesh objects.) Use Save a Copy (to retain the original file), remove the complex object(s), and try to print. If that doesn't work, make sure File >Document Setup and the File > Print dialog contain the correct settings for your output device.

Keep in mind that Illustrator's comprehensive Print dialog takes on many of the functions that belonged to the Page Setup and Separation Setup dialogs in versions of Illustrator prior to CS. But the current Print dialog gives you much more control over every part of the printing process.

If you're using transparency, or effects that contain transparency, you might want to preview how your art will print using the Flattener Preview panel (Window > Flattener Preview). For information on the Flattener Preview panel, and other ways to control flattening settings, see the *Transparency* chapter. Printing results will vary depending on these settings. For more technical help with printing and transparency, go to the Adobe website (www.adobe.com) and search for "Spot colors and transparency in Illustrator CS3" (without the quote marks).

More about controlling the size of your files

The major factors that can increase your file size are the inclusion of image objects, path pattern, brushes and ink pen objects, complex patterns, a large number of blends and gradients (especially gradient mesh objects and gradient-to-gradient blends), linked bitmapped images, and transparency. Although linked bitmaps can be large, the same image embedded as an image object is significantly larger. Even so, if you have the need to send your Illustrator file to another, all placed images (and fonts) must be included in order for the recipient to image it properly. Most service bureaus highly recommend delivering your files in Adobe Portable Document Format (PDF) as this will "package" your file, images, and fonts into a single, relatively small PDF file, which makes imaging much easier and more predictable (always check with your service provider in advance).

ACTIONS

Actions are a set of commands or a series of events that you can record and save as a set in the Actions panel. Once a set is recorded, you can play back the actions to automate complex or repetitive tasks (such as a placing registration marks or deleting all unused styles).

Select the action in the Actions panel and activate it by clicking the Play icon at the bottom of the panel, by choosing Play from the pop-up menu, or by assigning the action to a keyboard "F key" (function key) so you can play the action with a keystroke. You can select an action set, a single action, or a command within an action to play. To exclude a command from playing within an action, disable the checkbox to the left of the command.

In order to play some types of actions, you may have to first select an object or text. Load action sets using the pop-up menu.

Since you must record actions and save within an action set, begin a new action by clicking the Create New Set icon or by choosing New Set from the pop-up menu. Name the action set and click OK. With the new set selected, click the Create New Action icon, name the action, and click Record. Illustrator records your commands and steps until you click Stop. To resume recording, click on the last step, choose Begin, and continue adding to the action. When you've finished recording, you'll need to save the action file by selecting the action set and choosing Save Actions from the pop-up menu.

When you are recording, keep in mind that not all commands or tools are recordable. For example, the Pen tool itself is not recordable, but you can add the paths the Pen tool creates to an action by selecting a path and choosing Insert Selected Paths from the pop-up menu. Recording actions takes some practice, so don't get discouraged, and always save a backup file.

Although many of the practical aspects of working with Actions and Scripting is technically beyond the scope of this book, you can find plenty of help with these features in the "Automation_with_Illustrator.pdf" on the *Wow! CD*; this six-page excerpt is from Mordy Golding's *Real World Illustrator CS3* (Peachpit Press).

ADOBE BRIDGE AND ADOBE STOCK PHOTO

Adobe's Creative Suite 3 includes a file browser application called Adobe Bridge. Adobe refers to it as a "navigational control center" that gives you centralized access to your project files, applications, and settings. It's a bridge both in the sense of a command center *and* a link between different places. You can view, search, sort, manage, process, and share files from within Bridge, interfacing between the various Creative Suite applications.

With Bridge and an active Internet connection, you can access Adobe Stock Photos where you can search and purchase stock art and images. Tips, techniques, podcasts, interviews, and training videos are also available in Adobe Bridge Home by choosing File > Browse.

Resolution templates

If you're creating a batch of documents, and want them all to have the same resolution settings, Illustrator's new Templates feature makes it easy. Just set up a new document with the settings you want, and then save it as a template (.ait) file (File > Save as Template). Then you can base as many new documents on your template as you like—and they'll have your preferred resolution settings.

Adobe Stock Photos

In addition to helping you browse and manage the files already on your computer, Adobe Bridge is also your link to Adobe Stock Photos, a new feature that allows you to search for royalty-free images from a number of A-list stock photo agencies. You can find and purchase images using a shopping cart system, all from within Bridge.

The view from the Bridge: Adobe Bridge lets you browse and manage images and files with maximum convenience and control, all from a single centralized window

The Zen of Illustrator

Zen: *"Seeking enlightenment through introspection and intuition rather than scripture."* *

You're comfortable with the basic operations of your computer. You've gone through the Tutorials in the *User Guide* or *Illustrator Help*. You've logged enough hours using Illustrator to be familiar with how each tool (theoretically) functions. You might even understand how to make Bézier curves. Now what? How do you take all this knowledge and turn it into a mastery of the medium?

As with learning any new artistic medium (such as engraving, watercolor, or airbrush), learning to manipulate the tools is just the beginning. Thinking and seeing in that medium is what really makes those tools part of your creative arsenal. Before you can determine the best way to construct an image, you have to be able to envision at least some of the possibilities. The first key to mastering Illustrator is to understand that Illustrator's greatest strength comes not from its many tools and functions but from its extreme flexibility in terms of how you construct images. The first part of this chapter, therefore, introduces you to a variety of approaches and techniques for creating and transforming objects.

Once you've got yourself "thinking in Illustrator," you can begin to *visualize* how to achieve the final results. What is the simplest and most elegant way to construct an image? Which tools will you use? Then, once you've begun, allow yourself the flexibility to change course and try something else. Be willing to say to yourself: How else can I get the results that I want?

The second key to mastering Illustrator (or any new medium) is perfecting your hand/eye coordination. In Illustrator, this translates into being proficient enough with the "power-keys" to gain instant access to tools and functions by using the keyboard. With both eyes on the monitor, one hand on the mouse, and the other hand on the keyboard, an experienced Illustrator user can create and manipulate objects in a fraction of the time required otherwise. The second part of this chapter helps you to learn the "finger dance" necessary to become a truly adept power-user.

The ability to harness the full power of Illustrator's basic tools and functions will ultimately make you a true master of Adobe Illustrator. Treat this chapter like meditation. Take it in small doses if necessary. Be mindful that the purpose of these exercises is to open up your mind to possibilities, not to force memorization. When you can conceptualize a number of different ways to create an image, then the hundreds of hints, tips, tricks, and techniques found elsewhere in this book can serve as a jumping-off point for further exploration. If you take the time to explore and absorb this chapter, you should begin to experience what I call the "Zen of Illustrator." This magical program, at first cryptic and counterintuitive, can help you achieve creative results not possible in any other medium.

*Adapted from *Webster's New World Dictionary of the English Language*

Building Houses

Sequential Object Construction Exercises

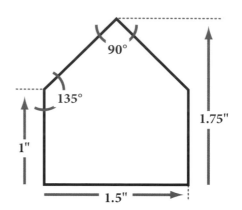

Overview: *Explore different approaches to constructing the same object with Illustrator's basic construction tools.*

1
 zenhouse.ai

2
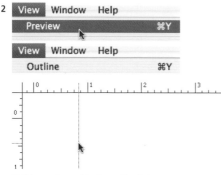

Pulling out a guide from the Ruler

3
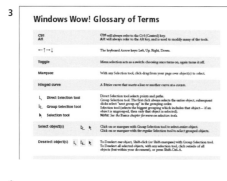

4

Hold down the Shift key to constrain movement to horizontal/vertical direction. For more modifier key help, see the end of this chapter for the "Finger Dance" lesson.

This sequence of exercises explores different ways to construct the same simple object—a house. The purpose of these exercises is to introduce you to the flexibility of Illustrator's object construction, so don't worry if some exercises seem less efficient than others.

So you can more easily follow along, set Units > General to Inches (from Preferences > Units & Display Performance). Also, please read through all of the recommendations below.

1 Use the zenhouse.ai file as a guide. Start with the file zenhouse.ai (copy it to your hard drive from the *Wow! CD*, in the Chapter 2 folder) as a guide when needed.

2 Work in Outline mode, and Show Rulers (View menu). Outline mode eliminates distractions like fills and strokes while it displays centers of geometric objects (marked by "×"). Rulers allow you to "pull out" guides.

3 Read through the *Wow! Glossary.* Please make sure to read *How to use this book* and the *Glossary* pull-out card.

4 Use "modifier" keys. These exercises use Shift and Option (Opt) or Alt keys, which you must hold down until *after* you release your mouse button. If you make a mistake, choose Undo and try again. Some functions are also accessible from the Context-sensitive menu. Try keyboard shortcuts for frequently-used menu commands.

Exercise #1:
Use Add Anchor Point tool

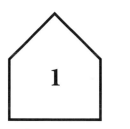

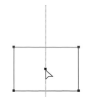

1 Open zenhouse.ai and create a rectangle and a vertical guide. Open zenhouse.ai. On the left corner where the side meets the peak, click to create a rectangle 1.5" x 1". Drag out a vertical guide and snap it to the center.

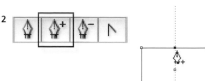

2 Add an anchor point on the top. With the Add Anchor Point tool, click on the top segment over the center guide.

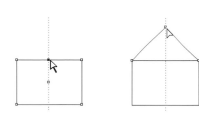

3 Drag the new point up. Use the Direct Selection tool to grab the new point and drag it up into position using the zenhouse as a guide.

Exercise #2:
Make an extra point

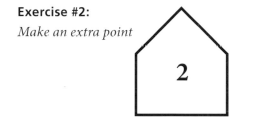

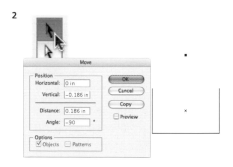

1 Create a rectangle, delete the top path and place a center point. Create a wide rectangle (1.5" x 1"). With the Direct Selection tool, select the top path segment and delete it. With the Pen tool, place a point on top of the rectangle center point.

2 Move the point up. Double-click on a selection tool in the Toolbox to open the Move dialog and enter a 1.25" vertical distance to move the point up.

3 Select and join the point to each side. Use the Direct Selection tool to select the left two points and Join (Object > Path > Join, or ⌘-J/Ctrl-J) them to the top point. Repeat with the right two points.

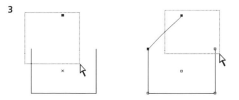

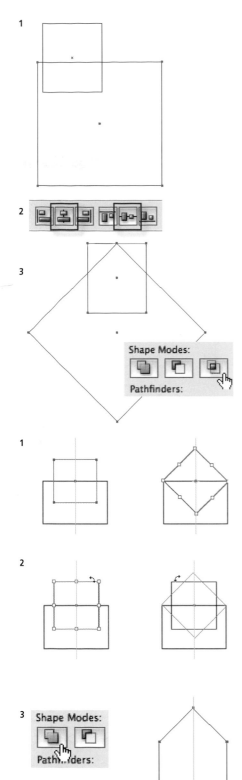

Exercise #3:
*Make two rectangles,
Rotate one, Align,
apply Intersect*

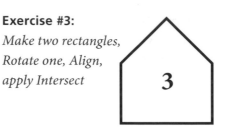

1 Make two rectangles and rotate the second. Click with the Rectangle tool to create a rectangle 1.5" x 1.75". Then click anywhere with the Rectangle tool to create a second rectangle, 3.1795" x 3.1795", and while it's selected, double-click the Rotate tool and specify 45°.

2 Align the rectangles. Select the two rectangles and, in the Control panel, click the vertical center and top Align icons. Then set the fill to white and stroke to black.

3 Apply the Intersect Pathfinder. In the Pathfinder panel (Window menu), click the Intersect shape mode. Switch to Preview mode (View menu) to see the results.

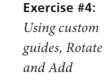

Exercise #4:
*Using custom
guides, Rotate
and Add*

1 Make two rectangles. Create a rectangle (1.5" x 1"), then drag out a vertical guide, snapping it to the center. Hold Option/Alt and, where the center guide intersects the top segment, click with the Rectangle tool. Enter 1.05" x 1.05".

2 Rotate the square. With the Selection tool, move your cursor along the square until you see a Rotate icon. Hold the Shift key and drag until the square pops into position.

3 Select and Add. Choose Select > Select All (⌘-A/Ctrl-A), then Window > Pathfinder and click the Add icon. Switch to Preview mode to see the single shape!

Exercise #5:

Use Add Anchor Points in a three-sided polygon

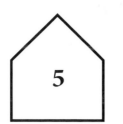

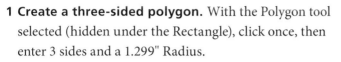

1 Create a three-sided polygon. With the Polygon tool selected (hidden under the Rectangle), click once, then enter 3 sides and a 1.299" Radius.

2 Use the Add Anchor Points command. With the polygon object still selected, choose Object > Path > Add Anchor Points.

3 Average the two left points, then Average the two right points. Direct-Select the two left points and Average them along the vertical axis (Context-sensitive: Average, or Object > Path > Average), then repeat for the two right points.

4 Delete the bottom point. With the Delete Anchor Point tool, click on the bottom point to delete it.

5 Move the top point down. Use the Direct Selection tool to select the top point, then double-click on the Direct Selection tool (in the Toolbox) to open the Move dialog and enter –.186" vertical distance, 90° for angle.

6 Slide in the sides towards the center. Use the Direct Selection tool to click on the right side of the house and drag it towards the center until the roofline looks smooth (hold down your Shift key to constrain the drag horizontally). Repeat for the left side of the house. Alternatively, select the right side and use the ← key on your keyboard to nudge the right side towards the center until the roofline looks smooth. Then, click on the left side to select it, and use the → key to nudge it towards the center. (If necessary, change your Keyboard Increment setting in the Preferences > General dialog.)

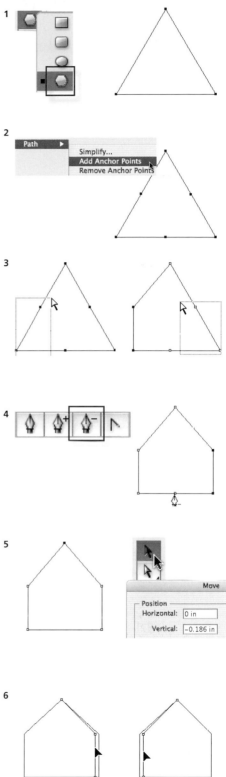

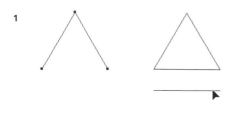

1

Exercise #6:
*Cut a path and
Paste in Front*

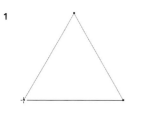

2

1 With zenhouse.ai, cut, paste, then move the bottom of a triangle. In the zenhouse.ai file, click with the Polygon tool and enter 3 Sides and a .866" Radius. With the Direct Selection tool, select and Cut the bottom path to the Clipboard, choose Edit > Paste in Front (⌘-F/Ctrl-F), then grab the bottom path and drag it into position.

2 Create the sides and move middle points into place. Direct-Select the two right points and join them, then repeat for the two left points. Finally, select the two middle points, and grab one to drag *both* up into position.

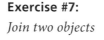

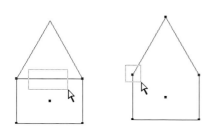

1

Exercise #7:
Join two objects

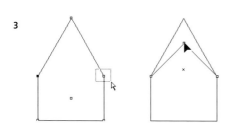

2

3

1 Make two objects. Click once with the Polygon tool, enter 3 Sides and a .866" Radius. Zoom in on the lower left corner and, with the Rectangle tool, click exactly on the lower left anchor point. Set the rectangle to 1.5" x 1".

2 Delete the middle lines and join the corners. Direct-Select marquee the middle bisecting lines and delete. Select the upper-left corner points and Average-Join by either Averaging, and then Joining the points (both from the Object > Path menu) or by pressing ⌘-Shift-Option-J/ Ctrl-Shift-Alt-J to average and join simultaneously. Select and Average-Join the upper right points.

3 Drag the top point down. Grab the top point, hold the Shift key and drag it into position.

Exercise #8:

Use Add Anchor Points, then Average-Join

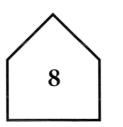

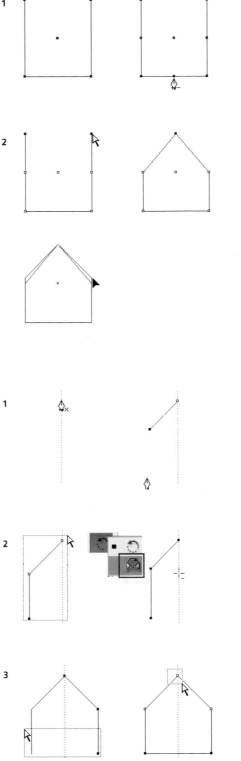

1 Using zenhouse.ai, make a rectangle, delete the top path, add anchor points, remove the bottom point. Create a tall rectangle (1.5" x 1.75") and delete the top path. Choose Add Anchor Points (Object > Path) and use the Delete Anchor Point tool to remove the bottom point.

2 Select and Average-Join the top points and move middles into position. Direct-Select the top two points and Average-Join (see Exercise #7, step 2). Then Direct-Select the middle points, grab one and, with the Shift key, drag them both into position on the zenhouse.

Exercise #9:

Reflect a Pen profile

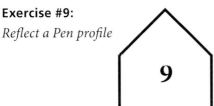

1 Create a house profile. Drag out a vertical guide, then reset the ruler origin on the guide. To draw the profile, use the Pen tool to click on the guide at the ruler zero point, hold down Shift (to constrain your lines to 45° angles) and click to place the corner (.75" down and .75" to the left) and the bottom (1" down).

2 Reflect a copy of the profile. Select all three points of the house profile. With the Reflect tool, Option/Alt-click on the guide line. Enter an angle of 90° and click Copy.

3 Join the two profiles. Direct-Select and Join the bottom two points. Then Direct-Select the top two points and Average-Join (by pressing ⌘-Shift-Option-J/Ctrl-Shift-Alt-J, or Average then Join from the Object > Path menu).

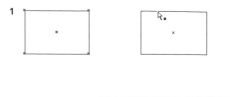

Exercise #10:
Use the Line tool and Align

10

1 Create a Rectangle. With the Rectangle tool, click on your Artboard and specify 1.5" x 1". Choose Select >Deselect, then click the top edge of the rectangle and Delete.

2 Create and align the peak. With the Line tool, click anywhere and specify a 1.75" Length and 90° Angle. Select both objects and, in the Control panel, click the vertical center and bottom Align icons, then Deselect.

3 Delete the bottom point and form the peak. Using Direct Selection, select the bottom line point and Delete. Then marquee the top point and one of the sides. In the Control panel, click the middle Anchors button to Connect the points. Repeat to form the other peak.

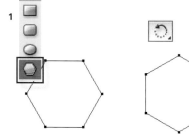

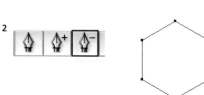

Exercise #11
Make a six-sided polygon

11

1 Create a six-sided polygon using zenhouse.ai. Open zenhouse.ai. Click with the Polygon tool and enter 6 Sides and a .866" Radius. Then double-click the Rotate tool and enter 30°. Align the peak of this object with the zenhouse.

2 Delete the bottom point. With the Delete Anchor Point tool, click on the bottom point to delete it.

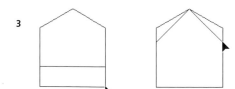

3 Move pairs of points. Use the Direct Selection tool to select the bottom two points. Grab one of the points and Shift-drag in a vertical line into position. Direct-Select, grab and Shift-drag the middle two points into position.

Exercise #12:

With Smart Guides, Rotate and make a Live Paint object

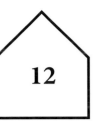

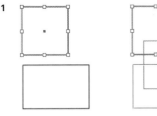
1

1 Make two rectangles. Enable View > Smart Guides. Create one rectangle 1.5" x 1", and one 1.05" x 1.05". Grab the center point of the square and drag it towards the center of the wide rectangle until you see "center" then move it up along this axis to the top edge until you see the words "intersect" and "align."

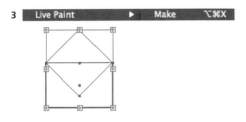
2

2 Rotate the square. With the square selected, double-click the Rotate tool and specify 45°.

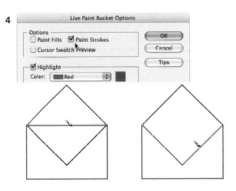
3

3 Make a Live Paint object. Select both objects and choose Object > Live Paint > Make.

4 Use the Live Paint Bucket to "paint out" the interior lines. Switch to Preview mode (View menu) and set the fill to white, stroke to None. Double-click the Live Paint Bucket and, in Options, disable the Paint Fills and enable Paint Strokes, and click OK. Choose None for stroke, then "paint" the interior triangular lines with None.

5 If you want to be able to easily paint the interior of the house as one object, delete the interior lines. Return to Outline mode (View menu). Notice that when you make a Live Paint object, it still maintains the separate shapes that made the original objects—even if you color the strokes separately. However, you *can* blend objects of the same style, like the white-filled house objects, into one object by eliminating the dividing lines.

So that the entire interior of the house operates as if it is one fill, you need to delete the triangular lines that divide the interior. Using the Direct Selection tool, marquee the interior lines and Delete. Switch back to Preview mode to see that the house is still intact.

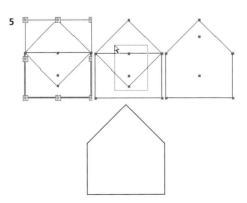
4

5

Of Grids & Lines
Four Ways to Create a Grid of Squares

Overview: *Find different ways to construct the same simple grid.*

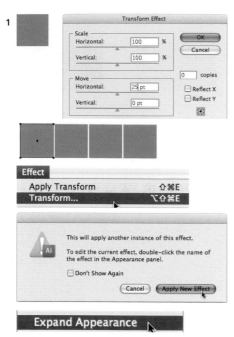

Make one square, apply Effect > Distort & Transform > Transform and specify a Move of 25 pt for Horizontal and 3 copies, then Effect > Transform to specify a move of 25 pt for Vertical and 3 copies; for editable squares, choose Object > Expand Appearance

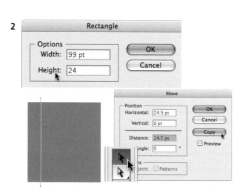

Clicking on the word Height or Width in a dialog will copy the other value; after making a vertical line and using Move to make a copy of it

There's rarely only one right way to create anything. Give different Illustrator experts a problem to solve, and they'll come up with different solutions. This clean logo designed by Jack Tom for Craik Consulting, Inc. provides a great opportunity to explore different ways to create a simple grid of blue squares separated by white lines.

Everybody's mind works differently, and the most obvious solutions to you might seem innovative to someone else. If design changes require you to rethink your initial approach (for instance, if the client wants the white areas of a logo to be holes that allow a background photo to show through), try to construct it another way.

1 Making separate small squares. With the Rectangle tool, click on your page and specify a 24 pt by 24 pt square. While it's still selected, choose a blue color from the Swatches panel. To create the horizontal row choose Effects > Distort & Transform > Transform. Specify a Move of 25 pt for Horizontal, and 3 for Copies and click OK. To fill out the grid vertically, again choose the Transform near the top of the Effects menu and click "Apply New Effect" when you see the warning. This time specify a Move of -25 pt for Vertical and 3 for Copies. If later you want to edit the rectangles separately, you can expand the live effect with Object > Expand Appearance.

2 Making one large rectangle with white lines on top.
This method is a bit longer than the others, but it also allows for more design flexibility. In constructing his actual logo, Jack Tom included white lines over one large blue square, so he could control exactly how and where each line interacted with the logo "figure." He deleted part of a line below the large, white oval, and he nudged other lines slightly, horizontally or vertically.

To make a large square, choose a blue fill, click with the Rectangle tool and specify 99 pt for Width and click the word Height to automatically fill in the same number as Width (99 pt). Hold the Shift key and draw a vertical line that starts above and extends below your rectangle, and set a Fill of None and white for Stroke. To make a second line, double-click a selection tool in the Toolbox and, in the Move dialog, enter 25 pt Horizontal, 0 for Vertical, and click Copy. Make the third line by pressing ⌘-D/Ctrl-D (which is Transform Again). For the cross lines, select your three lines, Group (⌘-G/Ctrl-G), double-click the Rotate tool, enter 90° and click Copy. To align the lines to the square, Select All (⌘-A/Ctrl-A), click the square (to designate the square as the object others align to) and, in the Control panel, click both the horizontal and vertical center Align icons.

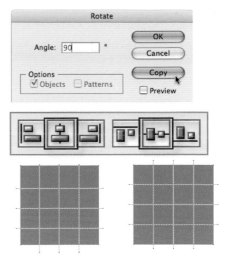

After creating the three vertical lines, using Rotate to make the horizontal copies, and aligning lines with the rectangle

3 Splitting the square using a grid. Another way to create this particular grid is to choose a blue fill and click with the Rectangle tool and specify 99 pt Width and Height. Now choose Object >Path >Split Into Grid and specify 4 rows, 4 columns; ignore the height and width but enter 1 pt for each Gutter.

Choosing Split Into Grid and specifying the parameters in the dialog

4 Using the Rectangular Grid tool. For this last simple version, set your Stroke to 1 pt White and select a blue Fill. Choose the Rectangular Grid tool (from the Line tool pop-up), click on the Artboard and specify 100 pt for both Width and Height. Enter 3 for each of the divider fields, and be sure to enable both "Use Outside Rectangle as Frame" and "Fill Grid," and click OK.

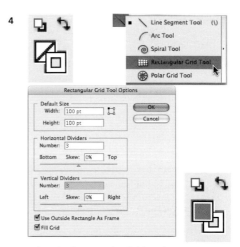

Using the Rectangular Grid tool

Zen Scaling *(with the Scale tool)*

Note: *Use the Shift key to constrain proportions.* **Zen Scaling** *practice is also on the* **Wow! CD**.

1 Scaling proportionally towards the top Click at the top, grab lower-right (LR), drag up

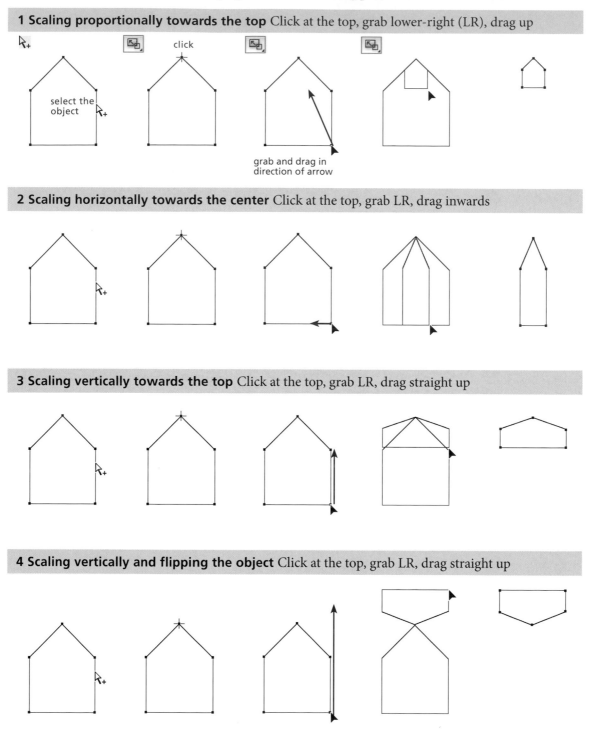

select the object

click

grab and drag in direction of arrow

2 Scaling horizontally towards the center Click at the top, grab LR, drag inwards

3 Scaling vertically towards the top Click at the top, grab LR, drag straight up

4 Scaling vertically and flipping the object Click at the top, grab LR, drag straight up

Zen Scaling *(with the Scale tool, continued)*

Note: *Use the Shift key to constrain proportions.* ***Zen Scaling*** *practice is also on the* ***Wow! CD***.

---

5 Scaling proportionally towards lower-left (LL) Click LL, grab upper-right, drag to LL

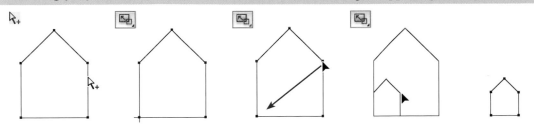

---

6 Scaling horizontally to the left side Click LL, grab lower-right (LR), drag to left

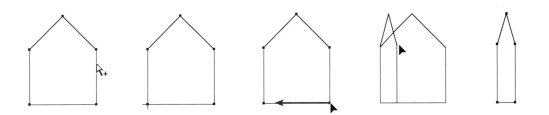

---

7 Scaling vertically towards the bottom Click center bottom, grab top, drag down

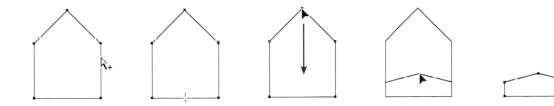

---

8 Scaling proportionally towards the center Click the center, grab corner, drag to center

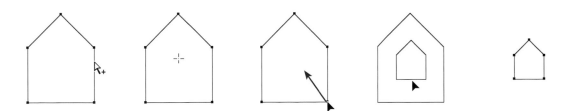

Or, to scale about the center, use the Scale tool to click-drag outside the object towards the center

Zen Rotation *(with the Rotate tool)*

Note: *Use the Shift key to constrain movement.* **Zen Rotation** *practice is also on the* **Wow! CD**.

1 Rotating around the center Click in the center, then grab lower-right (LR) and drag

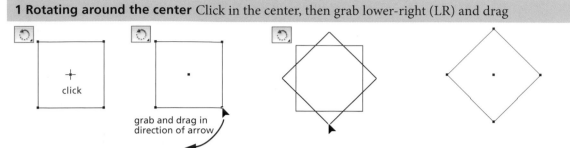

click

grab and drag in
direction of arrow

Or, to rotate about the center, use the Rotate tool to click-drag outside the object towards the center

2 Rotating from a corner Click in the upper left corner, then grab LR and drag

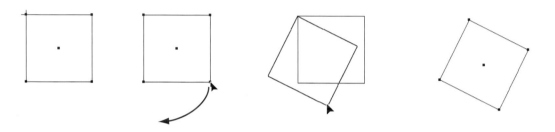

3 Rotating from outside Click above the left corner, then grab LR and drag

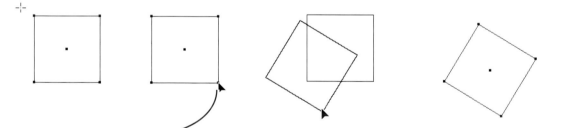

4 Rotating part of a path Marquee points with the Direct Selection tool, then use Rotate tool

Marquee the forearm with Direct Selection tool   *With the Rotate tool, click on the elbow, grab the hand and drag it around*

Creating a Simple Object Using the Basic Tools

Key: *Click where you see a RED cross, grab with the GRAY arrow and drag towards BLACK arrow.*

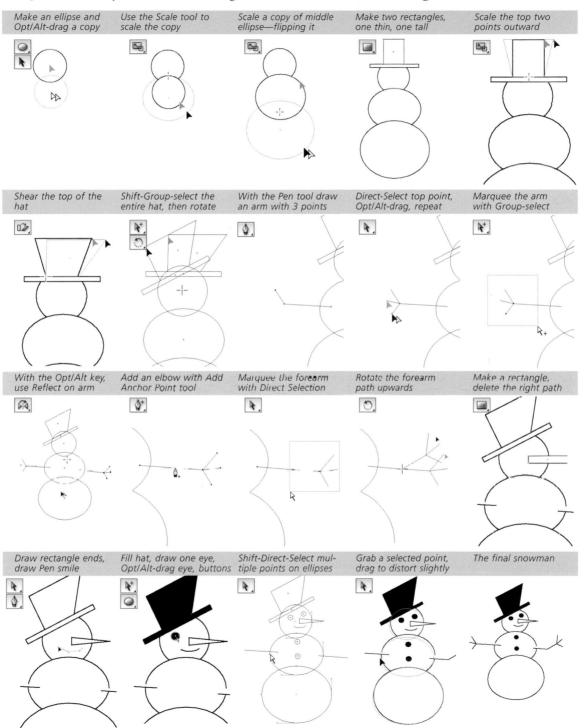

| Make an ellipse and Opt/Alt-drag a copy | Use the Scale tool to scale the copy | Scale a copy of middle ellipse—flipping it | Make two rectangles, one thin, one tall | Scale the top two points outward |

| Shear the top of the hat | Shift-Group-select the entire hat, then rotate | With the Pen tool draw an arm with 3 points | Direct-Select top point, Opt/Alt-drag, repeat | Marquee the arm with Group-select |

| With the Opt/Alt key, use Reflect on arm | Add an elbow with Add Anchor Point tool | Marquee the forearm with Direct Selection | Rotate the forearm path upwards | Make a rectangle, delete the right path |

| Draw rectangle ends, draw Pen smile | Fill hat, draw one eye, Opt/Alt-drag eye, buttons | Shift-Direct-Select multiple points on ellipses | Grab a selected point, drag to distort slightly | The final snowman |

A Finger Dance
Turbo-charge with Illustrator's Power-keys

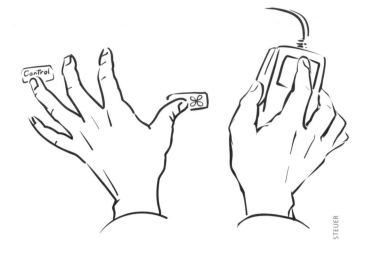

Overview: *Save hours of production time by mastering the finger dance of Illustrator's power-keys.*

Find a summary of Finger Dance power-keys on the pull-out quick reference card

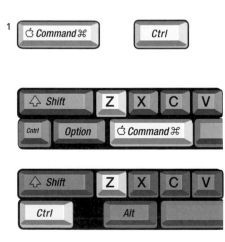

If you are using the mouse to choose your selection tools from the Toolbox, you need this lesson. With some time and patience, you'll be able to free up your mouse so that practically the only thing you do with it is draw. Your other hand will learn to dance around the keyboard accessing all of your selection tools, modifying your creation and transformation tools, using your Zoom and Hand tools and, last but not least, providing instant Undo and Redo.

This "Finger Dance" is probably the most difficult aspect of Illustrator to master. Go through these lessons in order, but don't expect to get through them in one or even two sittings. When you make a mistake, use Undo (⌘-Z/Ctrl-Z). Try a couple of exercises, then go back to your own work, incorporating what you've just learned. When you begin to get frustrated, take a break. Later—hours, days, or weeks later—try another lesson. And don't forget to breathe.

Rule #1: Always keep one finger on the ⌘/Ctrl key.
Even when you're using a new tablet with keyboard characters, in most cases, the hand you are not drawing with should be resting on the actual keyboard, with a finger (or thumb) on the ⌘/Ctrl key. This position will make that all-important Undo (⌘-Z/Ctrl-Z) instantly accessible.

Rule #2: Undo if you make a mistake. This is so crucial an aspect of working in the computer environment that I am willing to be redundant. If there is only one key combination that you memorize, make it Undo (⌘-Z/Ctrl-Z).

Rule #3: The ⌘/Ctrl key turns your cursor into the last used selection tool. In Illustrator, the ⌘/Ctrl key does a lot more than merely provide you with easy access to Undo. The ⌘/Ctrl key will convert any tool into the selection arrow that you last used. In the exercises that follow, you'll soon discover that the most flexible selection arrow is the Direct Selection tool.

Rule #4: Watch your cursor. If you learn to watch your cursor, you'll be able to prevent most errors before they happen. And if you don't (for instance, if you drag a copy of an object by mistake), use Undo and try again.

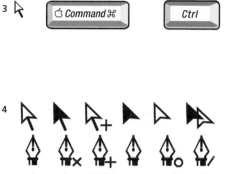

Rule #5: Pay careful attention to *when* you hold down each key. Most of the modifier keys operate differently depending on *when* you hold each key down. If you obey Rule #4 and watch your cursor, you'll notice what the key you are holding does.

Rule #6: Hold down the key(s) until after you let go of your mouse button. In order for your modifier key to actually modify your action, you *must* keep your key down until *after* you let go of your mouse button.

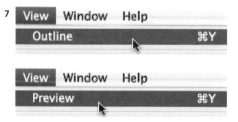

Rule #7: Work in Outline mode. When you are constructing or manipulating objects, get into the habit of working in Outline mode. Of course, if you are designing the colors in your image, you'll need to work in Preview, but while you're learning how to use the power-keys, you'll generally find it much quicker and easier if you are in Outline mode. Use the View menu, or ⌘-Y/Ctrl-Y to toggle between Preview (the default) and Outline modes.

Before you begin this sequence of exercises, choose the Direct Selection tool, then select the Rectangle tool and drag to create a rectangle.

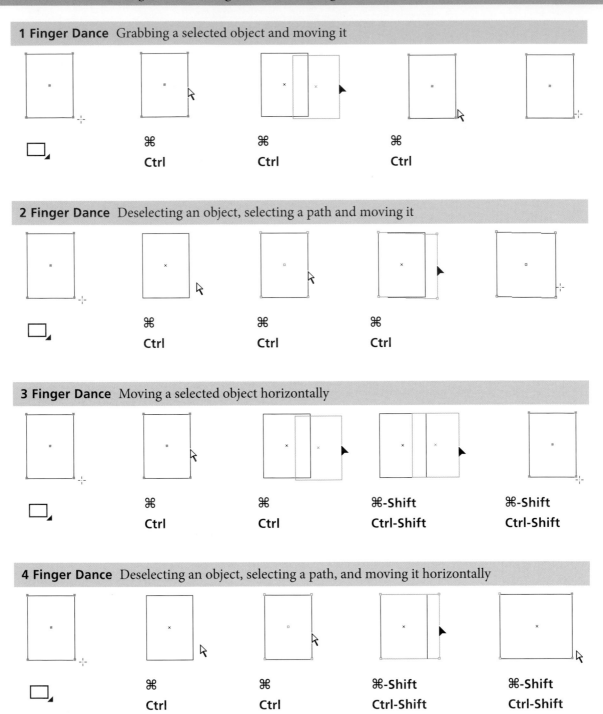

1 Finger Dance Grabbing a selected object and moving it

2 Finger Dance Deselecting an object, selecting a path and moving it

3 Finger Dance Moving a selected object horizontally

4 Finger Dance Deselecting an object, selecting a path, and moving it horizontally

THE FINGER DANCES

Before you begin this sequence of exercises, choose the Direct Selection tool,
then select the Rectangle tool and drag to create a rectangle.

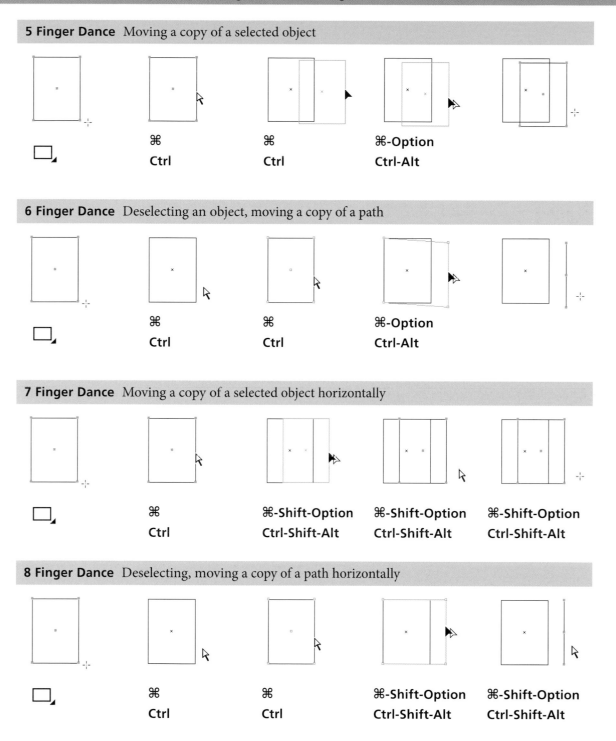

5 Finger Dance Moving a copy of a selected object

⌘	⌘	⌘-Option
Ctrl	Ctrl	Ctrl-Alt

6 Finger Dance Deselecting an object, moving a copy of a path

⌘	⌘	⌘-Option
Ctrl	Ctrl	Ctrl-Alt

7 Finger Dance Moving a copy of a selected object horizontally

⌘	⌘-Shift-Option	⌘-Shift-Option	⌘-Shift-Option
Ctrl	Ctrl-Shift-Alt	Ctrl-Shift-Alt	Ctrl-Shift-Alt

8 Finger Dance Deselecting, moving a copy of a path horizontally

⌘	⌘	⌘-Shift-Option	⌘-Shift-Option
Ctrl	Ctrl	Ctrl-Shift-Alt	Ctrl-Shift-Alt

Before you begin this sequence of exercises, choose the Direct Selection tool,
then select the Rectangle tool and drag to create a rectangle.

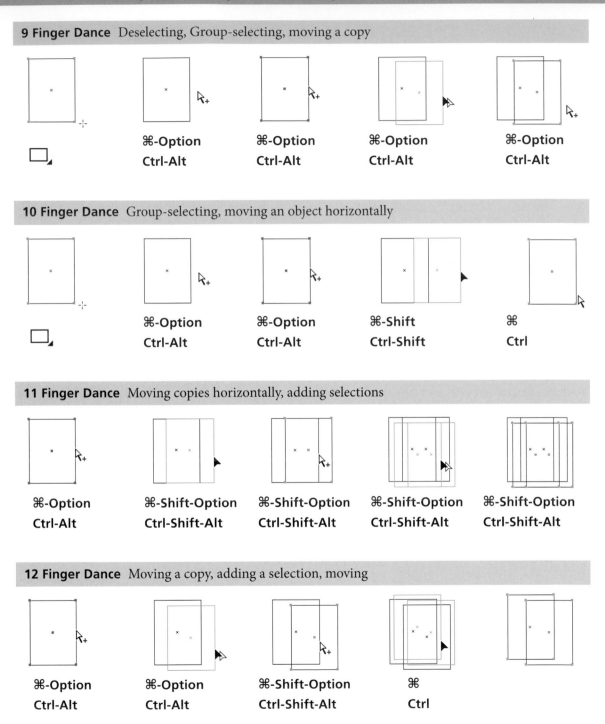

9 Finger Dance Deselecting, Group-selecting, moving a copy

| ⌘-Option | ⌘-Option | ⌘-Option | ⌘-Option |
| Ctrl-Alt | Ctrl-Alt | Ctrl-Alt | Ctrl-Alt |

10 Finger Dance Group-selecting, moving an object horizontally

| ⌘-Option | ⌘-Option | ⌘-Shift | ⌘ |
| Ctrl-Alt | Ctrl-Alt | Ctrl-Shift | Ctrl |

11 Finger Dance Moving copies horizontally, adding selections

| ⌘-Option | ⌘-Shift-Option | ⌘-Shift-Option | ⌘-Shift-Option | ⌘-Shift-Option |
| Ctrl-Alt | Ctrl-Shift-Alt | Ctrl-Shift-Alt | Ctrl-Shift-Alt | Ctrl-Shift-Alt |

12 Finger Dance Moving a copy, adding a selection, moving

| ⌘-Option | ⌘-Option | ⌘-Shift-Option | ⌘ |
| Ctrl-Alt | Ctrl-Alt | Ctrl-Shift-Alt | Ctrl |

3

An open path shown stroked (left), filled and stroked (center), and filled only (right); note that the fill is applied as if a straight line connected the two endpoints

Swapping fill and stroke

When you press the X key by itself, it toggles the Stroke or Fill box to *active* (in front of the other) on the Tools and Color panels. If you press Shift-X it swaps the actual *attributes* or contents of the Stroke and Fill boxes. For example, if you start with a white fill and a black stroke, you will have a black fill and a white stroke after you press Shift-X. **Note:** *Because gradients are not allowed on strokes, Shift-X will not work when the current fill is a gradient.*

The Align Stroke buttons in the Stroke panel (Center, Inside, Outside)

Drawing & Coloring

This chapter goes beyond the two previous in outlining the fundamentals of Illustrator's drawing and coloring tools and panels. In this chapter you'll also find information about the simpler parts of the new feature set that Adobe calls Live Color (see the *Live Color* chapter for more on these features). Once you've got these basics under your belt, you'll be ready to move on to the more advanced techniques in the following chapters.

STROKE AND FILL

Every object you draw in Illustrator has two components that can be styled—*stroke* and *fill*. *Fill* is what goes inside of a path. The chosen fill can be a color, a gradient, or a pattern, or even a fill of None (which means no fill of any kind). When you fill an open path (where the endpoints aren't connected), the fill is applied as if the two endpoints were connected by a straight line (even though they're not).

Stroke refers to the "outline" of your drawn object. So the fill is the space enclosed by a path, and that path can be stroked to make it look any way you want. You do this by assigning attributes to the path, including weight (how thick or thin it looks), line style (whether the line is solid or dashed), and the styles of line joins and line caps. You can also assign your path a stroke of None, in which case it won't have a visible stroke at all. (Dashed lines, joins, and caps are covered later in this chapter intro.) You can also control whether a stroke will align with the center, inside, or outside of a closed path. To do this, select a closed path and click the appropriate Align Stroke button in the Stroke panel to set the alignment of the stroke to the Center, Inside, or Outside of the path.

The many ways to fill or stroke an object

To set the fill or stroke for an object, first select the object and then click on the Fill or Stroke icon near the bottom of the Toolbox (toggle between fill and stroke using the X key.) To set the object's stroke or fill to None, use the "/" key, or click the None button on the Toolbox or the Color panel (the little white box with a red slash through it).

You can set the fill or stroke color you want using any of the following methods: 1) adjusting the sliders or sampling a color from the color bar in the Color panel; 2) clicking on a swatch in the Swatches panel; 3) using the Eyedropper tool to sample color from other objects in your file; 4) sampling colors from the Color Picker; 5) clicking on a swatch from the Color Guide panel; or 6) clicking the Fill or Stroke icons in the control bar. (To open the Adobe Color Picker, double-click the Fill or Stroke icon in the Toolbox or the Color panel.) In addition, you can drag color swatches from panels to objects (selected or not), or to the Fill/Stroke icon in the Toolbox.

WORKING WITH THE COLOR PANELS

There are now four different panels for working with color: Color, Swatches, Color Guide, and kuler (pronounced "cooler"—see Tip at right for more about kuler). By default, the panel dock only displays one panel at a time. To view multiple panels at once, you must drag each from the dock into your workspace or rearrange panels in your dock in Expanded view. You can also access each panel from the Window menu (see the first chapter, *Illustrator Basics,* to learn more about working with panels).

Color panel

The Color panel is a collection of tools that allows you to mix and apply color to your artwork. In addition to the sliders and edit fields for locating precise colors, this panel includes a None button (lower left) so you can set your Fill or Stroke to no color at all. There's also a color spectrum bar where you can click to select color and a black/white proxy.

The little 3D cube that often pops up next to your color is a Web Color Warning. Adobe maintains this simple feature even though most people agree that Web-safe

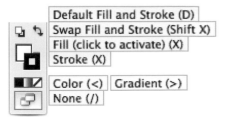

Fill and Stroke section of the Tools panel

Control bar fill and stroke

When you click on the fill or stroke icons in the control bar, you get the Swatch panel content. If you hold the Shift key, you get the Color panel sliders.

How cool is kuler?

kuler (lowercase) is Adobe's marketing name for an experimental technology from Adobe labs included only in the US and Int'l English builds of Illustrator. (See the *Live Color* chapter for more about kuler.)

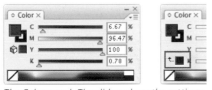

The Color panel. The sliders show the settings of the Fill or Stroke color—whichever is in front. Shown on the right is the Last Color proxy (outlined in red); when it appears, you can click it to return to the last color used before choosing a pattern or gradient, or setting a style of None

The Web Color and Out of Gamut Color warning area (outlined in red) and pop-up menu of the color panel.

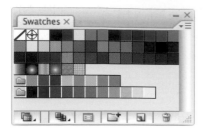

Swatches panel showing all swatches

Swatch Options for a global process color

The Swatches panel, shown in list view for color swatches only; the top two swatches are process colors; the middle two are spot colors; and the last two are global colors (at left with the document in CMYK mode, at right the same colors with the document in RGB mode)

The same swatches as in the previous caption, this time shown in large thumbnail view; the left two are process; the middle two are spot (includes a white triangle with a "spot"); the right two are global (includes a simple white triangle)

Swatch panel shortcuts

Hold ⌘/Ctrl when you click the New Swatch Button to make it a new Spot color. Hold ⌘-Shift/Ctrl-Shift when you click to create a new Global color. Hold Option/Alt to add the color in the Color panel as a swatch.

color is largely a non-issue at this point. Clicking this area of the Color panel allows you to quickly convert a color to the closest match of Web-safe color. If you're creating artwork for the Web, you may also wish to choose Web Safe RGB from the Color panel menu.

The Color panel's menu options also include Invert and Complement. Search for Invert or Complement in Illustrator Help for Adobe's explanation of these terms.

When you're creating artwork for print, if you choose or mix a color out of the CMYK gamut, an exclamation point appears on the Color panel. Illustrator will suggest to you an "In Gamut Color" that it thinks is a close match; click on the mini swatch to accept the suggestion.

Swatches panel

To save a color you've mixed in the Color panel, drag it to the Swatches panel, or just click the New Swatch button at the bottom of the Swatches panel. You can also create a new swatch by choosing New Swatch from the Swatches panel menu, or by choosing Create New Swatch from the Color panel pop-up menu.

Whenever you copy and paste objects that contain custom swatches or styles from one document to another, Illustrator will automatically paste those elements into the new document's panels.

The Swatch Options dialog box (which you can open by double-clicking any swatch or by clicking the Swatch Options button at the bottom of the Swatch panel) lets you change the individual attributes of a swatch—including its name, color mode, color definition, and whether it's a process, global process, or spot color (see the section following). For pattern and gradient swatches, the only attribute in the Swatch Options dialog box is the name.

Process, global, and spot colors

You can create three kinds of solid fills in Illustrator: process colors, global process colors, and spot colors. These three kinds of colors each appear differently in the Swatches panel, so they're easy to distinguish visually.

- **Process colors** are colors that are printed using a mixture of the four CMYK color values: Cyan, Magenta, Yellow, and Black. (If you're doing non-print work in RGB, your color mixture would use Red, Green, and Blue.)

- **Global process colors** are process colors that have an added convenience: If you update the swatch for a global process color, Illustrator will update that color for all objects that use it in the document. You can identify a global process color in the Swatches panel by the small triangle in the lower right corner of the swatch (when the panel is in Thumbnail view) or by the Global Color icon (when the panel is in List view). You can create a global process color by enabling the Global option in either the New Swatch dialog or the Swatch Options dialog. (The Global check box is disabled by default.)

- **Spot colors** are custom colors used in print jobs that require a premixed ink rather than a percentage of the four process colors. Specifying a spot color allows you to use colors that are outside of the CMYK gamut, or to achieve a more precise color match than CMYK allows. You can specify a color as a spot color in the New Swatch dialog box (by choosing Spot Color from the Color Type menu), or you can choose a spot color from a Swatch library, such as the various Pantone libraries (from the Swatch panel's Swatch Libraries Menu button choose Color Books). All spot colors are global, so they update automatically; and, when the Swatches panel is in Thumbnail view, they have a small triangle in the lower right corner, as well as a small dot or "spot." In List view, they're marked by the Spot Color icon.

Creating Color Groups

You can now create and save your own groups of colors with the New Color Group button located at the bottom center of the Swatches panel. To create a new color group, simply select multiple colors from the Swatches panel by Shift-clicking to select contiguous swatches, or by holding

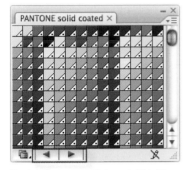

Swatch library panels have left/right arrow buttons at the bottom. Click an arrow to go to the next Swatch library (in the same panel)

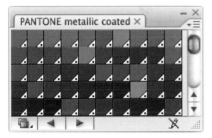

The swatches in this Pantone library all have white triangles with dots to show that they're both global and spot colors

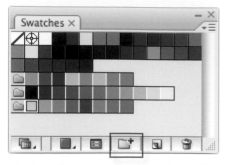

The New Color Group button makes it possible to organize your Swatches panel by grouping colors that you choose. You also specifiy the name for the group

When deleting swatches

When you click the Trash icon in the Swatches panel to delete se-lected swatches, Illustrator does *not* warn you that you might be deleting colors used in the docu-ment. Instead Illustrator will con-vert global colors and spot colors used to fill objects to non-global process colors. To be safe, choose Select All Unused and then click the Trash.

Save Swatch Library as ASE, found in the Swatches panel menu, makes it easy to save custom swatch libraries to use in other Adobe applications

⌘/Ctrl and clicking for non-contiguous selections. Then click the New Color Group button. Alternatively, select objects in your artwork that contain the colors you desire and then click the New Color Group button. You'll be given the opportunity to name your color group, and your new group will be saved and ready to use in the Swatches panel.

Custom swatch libraries

There are several places from which you can access swatch libraries. Probably the simplest method is to click the Swatch Libraries menu button, at the lower left of the Swatches panel (see Tip "Accessing the libraries" earlier in this section also).

Once you've set up your Swatches panel to your satis-faction, you can save it as a custom swatch library for use with other documents. This can help you avoid having to duplicate your efforts later on. Saving a swatch library is easy—click the Swatch Libraries menu button at the lower left of the Swatches panel and choose Save Swatches. This will, by default, save your swatch library to the Adobe Illustrator CS3 Swatches folder (for details about where swatch libraries are stored, search for Swatch Libraries in Adobe Illustrator Help).

Exchanging swatches

Adobe's Creative Suite allows you to easily share swatches between the different Adobe applications. So, you can save your Illustrator swatches for use in InDesign, or save your Photoshop swatches for use in Illustrator, and so on.

To save Illustrator swatches for use in other Adobe applications, set up your Swatches panel with the swatches you want and remove any extraneous ones. Then choose "Save Swatch Library as ASE" from the Swatches panel pop-up menu, and save the swatch library to a convenient location. Now you can load the swatch library you've saved (file name ending in .ase) into most other Adobe applications. Likewise, you can save swatch libraries from other applications to use in Illustrator (in .ase format). To load a swatch library in Illustrator, choose Other Library from the Swatch Libraries menu in the Swatches panel. You'll be presented with a dialog box that lets you locate the swatch library you've saved from another application.

Color Guide

In the Color Guide panel, you can generate groups of colors that Illustrator "thinks" will go well with your current color. It uses scientific "Harmony Rules" of color theory to make suggestions. The Color Guide panel is one of several enhancements in Illustrator that Adobe refers to collectively as Live Color. The Color Guide panel could be thought of as a kind of color laboratory where you can apply color theory rules to your source color.

The variation grid is the main area in the Color Guide panel, just below the Harmony Rules menu (be sure to first select Show Options in the Color Guide panel's pop-up menu). Vertically, this grid displays hues determined by the Harmony Rule you choose. Horizontally, you see variations of each color (or hue) in the harmony selection. The grid can be altered to display three different variations: Tints/Shades, Warm/Cool, or Vivid/Muted.

As one example of using the Color Guide, you could choose Complementary 2 from the drop-down Harmony Rules menu (a listing of classic color harmonics). This would give you analogous colors (colors adjacent on the color wheel) in the variation grid. In the example shown (top), we have our red source color and five complementary hues showing in the Harmony Rules menu area—six distinct hues. Notice how the variation grid shows those same five hues stacked vertically down the center of the grid? The source color is at the top with the other harmony colors underneath. To the left of each hue are shades (darker values) of that hue and to the right are tints (lighter values).

Using the buttons along the bottom of the Color Guide, you can limit the colors to a certain swatch library, access the Live Color dialog box (more about this in the

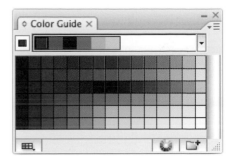

The Color Guide panel showing Tints/Shades (right/left) of a particular red (the source color) and its complements (greens)

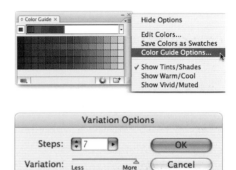

Color Guide Options

The Color Guide panel default setting gives you seven steps—seven shade samples to the left and seven tint samples to the right for your source color and for each color in the harmony which you've selected. However, you can change this by choosing "Color Guide Options" from the Color Guide panel pop-up menu and adjusting the number of Steps. The amount of Variation can also be altered here by adjusting the Less or More slider. Less will give you a smaller variance of Tints/Shades (or Warm/Cool, or Vivid/Muted). More will result in a greater variance between the steps shown.

From left to right: the Eyedropper tool, the cursor in normal sampling mode, in applying mode (Option/Alt), with Shift then Option/Alt key to add (not replace) appearances, and from type

Sampling from the desktop

Use the Eyedropper to sample attributes from any object on your computer's desktop, but keep in mind that the Eyedropper will only pick up RGB color when sampling from outside the current Illustrator document. To sample attributes from the desktop, first select the object whose attributes you want to change. Then select the Eyedropper tool, click anywhere on your document and continue to hold the mouse button down while you move your cursor over the desktop object you want to sample. Once your cursor is over the object, just release the mouse button and you'll see the sampled attributes applied to the selected object.

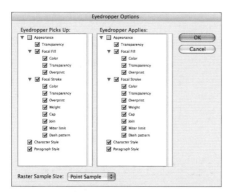

Eyedropper options give control over what to pick up and/or deposit. In addition to stroke, fill, color, and text formatting, you can use the Eyedropper to copy styles and type attributes (which are discussed later in the book).

Live Color chapter), and save a color group to the Swatch panel. After experimenting and arriving at colors that you like, you can apply the color to your artwork (stroke or fill) by dragging a color from the Color Guide panel or by selecting one or more objects in your artwork and then clicking a color in the variation grid.

THE TWO-IN-ONE EYEDROPPER

The Eyedropper tool allows you to copy appearance attributes from one object to another, including stroke, fill, color, and text attributes. It's true: the Eyedropper picks up *and* applies text formatting and has two modes: the *sampling* Eyedropper and the *applying* Eyedropper.

To copy attributes from one object to another using the Eyedropper, first select the Eyedropper from the Toolbox, and position it over an unselected object. You'll see that the Eyedropper is in sampling mode (it angles downward to the left). Click the object to pick up its attributes. Now position the Eyedropper over the unselected object to which you want to apply the attributes you just sampled, and hold down the Option (Mac)/Alt (Win) key. The Eyedropper will switch to applying mode: It angles downward to the right, and looks full. Click the object to apply the attributes sampled from the first object.

Alternatively, you can use the single-step method: First select the object with the appearance attributes you want to change, and then move the Eyedropper over the unselected object from which you want to copy attributes. Click to sample the unselected object's attributes and apply them to the previously selected object all at once. (With this method, you won't see the Eyedropper change from sampling to applying, since the whole process happens in one step.)

In addition to sampling color from objects, the Eyedropper can sample colors from raster and mesh images if you hold down the Shift key as you click. The Shift key can also modify the Eyedropper in other ways. By default, a regular click with the Eyedropper picks up all fill and stroke attributes (it picks up the complete appearance of an object, including Live Effects). Using the single-step method described above, adding the Shift key allows you to sample the *color only* (as opposed to sampling the other appearance attributes as well); this will apply the color you sample to the stroke or the fill, whichever is active in the Toolbox at the time you click. If you hold Shift-Option/Shift-Alt when you click, you'll *add* the appearance attributes of an object to the selected object's appearance—instead of just replacing it.

You can control which attributes the Eyedropper picks up and applies by using the Eyedropper Options dialog box (accessed by double-clicking the Eyedropper in the Toolbox). You can also control the size of an area the Eyedropper samples from raster images by using the Raster Sample Size menu at the bottom of the dialog box. Choosing Single Point will sample from a single pixel; 3 x 3 will pick up a sample averaged from a 3-pixel grid surrounding the point you click on; and 5 x 5 will do so for a 5-pixel grid. (Averaging helps you to get a more accurate sample of the actual color than the human eye can perceive.)

END OF LINES

Sometimes stroked lines seem to match up perfectly when viewed in Outline mode but they visibly overlap in Preview mode. You can solve this problem by changing the end caps in the Stroke panel. Just select one of the three end cap styles described below to determine how the endpoints of your selected paths will look when previewed.

The first (and default) choice is a Butt cap; it causes your path to stop at the end anchor point. Butt caps are essential for creating exact placement of one path against another. The middle choice is the Round cap, which rounds the endpoint in a more natural manner. Round caps are especially good for softening the effect of single line segments. The Projecting cap extends lines and dashes at half the stroke weight beyond the end anchor point. Cap styles also affect the shape of dashed lines (see illustration).

The Stroke panel with the cap/join section

At left, three lines shown top to bottom in Outline, Preview with Butt cap, Round cap and Projecting cap; at right, a 5-pt dashed line with a 2 pt dash and 6 pt gap shown top to bottom in Outline, then Preview with a Butt cap, Round cap, and Projecting cap

A dashed line with Butt caps (top) and the same dashed line with Round caps (bottom)

In CS3, a dashed line (top) is converted, as you'd expect, into outlines (bottom) when choosing Object > Path > Outline Stroke

A path shown first in Outline, then in Preview with a Miter join, Round join, and Bevel join

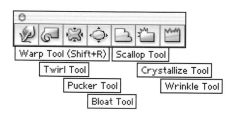

| Outline | Miter of 4x | Miter of 12x | Miter of 1x |

Objects with 6-pt strokes and various Miter limits, demonstrating that the angles of lines affect Miter limits

The Free Transform tool

The Liquify Distortion tools' tear off panel can be accessed from the Warp tool: see "Tear off panels" in the Illustrator Basics *chapter*

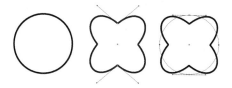

Using a Filter rather than an Effect allows you to edit your paths directly and will make screen redraw faster. Shown in the middle, Filter > Distort > Pucker & Bloat has been applied to a circle. On the right, Effect > Distort & Transform > Pucker & Bloat is illustrated.

Corner Shapes

The Join style in the Stroke panel determines the shape of a stroke line at its corner points. Each of the three styles determines the shape of the outside of the corner; the inside of the corner is always angled.

The default Miter join creates a pointy corner. The length of the point is determined by the width of the stroke, the angle of the corner (narrow angles create longer points; see illustration at left) and the Miter limit setting on the Stroke panel. Miter limits can range from 1x (which is always blunt) to 500x. Generally, the default Miter join with a miter limit of 4x looks just fine.

The Round join creates a rounded outside corner for which the radius is half the stroke width. The Bevel join creates a squared-off outside corner, equivalent to a Miter join with the miter limit set to 1x.

FREE TRANSFORM/LIQUIFY TOOLS, DISTORT FILTERS

You can use Illustrator's Free Transform tool to distort the size and shape of an object by dragging the corner points of the object's bounding box. You must first start dragging a bounding box corner point and then also hold down ⌘/Ctrl while continuing to drag. The shape of the object distorts progressively as you drag the bounding box corner points.

The suite of "Liquify" Distortion tools allows you to distort objects manually by dragging the mouse over them. The Warp, Twirl, Pucker, Bloat, Scallop, Crystallize, and Wrinkle tools work not only on vector objects, but on embedded raster images as well. Use the Option/Alt key to resize the Liquify brush as you drag.

Similar Distort features are found under both the Filter menu (choose the topmost of the two Distort submenus in the Filter menu) and the Effect menu (choose Effect > Distort & Transform). These particular features are somewhat different from the Liquify Distortion tools and offer some advantages. For instance, the ability to reapply the same effect with exact precision by choosing it again from the top of the filter menu (if you use the versions in the Effect menu, they are live, and can be saved as Graphic Styles; see the *Live Effects & Graphic Styles* chapter for more about these live effects). They can also be used to create in-betweens for animations in cases where blends might not give the desired results, or might be too cumbersome.

The Distort filters include Free Distort, Pucker & Bloat, Roughen, Tweak, Twist, and Zig Zag. All of these filters distort paths based on the paths' anchor points. They move (and possibly add) anchor points to create distortions. Enable Preview in the dialog box to see and modify the results as you experiment with the settings.

Many of the Free Distort functions can also be performed with the Free Transform tool. (To learn about the Free Transform tool, see the "Distorting Views" lesson later in this chapter.)

PATH SIMPLIFY COMMAND

More is not better when it comes to the number of anchor points you use to define a path. The more anchor points, the more complicated the path—which makes the file size larger and harder to process when printing. The Simplify command (Object > Path > Simplify) removes excess anchor points from one or more selected paths without making major changes to the path's original shape.

Two sliders control the amount and type of simplification. Enable Show Original as well as the Preview option to preview the effect of the sliders as you adjust them. The Preview option also displays the original number of points in the curve and the number that will be left if the current settings are applied.

Adjust the Curve Precision slider to determine how accurately the new path should match the original path. The higher the percentage, the more anchor points will remain, and the closer the new path will be to the original. The endpoints of an open path are never altered. The Angle Threshold determines when corner points should become smooth. The higher the threshold, the more likely a corner point will remain sharp.

Object > Path > Simplify can be used to reduce the number of points and to stylize type

The Path Eraser tool   *The Eraser tool (Shift+E)*

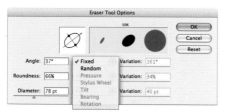

The Eraser Tool Options dialog box allows you to shape your eraser before using it.

ERASING VECTORS

Erasing doesn't necessarily mean correcting mistakes in the drawing process. Erasing, or taking away, can be an important part of your drawing's evolution. Like a sculptor, you can not only "add to" but also "take away" in order to form objects.

Illustrator has two different vector "erasing" tools. The Path Eraser tool removes sections from selected paths and the Eraser tool subtracts from objects.

The Path Eraser Tool

The Path Eraser tool will remove parts of a selected path (you must first select the path with any of the selection tools). By dragging along the path, you can "erase" or remove complete sections. You must drag along the path—when erasing diagonal or perpendicular to the path, results are less predictable.

The Eraser Tool

The Eraser tool removes a swath from vector objects as you "slice through" them. If a vector object is selected, the Eraser tool will affect only that selected object. If there is nothing selected, all vector objects that are touched by the Eraser tool will be affected (through all layers). The Eraser tool does not affect placed raster images or text. You can, however, convert text to paths (Type > Create Outlines) and then apply the Eraser tool. Also, some objects must be expanded before erasing parts of them (symbols, envelopes, graphs, blends, and meshes).

Double-clicking the Eraser tool opens the Eraser Tool Options dialog. Here, you can adjust the Angle, Roundness, and Diameter of your eraser. You can also use the [and] keys to decrease and increase Eraser brush size.

The pop-up list to the right of each option lets you control variations in the shape of the tool. The list of variations includes Fixed, Random, Pressure, Stylus Wheel, Tilt, Bearing, and Rotation (some options apply only when using graphics tablets and drawing styli). For more, go to Illustrator Help and search using keyword "Eraser."

Tiffany Larsen

Tiffany Larsen used custom patterns to dress the Big Bad Wolf in realistic fabric textures. The gingham dress pattern was created by drawing a checkerboard of squares with the Rectangle tool. Within the checkerboard, Larsen drew smaller squares of various sizes to simulate a mottled appearance. She then masked the grouped checkerboard into the size she wanted and dragged it to the Swatches panel to create a pattern. To make the lace (shown above on a black background), Larsen drew several circles (white Fill, no Stroke) within a square (white Fill, no Stroke). With the Direct Selection tool, she selected the square and circles and made the selection into a compound path (Object > Compound Path > Make) to create transparent holes (see the *Advanced Techniques* chapter for more on masks). Larsen made the selection into a pattern by choosing Edit > Define Pattern. Using the Stroke panel, Larsen made the stitching a 1-pt dashed line with a 2-pt gap.

Simple Realism

Realism from Geometry and Observation

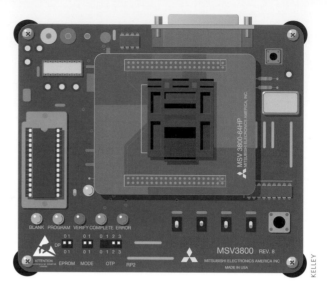

Overview: *Draw a mechanical object using the Rectangle, Rounded Rectangle, and Ellipse tools; use tints to fill all of the paths; add selected highlights and offset shadows to simulate depth.*

1

The default Fill and Stroke in the Tools panel; setting the default stroke weight for objects

Creating rounded rectangles and ellipses to construct the basic forms

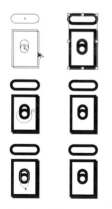

Option-Shift/Alt-Shift-dragging a selection to duplicate and constrain it to align with the original; using the Lasso tool to select specific points; Shift-dragging to constrain and move the selected points

Many people believe the only way to achieve realism in Illustrator is with elaborate gradients and blends, but this illustration by Andrea Kelley proves that artistic observation is the real secret. Using observation and only the simplest Illustrator techniques, Kelley drew technical product illustrations of computer chip boards for a handbook for her client, Mitsubishi.

1 Re-creating a mechanical object with repeating geometric shapes by altering copies of objects. Most artists find that close observation, not complex perspective, is the most crucial aspect to rendering illustrations. To sharpen your skills in observing the forms and details of objects, select a simple mechanical device to render in grayscale. First, create a new Illustrator document. Then experiment with the Ellipse, Rectangle, and Rounded Rectangle tools to draw the basic elements of the device. After you've made your first object—with the object still selected—click on the Default Fill and Stroke icon in the Tools panel, open the Stroke panel (Window > Stroke), and choose a stroke weight of 0.75 pt using the Weight pop-up menu. All objects you make from that point on will have the same fill and stroke as your first object.

Because mechanical and computer devices often have similar components, you can save time by copying an object you've drawn and then modifying the shape of the copy. You can easily align your copy with the original by holding the Opt-Shift/Alt-Shift keys while dragging out the copy from the selected object to the desired location. Smart Guides (View menu) can also help with alignment.

To illustrate a series of switches, Kelley dragged a selected switch (while holding Option-Shift/Alt-Shift to copy and constrain its movement), stretched the switch copy by selecting one end of the switch knob with the Lasso and dragged it down (holding the Shift key to constrain it vertically). She repeated this process to create a line of switches with the same switch plate width, but different switch knob lengths.

2 **Using tints to fill the objects.** At this point, all the objects are filled with white and have a stroke of black. Select a single object and set the Stroke to None and the Fill to black using the Color panel (Window > Color). Open the Swatches panel (Window > Swatches) and Option-click/Alt-click on the New Swatch icon to name it "Black-global," and enable the Global option. Click OK to save your new color. Then create a tint using the Tint slider in the Color panel. Continue to fill individual objects (be sure to set their Stroke to None) using Black Spot as the fill color, and adjust the tints for individual objects using the Tint slider until you are happy with their shades. Kelley used percentages from 10% to 90%, with most of the objects being 55% to 75% black.

3 **Creating a few carefully placed highlights.** Look closely at the subject of your drawing and decide where to place highlights. For lines that follow the contour of your object, select part or all of your object's path with the Direct Selection tool, copy (Edit > Copy) and Paste in Front (Edit > Paste in Front) that path or path section. Using the Color panel, change the Fill of your path to None and use the tint slider to change the Stroke to a light value of gray. While the highlight's path is still selected, you can reduce or increase the width of your

2

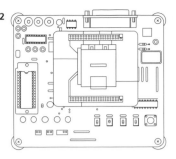

The drawn object prior to filling selected paths with gray

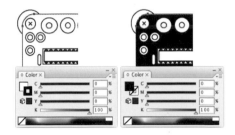

Left, the selected path set to the default stroke and fill colors; right, the selected object set to a fill of Black and a stroke of None

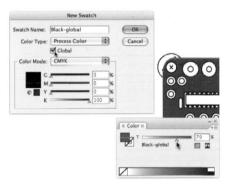

Creating a new custom global color that will then appear in the Swatches panel; setting the selected path to a fill of 70% Black using the Tint slider in the Color panel

Individual paths filled with tints of Black Spot in a range from 10% to 90%

3

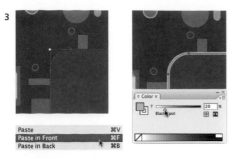

Using Paste in Front on a selected, copied path to duplicate it directly on top; changing the Stroke and Fill of the duplicate path to create a highlighted outline

Using the Stroke panel Weight field to increase or decrease the width of the highlight path

Placing small circles with a Fill of 0% black (white) and a darker inset curved path to simulate depth; Option-Shift/Alt-Shift-dragging a selected path to duplicate the path and constrain its movement

4

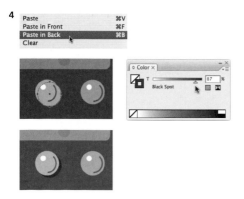

Copying a dial and choosing Paste in Back; using Arrow keys to offset the copy; setting the Fill "T" tint to 87% black to create a shadow from the copy

stroke using the Weight field of the Stroke panel. If you need to trim the length of a highlight, cut its path with the Scissors tool and then select the unwanted segments with the Direct Selection tool and delete them.

For some of the knobs and dials on her chip, Kelley used circular highlights with a value of 0% black (white) and an inset curved path with a darker value to simulate depth. Once you are satisfied with the highlights on a particular knob, select the paths (both the highlights and the knob) and hold down the Option/Alt key while dragging the objects in order to duplicate them (hold down Option-Shift/Alt-Shift to copy and constrain the paths as you drag them).

For her highlights, Kelley used lines that varied in weight from .2 to .57 pt and colors that varied in tint from 10 to 50%. She also used carefully placed white circles for some of the highlights. Try experimenting with different Cap and Join styles in the Stroke panel (see the "End of Lines" section and figures in the introduction to this chapter for more on Caps and Joins).

4 **Creating shadows.** Follow the same procedure as above, but this time use darker tints on duplicated paths pasted behind in order to create shadows. Select a path to make into a shadow, copy it, and use Edit > Paste in Back to place a copy of the path directly behind the original path. Use your Arrow keys to offset the copy, and change the Fill to a darker tint using the Color panel.

Consider using Effects to create shadows and highlights. See the *Live Effects & Graphic Styles* chapter for information on building multi-stroke appearances and saving them as styles that you can use on other artwork.

Symbols for faster updating and smaller files

Define artwork as a symbol if you want to easily update all instances of that artwork at once (symbols also result in smaller files when you export the illustration as a Flash file). See the *Brushes & Symbols* chapter to learn more about Symbols.

ROSTOMIAN

Zosia Rostomian / The Sharper Image®

Using a clever mixture of custom gradients and patterns from the Swatches library, Zosia Rostomian created a sophisticated illustration. Rostomian often has to create many product illustrations within a limited time and the pattern library speeds the process along. First Rostomian added patterns to the Swatches panel. She clicked on the Swatch Libraries Menu button at the bottom left corner of the Swatches panel and selected Patterns > Basic Graphics > Basic Graphics_Dots. She selected

the object and filled it with a dotted pattern from the Swatches panel. She experimented until she found a pattern close to what she needed. With the filled object selected, she chose Object > Transform > Scale. Rostomian checked Uniform, entered a percentage, and then under Options, she selected Patterns. She clicked the preview button and experimented with various percentages until the pattern was perfectly scaled. For more on her drawing technique, see her galleries in the *Blends, Gradients & Mesh* chapter.

Distorting Views

Using Free Transform for Productivity

ATTEBERRY

Overview: *Draw basic parts in a "normal" front view, then Free Transform copies for specific illustrations or frames; use Free Transform for creating perspective depth.*

Assembling parts into separate groups, avoiding the need to redraw for every view of the subject

1

Assembled character before using Free Transform to pose the mask

Creating characters that will adopt varying poses throughout a story or animation requires some special preplanning. To avoid drawing the complex elements over and over, Kevan Atteberry creates modular parts for his characters, placing any complex parts in a "neutral" position, then uses the Free Transform tool to position the character parts as needed for each illustration. He also draws elements flat that would be time-consuming to draw in perspective, using Free Transform to adjust them.

1 Drawing the bugs' masks facing front, then transforming them into expressive positions. Because the bugs' masks need to convey the emotion of the story, they are the most complex parts. Atteberry constructed them in a head-on position, using a combination of the Brush tool or Pencil tool for the loose drawing, and compound paths and blends to shape and color them (to learn more about blends, see the *Blends, Gradients & Mesh* chapter). He finally Grouped (⌘-G/Ctrl-G) all the elements for a mask in order to transform the mask as a single unit.

2 Transforming the masks into expressive positions. Atteberry preserved the original masks and worked on duplicates. He next transformed the masks to appear in their final position for the illustration. With a mask copy selected, he chose the Free Transform tool (E). This would allow him to scale, rotate and distort the mask into place without his having to call upon separate Transform commands. The key to using the Free Transform tool is knowing how to use the modifier keys with it. Atteberry hovered the cursor just outside the bounding box until he saw the curved, double-headed arrow letting him know a click-drag would rotate the object. To distort it, he clicked on a corner of the bounding box, then added the ⌘/Ctrl key. (It is important that you click before adding the modifier key—otherwise you are turning your Free Transform tool into the Selection tool temporarily.) When he saw the arrow turn into a single arrowhead, he dragged on the corner to distort that area of the mask. By clicking on a middle bounding box handle and then ⌘/Ctrl-dragging, he could skew the mask along one side. Adding the Option/Alt key would allow the object to be skewed in two directions at once. He scaled the mask by clicking on any handle on the bounding box to get the double-arrow cursor and dragging without using a modifier key, or he constrained the proportions as he was scaling it by adding the Shift key. Adding the Option/Alt key scaled the object around its center point. In this fashion, Atteberry positioned the masks to fit each body for the illustration (or frame). He also used the Free Transform tool on some of the bug bodies and limbs to depict movement.

3 **Using Free Transform to add perspective.** For this illustration in the bugs' series, Atteberry created the tiles for the floor by drawing them individually on a flat surface. He gave the tiles depth by placing a solid rectangle at the bottom, with black-filled tile objects on a layer above. He grouped and copied the tiles, offsetting the copy just enough that the black tiles, to which he applied a Gaussian Blur, became the shadows of the tiles. Selecting both groups of tiles, he again chose the Free Transform tool. This time he clicked on a top corner point and then used the ⌘-Option-Shift (Mac)/Ctrl-Alt-Shift (Win) keys, dragging horizontally, to transform in perspective.

2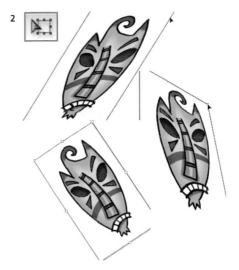

Using the Free Transform tool, with and without modifier keys, to rotate, skew, scale, and distort

The character's basic, reusable parts transformed to fit the needs of this illustration or frame for an animation

3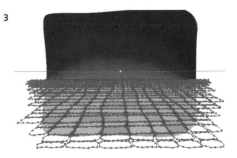

Tile flooring transformed in single-point perspective with the Free Transform tool

Distort Filter Flora

Applying Distort Filters to Create Flowers

GRACE

Overview: *Create rough circles; duplicate, resize, and rotate circles to construct a rose; fill with a radial gradient; apply various Distort filters to copies; recolor with Live Color.*

1

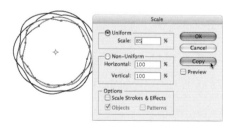

Setting the Pencil Tool Preferences; drawing two rough circular paths

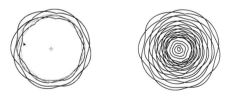

Using the Scale tool dialog window to create a reduced-size pair of circles nested within the first pair of circles

(Left) Using the Rotate tool to rotate the last-created pair of circles; (right) the complete construction of the flower before coloring—the flower center consists of a few small circles

Artist Laurie Grace used two roughly drawn circular paths and a series of Distort filters to construct the delicate flowers in her illustration, which she colored with various radial gradients. (See examples using "live" filters in the *Live Effects & Graphic Styles* chapter.)

1 Drawing circular paths; resizing and rotating path copies to create a rose. To draw two rough circular paths, in a new Illustrator document, double-click on the Pencil tool to bring up Pencil Tool Preferences. So that your drawn path will most closely follow your rough Pencil scribbles, in the Tolerances section, set Fidelity to 0.5 pixels and Smoothness to 0. In the Options section, leave all three boxes unchecked. Using the Toolbar or Color panel, set a Fill of None and a Stroke of Black. Draw a roughly circular path an inch or so in diameter, holding the Option (Mac)/Alt (Win) key as you near the end of the circle to automatically close the path. Then draw another rough circle just within, or overlapping, the first circle.

To select the two paths, drag around them with the Selection tool or Lasso tool. To create a duplicate pair of circles that is smaller than and nested within the first pair, double-click on the Scale tool, set a percentage less than 100 (Grace used 85%), and click the Copy button. With the last pair still selected, choose the Rotate tool and click-drag on the image in the direction of the rotation you want.

Continue to resize/copy and rotate selected pairs of circles until the flower form you are building is almost filled with circles. To vary the petal placement in the final rose, continue to rotate some of the pairs after you've created them. Then, for the center of the rose, click on the Pencil tool and draw a few small, nested circles. Use the Lasso tool or the Selection tool to select all the paths in the rose construction, and choose Object > Group.

2 Coloring the flower using a radial gradient. To create an effect that mimicked the petals of real flowers, Grace applied a custom radial gradient to her rose. From the Swatches panel (click the Swatches icon, or choose Window > Swatches), click and hold the "Show Swatch Kinds menu" button and choose "Show Gradients Swatches." Next, click on the orangey "Radial Gradient 2" swatch. To change the colors of the gradient, you need both the Gradient and Color panels open (from the Window menu, or drag them from the dock), click once on the left gradient slider (the beginning point of the gradient) in the Gradient panel, and adjust the color sliders in the Color panel. (For her left slider Grace chose 100% M, and moved the Y slider to 0%.) Next, click on the right gradient slider (the last color in the gradient) and adjust its color sliders in the Color panel; Grace chose 34% M (0% Y). To increase the amount of 100% magenta in your filled objects, drag the left slider to the right and release it where you like (Grace's Location setting was approximately 45%). Finally, create your new Gradient swatch by clicking on the "New Swatch" button in the Swatches panel. Name your swatch (Grace chose "Pink Flower Gradient") and click OK. With the rose illustration selected, use the ⌘-H/Ctrl-H toggle to hide the edges of your selection. Set the Fill to "Pink Flower Gradient" and the Stroke to None. (For more on Gradients, see the *Blends, Gradients & Mesh* chapter.)

2

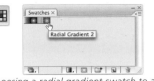

Choosing a radial gradient swatch to adjust

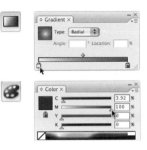

Adjusting the color settings of the beginning point gradient slider

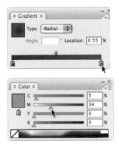

Adjusting the color settings of the ending point gradient slider

Repositioning the beginning gradient slider

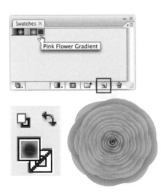

(Top) Creating a new Gradient swatch; (bottom, left and right) setting Fill to the "Pink Flower Gradient" swatch and Stroke to None

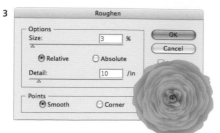

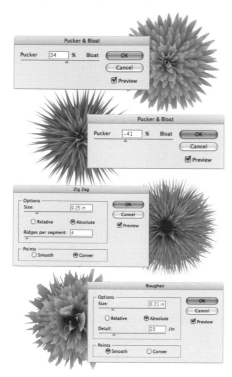

Settings for the Roughen filter; the final rose

Applying additional distortion filters to copies of the final rose illustration

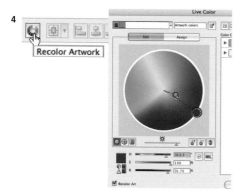

After selecting flowers, clicking the Recolor Artwork button, then editing colors with Live Color

3 Applying the Roughen filter. To create a realistic rough-edged petal effect, Grace used the Roughen filter. With the rose selected, (and with selection edges hidden), choose Filter > Distort > Roughen. Experiment with Options; Grace set Size to 3%, Detail to 5/in, and Points to Smooth. Enable the Preview checkbox to see the effect of the filter as you work. Click OK to apply your settings.

Grace used her final rose to create some of the other flowers in her illustration by applying more Distort filters to copies of the rose (be sure to enable the Preview checkbox for each filter as you work). Duplicate the entire rose by holding down the Option (Mac)/Alt (Win) key as you use the selection tool to drag it to a new location. With the duplicate still selected, choose Filter > Distort > Pucker & Bloat, enable Preview, and set the Bloat to 33%. Click OK to apply. On another copy of the rose, apply a Pucker & Bloat setting of –40 Pucker. With a third copy of the rose selected, choose Filter > Distort > Zig Zag and set Size to .25 in, choose Absolute, set Ridges to 5 and choose Corner in the Points section. With a fourth copy of the rose, use Filter > Distort > Roughen again. Set Size to .21 in, choose Absolute, set Detail to 23/in, and select Smooth in the Points section. (Remember, use ⌘-H/Ctrl-H if you need to see your selection edges once again.)

4 Changing the flower colors using Live Color. To change the colors of a flower or group of flowers, select the objects you want to change and click the Recolor Artwork button in the Control panel. Next, in the resulting Live Color dialog, choose the Edit tab and make sure Recolor Art is enabled. Each of the circles that you see within the smooth color wheel is a color marker that represents a color in your flower. To edit a color, you can move its color marker within the color wheel, change the Brightness or HSB sliders, or experiment with the other color adjustment options in Live Color. When you are satisfied with your colors, click OK. The new gradients that you created will be applied to your selected objects, and will be automatically saved in your Swatches panel.

Laurie Grace

Continuing with the flower theme she created in the previous lesson, Laurie Grace made some adjustments to color and size used for some of the flowers. She created variations on the other flowers by using Filter > Distort > Roughen. She created more flowers using the Pen tool to draw individual petals. She Option-clicked on the Rotate tool (Alt-click for Windows), entered 30° and clicked Copy. She used ⌘-D (Ctrl-D for Win) to continue the rotation around 360°. To add to the decorative design for the greenery, she used the Pen and Pencil tools to draw the stems and leaves. She then used Filter > Distort > Zig Zag and Twist on some of the pen lines and leaves. She added color by creating some gradient mesh objects (see the *Blends, Gradients & Mesh* chapter).

GRACE

Isometric Systems

Tools & Formulas for Isometric Projection

Overview: *Create detailed, to-scale drawings of three sides of an object; use an isometric formula to transform the objects; assemble with Selection tool and Snap to Point; create objects that aren't boxes.*

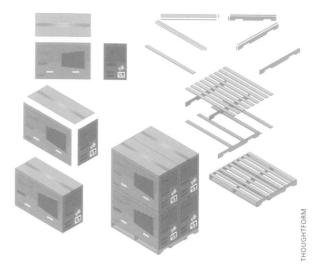

THOUGHTFORM

1

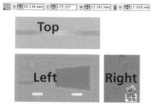

Top, left, and right faces that have more than one component are first grouped individually, and always positioned with the side on the left and the front on the right

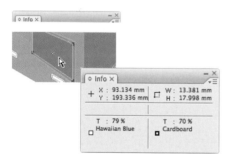

Using the Control or Info panels for drawing to scale

Ellipses are contained by boxes

To construct an elliptical object in isometric view, first make a rectangle to fit one side of the "box." Scale, shear, rotate, and join the rectangle to the rest of the object. Now draw an ellipse inside the rectangle, touching at all edges. Delete the rectangle.

Technical illustrations and diagrams are often depicted in isometric view. Adobe Illustrator has several features which can help you assemble and transform objects in isometrics. Kurt Hess created and transformed the diagrams on these pages using a three-step ISO formula.

1 Creating detailed renderings of the front, side and top views of your object to scale. When you're ready to begin a technical drawing, you'll want to decide upon your "General" Units in Preferences, setting it to a type that represents the larger units the actual item is measured in. For example, 4 mm on paper might represent one inch of the object's actual size. If you then set the "Keyboard Increment" in General Preferences to 1 mm, you can use the arrow keys to move a line or object to match .25 inches of the item's physical measurement. Use the Control panel or the Info panel (Window>Info) to read width and height between selected points on items already drawn, and to enter measurements directly. Enable View>Snap to Point for assistance in joining edges, and View>Smart Guides to help you locate angles and intersecting nodes. Draw the component parts of the item that will be visible (usually front, top and one side) face on, in flat, 2D perspective, then Select and Group (⌘-G/Ctrl-G) the elements of each side in preparation for transforming them into an isometric projection.

2 Using an isometric formula to transform your objects, then assembling the elements. To assemble your elements into an isometric view, you can use the transform tools (Scale, Shear, Rotate) in the Toolbox, Object > Transform, or the Transform panel. To assemble the box, select all three views and double-click on the Scale tool to scale them 100% horizontally and 86.6% vertically. Next select the left face, and shear it at a –30° angle. If you've drawn the top to align with the left (figure A), shear it and the right face at 30°. Now rotate the right 30° and the top and left –30°. If you've drawn the top to align with the right (figure B), then shear the top with the left instead (–30°), the right still at 30°. Then rotate the top and right 30°. The left still rotates at –30°. The chart at right shows angles of direction.

To assemble the top, right and left, use the Selection tool to grab a specific anchor-point from the right view that will contact the left view, and drag it until it snaps into the correct position (the arrow turns hollow). Next, select and drag to snap the top into position. Finally, select and group the entire object for easy reselection.

3 Drawing elements beyond the basic box. To create this wooden pallet, create one top slat and one end. The right face will always wind up aligned with the 30° axis (see illustration, right), although it will not always represent the "front" of the object in the real world. Scale as before. If you've drawn the top to align with the left (figure A), shear it and the right face at 30°, and the left at –30°. Rotate the right 30° and the top and left –30°. If you've drawn the top to align with the right (figure B), then shear the top with the left (–30°), and the right at 30°. Rotate the top and right 30°. The left rotates at –30°. Duplicate and drag each element into position for the opposite side. Join as if they were the top and right side of a box. Create the in-between slats by selecting the end pieces, then double-click the Blend tool to choose Specified Steps (for Spacing) and enter the number of slats (for help, see the *Blends, Gradients & Mesh* chapter).

	Shear—Rotate		Shear—Rotate
Right	+30 +30	Right	+30 +30
Top	+30 -30	Top	-30 +30
Left	-30 -30	SLeft	-30 -30

Using the Scale tool and the Transform panel, applying the formula according to whether the top is aligned with the Left (A) or the Right (B)

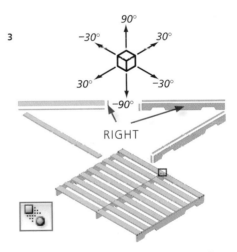

Shear and Rotate, then join sides along angle axes, using the Selection tool and dragging an anchor point until the arrow becomes hollow and the edges snap together (View > Snap to Point)

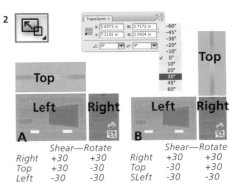

Assembling parts, determining what part will be viewed on the (positive) 30° axis; duplicating pieces, sliding into position and using the Blend tool with Specified Steps to complete a pallet

Automated Isometric Actions!
Rick Henkel of ThoughtForm created *WOW Actions* that automate formulas for isometrics (on the *Wow! CD*).

Intricate Patterns

Designing Complex Repeating Patterns

Advanced Technique

Overview: *Design a rough composition; define a confining pattern boundary and place behind all layers; use the box to generate crop marks; copy and position elements using crop marks for alignment; define and use the pattern.*

Top, arranging pattern elements into a basic design; bottom, adding the pattern tile rectangle behind the pattern elements

Creating crop marks based on selection of the pattern tile rectangle

Included with Illustrator are many wonderful patterns for you to use and customize, and *Illustrator Help* does a good job of explaining pattern-making basics. But what if you want to create a more complex pattern?

A simple trick with crop marks can help to simplify a tedious process of trial and error. With some help from author and consultant Sandee Cohen, Alan James Weimer used the following technique to design an intricate tile that prints seamlessly as a repeating pattern.

1 Designing your basic pattern, drawing a confining rectangle, then creating crop marks for registration. Create a design that will allow for some rearrangement of artwork elements. *Hint: Pattern tiles cannot contain linked images—to include a linked image in a pattern, select it and click Embed Image in the Control panel.*

Use the Rectangle tool to draw a box around the part of the image you would like to repeat. This rectangle defines the boundary of the pattern tile. Send the rectangle to the bottom of the Layers panel or to the bottom of your drawing layer (Object > Arrange > Send to Back). This boundary rectangle, which controls how your pattern repeats, must be an unstroked, unfilled, nonrotated, nonsheared object. Make certain this rectangle is selected, and select Filter >Create >Crop Marks. Last, Ungroup these marks (in the next step, you'll use the crop marks to align elements that extend past the pattern tile).

2 **Developing the repeating elements.** If your pattern has an element that extends beyond the edge of the pattern tile, you must copy that element and place it on the opposite side of the tile. For example, if a flower blossom extends below the tile, you must place a copy of the remainder of the blossom at the top of the tile, ensuring that the whole flower is visible when the pattern repeats. To do this, select an element that overlaps above or below the tile and then Shift-select the nearest horizontal crop mark (position the cursor on an endpoint of the crop mark). While pressing the Shift-Option or Shift-Alt keys (the Option/Alt key copies the selections and the Shift key constrains dragging to vertical and horizontal directions), drag the element and crop mark upward until the cursor snaps to the endpoint of the upper horizontal crop mark. Enabling Smart Guides (from the View menu) can help you find the correct horizontal and vertical alignment when you are dragging objects. (For any element that overlaps the left or right side of the tile, select the element and the vertical crop mark and hold down Shift-Option/ Shift-Alt as you drag them into position.)

3 **Testing and optimizing your pattern.** To test your pattern, select your pattern elements (including the bounding rectangle), and either choose Edit >Define Pattern to name your pattern, or drag your selection to the Swatches panel (then double-click the swatch to customize its name). Create a new rectangle and select the pattern as your fill from the Swatches panel. Illustrator will fill the rectangle with your repeating pattern. If you redesign the pattern tile and then wish to update the pattern swatch, select your pattern elements again, but this time Option-drag/Alt-drag the elements onto the pattern swatch you made before.

2

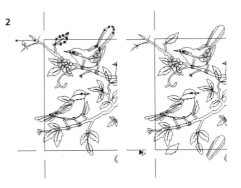

Left, selecting the flower blossom and horizontal crop mark; right, after dragging a copy of the flower blossom and crop mark into position at the top of the pattern tile artwork

Finished artwork for the pattern tile, before turning into a pattern swatch in the Swatches panel

3

Making a new swatch using Edit >Define Pattern

Speeding redraw with patterns

Speed redraw for an object filled with a complex pattern by setting the object to Outline mode using the Layers panel (see the *Layers & Appearances* chapter for details on how to do this).

Color Guidance

Inspiration from the Color Guide Panel

Advanced Technique

Overview: *Set up the Color Guide panel to generate color groups; creae and save color groups based on harmonies in the Color Guide panel; apply, modify and save color groups from within Live Color.*

In this "Day at the Circus" poster (created for a children's fundraising event), illustrator Hugh Whyte used a very specific palette of colors. Using Illustrator's Color Guide panel, it's simple to generate and save color groups of new palettes based on existing colors. Live Color allows you to apply your new color groups to an existing image, and then continue to experiment with how colors are applied.

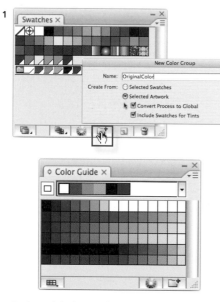

Saving original artwork colors as a color group in the Swatches panel, which automatically places a selected color group with variations into the Color Guide panel

1 Setting up the Color Guide panel to base new color versions on the original. For your first attempt, use the Circus image on the *Wow! CD*, or one that has a limited number of colors, to avoid having too many swatches in your original artwork to handle easily. Since you'll be working with both your Swatches and Color Guide panels, drag them away from the dock to float free for easy viewing. Select the artwork and, in the Swatches panel, click on the New Color Group button in order to have the colors that are currently in your artwork saved as a group to work with in the Color Guide panel. When the New Color Group dialog opens, keep the default settings and rename this color group "Original Color." Deselect your artwork. In order to base your color group creations on your original color relationships, click on the small folder icon beside your color group swatches to select the entire group so that it shows up in the Color Guide panel.

2 Creating color groups in the Color Guide panel and saving them to the Swatches panel. Next, you're going to create a variety of color groups in the Color Guide panel. Notice that your original artwork colors run down the middle of the Color Guide's panel of swatches. To the right are lighter versions of these colors (tints), and to the left are darker versions (shades). Select the top color in the third row from the right, then Shift-click to select the entire row vertically (⌘-click/Ctrl-click for non-contiguous colors). Click on the Save to Swatches panel button. Now change the relationship between the colors by clicking on the Color Guide's pop-up menu and choosing Show Warm/Cool. Again select the third vertical row from the right and save this new cooler color group to the Swatches panel. Select the group by clicking on its folder icon, select Color Group Options from the Swatches panel pop-up menu, and rename it something like "Cooler Original" by typing a new name in the dialog that appears. Select this group to place it in the Color Guide panel as the new base group for the Harmony Rules. (For the rest of this lesson, you will create color groups based on this base group. However, you can click on any swatch, then click on the "Set base color to the current color" button on the Color Guide panel to change the current color group; changing the base color will affect all of the Harmony Rules that are based on it.)

Click on the Color Guide arrow to the right of your current colors to make another color group, choosing one of the Harmony Rules, such as the Left Complement shown here. Save and rename that group "Left Complement from Cooler." Be aware that if you create new color groups with fewer swatches than your original artwork, you will be reducing the color variation in your artwork. A Harmony Rule contains no more than five swatches, but the panel contains variations based on those five swatches. You can drag any swatch from either the Color Guide or Swatches panels into any saved color group in the Swatches panel. You can also drag colors out of a color group in the Swatches panel.

2

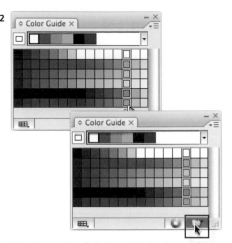

Selecting a tint of all the original colors and saving the new color group to the Swatches panel

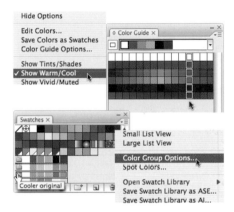

Changing the view of swatches in the Color Guide panel from the menu, selecting, saving and renaming a new color group

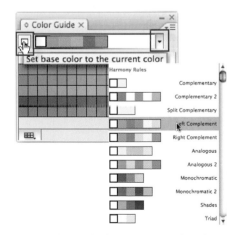

Setting a base color for a Harmony Rule and selecting a new Harmony Rule from the Color Guide list box

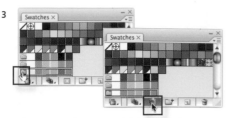

Selecting a color group with its folder icon so no color is actually selected or applied, and entering Live Color using the Edit or Apply Color Group button

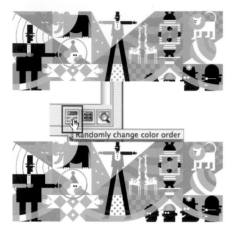

Using Randomly change color order button on the Assign tab

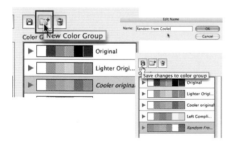

Saving a new color group OR saving changes to an existing color group

Random assignment of saturation and brightness to the pastel color group

3 Applying color groups and creating new ones using Live Color. To protect your original work, choose File > Save As and give your file a new name. (Whenever you create a version you like, repeat saving the file with another file name to protect what you've already created.) Select your artwork and then select the Cooler Original color group by clicking on the folder icon next to it. If you accidentally click on a swatch instead of the color group folder icon, and that color is applied to your artwork, choose Undo. You want to click only on the folder icon so a border shows up around your swatch group, but no color is selected.

Click on the Edit or Apply Color Group icon to enter Live Color. By default, Black and White are protected from being changed by any of the colors in your selected color group. The Cooler Original swatches replace the remaining colors with a random selection of the group's swatches. If you want to try a new version, click on the Assign tab and then on the "Randomly change color order" button. This command assigns any of the swatches from the Color Group to any of the color bars. You can keep clicking until you see a combination you like, but be sure to do this carefully, because there is no Undo in Live Color, so there's no way to return to a combination you liked. Therefore, every time you find a combination that appeals to you, click on the Save New Color Group button and save that combination as a new color group. Double-click on the name to rename it. Be careful not to click on the "Save changes to color group" button (the floppy disk), unless you want to overwrite the color group you had selected and that now has its name in italics. If you don't like the direction your changes are headed, click back on a saved color group you liked for a fresh start at generating different color versions. Whenever you find a version you want to apply, click OK and save it as a new file name. If you want to save your new color groups without changing the art, disable Recolor Art or click on "Get colors from selected art," and then click OK.

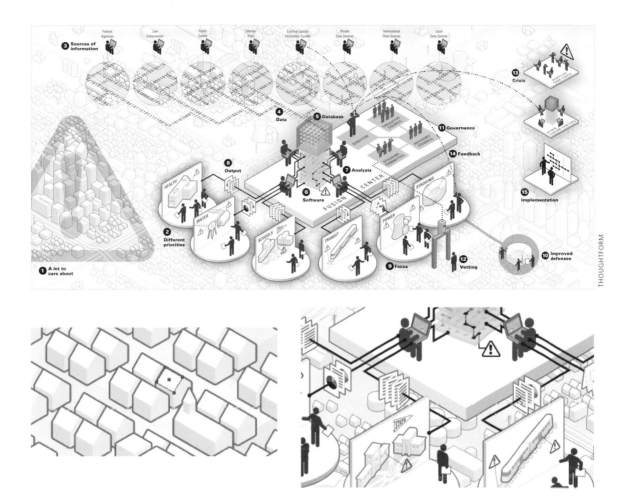

Rick Henkel / ThoughtForm Design

When Rick Henkel created this illustration of a system for information sharing, he chose an isometric view, which is commonly used in technical drawings. He first created a background "grid" of colored squares in isometric view, then overlaid basic objects of varying shapes to represent the city. He next built up the platforms for areas the system connects to, with lines and dots to form the connection. Henkel and other illustrators at ThoughtForm Design store "libraries" of objects such as these for the city, the platforms, and the figures, ready to be reused when different projects require them. They save files according to the object's category, allowing Henkel to concentrate on creating an illustration that provides an unobstructed view of the flow of information, a view isometrics is especially suited to. Adding effects such as transparency and glows not only creates a pleasing design, but also highlights important information for the viewer.

4

Beyond the Basics

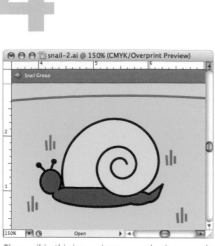

The snail in this image is a group that's currently in Isolation Mode. The gray Isolation Mode bar at the top of the window displays the name of the group, and the other elements of the image—green background, blades of grass, and skyline—are all dimmed, indicating that they're locked and only the snail group can be edited.

Controlling isolation mode

When you have a group selected, the Control panel has a button that will also allow you to enter isolation mode. You can use the same button to exit isolation mode as well.—*Mordy Golding*

Layers panel and isolation

While you're in Isolation Mode, only the artwork in the group 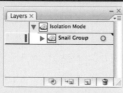 or sublayer that's isolated will be visible in the Layers panel. Once you exit Isolation Mode, the other layers and groups will once again appear in the Layers panel.

In the preceding chapters you've learned the basics of drawing and coloring in Illustrator. This chapter will take you beyond the basics into the world of compound paths and compound shapes (including the Pathfinder panel), Live Trace, and Live Paint. Live Trace lets you transform a raster image into a detailed, accurate set of vector paths that remain live and editable. Live Paint allows you to paint areas of a vector graphic more intuitively, as if you were painting by hand on paper or canvas.

This chapter begins with a look at a feature called Isolation Mode, which can be confusing (or even scary) if you encounter it without knowing what it is and how it works, but which is a helpful part of working with groups in general, and Live Paint in particular.

USING ISOLATION MODE

Whenever you work with a group of objects of any kind, you can enter Illustrator's Isolation Mode to edit members of that group without taking the risk of unintentionally editing anything else. Isolation Mode has been improved (it's easier to use and less confusing), and its implementation greatly expanded since it was first introduced. But it's still possible to trigger Isolation Mode accidentally, especially if you're not familiar with it. For that reason alone, it's important to know how it works and how to get out of it if you find yourself there unexpectedly.

Suppose you have some artwork that's already grouped. To enter Isolation Mode, just choose the Selection tool and then double-click any of the objects in your existing group. You'll see a gray bar with the name of the group appear at the top of your document window, which tells you you've just entered Isolation Mode. Meanwhile, everything on your Artboard *except* the group you've just isolated will be dimmed, indicating that all other objects have been locked. From this point on, anything you add to your Artboard will automatically be considered part of the isolated group. In Isolation Mode, any edits that you make, including creating new objects and deleting objects, will affect the group.

When you're ready to leave Isolation Mode, there are several ways to exit: Click anywhere in the gray Isolation Mode bar, at the top of the screen; double-click anywhere on the Artboard outside of the Isolated artwork; click the Exit Isolated Group button in the Control panel; or choose Exit Isolated Group from the contextual menu by right-clicking or Control-clicking (Mac). The gray bar will disappear, and you'll be working under normal grouping rules again. Also note that you can always disable the "Double-click to Isolate" box in Preferences > General to avoid accidentally entering Isolation Mode.

Even if you didn't consciously create a group using the Group command, you can enter Isolation Mode for groups of objects such as blends, compound shapes, or Live Paint objects.

In addition to groups, you can also isolate any sublayer. Just select the sublayer in the Layers panel, and choose Enter Isolation Mode from the Layers panel menu. (But note that top-level layers can't be isolated.) Exiting Isolation Mode for a sublayer works the same as it does for groups, except there's no Exit button in the Control panel. Editing symbols also takes place in Isolation Mode—for more on working with symbols in Isolation Mode, see the intro to the *Brushes & Symbols* chapter.

COMPOUND PATHS & COMPOUND SHAPES

It's often easier to create an object by combining two or more relatively simple shapes than it would be to draw the more complex result directly. Fortunately, Illustrator has tools that let you easily combine objects to get the results you want.

There are two effective ways to combine objects: 1) compound shapes, which remain "live" and editable; and 2) Pathfinder commands, which are "destructive" and permanent, so that shapes can't be returned to their orignal editable state (except by using Undo).

Isolation limitations

While in Isolation Mode, Outline View is not available, and you can only Show/Hide or Lock/Unlock objects by using the Layers panel.

Left to right: two ovals (the inner oval has no fill, but appears black because of the black fill of the larger oval behind it); as part of a compound path the inner oval knocks a hole into the outer one where they overlap; the same compound path with inner oval, which was Direct-Selected and moved to the right to show that the hole is only where the objects overlap

Compounds operate as a unit

Compound shapes and compound paths don't have to overlap to be useful; apply a "compound" to multiple objects whenever you want them to operate as a unit, as if they were one object.

Expand compound shapes?

- If a compound shape is so complex that interacting with it is noticeably slow, expand it.
- Anything that relies on bounding boxes will behave differently on the expanded shape if that shape has a smaller bounding box than the editable compound shape. This affects all the Align commands and certain transformations.
- You must expand a compound shape before using it as an envelope. See the *Live Effects & Graphic Styles* chapter for more.

—*Pierre Louveaux*

This artwork by Gary Newman is an example of separate outlined letters made into a compound path so they operate as a unit; he then used the compound path as a mask.

The "Making a Typeface" lesson in the Type *chapter demonstrates how Caryl Gorska created her own letterforms, including letter counters (holes cut into your letter forms for the center of letters) using Pathfinder Shape modes, then expanded into compound paths.*

Compound paths or shapes?

The quick answer to this question is to use compound paths on simple objects for basic combining or hole-cutting. Use compound shapes on more complex objects (such as live type or effects) and to more fully control how your objects interact.

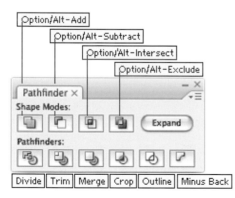

The Pathfinder panel contains two sets of commands that you can apply: Shape modes (as in Compound Shapes), and Pathfinders (which are destructive); see the figures on the next few pages for visual examples of what these commands do, and see the "Pathfinder panel" section later in this chapter for more explanation about using the Pathfinder panel.

Compound paths

A compound path consists of one or more paths that have been combined so they behave as a single unit. One very useful aspect of compound paths is that a hole can be created where the original objects overlapped. These holes are areas cut out from others (think of the center of a donut, or the letter **O**), through which you can see objects.

To create a compound path, e.g., a donut, or the letter **O**, draw an oval, then draw a smaller oval that will form the center hole of the **O**. Select the two paths, and then choose Object > Compound Path > Make. Select the completed letter and apply the fill color of your choice—the hole will be left empty. To adjust one of the paths within a compound path, use the Direct Selection tool. To adjust the compound path as a unit, use the Group Selection or Selection tool.

In addition to creating holes in objects, you can use compound paths to force multiple objects to behave as if they were a single unit. An advanced application of this is to make separate objects behave as one unit to mask others. For an example of this using separate "outlined" type elements, see the figure "Careers" by Gary Newman.

Holes and fills with compound paths

For simple holes, the Compound Path > Make command will generally give the result you need. If your compound path has multiple overlapping shapes, or you're not getting the desired holes in the spaces, take a look at Fill Rules.pdf on the *Wow! CD*. Or, try using compound shapes (described in the next section), which give you complete control. Certain results can be obtained only by using compound shapes.

Compound shapes

It's often easier to create an object by combining two or more relatively simple shapes than it would be to draw the more complex result directly. Fortunately, Illustrator has tools that let you easily combine objects to get the results you want.

A compound shape is a live combination of shapes using the Add, Subtract, Intersect, and/or Exclude Pathfinder operations. See the figures on this page for examples of how they work.

You can make compound shapes from two or more paths, other compound shapes, text, envelopes, blends, groups, or any artwork with vector effects applied to it. To create a compound shape, choose Window > Pathfinder to display the Pathfinder panel. Then select your objects, and choose Make Compound Shape from the Pathfinder panel menu. To assign a particular Shape Mode, select one of the components of your compound shape and click on the corresponding Shape mode button on the top row of the Pathfinder panel.

Note: *Simply selecting your* ungrouped *objects and clicking one of the Shape Mode buttons creates a compound shape and applies the shape you've chosen to the objects.*

Add to Shape Area (For this example as well as the ones below, the first column shows the original shapes; the second column shows the results of the operation shown in Preview mode; and the third column shows the resulting objects selected, so you can see the effects of the operation more clearly.)

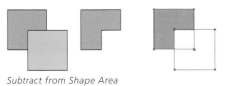

Subtract from Shape Area

Intersect Shape Area

The pros and cons of compound shapes

You can combine complex objects using compound shapes so that they remain editable. As you know by now, compound shapes allow you to combine objects in a variety of ways using Add, Subtract, Intersect, and Exclude. While keeping these Shape modes live, you can also continue to apply (or remove) Shape modes, or a wide variety of effects, to the compound shape as a unit. In later chapters, as you work with live effects such as envelopes, warps, and drop shadows, remember that you can integrate effects into your compound shapes while retaining the ability to edit your objects—even if they are editable type. Compound shapes can also be brought into Photoshop (see the "Shape Shifting" lesson in the *Illustrator & Other Programs* chapter).

Exclude Shape Area

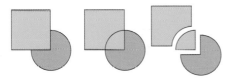

Divide Pathfinder (For this example as well as the ones below, the first column shows the original shapes; the second column shows the results of the operation shown in Preview mode; and the third column shows the resulting objects selected and/or moved apart, so you can see the effects of the operation more clearly.)

Remember: the power of compound shapes does come at a cost. Compound shapes require Illustrator to perform many calculations on your behalf, so as a result too many compound shapes or too many operations or effects applied to compound shapes can slow down the screen redraw of your image. Although compound paths are

Trim Pathfinder

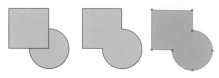

Merge Pathfinder (Note that Merge only functions correctly if both objects are the same color; otherwise it works the same as Trim.)

Crop Pathfinder

Outline Pathfinder (Note that after performing the Outline operation, Illustrator applies a stroke of 0 by default. Here, we've manually applied a 2-pt stroke.)

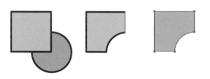

Minus Back Pathfinder

GIBLIN

You don't have to be a rocket scientist to use Live Trace in combination with Live Paint (discussed in the section following this one)—the two features were designed to work hand in hand. To create the colored rocket above, Ian Giblin began with the scanned drawing on the left, then used Live Trace to create the tracing in the middle. After he converted the tracing to a Live Paint group, it was easy to color the rocket using the Live Paint Bucket.

much less powerful or flexible, they won't slow down your redraw. So if you're working with simple objects, it's best to use compound paths instead.

Pathfinder panel

The Pathfinder panel (see figures starting on the previous pages) includes the top row of Live Shape commands and the lower row of permanent Pathfinder commands. You can use the Pathfinder commands Divide, Trim, Merge, Crop, Outline, and Minus Back to permanently combine or separate selected objects. The top row, Live Shape modes, can also be effectively applied as permanent Pathfinder commands. One way to do this is to hold Option/Alt as you click any of the Shape buttons. If you've already applied the live shape, you can make that into a permanently applied pathfinder effect by selecting the objects and clicking the Expand button in the Pathfinder panel.

The Divide, Trim, Merge, Crop, and Outline Pathfinder commands are used to separate (not combine) objects—think of them as cookie cutters. Before you can use them, the Trim and Merge commands require that you fill objects.

Unlike objects you create using compound shapes, the results you get when you apply the Pathfinder commands alter your artwork permanently. So Pathfinder commands are preferable when you need to perform further operations on the altered paths. For example, if you apply the Divide Pathfinder as shown in the figure at left, you can then pull the resulting pieces apart, or continue to manipulate them. In contrast, you couldn't separate the two pieces resulting from the Exclude Shape Area operation, because the underlying paths aren't really altered.

USING LIVE TRACE

Have you ever wished you could automatically transform a raster image—such as a photo or a scanned drawing—into a detailed, accurate set of vector paths? Illustrator's Live Trace feature grants your wish. In a matter of minutes (and in some cases, seconds) Live Trace renders your original image into vector graphics that can then be edited, resized, and otherwise manipulated without distortion or loss of quality.

Live Trace gives you complete control over the level of detail that is traced. Live Trace options include the ability to specify a color mode and a palette of colors for the tracing object, fill and stroke settings, the sharpness of corner angles, blurring and resampling controls, and more. Tracing Presets allow you to store a set of tracing options for quick access the next time you need them.

Best of all, the tracing object you create with Live Trace remains live (that's why they call it Live Trace), so you can adjust the parameters and results of your tracing at any time. Once you're happy with your Live Trace object, you can work with it as vector paths or you can choose to convert it to a Live Paint object and take advantage of the new Live Paint Bucket's intuitive painting capabilities.

The basics of Live Trace

To trace an image using Live Trace, start by opening or placing the file that you'll be using as your source image. Once you've selected the source image, you can choose to trace the object using the default settings just by clicking Live Trace in the Control panel, or choosing Object > Live Trace > Make. If you'd like to have some control over the options for Live Trace before you trace the image, click the Tracing Presets and Options button in the Control panel (it's a small black triangle to the right of the Live Trace button) and select Tracing Options. (You can also access the Tracing Options by choosing Object > Live Trace > Tracing Options.) Search "live trace" in Help > Illustrator Help for a rundown of the various options in the Tracing Options dialog. You can enable the Preview checkbox to see what your tracing will look like before you actually execute it, but be aware that this can slow you down considerably.

Before you execute your tracing, you can choose a tracing preset in the Tracing Options dialog (from the Preset menu), or by clicking on the Tracing Presets and Options

The Tracing Options dialog is an essential stop if you want to have any control over the results of your tracing

You can manage your tracing presets from within the Tracing Presets dialog.

The Raster View (left) and Vector View (right) buttons in the Control panel

ATTEBERRY

See Kevan Atteberry's Galleries using Live Trace later in this chapter

In many cases, regardless of what Raster View setting you choose in Tracing Options or the Control panel, your original source image may not be clearly visible unless you set the Vector View to either No Tracing Result or Outline.

> No Tracing Result
> Tracing Result
> Outlines
> Outlines with Tracing

Tracing paper

Adobe has published a technical white paper on Live Trace entitled *Creating Vector Content: Using Live Trace.* You can find it as creating_vector_content.pdf on the *Wow! CD.*

Click the Live Trace button in the Control panel to trace using the default settings

The Tracing Presets and Options button in the Control panel lets you open the Tracing Options dialog or choose a tracing preset

☐ Ignore White

New in CS3, the Ignore White checkbox in the Tracing Options lets you automatically remove a white background from your tracing object

Tracing object names

All tracing objects appear in the Layers panel with the default name "Tracing"—until you re-name them, expand them, or convert them to Live Paint objects.

button in the Control panel. If you create a Live Trace setting that you think you'll want to apply to other images in the future, you can save time by saving your current settings as a custom tracing preset.

To create a custom tracing preset, set your options in the Tracing Options dialog and then click the Save Preset button. Illustrator prompts you to type a name for your new preset. Once you do that and click OK, your new preset will be available from the Preset pop-up menu in the Control panel when you have either a raster object or a Live Trace object selected. (Your preset will also be available from the Preset pop-up menu in Tracing Options.) To manage your tracing presets, choose Edit > Tracing Presets to access the Tracing Presets dialog, where you can edit or delete existing presets, create new ones, or click Export to save your presets to a file that can be shared with other users. (To load presets from an exported file, just click the Import button and locate your saved preset.)

When you've set the tracing options the way you want them, click Trace, and then sit back and watch the Live Trace feature go to work. Once Live Trace has traced your image for you, you can change the way the tracing object is displayed, or adjust the results of the tracing.

Changing the display of a Live Trace object

Because Live Trace is live by definition, your original source image remains untouched. So there are really two parts to a Live Trace object: the original source image, and the tracing that results from Live Trace. Though only the tracing result is visible by default, you can change how both parts of the Live Trace object are displayed.

Start by selecting the Live Trace object. Once you've done that, you can change whether (and how) the original source image is displayed by choosing Object > Live Trace or clicking the Raster View button in the Control panel. Select one of the four options: No Image to completely hide the source image; Original Image to display the source image underneath the tracing result; Adjusted Image to display the image with any adjustments applied during the tracing process; or Transparent Image to see a "ghost" of the source image.

With the Live Trace object selected, you can also change how the tracing result is displayed by choosing Object > Live Trace or clicking the Vector View button in the Control panel. Select one of the four options: No Tracing Result to completely hide the result of the tracing; Tracing Result to display the full tracing result; Outlines to display only the outlines of the tracing object; or Outlines with Tracing to see the tracing result with outlines visible.

Adjusting the results of a Live Trace

Of course, because your Live Trace object is live, you can adjust the results of the tracing whenever you want. Simply select your Live Trace object and choose a new preset from the Control panel preset pop-up menu; or, click the Tracing Options button in the Control panel; or choose Object > Live Trace > Tracing Options. If you choose Tracing Options, you'll get the same Tracing Options dialog you saw before you traced the object, and you can continue to adjust and change any of the options at will. Then, just click Trace to reapply. Also note that you can adjust certain basic options for your tracing result (namely Threshold and Min. Area) right in the Control panel, without even entering the Tracing Options dialog.

Using swatch libraries with Live Trace

You can create a special swatch library with only the colors you want in your tracing, and then specify it in the Tracing Options dialog by choosing its name from the panel pop-up. You can also specify any existing swatch library. In either case, just make sure you have the swatch library open before you open the Tracing Options dialog, or else its name won't appear in the panel pop-up.

Converting to a Live Paint object or set of paths

Live Trace is designed to work hand in hand with the new Live Paint feature (see the section on Live Paint following this one). Once you're happy with your tracing object, you

The options in the Raster View menu

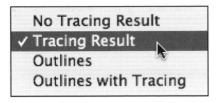

The options in the Vector View menu

Testing a trace

Save a small, representative, cropped version of your image and test your Live Trace settings with that small file. Save your settings, and then apply them to your large file! *—Kevan Atteberry*

Quick conversion

You can make a tracing and convert it to Live Paint or a set of paths in one step. Just choose Object > Live Trace > Make and Convert to Live Paint or Object > Live Trace > Make and Expand. (Or Option/Alt-click the Trace button to convert directly to a set of paths.)

Releasing a tracing object

If you want to get rid of a tracing object—but keep the original placed image where it is—all you have to do is release the tracing object by selecting it, and choosing Object > Live Trace > Release.

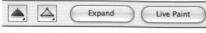

The Expand and Live Paint buttons in the Control panel

can easily convert it to a Live Paint object so that you can color it intuitively using the Live Paint Bucket. You can also convert the tracing object to paths if you want to work with the elements of the traced artwork as separate objects.

Whether you're converting to Live Paint or to paths, keep in mind that your tracing will no longer be live and editable after you perform this step, so don't convert your tracing until you're satisfied with it. To convert the tracing to a Live Paint object, just select the object and click the Live Paint button in the Control panel (or use Object > Live Trace > Convert to Live Paint). To convert the tracing to a set of grouped paths, click the Expand button in the Control panel or choose Object > Live Trace > Expand.

When you expand your tracing, you can choose to preserve your current display options by choosing Object > Live Trace > Expand as Viewed. In that case, your Raster and Vector View settings will determine what's visible after you expand. So, for example, if your Vector View is set to Outlines, and you set the Raster View to No Image, after you choose Expand as Viewed you'll get a set of paths with no stroke and no fill, and no visible source image either. On the other hand, if you want to preserve the source image to be used as a guide for the paths after you've expanded them, you could set your Raster View to Original Image. At that point, when you choose Expand as Viewed, your source image will also be preserved and grouped together with the new paths.

WORKING WITH LIVE PAINT

With Illustrator's Live Paint function, you can instantly apply color, gradients, and other fills to any enclosed space in your artwork, without having to make sure it's defined as a separate vector object first. That lets you paint shapes and spaces the way your eye sees them—just as you would if you were coloring a drawing by hand.

Painting the intuitive way

Suppose you draw three squares, arranged so that the space between them forms a triangle, as in the example at right. Under normal Illustrator rules, you wouldn't be able to color that triangle because it doesn't exist as a separate vector object. It's just the empty space between the squares. That's where Live Paint comes in. Live Paint says, in effect, "If you don't like the rules, change them!" Just designate the objects you want to paint as a Live Paint Group. Suddenly, you can paint any enclosed area you want, whether or not it's a discrete vector object.

Three squares arranged to form a triangular space in the middle

So here's how to paint the empty triangular space. First, select the three squares with the Selection tool. Then choose the Live Paint Bucket tool (it lives just below the Eyedropper in the Tools panel) and click on the selected squares to turn them into a Live Paint Group. (You can also turn selected objects into a Live Paint Group by choosing Object > Live Paint Make, or via the keyboard command ⌘-Option-X/Ctrl-Alt-X.) You'll notice a special bounding box around the squares, with little star-shapes in its handles. This bounding box distinguishes a Live Paint Group from an ordinary Group.

Clicking a selected group with the Live Paint Bucket turns it into a Live Paint Group. Note the helpful tool tip that appears next to the cursor

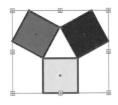

When you select a Live Paint Group with the Selection tool, you'll see this special bounding box

Next, choose a bright green color as a fill, and then move the Live Paint Bucket over the triangular space. The triangle becomes highlighted, showing that the area is available for painting. Click on the triangle, and presto—the triangle fills with the chosen color.

By the way, you can change the way the Live Paint Bucket behaves by double-clicking on its icon in the Tools panel. This opens the Live Paint Bucket Options dialog, where you can set options such as whether the Bucket paints fills, strokes, or both, and you can set the color and size of the highlight you see when you position the Bucket over a paintable area. Also, keep in mind that you can always edit the paths in Live Paint Groups using the Pen tool or other tools.

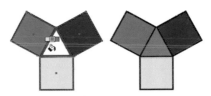

Left: When you position the Live Paint Bucket over an area that can be painted, a highlight appears around the area. Right: After clicking with the Bucket, the area fills with color

Painting strokes with Live Paint

As mentioned in the previous section, you can use the Live Paint Bucket to paint strokes as well as fills. Just make sure the Paint Strokes checkbox is enabled in the Live Paint Options dialog, and the Live Paint Bucket will

Access the options for the Live Paint Bucket by double-clicking on it in the Tools panel

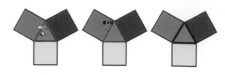

Left: The Live Paint Bucket is positioned to paint the fill. Middle: When the cursor is positioned to paint the stroke, note that the cursor changes from a bucket to a little paintbrush, in addition to highlighting the stroke. Right: After painting the strokes on all three sides of the triangle

Left: the original butterfly outline. Middle: Live Paint lets you select and paint the area of the wing around the two spots. Right: the fully painted butterfly

Cursor swatch preview

The Live Paint Bucket's "cursor swatch pre- view" feature lets you quickly cycle through color choices in the Swatches panel—both within and between color groups. The preview is visible anytime you choose a color from the Swatches panel to paint with. The middle square is the selected color, and the squares on either side are its neighbors in the Swatches panel—use the left and right arrow keys to move to the previous or next swatch, and the up and down arrow keys to move between color groups and the general group of swatches. You can always make the swatch preview go away by double-clicking the Live Paint Bucket and disabling the Cursor Swatch Preview checkbox in Live Paint Options (it's turned on by default).

apply whatever Stroke attributes you've defined before you click with the Bucket. When painting the stroke, make sure to position the bucket so that the stroke is highlighted rather than the fill.

Also, even if you haven't enabled the Paint Strokes checkbox in Live Paint Options, you can always paint strokes at will by holding down the Shift key as you click with the Bucket.

Keep in mind that the stroke attributes currently specified in the Stroke panel (or Control panel) will determine the look of the stroke the Bucket paints, so be sure to set them where you want them before you click.

The flat world of Live Paint

One of the rules that falls by the wayside when you're working with a Live Paint Group is the idea of stacking order. Within a Live Paint Group, everything is treated as if it's at the same level.

Here's an example. The simple butterfly figure at left is ready to be colored using Live Paint. Notice that when the Live Paint Bucket is moved over the left wing, Illustrator highlights the area of the wing surrounding the two spots, allowing you to paint the main part of the wing without also coloring in the spots. (You can color the spots separately by moving the Bucket directly over them.) Under the normal rules of Illustrator, you'd have to make sure that the two spots were stacked above the wing shape so you didn't paint over them when you colored the wing. But in the flat world of Live Paint, Illustrator understands that the spots are separate entities, and allows you to simply color around them.

Choose your fill (or go with no fill)

We've seen how Live Paint can apply color to enclosed spaces—but the Live Paint Bucket can paint all kinds of fills, not just solid colors. That means you can choose to paint with a gradient, a pattern, or even no fill at all.

Create two overlapping solid-filled circles, and make them into a Live Paint Group. Now you can fill the intersection between the two circles with a gradient (by choosing a gradient swatch from the Swatches panel, and clicking on the intersection with the Live Paint Bucket). You can even fill the intersection with None, and the intersection will become a hole that lets you see objects or fills below. For an example of what you can do by painting with no fill, see Sandee Cohen's "Fixing a hole" tip.

Putting the "Live" in Live Paint

The "Live" part of Live Paint means that your painting remains editable and changes along with your objects when you resize them, transform them, or move them around. When you move or resize your two overlapping circles, the intersection maintains its fill even as it changes size, shape, and position along with the circles.

Adding paths to a Live Paint Group

After you've created a Live Paint Group, you may decide that you'd like to add some paths to it. Fortunately, it's easy to add new members to a Live Paint Group.

Suppose you want to add stripes to the body of the butterfly example. One way to add them is to draw stroked lines using the Pen or Line tools. Next, select the lines along with the butterfly Live Paint Group, and click the Merge Live Paint button in the Control panel (or choose Object > Live Paint > Merge). The six lines are added to the Live Paint Group, where they serve as three stripes that you can easily paint.

However, there's an even easier way to add new paths to a Live Paint Group—by working in Isolation Mode, as discussed at the beginning of this chapter.

Using the Selection tool, double-click on any object in an existing group (or in this case a Live Paint Group). You'll see the gray bar with the current name of your group (as shown in the Layers panel) appear at the top of your window, which tells you you've just entered Isolation Mode. Once you see the gray bar, your group has been isolated and anything you add to your Artboard will automatically be considered part of the group.

Left: positioning the Bucket over the intersection of the circles. Right: after clicking on the intersection to fill it with a rainbow gradient

Left: the original circles. Middle: moving the red circle below the green one. Right: changing the size and shape of both circles. The intersection keeps its gradient fill even as it moves around

Fixing a hole

With Live Paint objects, you can create a transparent "hole" in an object simply by choosing the None swatch and using the Live Paint Bucket to fill an area (such as the center of this donut) with None! —*Sandee Cohen*

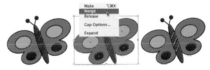

Left: adding six lines to the butterfly's body. Middle: adding the new paths to the butterfly's Live Paint Group. Right: painting the spaces between the lines orange to create three stripes

Reapplying fills

Unfortunately, if you move a path so that an enclosed painted area becomes unpainted, Illustrator doesn't remember that the region was filled with a color prior to the edit. Moving the path back to its original position will not bring the fill back and you'll need to reapply the fill color.—*Mordy Golding*

Left: the bananas before coloring. Right: the circle indicates the gap that's causing color to flood outside the bananas.

The Gap Options dialog

Once the gap was no longer a problem, it was easy to paint the bananas yellow

Check the Gap Detection box and the Preview box in the Gap Options dialog, then choose green for the highlight color

So in the case of the butterfly, double-clicking part of the butterfly with the Selection tool will put you in Isolation Mode. You can now draw your stripes and they will automatically become part of the Live Paint Group for the butterfly. To exit Isolation Mode, click the gray bar, or double-click on the Artboard (or on any objects that aren't within your group).

Live Paint's Gap Options

As you've seen, Live Paint lets you apply color to any enclosed area. But the key word there is *enclosed*. What happens when the area you're trying to paint isn't completely sealed off? What if there are one or more small openings between the paths surrounding the area, causing it to spring a leak? That's where Illustrator's handy Gap Options dialog comes in.

At left is an example developed by author and trainer Sandee Cohen. Sandee created this pair of bananas by tracing a raster image with Live Trace. Sandee then converted the tracing to a Live Paint group and attempted to paint the bananas yellow. But as you can see in the right-hand image, when she clicked on the bottom banana with the Live Paint Bucket, color flooded outside the banana because of a small gap toward the end of the banana. (It's indicated with a red circle.) To fix this problem, Sandee selected the bananas and then opened the Gap Options dialog by choosing Object > Live Paint > Gap Options.

Using the drop-down menu labeled "Paint Stops at" located at the top of the dialog, Sandee changed the setting from Small Gaps to Large Gaps. This caused Live Paint to ignore the relatively small gap at the end of the banana, and let her paint the banana yellow, just as if the gap weren't there. If Sandee had wanted to be even more precise, she could have specified an exact size for how large a gap would have to be before Live Paint would recognize it as an opening. To do so, she'd enable the Custom checkbox and enter a number in the field.

If you don't have any Live Paint Groups selected when you open the Gap Options dialog, whatever settings you

choose will become the defaults for any new Live Paint
Groups you create before you change the settings again.

You can also use the Gap Options dialog to detect
gaps in your artwork. Let's look at the example of the
three squares again. Suppose that when you try to paint
the triangle you can't get the triangle to highlight when
you move the Live Paint Bucket over it. That's a good
sign that maybe the squares weren't exactly flush. In that
case, you can use the Gap Detection feature to see where
the problem is, as shown at left. Select the squares, open
the Gap Options dialog, check the Preview checkbox
and choose Green as the highlight color from the "Gap
Preview Color" drop-down menu. At right is the resulting
preview, showing the troublemaking gaps highlighted in
green. At this point, it's easy enough to move the squares
a little closer together to eliminate those gaps.

Illustrator will even close gaps for you automatically
if you click the "Close gaps with paths" button at the bottom of the dialog. But be aware that Illustrator always
uses straight paths to close gaps in the selected objects.
Make sure straight paths are really what you want in
those locations, and check your results closely.

When you convert a Live Trace object to Live Paint,
Gap Detection will be turned off, even if you turned it on
before converting. Just re-enable it if you need it.

How to expand (or release) Live Paint Groups

Once you've finished coloring a Live Paint Group, you
may find that you're ready to move on and do other things
to the objects in the group—some of which will require
taking them out of the realm of Live Paint. For example,
you may want to be able to work with the objects in the
group as separate elements once you've colored them.
That's where expanding comes in.

When you select your Live Paint Group and choose
Object > Live Paint > Expand (or click the Expand button in the Control panel), the selected objects will be
converted to ordinary vector paths. Their appearance will
stay the same as before, but they will no longer be Live

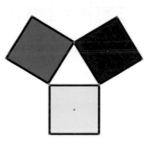

*The little green dots at the corners of the tri-
angle reveal where the gaps are*

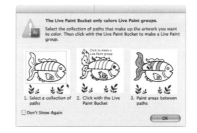

*If you click with the Live Paint Bucket and you
haven't selected any paths, you'll see the (very
informative) dialog shown above.*

Splitting Live Paint groups

With Live Paint groups that are
made up of many complex paths,
gap detection will impede performance. You will experience
better performance by splitting
very large Live Paint groups into
several smaller Live Paint groups.
—*Mordy Golding*

Coloring multiple areas

You can use the Live Paint Bucket
tool to color multiple areas with a
single color in one step by clicking
in one area and dragging across
additional contiguous areas.

Deleting can make holes too!

There's another way to make a
donut hole: use the Live Paint Selection tool to select and delete!

Using the Live Paint Selection tool to select one piece of a line

Selecting and deleting the four line segments around the middle square

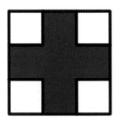

After deleting the four segments, painting the four corner squares white to make the red cross stand out

Paint objects, and they'll be rendered into separate filled and stroked paths that behave according to the "normal" rules Live Paint allowed you to break.

On the other hand, you may find that you'd like to revert the objects in your Live Paint Group back to their pre-Live Paint state. Maybe you'd like to rework them a little before you paint them, or you decide you'd like to color them the old-school way, without using Live Paint. No problem—just choose Object > Live Paint > Release (or click the Release button in the Control panel) and your objects will be converted back to ordinary paths.

Editing paths the intuitive way

You've seen how Live Paint lets you color spaces the way the eye sees them. But Illustrator also allows you to edit paths the same way. You can use the Live Paint Selection tool (which lives next to the Live Paint Bucket in the Tools panel) to select and alter specific parts of paths based on the way they look (instead of how they were constructed).

You can set options for the Live Paint Selection tool by double-clicking, just like the Live Paint Bucket. Before moving on to the next step, you'll want to open the Live Paint Selection Options dialog to make sure you're able to select strokes as well as fills. You'll be working with a red object in the next step, so change the highlight color to something you can see against a red fill, such as green.

First, create a grid of nine squares by drawing a large red square with a black stroke, and then overlaying this big square with four intersecting black-stroked lines on top. Then convert the whole grid into a Live Paint Group.

Now, by choosing the Live Paint Selection tool and moving it over the divider lines, you can select the smaller segments of the lines that were formed as they crossed each other. At this point, you only have to select and delete four of those small segments to end up with the cross-shaped object in the center of the large square. Then you can use the Live Paint Bucket to paint the four corner squares white, and presto—the result is a red cross on a white background.

GRAHAM

Cheryl Graham

Live Trace is an ideal complement to Cheryl Graham's high contrast drawing style. Graham added her photo to the page (File > Place) then clicked the Live Trace button in the Control panel. She used this Default preset knowing that the Mode setting of Black and White would produce the desired effect (middle detail). Graham then retraced the photo using the Control panel buttons, this time lowering the Threshold. To create a larger area of white, she lowered the Threshold to 90. To bring out greater detail around the eyes and hair, she set Path Fitting to 1px

with a Minimum Area of 4px.(bottom detail). Satisfied with the results, she clicked Trace. Graham did not save these settings because every photo usually requires a different combination of Tracing Options and plenty of experimentation. Graham clicked the Expand button in the Control panel to convert the Live Trace object to editable paths. She refined the paths with the Smooth Tool. Using the Pen tool and variations of the default Art Brush Calligraphy 1, she drew in the remaining details of the portrait. (See her gallery in the *Brushes & Symbols* chapter for more about her drawing technique).

Cutting & Joining
Basic Path Construction with Pathfinders

FOX / BLACKDOG (Art Director: Jeff Carino, Landor Associates)

Overview: *Design an illustration using overlapping objects; use the Pathfinder panel to join and intersect objects, join lines to circles, and cut objects from other objects.*

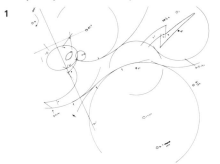

Fox's inked sketch drawn with a compass
NOTE: Fox created his image in reverse. As a last step, he used the Reflect tool to flip the final image (see the *Zen* chapter for help reflecting).

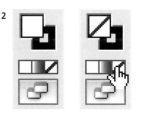

Using the Tools panel to set the Fill to None before starting to draw

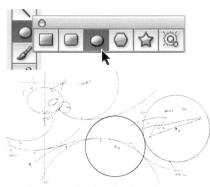

Drawing constrained circles from the center with the Ellipse tool (by holding Shift-Option/Shift-Alt) to trace over the placed template

To redesign the classic "9 Lives" cat symbol that has appeared on Eveready batteries for over 50 years, Mark Fox began with a hand-drawn sketch. Once his sketch was approved, he inked the sketch with a Rapidograph pen and a compass, and then reconstructed the ink image in Illustrator using permanent (destructive) Pathfinder commands. The top row of Pathfinders are actually *Shape* modes that allow you to keep the objects "live" so you can make adjustments. To apply these shape modes permanently so that you can move on to the next step, select the objects and click the Expand button. Alternatively, you can apply any Shapes mode permanently in one step by holding Option/Alt when you first click the Shape icons. The bottom row of Pathfinder icons are always permanent. *Especially* when you work with permanent Pathfinders, save incremental versions of your image as you work.

1 Creating a sketch and placing it as a template layer. Fox used a compass to create a precise drawing constructed of fluid curves. Using his inked sketch as a template, Fox then used the Ellipse tool to recreate his compass circles in Illustrator. Create your own sketch using traditional materials and then scan it, or sketch directly into a painting program (such as Painter or Photoshop). Save your sketch as PSD or TIF format, and place it into a new Illustrator document as a template. To do this, choose File > Place to locate the image you wish to use as a template, then enable the Template option and click Place (see the *Layers* chapter for more on templates).

2 Hand-tracing your template using adjoining and overlapping objects. In order to see your objects as you work, before you begin drawing make sure that you're in Preview mode (View menu), and set your Fill to None and Stroke to Black. Now use the Ellipse and Rectangle tools to create the basic shapes that will make up your image. Fox used some circles to form the shapes themselves (like the rump of the cat), and others to define the areas that would later be cut from others (like the arc of the underbelly). To create perfect circles or squares hold the Shift key while you draw with the Ellipse and Rectangle tools. By default, ellipse and rectangles are drawn from a corner. In order to draw these objects from a center point, hold down the Option/Alt key as you draw. To create a circle from its center point, you'll need to hold down the modifier keys Shift-Option/Shift-Alt as you draw—don't release the modifier keys until after you release your mouse button. Because Fox measured everything in millimeters in his inking stage, he created his circles numerically. With the Ellipse tool, Fox Option-clicked/Alt-clicked on each center point marked on his template, entered the correct diameter for Width and Height, and clicked OK.

3 Constructing curves by combining parts of different circles. Once your paths are drawn and in position, use the Pathfinder panel to combine portions of different circles to create complex curves. After drawing basic circles, use the Line Segment tool to draw a line through the circles at the point where you want to join them, and choose Object > Path > Divide Objects Below. Then select the sub-sections of the divided circles that you don't want and delete. To join separate adjoining curves, click the Add to shape area Pathfinder icon. To apply Add permanently, click the Expand button.

4 Constructing objects using the Intersect Pathfinder command. If the area you wish to keep is the portion where objects overlap, use the Intersect command. Fox

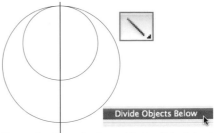

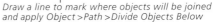

Draw a line to mark where objects will be joined and apply Object > Path > Divide Objects Below

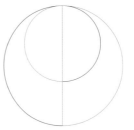

Select and delete unwanted portions of objects that won't be part of the final curve

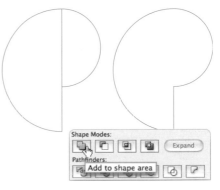

Once only the elements you wish to be joined remain, select them and click the Add to shape area Pathfinder icon (later click the Expand button to apply Add permanently)

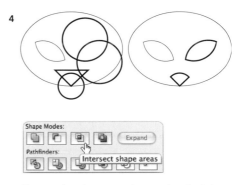

Constructing the eyes and nose using the Intersect Shape Areas Pathfinder command

Drawing one line from an anchor point on the circle and another angled line slightly removed

Creating a perpendicular copy of the angled line by double-clicking the Rotate tool, specifying a 90° Angle, and clicking Copy

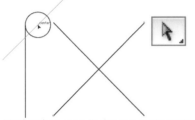

Moving the perpendicular copy to the circle's center and then making it into a guide

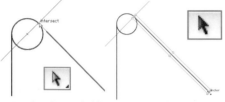

Moving the angled line tangent to the circle using the guide, then lengthening the line

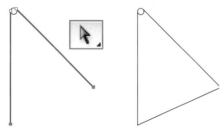

Selecting the two end anchor points of the lines and closing using Join to connect the lines

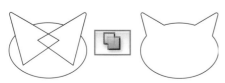

Using the Add to Shape Pathfinder command to attach the circle to the angled shape, then the completed ears to the cat-head ellipse

used Intersect to create the eyes and the nose of the cat. To make the eye shape, he drew a circle and then created a duplicate by holding Option/Alt as he moved it with the Selection tool. He then positioned the two circles so the overlap created the desired shape and selected both circles. Fox applied Intersect shape areas and Expand in one step by holding Option/Alt when he clicked the Intersect icon.

5 Attaching lines to circles. Fox connected angled lines to a tiny circle to form the cat's ear. To smoothly attach lines to circles, the lines need to lie "tangent" to the circle (touching the circle at only one anchor point). To work with precision, turn on Smart Guides (View menu).

Start with the Ellipse tool and draw a small circle. To create the first tangent line, choose the Line Segment tool, and place the cursor over the left side anchor-point of the circle. When you see the word "anchor point" click-drag downward from that anchor point to draw a vertical line.

Creating a tangent line that doesn't begin at an anchor point is trickier. Start by drawing another line slightly apart from the circle, but at the angle you desire (holding the Shift key constrain movement to horizontals, verticals, and 45° angles). To help you find the tangent point for this line, you need to create a line perpendicular to it. With your angled line selected, double-click the Rotate tool, enter 90°, and click Copy. Use either the Direct Selection or Group Selection tool to grab this perpendicular copy of your line near the middle and drag it toward the center of your circle; release the mouse when you see the word "center." With this line still selected, make it into a guide with View > Guides > Make Guides. Now select your angled line by marqueeing it with the Direct Selection tool, or click it with the Group Selection tool. Finally, with either the Direct Selection or Group Selection tool, grab the top anchor point and drag it to where the perpendicular guide meets the circle; release the mouse when you see the word "intersect."

To adjust the length of either line, switch to the Selection tool, select the line, and drag the bounding box from the middle end handle at the open anchor point.

The Add to Shape Pathfinder ignores lines, so to attach the lines to the circle, first connect the lines together to form a two-dimensional shape. Using the Direct Selection tool, marquee the two open anchor points and choose Object > Path > Join (⌘-J/Ctrl-J) to connect the points with a line.

Finally, to unite your angled shape with the circle, select them both, hold Option/Alt, and click the Add to Shape Area Pathfinder icon. Fox also used Add to Shape Area to join the ears to the head (he rotated the first ear into position, and used the Reflect tool to create a copy for the other ear—see the *Zen of Illustrator* chapter for help with rotation and reflection).

6 **Cutting portions of paths with other objects.** To create the rear flank of the cat, Fox used a large object to cut an area (subtract) from another circle. Use the Selection tool to select the path you'll use as the cutter and bring it to the top of the stacking order (in the exact position) either by choosing Object > Arrange > Bring to Front, or Edit > Cut and then Edit > Paste in Front (⌘-F/Ctrl-F). Select the cutter object and the objects you want to cut and click the Subtract from shape area Pathfinder icon.

Better to see Pathfinders...

If your objects are styled  with a stroke and no fill, you can swap the Fill and Stroke styling to better see the effects of a Pathfinder command. To do this, with objects selected, click on the Swap Fill and Stroke arrows in the bottom section of the Tools panel. Click again to swap it back.

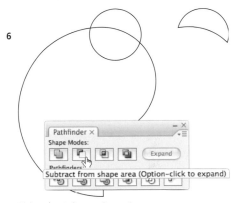

Using the Subtract from shape area to cut one object from others

Manually cut with Scissors

Although it's not as precise as using a line and "Divide Objects Below," you *can* use the Scissors tool to cut any path, including open paths. Turn on Smart Guides (View menu) and click with the Scissors tool when the word "Path" appears to place two coinciding points on the path. To separate the points, first deselect the path entirely. Then, with the Direct Selection tool, click on top of the new points to select only the top point. Then you can move or delete the selected point.

Divide & Color

Applying Pathfinder Divide & Subtract

Overview: *Design an illustration using overlapping elements; create individual paths using Divide, and delete unnecessary paths; using Subtract to cut "holes" and create Compound Paths; Divide again and assign colors to divided objects.*

PIRMAN / PHOTO: JOSHUA MCHUGH

1

Creating the basic elements using the Rectangle and Ellipse tools

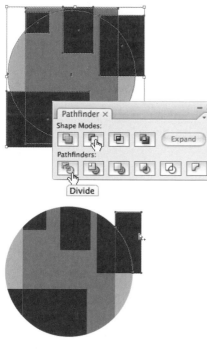

(Top) Selecting all paths and clicking on Divide in the Pathfinder panel; (bottom) selecting and deleting unnecessary paths

Illustrator's Pathfinder panel provides many ways to combine objects. To create this disco clock for a Worldstudio Foundation's "Make Time" benefit, John Pirman used the Divide and Subtract Pathfinder options to permanently alter his objects. This allowed him to adjust colors within each of the divided areas in his illustration.

1 Creating and positioning paths; dividing overlapping paths. Pirman created a circle and a number of rectangles to serve as the background (and later as the objects to Divide his figure shapes) for his clock face design. In a new Illustrator document, draw a filled circle with no Stroke using the Ellipse tool (hold the Shift key to constrain the ellipse to a circle). Then use the Rectangle tool to draw a few rectangles filled with different gray values, and a stroke of None. Use a selection tool to move the rectangles around until you are satisfied with an arrangement of rectangles in relationship to the circle. Next, choose Select > All, then open the Pathfinder panel (Window > Pathfinder) and click the Divide button (in the panel's bottom row). All overlapping paths will split into separate, editable objects. To delete the extra paths outside of this "divided circle" shape, first choose Select > Deselect, then select them, and press Delete.

2 Using Subtract to create "holes" and Divide again. Next, Pirman drew a series of silhouetted human figures with the Pen and Pencil tools and arranged them in relation to the background. For figures that included enclosed "negative space" (such as an arm partially touching another part of the body) he used Pathfinder Subtract to cut the areas as "holes," so objects behind would show through. To cut enclosed areas into permanent holes, first make sure that your enclosed paths are on top of the rest of the figure. Next, set solid fills for all the objects, with no strokes. Then select your figure and the enclosed spaces and hold Option/Alt while you click on Subtract in the Pathfinder panel (holding Option/Alt while applying a Pathfinder in the panel upper row makes that Pathfinder action permanent). Your figure with holes has now become a Compound Path. Use the Selection tool to reposition the figure, the Group Selection tool to reposition the holes, or the Direct Selection tool to edit the paths.

Pirman created a color swatch group of blues, greens, and white to apply to his figures. He then positioned each figure over his "divided circle" background and used his background objects to divide the figures. To do this, choose different color fills for your figures and arrange them in front of your divided background (the stacking order doesn't matter). Next, select all your paths (Select > All) and click Divide in the Pathfinder panel. As before, all of the overlapping paths will now be split into individual paths. Use the Group Selection tool to select and delete paths outside of your background shape, and then to select individual sections of the figures in order to change the fill color. Pirman used colors of similar value to visually integrate the divided figures.

With his figures divided, Pirman then used his palette colors to recolor the various divided sections of the figures and continued to make adjustments to the background. To do this, color all of the paths that make up the fully divided illustration using your color palette. Using the Group Selection tool, click on the individual paths within the circle shape and style with any Fill color you like (see how to recolor an entire image with Live Color in the *Live Trace, Live Paint, & Live Color* chapter).

2

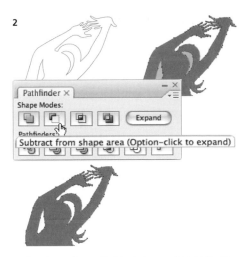

Drawing a figure that includes enclosed objects defining "negative space" (top left), selecting all the objects that create the figure and applying Pathfinder > Subtract while holding Option/Alt (top right); the figure now as a Compound Path

Filled figures; positioning the colored figure paths over the divided circle background

The process of styling individual objects with different colors.

Live Tracing Logos

Using a Rasterized Logo for Live Trace

ONE WAVE YOGA
JOLYNNE ROORDA

Overview: *Rasterizing a vector logo to start fresh, thereby creating cleaner, more economical paths; using Live Trace to acquire clean vector paths and reconstruct the logo.*

1

The first version of the logo, long-since replaced by later versions

Imprecise paths required simplifying for easier future modifications

Selecting the One Color Logo preset from the Live Trace functions on the Control panel

Black paths selected for recoloring after clicking on the Expand button on the Control panel

Illustrator's Live Trace preset "One Color Logo" can be very successful in reconstructing vector logos from rasterized images. Although Jolynne Roorda actually had the vector version of this logo, it had been through several revisions and she wanted to produce a version that was more cleanly constructed. She decided it would be quickest to rasterize the current version of the logo and use Live Trace to retrace the logo with more precise paths.

1 Rasterize the logo and use Live Trace to vectorize it again. Roorda opened the file containing the logo and duplicated the artwork layer. She selected the logo and rasterized it at a high enough resolution for smooth curves. She then used the drop-down list box on the Control panel to select the One Color Logo preset. This preset closely traces the original, but ignores White so the background becomes transparent. The Black and White Logo preset leaves White as part of the tracing, and the "[Default]" preset uses a lower Threshold and traces more loosely. If Roorda hadn't been happy with the default settings for the One Color Logo preset, she could click on the Tracing Options dialog button, check Preview and adjust the settings until she was happy with the results.

After tracing the logo, Roorda clicked on the Expand button on the Control panel to turn the tracing back into basic paths. She knew the logo would be used in many different situations and wanted to ensure that no one would have difficulties opening or printing the file using older software. She then selected the black-filled area and recolored it with the company's turquoise.

VALENZUELA

Judy Valenzuela

As one of a deck of Tarot cards, Judy Valenzuela began the chair with a hand-drawn and scanned sketch. She wanted the look of spontaneity, and knew Live Trace would maintain this look and be modifiable as a vector object. She chose Inked Drawing as the Preset. Its looser tracing would keep the sketch flowing. She adjusted the Threshold from the default 180 to 245 to fill the lines that were being missed, and checked Ignore White. Before converting the chair to a Live Paint object, Valenzuela clicked on Expand. Because Live Paint on a loose tracing may not create the desired closed shapes, Valenzuela knew there would be gaps that could cause Live Paint to overfill her Empress chair, and Expand would close those gaps. In keeping with the spontaneous feeling of the subject, she then added calligraphic brush strokes, lesser shapes she hand-drew or transformed, and drop shadows to float the objects in space. Lastly, she added text to complete the card.

Coloring Sketches

From Sketch to Live Trace and Live Paint

Overview: *Import a sketch into Illustrator; apply Live Trace; convert to a Live Paint Group; color with Live Paint Bucket.*

JOLY

1

The first rough draft of the robot sketch

The refined version of the sketch

Dave Joly drew this robot character as a visualization exercise for an animation project. Joly started by creating a rough sketch by hand. In Illustrator, Joly found that the new Live Trace and Live Paint features were like an express route between his sketch and a polished Illustrator drawing. Live Trace and Live Paint are well integrated for the task of filling sketches with color.

1 **Drawing the initial robot concept.** Joly sketched the robot using the natural media tools in Corel Painter. He then removed stray details and solidified the linework to make the image easier to trace later. When he finished, he saved the image as a Photoshop file.

Although Joly chose to start and edit his original drawing in Painter, you can also sketch an idea on paper and scan it into your computer. If necessary, you can clean up the sketch of your scan in an image editor such as Adobe Photoshop before moving it to Illustrator.

2 Tracing with Live Trace. In Illustrator, you can open a Photoshop image as a new document by choosing File > Open, or add it to an existing Illustrator document by choosing File > Place. Select the image on the Artboard and click the Live Trace button on the Control Panel.

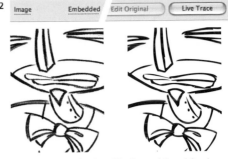

Applying Live Trace doesn't just trace the image; it also creates a Live Trace object consisting of both the original image and the tracing. Unlike a hand-tracing, you can change the tracing options to alter the results at any time without starting over. On the Control panel, choose a tracing preset from the Presets pop-up menu, or click the Options button to open the Tracing Options dialog where more Live Trace options are available. The default tracing preset creates high-contrast black and white line art that is well-suited for Live Paint. As a result, Joly did not need to change any Live Trace options for this project.

Image options displayed in Control Panel (top) for selected image (bottom left); the image after clicking the Live Trace button (bottom right)

Control Panel for selected Live Trace object; Options button (for Tracing Options) highlighted

3 Filling areas with Live Paint. With the tracing selected, Joly clicked the Live Paint button in the Control Panel to convert it from a Live Trace object to a Live Paint Group. The object no longer contained the original image or allowed easy retracing, but it gained Live Paint attributes: Joly could fill and stroke any naturally enclosed areas in the Live Paint Group without having to draw a path to hold each fill. Joly selected the Live Paint Bucket and chose a Fill swatch from the Control Panel. Whenever Joly positioned the Live Paint Bucket over an area that could be painted using Live Paint, a red outline appeared to indicate a Live Paint region. If he wanted to paint the area outlined in red, he clicked the region or dragged across multiple regions.

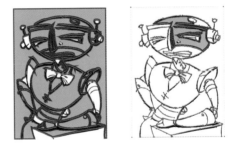

Control Panel for selected Live Paint Group; Options button (for gap options) highlighted

Clicking the Live Paint Bucket on the robot's face with no gap detection (left) and after applying gap detection for large gaps (right)

Initially, gaps between the hand-drawn black lines let color spill into surrounding areas. Joly chose Edit > Undo to remove the spilled paint, and then clicked the Options button on the Control Panel to open the Gap Options dialog. Here, you can specify the size of gap to automatically close by using the Paint Stops At pop-up menu or the Custom field. If you enable the Preview checkbox,

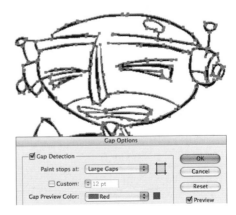

Gap Options dialog with gaps highlighted in red on Artboard because Preview is checked

4

Additional details that Joly drew as paths in front of the Live Paint object; the Live Paint object's fills have been removed here for clarity

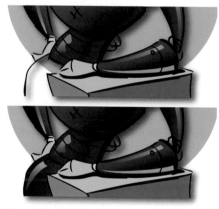

Very wide gap in lower left corner (top) and the blue filled path Joly drew (bottom)

Live Paint Group border with Group Isolation Mode off (top left) and on (top right); the mode is controlled by the Group Isolation button (highlighted) on the Control Panel (bottom)

red dots on the Artboard mark the gaps detected by your Gap Options settings. For this project, Joly found that the Large Gaps setting worked well.

4 **Completing the drawing.** Joly rapidly colored the rest of the sketch using the Live Paint Bucket, changing the fill swatch as needed and clicking or dragging across Live Paint areas he wanted to fill. Joly also drew additional paths to add new details, highlights, and shading.

Some regions, like the hip at the bottom left of the illustration, had gaps that were too large for the automatic gap detection settings. Joly drew new paths for those few areas.

Joly drew his additional paths separately from the Live Paint object, filling them using the traditional method of selecting each path with the Selection tool and then clicking a swatch. However, it's possible to add paths to an existing Live Paint Group by entering Group Isolation Mode. With a Live Paint Group selected, click the Isolate Group button on the Control Panel to enter Group Isolation Mode (the border of the Live Paint Group becomes gray). When a Live Paint Group is in Group Isolation Mode, drawing a new path adds it to the selected Live Paint Group; you can then paint the new path using the Live Paint Bucket. Click the Group Isolation Mode button again to exit Group Isolation Mode.

Filling and Stroking with the Live Paint Bucket

You can control whether the Live Paint Bucket paints fills or strokes. In the toolbox, double-click the Live Paint Bucket to open the Live Paint Bucket Options dialog, and enable or disable the Paint Fills and Paint Strokes checkboxes. If only one checkbox is enabled, pressing Shift temporarily reverses what happens when you click with the bucket. For example, by default, clicking paints fills and Shift-clicking paints strokes. With both checkboxes enabled, clicking the Live Paint Bucket automatically paints a stroke or a fill, depending on how close the bucket is to an edge.

Lance Jackson

Lance Jackson created these portraits for a San Francisco Chronicle special section on high-profile CEOs. Jackson first drew pencil sketches of the CEOs on paper. He scanned his sketches, saved them as JPEG files, and applied Live Trace to the JPEG images in Illustrator. He adjusted Live Trace settings such as Threshold to trace the precise tonal range he wanted from each sketch. Jackson expanded the Live Trace results in order to edit paths and apply additional fills as needed.

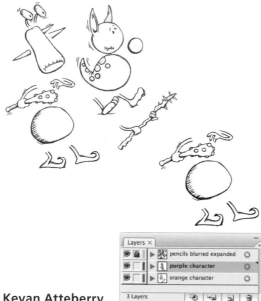

Kevan Atteberry

Illustrator Kevan Atteberry drew a sketch with a traditional paper and pencil sketch of "Lurd pieces" (top left). Atteberry creates characters in pieces so he has the flexibility to place part of a character behind another, to tweak positioning of a posture, and so forth. In the past he would just lay his scanned line drawing in layers above the colored objects (created with shaped blends), but he now applies Live Trace to his drawings first. Because each image requires slightly different settings, and because it can take a while for Live Trace to preview the changes of settings, Atteberry devised an ingenious workflow. When scanning an illustration, he also saves a small representative detail of the image. He began by placing and selecting the small Lurd detail in Illustrator, then he chose Object > Live Trace > Tracing Options. In Tracing Options, he enabled Preview, set the mode to Grayscale with the Max colors of 4, and then experimented with the blur settings so the extraneous marks for the Lurds were

minimized, while the line shape of the pencil drawing remained preserved. Saving these settings (Save Preset), he clicked Trace. Placing the main drawing, he again entered Tracing Options, chose his new settings from the Preset pop-up, and clicked Trace. Atteberry applied Object > Expand, turning the traced object into separate vector objects filled with black, white, and two grays (a detail shown above the Layers panel). To delete the whites, he clicked on one with the Direct Selection tool, chose Select > Same > Fill Color, and deleted. Because he wanted the grays to darken the colors he would be adding (not just laying gray over the colors), he used Select > Same > Fill Color to select both of the grays. In the Control panel he changed the blending mode from Normal to Multiply and reduced the Opacity to 58% (click and hold the triangle to the right of Opacity). Creating layers underneath, Atteberry used the Pen and Pencil tools with blends (see his lesson in *Blends, Gradients & Mesh*) to color the parts.

ATTEBERRY

Kevan Atteberry

Using his compositional sketch as a guide (right) and his "Lurd parts" from the Gallery opposite, Illustrator Kevan Atteberry assembled his composition. Before assembling the parts, however, Atteberry selected each "part" made up of the expanded Live Trace line work along with the inner solid shapes and shaped blends (see his lesson in the *Blends, Gradients & Mesh* chapter) and grouped (⌘-G/ Ctrl-G). This allows Atteberry to click on each part with the Selection tool to select all of it. He can then move parts easily, reorder them in the Layers panel, and form the characters. Once the characters are formed, he places them within the scene created from shaped blends.

Trace Techniques

Using Live Trace for Auto & Hand-Tracing

Advanced Technique

Overview: *Use the same image as a foundation for both a background created using Live Trace and a hand-traced foreground.*

Swatches panel before and after removing unused swatches

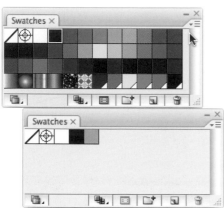

The original photograph Crouse used as the starting point for both the Live Trace background and hand-traced foreground

Scott Crouse drew this portrait of George Jenkins, the founder of Publix Markets, as part of a series of exterior murals for the Publix grocery store chain. To communicate the warm, friendly personality of "Mr. George," Crouse applied his personal illustration style as he hand-traced the portrait from a photograph. The background image did not need to be as distinctive, so Crouse saved time by using the Live Trace feature to create it from the same photograph. For easier hand-tracing, Crouse simplifies images by limiting tonal levels and removing distracting stray bits; in many cases Live Trace can replace Photoshop for this preparatory task.

1 Preparing the document. Crouse chose Select All Unused from the Swatches panel menu, and then he clicked the trash can icon in the Swatches panel to delete the selected swatches. Removing all unused swatches from the document made it easier to see the swatches that will be created later by Live Trace.

Crouse chose File > Place to select the original photograph of Mr. George and add the photo to the page.

2 Copying the image layer. To separate the foreground and background images, you can duplicate them while keeping them aligned. Drag the original layer (not just the image) to the New Layer icon in the Layers panel, then double-click the name to rename it.

To prevent changes to layers other than the one you're editing, click the lock column to lock any layers not in use. The background is edited in the next step, so lock the foreground layer at this time.

3 Tracing the background. Crouse selected the photo and chose Object > Live Trace > Tracing Options. You can produce results similar to Crouse's by applying settings like these: For Mode, choose Grayscale; for Max Colors, enter 3 (some images need more levels); and select Output to Swatches. Leave other options at their default settings. Click Trace to commit the settings. The tracing is live, so you can change the settings at any time by choosing Object > Live Trace > Tracing Options.

4 Adjusting the background graphic's colors. To keep the viewer's focus on the subject, Crouse gave the background a light, low-contrast appearance. Selecting Output to Swatches in Step 3 added colors to the Swatches panel as global swatches applied to the Live Trace object. This is valuable because editing a global swatch updates all of its applied instances. To edit any of the new global swatches created by Live Trace, double-click them. In this case, the gray tones were changed to colors and lightened overall.

5 Simplifying the foreground copy for hand-tracing. In the Layers panel, lock the background layer and unlock the foreground. Select the foreground image and click the Tracing Options button on the Control Panel to edit the Live Trace settings for the selected image. Here, Max Colors was changed to 7, Blur to 1 px, Resample to 150 dpi, Path Fitting to 1 px, and Minimum Area to 10 px. The optimal values depend on the resolution of the image, so try different settings until you see what you want.

Layers panel before (top) and after (bottom) duplicating the image layer and locking the foreground layer

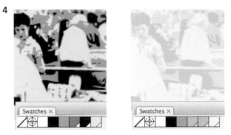

Tracing Options dialog

Before (left) and after (right) editing swatches output by Live Trace; white corners signify global swatches

Tracing Options button on the Control Panel, located to the right of the Preset pop-up menu

Detail of original image (left) and after adjusting for hand-tracing using Live Trace (right)

6

The Rasterize dialog

The Layers panel with the foreground tracing image layer set up as a template, and a new layer added to contain the hand-tracing

7

Completed tracing over the dimmed template (top), and with the template hidden to reveal the actual background (bottom)

6 Rasterizing the hand-tracing template. The Live Trace object contains many vector objects which could slow redraw. Converting it to a raster object simplifies the object and speeds screen redraw during hand-tracing. To rasterize the Live Trace object, select it and choose Object > Rasterize. Medium Resolution is a good compromise between a decent display speed and the ability to trace at high magnifications.

In the Layers panel, double-click the layer containing the foreground tracing image, select Template, and click OK. This locks and dims the layer, putting it in an ideal state for hand-tracing. Click the New Layer button to provide a layer to contain the paths that will be hand-traced.

7 Hand-tracing the foreground. Crouse used the Pen tool to hand-trace the template image, resulting in the foreground portrait. The goal of hand-tracing is to produce a personal interpretation of the original image, so Crouse didn't follow the template exactly; he added, edited, or removed paths as needed. Through his linework, Crouse enhanced and advanced the desired mood and feeling of the illustration and the physical and facial expressions of the subject.

When he was satisfied with his hand-tracing, Crouse used Save As to save a copy of his working file. With the original version saved, in this final copy of the file he deleted the hand-tracing template layer, leaving his hand-traced foreground over the Live Trace background.

Pre-processing a tracing image in Photoshop

Live Trace works by creating paths along significant changes in contrast. In some photos, the areas you want Live Trace to trace may not contain enough contrast. To address this, open the image in Photoshop and apply a Curves adjustment layer to increase or decrease image contrast or make other changes as needed. After you edit a placed image outside of Illustrator, use the Links panel in Illustrator to update the image link and the Live Trace object will also update.

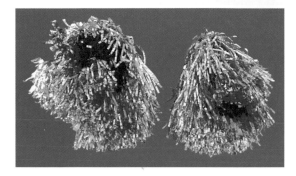

Scott Crouse

Using many of the same techniques as in Trace Techniques, Scott Crouse created this Illustrator CS2 rendering of a Miami Dolphins cheerleader. Crouse used Live Trace to trace a major foreground element—the pom-poms. The pom-poms are so complex that hand-tracing them would take too much time. Crouse realized that using Live Trace to trace the pom-poms would be much faster, and because of the random nature of the pom-poms, the Live Trace results would not be that different from hand-tracing them. Crouse first hand-traced the cheerleader with the Pen tool, but not the pom-poms. He then isolated the pom-poms from the rest of the original photo so that Live Trace would provide a clean outline of just the pom-poms. He did this by opening the original photo in Photoshop, tracing the outline of the pom-poms,

and then applying a single green fill color to everything but the pom-poms. For more control over the final colors, Crouse also used Photoshop to apply a Posterize adjustment layer and the Median filter. He also converted the image to Indexed Color using a 14-color Adaptive palette. He opened the edited Photoshop file in Illustrator and applied Live Trace. He used default Live Trace options with the following exceptions: He set the Mode to Color, the number of colors to 14, and enabled the Output to Swatches checkbox. Crouse then edited the swatches created by Live Trace to brighten them. Finally, he deleted the green area and positioned the traced pom-poms over the rest of the drawing he hand-traced earlier.

HANSEN

Scott Hansen

For this cover of *Game Developer*, a magazine targeted at people in the video gaming industry, Scott Hansen used Live Trace to trace his sketch of a graduate (above right). Hansen wanted to portray a recent graduate considering his options in video gaming: to be a programmer, designer, or artist. Using the version he made with Live Trace as a starting point, Hansen created additional enclosed portions within the original traced objects to define areas that he intended to

be filled with different colors or tones. Hansen also "cleaned up" the traced objects that contained a lot of extra "burrs" and points. He used the Delete Anchor Point and Smooth tools to smooth the ragged sections (the final cleaned up version in Outline mode shown directly above). As with most of his projects, Hansen created the finishing details in Photoshop (see the *Illustrator & Other Programs* chapter for more on bringing Illustrator objects into Photoshop).

Scott Hansen

Before departing on a national tour, electronic music duo Dusty Brown commissioned artist Scott Hansen to create a promotional tour poster. To distress graphic pattern elements in the composition, Hansen wanted to create a vector paint stroke. He painted a real media paint stroke, scanned it, and placed it into Illustrator. Selecting the stroke, he used Live Trace to turn the paint mark into a black vector object (top black mark). So that the mark better fit the objects to which he would apply it, he used the Free Distort tool, and rotated and stretched the mark. Then, using the Direct Selection tool, he deleted some of the detailed portions of the mark, and repositioned other parts. When the stroke better matched what he had in mind, he clicked the Merge icon in the Pathfinder panel to form the final stroke (bottom mark). He brought the stroke into Photoshop as a Shape and filled it with the same cream color as the background. He duplicated the shapes on layers above the pattern elements so that they hid portions of the blue and red patterns underneath (see *Illustrator & Other Programs* for more on shapes and Photoshop).

"B" Paintbrush tool; a brush in the Control panel

Brushes & Symbols

Using Brushes and Symbols, you can create the equivalents of many traditional illustration tools, such as pens and brushes that drip and splatter, colored pencils and charcoals, calligraphy pens and brushes, and spray cans that can spray anything—from single color spots to complex artwork. You can use these tools with a pen and tablet, or with a mouse or trackball.

In addition to the Brushes examples in this chapter, you'll find numerous step-by-step lessons and Galleries involving Brushes throughout the book.

BRUSHES

There are four basic types of Brushes: Calligraphic, Art, Scatter, and Pattern. You can use Brushes for everything from mimicking traditional art tools to painting with complex patterns and textures. You can either create brush strokes with the Brush tool, or you can apply a brush stroke to a previously drawn path.

Use Calligraphic Brushes to create strokes that look like they're from a real-world calligraphy pen or brush, or to mimic felt pens. You can define a degree of variation for the size, roundness, and angle of each "nib." You can also set each of the above characteristics to be Fixed, Pressure, or Random.

Art Brushes consist of one or more pieces of artwork that get stretched evenly along the path you create with them. You can use Art Brushes to imitate drippy, splattery ink pens, charcoal, spatter brushes, dry brushes, watercolors, and more.

The artwork you use to create an Art Brush can represent virtually anything: the leaves of a tree, stars, blades of grass, and so on. Use Scatter Brushes to scatter copies of artwork along the path you create with them: flowers in a field, bees in the air, stars in the sky. The size, spacing, scatter, rotation, and colorization of the artwork can all vary along the path.

Pattern Brushes are related to the Patterns feature in Illustrator. You can use Pattern Brushes to paint patterns along a path. To use a Pattern Brush, you first define the tiles that will make up your pattern. For example, you can create railroad symbols on a map, multicolored dashed lines, chain links, or grass. These patterns are defined by up to five types of tiles—side, outer corner, inner corner, start, and end—that you create, and one of three methods of fitting them together (Stretch to Fit, Add Space to Fit, and Approximate Path).

Artwork for Creating Brushes

You can make Art, Scatter, and Pattern Brushes from simple lines and fills, and groups of objects created from them, as well as blends and some live effects. Some complex artwork cannot be used for making brushes; artwork that can't be used in brushes include gradients, mesh objects, raster art, and advanced live effects such as 3D.

Working with Brushes

Double-click the Paintbrush tool to set application-level preferences for all brushes. When using Fidelity and Smoothness, lower numbers are more accurate, and higher numbers are smoother. Check the "Fill new brush strokes" option if you want the brush path to take on the fill color in addition to the stroke color. When Keep Selected and Edit Selected Paths are both enabled, the last drawn path stays selected; drawing a new path close to the selected path will redraw that path. Disabling either of these options will allow you to draw multiple brush strokes near each other, instead of redrawing the last drawn path. Disabling Keep Selected deselects paths as they are drawn, while disabling Edit Selected Paths turns off the adjusting behavior of the Brush tool even when it is near selected paths. If left enabled, the Edit Selected Paths slider determines how close you have to be in order to redraw the selected path, as opposed to drawing a new path. The lower the number, the closer you must be to the selected path to redraw it.

Closing a brush path

To close a path using the Brush tool, hold down the Option /Alt key *after* you begin creating the path, then let go of the mouse button just before you're ready to close the path.

Reversing brush strokes

To change the direction of a brush stroke on an open path, first select the path and then click on an endpoint with the Pen tool to establish the new direction toward that point. —*David Nelson*

Auto-replacing brush objects

To replace all applications of a brush, hold Option/Alt and drag one brush over another in the Brushes panel (you may wish to duplicate the brush being replaced first). —*David Nelson*

Scaling brushes

To scale artwork that contains paths with applied brushes, enable Scale Strokes & Effects in Preferences > General, or in the individual transformation dialogs (Scale, Rotate, etc.).

Including brush characteristics in brush name; using List View to make brushes easier to find

Scatter Brush artwork can be easily separated onto individual layers for use in animation. For details about distributing artwork to layers, see the "Release to Layers" section in the *Web & Animation* chapter introduction.

But it says I have pressure...

In previous versions of Illustrator, if you didn't have a pressure-sensitive tablet connected to your computer, you wouldn't see possible pressure settings in Calligraphic and Scatter Brush Options. Now you can actually see (and might be able to select) these pop-up options even if you're not connected to a tablet. However, unless you're connected to a tablet supporting the various pressure and tilt options, these settings will not affect your brush marks.

More about brushes

• Pasting a path that contains a brush will add the brush to the Brushes panel.

• Convert an applied brush into editable artwork by selecting the path and choosing Object > Expand Appearance.

• Drag a brush out of the Brushes panel to edit the brush art.

• To create a brush from an applied brush path, blend, gradient, or gradient mesh, expand it first (Object > Expand).

To edit a brush, double-click it in the Brushes panel to change Brush options; or, drag it out of the Brushes panel to edit the brush and then drag the new art into the Brushes panel. To replace a brush, press Option/Alt and drag the new brush over the original brush slot in the Brushes panel. Then in the dialog, you can either replace all instances of the applied brush already used in the document with the newly created brush, or create a new brush in the panel.

Keep in mind that if you change the options for a brush, and in the dialog choose to "Leave strokes," then the strokes created previously by that brush are no longer connected to that brush. In order to make changes to strokes no longer connected to a brush in the panel, you must access "Stroke Options" either by clicking the "Options of Selected Object" button, choosing it from the Brushes panel menu, or double-clicking the Stroke in the Appearance panel.

There are four colorization methods (None, Tints, Tints and Shades, and Hue Shift) you can use with Brushes. "None" uses the colors of the brush as they were defined and how they appear in the Brushes panel. The Tints method causes the brush to use the current stroke color, allowing you to create any color brush you like, regardless of the color of the brush depicted in the Brushes panel. Click on the Tips button in the Art Brush Options dialog for detailed explanations and examples of how all four color modes work.

When drawing with a pressure-sensitive stylus (pen) and tablet, using the Calligraphic Brush tool and a pressure setting in the options dialog, you'll be able to draw with varying stroke thickness and brush shape, according to the pressure you apply to the tablet. If your tablet supports Tilt, in the Calligraphic Brush Options dialog, choose Tilt from one of the parameter pop-ups and increase the variation. For particularly dramatic results, set the Angle for tilt with a flattened shape brush with a large variation. Then the angle at which you hold your pen will affect the brush stroke, producing a dramatic variation in brush-mark thickness (and or shape) as you draw. For Scatter brush pressure settings, you can vary the size, spacing, and scatter of the brush art. If you don't have a tablet, try choosing Random settings in Calligraphic and Scatter Brush Options.

SYMBOLS

Symbols are special pieces of artwork that you create and store in the Symbols panel. From this panel, you can then add one or more copies (called *instances*) of the symbols into your artwork. When you make changes to a symbol, those changes are automatically applied to all the instances of that symbol.

Symbols can be made from almost any art you create in Illustrator. The only exceptions are a few kinds of complex groups (such as groups of graphs) and placed art, which must be embedded (not linked).

Illustrator CS3 adds a variety of new controls, in both the Control panel and the Symbols panel, to make working with Symbols more convenient than ever.

The Symbols panel

The Symbols panel, like the Brushes panel and the Swatches panel, has a handy Libraries Menu button in the lower left corner of the panel, which lets you easily load other libraries of Symbols or save the symbols currently in the panel as a new library.

The Place Symbol Instance button places a new instance of the currently selected Symbol onto the page. The Break Link to Symbol button makes the selected instance independent. It is now an ordinary piece of artwork and no longer an instance of a symbol. You can then drag this piece of artwork back into the Symbols panel to create a new symbol, or you can replace the original parent symbol with this new version by Option/Alt-dragging the new symbol on top of the old one.

The New Symbol and Delete Symbol buttons round out the panel. (See the Tip "Options Trading" at right for a change in how the New Symbol button functions.)

Eraser tool on brushed paths

Applying the new Eraser tool to brushed paths may not necessarily give you the results you expect. See the "BSutherland-Eraser1-brushes" folder on the *Wow! CD* for a more detailed explanation and some workarounds.

Create symbols on the fly

You can create a new symbol quickly and easily just by selecting some art and then hitting the F8 key. The new symbol is added to the Symbols panel, and the selected art is automatically replaced by an instance of the newly created symbol. —*Jean-Claude Tremblay*

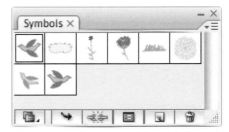

The buttons at the bottom of the Symbols panel, from left to right: Symbol Libraries Menu, Place Symbol, Break Link to Symbol, Symbol Options, New Symbol, and Delete Symbol

Options trading

When you click on the New Symbol button in Illustrator CS3, the Symbol Options dialog opens by default. If you want to skip the Symbol Options dialog, you need to Option/Alt-click the button. (It worked the other way around in previous versions of Illustrator, so don't get confused!)

The Instance Name field in the Control panel

The Edit Symbol, Break Link, and Duplicate buttons in the Control panel

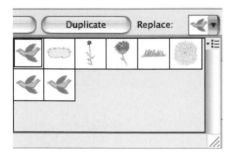

The Replace control in the Controls panel, and the drop-down version of the Symbols panel that displays when you click it

The other controls visible in the Control panel when a symbol is selected, from left to right: Opacity, Recolor Artwork, Align, and Transform

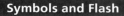

The icon next to the Instance Name field reflects whether the Symbol is specified as a Graphic or a Movie Clip in the Symbol Options dialog (see the tip later)

Symbols and Flash

Symbols represent the best way of using Illustrator for Flash animation. To learn more about working with symbols and Flash, see the *Web & Animation* chapter.

Another handy new control is the Select All Instances command in the Symbols panel menu, which instantly selects all instances in your document of whichever Symbol is currently chosen.

Symbols and the Control panel

When you select an instance of a symbol, you'll see the Control panel change to offer you several useful controls, including a field where you can assign that specific instance its own name. There's also an Edit Symbol button that takes you into Isolation mode (which is discussed in the following section), a Break Link button that severs the link between the selected instance and the parent symbol it's associated with, and a Duplicate button that creates a quick copy in the Symbols panel of the parent Symbol for the selected instance.

The Replace control in the Control panel offers you a handy drop-down version of the Symbols panel, where you can choose another symbol to replace the selected one. (This might save you the step of opening the Symbols panel itself, and help reduce clutter on your screen.)

Editing Symbols (Working with Isolation Mode)

Editing symbols is now much easier than it was in the past. You can edit a symbol by doing any of the following things: double-clicking a symbol in the Symbols panel; double-clicking an instance of a symbol on the Artboard; clicking the Edit Symbol button in the Control panel; or choosing the Edit Symbol command in the panel menu.

Once you perform any of those actions, Illustrator will open the symbol in Isolation mode for easier editing. If Isolation mode is a new concept for you, see the *Beyond the Basics* chapter for a primer on what it is and how it works. Remember that there are several easy ways to exit Isolation mode when you're done editing, or if you find yourself there by accident: Click anywhere in the gray Isolation mode bar, at the top of the screen;

double-click anywhere on the Artboard outside of the Isolated symbol; click the Exit Isolated Group mode button in the Control panel; or choose Exit Isolated Group from the contextual menu by right-clicking or Control-clicking (Mac).

After you exit Isolation mode, any changes you made to the Symbol will immediately be reflected in the parent symbol in the panel as well as any and all instances of the symbol on the page.

Working with the Symbolism Tools

There are eight different Symbolism tools. Use the Symbol Sprayer tool to spray selected symbols onto your document. A group of symbols sprayed onto your document is called a *symbol instance set* and is surrounded by a bounding box (you can't select individual instances inside a set with any of the selection tools). Then use any of the other Symbol tools—the Symbol Shifter, Scruncher, Sizer, Spinner, Stainer, Screener, or Styler—to modify symbols in the symbol instance set.

To add symbols to an existing instance set, select the instance set. Then, from the Symbols panel, select the symbol to be added—which can be the same as or different from the symbols already present in the instance set—and spray. If you're using the default Average mode, your new symbol instances can inherit attributes (size, rotation, transparency, style) from nearby symbols in the same instance set. See *Illustrator Help* for details about the Average versus User Defined modes.

When you add or modify symbol instances, it's important to make sure you have selected both the symbol instance set and the corresponding symbol(s) in the Symbols panel. If you don't, the Symbolism tools can easily appear to not be working. To remove symbols from an existing instance set, hold down the Option/Alt key and click on the symbols with the Symbol Sprayer tool. Specific details on how to create and modify symbols are covered in depth in the "Symbol Basics" lesson later in this chapter.

Symbols to layers

Symbol artwork can be easily separated onto individual layers for use in animations. Select and target the Symbol artwork layer, then choose Release to Layers (Sequence) from the Layers panel menu. For more, see "Release to Layers" in the *Web & Animation* chapter introduction.

Symbols sprayed, sized, and stained

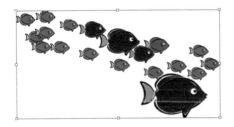

Symbols added using User Defined mode; new symbols are all same color and size

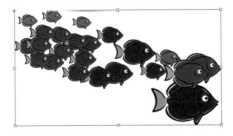

Symbols added using Average mode; new symbols inherit average color and size from symbols nearby (as defined by the brush radius)

Changing tool diameter

Instead of accessing the Symbolism Tools Options dialog to change a tool's diameter, you can use the square brackets on your keyboard to interactively resize the diameter of the symbolism tool in use. Use [(left bracket) to decrease and] (right bracket) to increase. —*Vicki Loader*

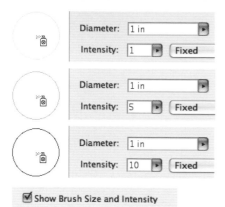

☑ Show Brush Size and Intensity

When Show Brush Size and Intensity is enabled, the intensity of the Symbolism tool is indicated by the shade of gray of the brush size circle

Changing symbol intensity

Press Shift-[to decrease (or press Shift-] to increase) a Symbolism tool's intensity.

Symbol intensity vs. density

The Symbolism Intensity option controls how fast symbol instances get sprayed onto the page. The Density option controls how closely they are spaced. You can also change the Density later. Simply select the Symbol instance set, then adjust the Density slider.

SYMBOLS VS. SCATTER BRUSHES

Symbols are more flexible than Scatter Brushes in terms of the types of changes you can make to them after they are applied; they can represent a greater variety of artwork (such as raster images or gradient-filled objects). However, there is one advantage to using Scatter Brushes: They allow you more control while drawing with a pressure-sensitive tablet.

Using the Symbolism tools, you can change many attributes (such as size, rotation, and spacing) to individual symbols in an instance set. Using Scatter Brushes, attributes will be applied to the whole set—you can't change attributes for single objects in a set. With Symbols, you can redefine the original artwork stored in the Symbols panel and have all the instances on the Artboard reflect those changes. Scatter Brushes also allow you to update the original artwork after you make changes (see the Tip "Auto-replacing brush objects," earlier in this chapter). Using Symbols, you can remove individual instances from a symbolism instance set. You can't delete Scatter Brush objects without first expanding the artwork.

Unlike other types of vector artwork, the art objects inside Symbols are not affected by the Scale Strokes & Effects preference. Scatter Brush artwork responds in its own unique way. For details, see the file "Scaling & Scatter Brushes.ai" on the *Wow! CD*.

Symbol type: graphic or movie?

You may notice two buttons in the Symbol Options dialog labeled Type: Graphic or Movie clip. Surprisingly, the default is Movie Clip. But don't worry: This setting only matters if you're bringing objects into Flash, and can be changed from within Flash itself. If you're not going to be working with your objects in Flash, you can safely disregard it. See the *Web & Animation* chapter for more information about working with Flash and symbols.

Cheryl Graham

Cheryl Graham created this vibrant painterly portrait with a custom Art Brush
designed to mimic a smudged stroke
made with a charcoal stick. To make
the "Dreadlock" Art Brush, Graham
drew ellipses in different sizes with the
Ellipse Tool (left detail). She selected the
ellipses and applied Pathfinder > Add
(middle detail). She then selected the
Warp Tool and smudged the edges of the
ellipse grouping (right detail). She often
resized the Warp tool by holding down
the Option key (Alt for Win) while dragging on the Artboard with the tool to
change its diameter. Graham selected the
artwork and dragged it to the Brushes
panel to make an Art Brush and chose
Hue Shift to enable quick color changes.
She first drew the individual strands of
hair with the Dreadlock brush. To make
a basic face shape, she drew additional
paths with the Pen and Pencil tools. She
further defined the face using the Dreadlock and default Calligraphy 1 brushes
modified in a variety of ways. As Graham
painted, she increased or decreased
the stroke width of the brushes to dramatically vary the shape and size of the
brushes. Occasionally she applied a Live
Effect to a brush stroke (Effect > Distort
& Transform > Tweak) or used the Rotate,
Shear, and Scale Tools. Graham applied
Transparency and Blending modes such
as Overlay, Multiply, and Screen, to many
of the brushes and shapes. She alter-

GRAHAM

nated between all of these methods as she
built this dynamic portrait. (See the *Live Effects
& Graphic Styles* and *Transparency* chapters to
learn more about using these features.)

Brushes & Washes

Drawing with Naturalistic Pen, Ink & Wash

Overview: *Adjust the Paintbrush tool settings; customize a Calligraphic brush; start from an existing image; experiment by using other brushes to stroke the paths and add washes.*

The default Layer 1 renamed Ink, and the original fountain photo placed as an Illustrator template layer below the drawing

The original photo (left), brush strokes drawn over the dimmed template photo (center), and the template hidden (right)

Maintaining your pressure

Only brush strokes *initially* drawn with pressure-sensitive settings can take advantage of pressure-sensitivity. Also be aware that you may alter the stroke shape if you reapply a brush after you experiment with another.

It's easy to create spontaneous painterly and calligraphic marks in Illustrator—and perhaps with more flexibility than in any other digital medium. Sharon Steuer drew this sketch of Place des Vosges in Paris, France using a pressure-sensitive Wacom tablet and two different Illustrator brushes. She customized a brush for the thin, dark strokes, and used a built-in brush for the underlying gray washes. When you use a pressure-sensitive, pen-like stylus and tablet to create highly variable, responsive strokes, you can edit those strokes as *paths,* You can also experiment by applying different brushes to the existing paths.

1 If you're using existing artwork as a reference, import it as a template layer. You can start drawing on a blank Illustrator Artboard, but if you want to use a sketch, scanned photo, or digital camera photo as a reference, set it up as a non-printing template layer. For her template image, Steuer used a scanned TIFF photo of Place des Vosges. To place an image as a template layer, choose File > Place, locate your file, enable the Link and Template checkboxes, and click the Place button. If the image imports at too large a size, unlock the template layer, enter a more reasonable Width value in the Transform panel, and press ⌘-Return/Ctrl-Enter to resize it proportionally.

Toggle between hiding and showing the template layer using ⌘-Shift-W (Mac)/Ctrl-Shift-W (Win), or by clicking in the visibility column in the Layers panel (the icon for a template layer is a tiny triangle/circle/square, instead of the Eye icon). Illustrator automatically dims the image to make your drawing easier to see.

You can customize the template layer by double-clicking its layer and changing options in the Layer Options dialog. When you import an image as a template, Illustrator automatically enables the Template, Lock, and Dim check boxes for you. You can't disable the Lock checkbox if the Template checkbox is enabled, but you can still unlock it in the Layers panel.

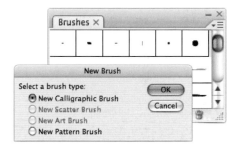

Customizing the template layer options

2 Setting your Paintbrush Tool Preferences and customizing a Calligraphic brush. In order to sketch freely and with accurate detail, you'll need to adjust the default Paintbrush tool settings. Double-click the Paintbrush tool in the Tools panel to open Paintbrush Tool Preferences. Drag the Fidelity and Smoothness sliders all the way to the left so that Illustrator records your strokes precisely. Make sure "Fill new brush strokes" is disabled; you don't need to change the other settings.

Customizing the Paintbrush Tool Preferences

To create a custom brush, click the New Brush icon at the bottom of the panel and click OK for a New Calligraphic Brush. Experiment with various settings, name your brush, and click OK. For this piece, Steuer chose the following settings: Angle=90°/Fixed; Roundness=10%/Fixed; Diameter=4 pt/Pressure/Variation=4 pt. If you don't have a pressure-sensitive tablet, try Random as a setting for any of the three Brush Options, since Pressure won't have any effect. The Paintbrush uses your current stroke color (if there isn't a stroke color, it will use the previous stroke color or the fill color). Now draw. If you don't like a mark: 1) choose Undo to delete it, 2) use the Direct Selection tool to edit the path, or 3) select the path and try redrawing it using the Paintbrush (to hide or show selection outlines, choose View>Hide/Show Edges). To edit a brush, deselect everything (Edit>Select

Creating a new Calligraphic brush

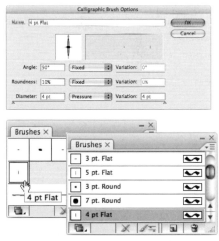

Angle, Roundness, and Diameter can be set to respond to pressure, to vary randomly, or to remain fixed; the new brush in the Brushes panel viewed with tool tips and in List View

3

Strokes made with Steuer's customized 4-pt flat brush (left); applying Adobe's default 3-pt Round brush (center), then a 1-pt Oval brush

4

The original drawing before adding a wash

A new layer (wash) created for wider wash strokes to appear under existing darker strokes on the Template placeholder layer

The gray wash strokes underneath the wider dark strokes, and the brush used to draw them

All), double-click the brush in the Brushes panel, and make changes. Illustrator will ask you if you want to apply the new settings to strokes you've already drawn with this brush; click Apply to Strokes if you want to do this or click Leave Strokes to apply the new settings only to new strokes that you'll create from this point forward, divorcing the original strokes from the edited brush. It's safer to edit a copy of a brush; to do this, drag it to the New Brush icon to duplicate it, and then edit the copy.

3 Experimenting with your artwork. Save any versions of your artwork that you like. Now try applying different brushes to specific strokes and to the entire piece. Access additional brushes from the Brush Libraries Menu button in the Brushes panel. In this step, two default brushes are applied to the same strokes as the custom brush.

4 Adding a wash. For this piece, Steuer added depth by introducing gray washes underneath the dark brush strokes. To easily edit the wash strokes without affecting the dark ink strokes, create a new layer, and draw your wash strokes into this layer between the ink and template layers. To avoid altering other layers while you brush in the washes, you may want to lock all layers except the one on which you're drawing. To do this, Option-click or Alt-click the wash layer's Lock icon.

Select or create a brush suitable for washes, and select a light wash color. Steuer used the Dry Ink 2 brush from the Artistic_Ink brush library included with Illustrator. In the Layers panel, click the wash layer to make it the current drawing layer, and paint away.

Drawing transparent brush strokes

By default, brush strokes are opaque. You can also draw with semi-transparent brush strokes, which you can use to simulate some types of inks or watercolors; where marks overlap, they become richer or darker. See the lesson "Transparent Color" in the *Transparency* chapter.

Sharon Steuer

This sketch is an extended version of the pen and ink drawing in the previous lesson. In this version, Steuer wanted to add young Noah riding a bicycle past the fountain. A photo of Noah on a carousel motorcycle was a perfect reference for the sketch, but the photo wasn't facing the right direction. To flip the photo, Steuer selected the image, chose Object > Transform > Reflect, and selected the Vertical Axis option. However, the fountain drawing's existing strokes occupied the area where she wanted to add Noah. Steuer solved this using a technique that isn't available with conventional ink: She used the Pencil tool to draw a path over the existing drawing, and filled the path with white to bring back the color of the paper. This restored an empty area where she could

add the drawing of Noah, so it looked like it was there from the beginning. Steuer drew Noah on a separate layer, allowing easy editing independent of the rest of the drawing.

JACKMORE

Lisa Jackmore

Inspired by a crumpled page from an antique garden notebook, Lisa Jackmore created a faded, textured appearance in this illustration as though pencil marks were still visible after they had been erased. Jackmore first made a panel of custom Art Brushes consisting of original and altered default Art Brushes. She created textures for the background by drawing scribble marks with the Pencil tool (using different stroke widths). For each scribble, she selected it and then dragged it into the Brushes panel to create a new Art Brush, and chose the Hue Shift colorization method so that she could vary the brush color as she drew with the art brush. Jackmore drew the vine and bird bath with a pressure-sensitive drawing tablet using varying widths of the Chalk Scribble and Thick Pencil Art Brushes. Jackmore double-clicked on the brush copy icon and in the Art Brush Options dialog, changing the percentage to vary the width. Before drawing with these brushes, she disabled "Fill New Brush Strokes" and "Keep Selected" in the Paintbrush Tool Preferences. This allowed her to draw multiple paths close to each other so she didn't accidentally redraw the previous line. Jackmore then deleted any extra points within the brush strokes by tracing over a selected brush stroke with the Smooth tool.

JACKMORE

Lisa Jackmore

To create the brush details in this image, Lisa Jackmore modified custom Art Brushes that she named scribble brushes (used in the drawing opposite). She selected some of the scribble brushes and reduced the opacity by clicking Opacity in the Control panel. Jackmore made an Art Brush to build the frame by drawing a path with the Pen tool. She altered the path with a combination of the Reflect and Shear tools. Jackmore Direct-selected points along the path and reapplied the Reflect and Shear tools to achieve an ink pen look. Then she selected the path and dragged it to the Brushes panel to make an Art Brush. Jackmore created the texture in the brown oval using a brush made of multiple strokes with the Thick Pencil Art Brush. She grouped the strokes and dragged the group to the Brushes panel to make the Art Brush. She made a clipping mask to contain the large brush stroke within the oval (middle detail). To reduce the size of the brush, she double-clicked on the brush in the Brushes panel and decreased its width.

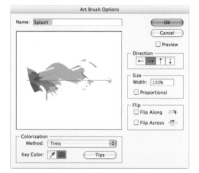

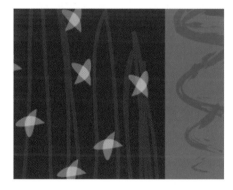

Michael Cronan

To capture the color, ethnic influence, and spirit of San Francisco's popular landmarks, Michael Cronan not only relies on Art Brushes collected over the years, but creates his own. To represent the Japanese Tea Garden, Cronan focused attention on the koi pond, creating the grasses with the Pencil brush and the multi-tones of the shrubbery with the Charcoal Brush (Open Brush Library > Artistic). He created a custom Splash brush that included transparency to represent the koi breaking the surface of the pond. Dry Ink and Chalk brushes added to the strong texture in this poster. Cronan also drew individual filled objects that he duplicated repeatedly in order to create pattern texture. By drawing loosely with the Pencil tool and using Pathfinder commands to break objects into abstract patterns, Cronan created informality and freshness in traditional vector drawing that enchanced the Art Brushes' strokes.

Michael Cronan

Continuing with his series of posters for San Francisco parks, Michael Cronan created Marina Green with his collection of Art Brushes, Scatter Brushes, and Pattern Brushes. He made extensive use of brushes that mimic traditional media. Adobe Illustrator has provided many of these with the program over the years, such as Dry Ink, Charcoal, and Pencil. With Scroll Pen 5 he could draw a variety of elements, from dragon hair to the Golden Gate Bridge and the grassy texture of the Marina Green. He renamed "Scroll Pen 5" to a more descriptive "Scroll Pen Variable Length" in order to find it easily in his Brushes panel. He created a Scatter Brush for the background stars on the Marina Green strip, and modified a Scatter Brush made from a flying beetle image that he used for one of the kites. A Polynesian design made a Pattern Brush that Cronan used to construct the dragonfly kite's tail, which he drew with the Pencil tool. He also drew vector objects and basic shapes for some of the elements, and colored them with solid or gradient fills.

Pattern Brushes

Creating Details with the Pattern Brush

MAXSON

Overview: *Create the parts that will make up a Pattern brush separately; place the parts in the Swatches panel and give them distinctive names; use the Pattern Brush Options dialog to create the brushes.*

Fitting Pattern brushes

Pattern brushes can still be scaled, flipped, and fit along a path after the brush has been created by double-clicking on the brush in the Brushes panel, which opens the Pattern Brush Options dialog.

1

Creating one zipper tooth, using the Blend tool for the highlight, expanding the object to be acceptable for a Pattern brush, then positioning a duplicate to mimic the teeth

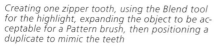
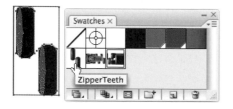

Selecting bounding box and objects, dragging objects for Pattern brushes into the Swatches panel, and naming them

While many Illustrator Brushes mimic traditional art strokes, Greg Maxson often concentrates his efforts on creating Pattern brushes that eliminate the tedious creation of the practical objects he often illustrates. For this product illustration, Maxson saved many hours by creating two zipper brushes, one for just the basic teeth of a zipper, and one that included the zipper pull and stop. Because he would be able to use these brushes over and over again, Maxson knew a little time creating a Pattern brush would save him a lot of time in the future.

1 Creating the parts of the zipper separately.
Maxson first created the zipper teeth. He drew a simple rounded rectangle for the base, and then drew a small, light oval on top of a larger black oval that would become the highlight. Maxson selected both objects and double-clicked on the Blend tool to choose Specified Steps, thus controlling the brush's complexity. He used the keyboard shortcut ⌘-Option-B/Ctrl-Alt-B to blend the highlight, which he placed on the base. Because Pattern brushes cannot be made from objects containing blends, he chose Object > Expand to convert the object to a grouped collection of paths. (See the *Blends, Gradients & Mesh*

chapter for more on blends.) Maxson duplicated the zipper "tooth" and positioned the copy as it would be in a real zipper. He then drew a no-stroke, no-fill bounding box behind the teeth to add space around each pair of teeth equal to the space between each tooth, thus keeping the teeth spaced evenly.He selected all the objects and chose Edit > Define Pattern. He gave the swatch a name he would recognize when he built the Pattern brush. Pattern swatches are the "tiles" that make up a Pattern brush.

Maxson then created the stop and pull for the zipper. To create the illusion of the pull and stop overlapping the teeth, he layered them on top of copies of the teeth he had already made. He made sure that the stop and pull were facing in the correct direction relative to the zipper pattern tiles (which run perpendicular to the path), and individually placed them in the Swatches panel.

2 Making and using the Pattern brushes. To make the first Pattern brush for the zipper teeth. Maxson opened the Brushes panel's pop-up menu and selected New Brush. He then chose New Pattern Brush, which opened the Pattern Brush Options dialog. He gave his Pattern brush a descriptive name, chose the first box in the diagram (the side tile), and then selected the Pattern swatch that represented the teeth alone. When a thumbnail of the Pattern swatch he had chosen (the teeth) showed in the first box, and the other boxes were left empty, he clicked OK to place the brush in the Brushes panel.

To create the version with the stop and pull, he again selected New Brush from the Brushes panel, and chose the same teeth pattern for the Side Tile. Skipping over the corner tiles, he chose the Zipper Pull swatch as the Start Tile, and the End Tile for the Zipper Stop swatch. He named his new Pattern brush so he would know it was built from all three swatches and clicked OK.

To use his new brushes, Maxson drew a path for each zipper. The long, vertical zipper used the brush with pull and stop, while the short zipper used the brush with only teeth, since the pull required a unique illustration.

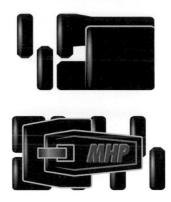

Creating zipper stop and pull, oriented in the outward-facing position Pattern brushes use for their tiles

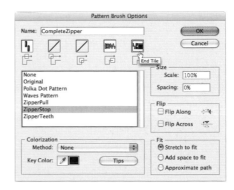

2

Creating a new Pattern brush with only a Side Tile repeated along the length of the path to make the zipper with just teeth

Creating a Pattern brush with Start and End tiles for the zipper with the pull and stop

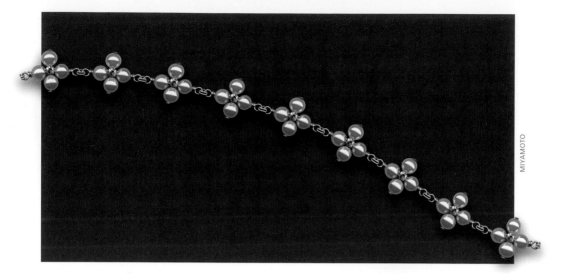

MIYAMOTO

Nobuko Miyamoto / Yukio Miyamoto

Making this intricate beaded necklace at first glance would seem impossibly difficult, but with the use of a Pattern brush, the necklace virtually draws itself. Nobuko Miyamoto designed the necklace and created the bead element (detail above) with a mixture of blended and solid filled objects. Careful attention was paid to the ends of the bead to ensure that when each bead lined up with the next one there would be a seamless connection between them. To make the chained ends, she selected the chain object and dragged a copy (Shift-Option/ Shift-Alt) to the other side of the bead. With the chain selected, she chose the Reflect tool and clicked above and below

the chain to reflect the chain vertically. Yukio Miyamoto then created the Pattern brush with the bead element. He selected and grouped the bead. Yukio clicked the New Brush icon at the bottom of the Brushes panel, selected New Pattern Brush, and clicked OK. In the Pattern Brush Options dialog, he kept the Colorization method as None, and then under Fit he chose Stretch to Fit. To make the necklace, Nobuko drew a path with the Brush tool and selected the bead Pattern brush in the Brushes panel to apply the brush. Now with the bead as a Pattern brush, the necklace can be easily adjusted to any length or path.

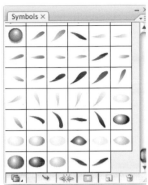

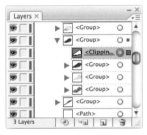

RLSimonson © 2005

SIMONSON

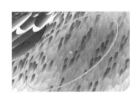

Rick Simonson

When Rick Simonson wanted to create a high level of verisimilitude in his Chipping Sparrow illustration, he turned to Illustrator's symbols as the obvious way to create the hundreds of feathers and seeds he would need. He drew closed paths for single feathers in the different colors and positions necessary to fill the bird's body. He added dimension to the feathers with gradient fills, and he duplicated and rotated some feathers to follow the growth pattern of real feathers. He then Option-clicked/Alt-clicked on the New Symbol icon on the Symbols panel to add the selected object without open-

ing the Symbol Options dialog. Simonson drew the main body of the bird, and began filling small areas with layers of feathers, using the Symbol Sprayer with short strokes to manage their placement. To get the look he wanted, he often added feathers one by one instead of in looser symbol sets. He also applied clipping masks to further shape areas of feather symbols (see the *Advanced Techniques* chapter for more about clipping masks). To create the glare and the shading he used the Transparency panel to reduce opacity and add transparency masks (see the *Transparency* chapter). He used the same methods for adding the seeds.

Symbol Basics

Creating and Working with Symbols

Overview: *Create background elements; define symbols; use Symbolism tools to place and customize symbols.*

The concept sketch

The background and symbol artwork

Kaoru Hollin created this Tropical Card for Adobe to use as sample art that would show the power and variety of effects possible using the new Symbolism tools. After creating a concept sketch, Hollin defined a library of symbols and then used the Symbolism tools to place and customize the symbols, almost as though they were brushes.

1 Creating the Background art. Based on her sketch, Hollin created the background art using eight simple layered objects, filled with gradients. To create the luminous colors, Hollin applied varying amounts of transparency to each of the objects. Hollin then added depth and richness to the water by applying Effect >Stylize >Inner Glow to the upper water curve, and Outer Glow to the lower water curve. Gradients, transparency, and effects are discussed in detail later in the book.

2 Creating symbols. Hollin created the artwork for each of the 20 symbols that she would use to create the piece. To turn a piece of artwork into a symbol, select the artwork and either drag it onto the Symbols panel, or press F8; Illustrator automatically takes your artwork on the Artboard and swaps it for an instance of the symbol. To keep your original artwork on the Artboard, hold down the Shift key as you drag it onto the Symbols panel.

3 Applying symbols. After creating a new layer for the fish, Hollin selected the fish symbol in the Symbols panel and created the school of fish with a single stroke of the Symbol Sprayer tool. You can experiment with the Symbol Sprayer by adjusting the Density and Intensity settings (double-click on any Symbolism tool to access the Symbolism Tool Options), and the speed of your spray strokes. Don't worry about getting an exact number or precise placement for each symbol as you spray; you can fine-tune those and other symbol attributes using other Symbolism tools.

4 Resizing symbols. To create a sense of depth, Hollin used the Symbol Sizer tool to make some of the fish smaller. By default, the Sizer tool increases the size of symbols within the tool's brush radius. To make a symbol smaller, hold down the Option/Alt key as you brush over it with the Symbol Sizer tool.

To make the diameter of a Symbolism tool visible, double-click on any Symbolism tool and enable the Show Brush Size and Intensity option. As for brushes, use the] key to make the Symbolism tool diameter larger and the [key to make it smaller.

5 Modifying symbol transparency and color. To modify the appearance of symbols, use the Symbol Screener,

2

The artwork for the 20 symbols that were used to complete the piece

3

The raw fish after being sprayed on with the Symbol Sprayer tool

The Symbolism tools tear off panel; see "Tear off panels" in the Illustrator Basics chapter

To access the other Symbolism tools, hold down Control-Option-click or Alt-right-click and drag toward the tool you want to use until the Tool icon changes. —Mordy Golding

4

Hollin used the Symbol Sizer tool to make some of the fish smaller and to add depth

5

The Symbol Stainer tool set to random was used to vary the color of the fish

6

Use the Symbol Spinner tool to adjust the rotation of symbols

7

After using the Symbol Shifter tool with a smaller brush size to adjust the fish positions

8

The final fish after more fine-tuning with the Symbol Sizer, Shifter, and Spinner tools

Symbols stacking order

To change the stacking order for your symbols, use the Symbol Shifter tool and:

- Shift-click the symbol instance to bring it forward.
- Option-Shift-click or Alt-Shift-click to push the symbol instance backward.

Stainer, and Styler tools. The Screener tool adjusts the transparency of symbols. The Stainer tool shifts the color of the symbol to be more similar to the current fill color, while preserving its luminosity. The Styler tool allows you to apply (in variable amounts) styles from the Graphic Styles panel. See *Illustrator Help* for details about the coloring modes and application methods of these tools.

Hollin used the Symbol Stainer tool, set to Random, to tint the fish a variety of colors with just one stroke. Later, she also used the Stainer tool on the hibiscus and starfish, and the Screener tool on the butterflies.

6 Rotating symbols. To make the first rough adjustment to the orientation of the fish, Hollin used the Symbol Spinner tool set to User Defined (which sets the spin based on the direction that the mouse is moved). See "Working with Symbols" in the Introduction to this chapter and *Illustrator Help* for an explanation of the User Defined and Average modes.

7 Moving symbols. Hollin used the Symbol Shifter tool with a smaller brush size to adjust the position of the fish.

The Shifter tool was not designed to move symbols large distances. To maximize symbol movement, first make the brush size as large as you can—at least as large as the symbol you wish to move. Then drag across the symbol, as though you were trying to push the symbol with a broom.

8 Deleting symbols. At this point, Hollin felt there were too many fish in the school. To remove the unwanted fish, Hollin used the Symbol Sprayer tool with the Option/Alt key held down. She chose a narrow brush size and clicked on the fish to be removed.

Finally, in order to make the school of fish conform more to the shape of the waves in the background, Hollin used the Symbol Sizer, Shifter, and Spinner tools to make further adjustments.

POWE.L

Gary Powell

Gary Powell created this illustration using his own set of custom symbols. He began with a template layer and hand-traced two pine cones and a simple branch. He combined the three into a new variation. Once he finished with the variations, he grouped and dragged them into the Symbols panel. With just five symbols, Pow-ell used the Symbol Sprayer tool and the Symbol Spinner tool to randomly spray branches into the scene and rotate them into position. As a finishing touch, he found the cloud symbol in the Nature Symbol Library, sprayed in a few clouds, and then used the Symbol Sizer tool to give them a sense of depth.

Symbol Libraries

Making Symbols and a Symbol Preset File

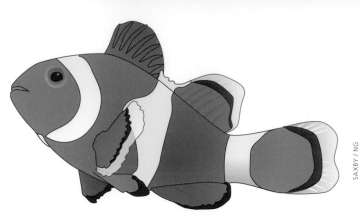

SAXBY / NG

Overview: *Create artwork; add it to the Symbols panel; save the file as a Symbol Library that can be accessed from Illustrator's Symbols panel.*

1

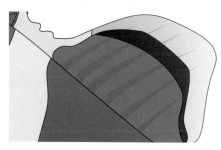

The original image (photo by Richard Ng for iStock Photo, www.istockphoto.com/richard_ng)

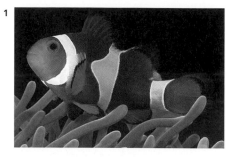

Enlargement of the dorsal fin showing the fin filled with a gradient at 75% opacity and fin rays filled with black at 12% opacity

Live Trace blues

Using Live Trace produces vector art from photographs automatically, but you'll probably need to tweak settings in Tracing Options to avoid complex artwork with extra objects, points and lines (for more information about working with Live Trace see the *Beyond the Basics* chapter).

To facilitate communication about environmental issues among scientists and environmentalists, the University of Maryland's Center for Environmental Science designed a library of symbols for use in reports, web sites and multimedia. These symbols, numbering over 1500, are free of copyright and royalty restrictions. A sampling of the symbols are included in the *Special Wow! CD IAN Symbol Pack Appendix* and on the *Wow! CD* (in the Software Demos&Links folder). For the latest update to the symbol library files, go to http://ian.umces.edu.

1 Importing and tracing an image and painting objects with gradient fills. Many sources exist for images that you can access and download from the Internet, providing a treasure-trove of visual inspiration for your symbols. Designer Tracey Saxby placed a clownfish photograph from iStockphoto (www.istockphoto.com/richard_ng) on a template layer and began tracing using the Pen and Pencil tools. If you plan to create a symbol library—a file that you access as an additional Symbols panel in Illustrator—consider keeping the artwork simple, using as few points, lines, and fills as necessary to create an expressive image. By keeping artwork simple, your symbols will be smaller in file size, making them load faster if you incorporate them in a Flash movie or in another kind of digital file.

Saxby completed the clownfish by painting the objects with linear and radial gradient fills. You can also experiment with reducing opacity and applying feathering

(Effect > Stylize > Feather) to some objects, like fins or feathers, to lend transparency to the artwork and to fade the artwork into the background behind the symbol.

2 Creating an Illustrator symbol from the artwork and organizing the Symbols panel. Once she completed the artwork, Saxby opened the Symbols panel. She selected the clownfish artwork, dragged it into the Symbols panel, and then double-clicked the symbol's thumbnail to open the Symbol Options dialog where she entered "Clownfish" in the Name field.

You can rearrange the order of symbols in the Symbols panel to make it easier for you or others to find a needed symbol. To reposition a symbol, drag the symbol to a new location in the panel. Also consider naming your symbols and having Illustrator arrange them alphabetically. To do this, select the Symbols panel menu and then select Sort by Name. (Illustrator is sensitive to initial caps in symbol names; Zebrafish will precede angelfish in the Symbols panel when you select Sort by Name.)

3 Saving the symbol file as an Illustrator symbol library and opening the library. To quickly access your symbol file in the future, save it as custom Symbol Library. To do this, choose Save Symbol Library from the Symbols panel's pop-up menu, and save it to the default "Symbols" location. To then access this library in the future, click on the Symbol Library Menu button (in the bottom left of the Symbols panel) and choose your library from the User Defined menu at the bottom of the list.

Loading a Library from Bridge CS3

Do you know that you can load document-specific libraries as you browse using Bridge CS3? If you hold down the Control key (Mac) or right-click on a thumbnail of any native Illustrator document, near the bottom of the contextual menu you will see "Open as AI Library" with option to load either Brushes/Swatch/Symbol/Graphic from that file. —*Jean-Claude Tremblay.*

The Symbols panel after the artwork has been dragged to the panel to create a new symbol

The Symbol Options dialog after the new symbol has been double-clicked in the Symbols panel

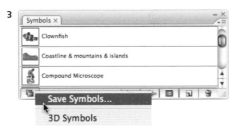

Top, the Sort by Name selection from the Symbols panel menu; bottom, the Symbols panel with the clownfish symbol among the symbols organized alphabetically using the panel menu's Sort by Name option

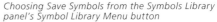

Choosing Save Symbols from the Symbols Library panel's Symbol Library Menu button

Accessing symbols from the bottom of the Symbol Library Menu button in the Symbols panel

Nature's Brushes

Illustrating Nature with Multiple Brushes

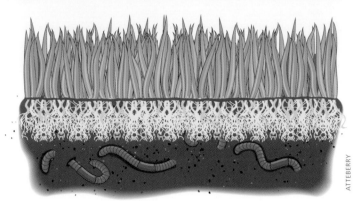

Overview: *Draw artwork and create an art brush; use Paintbrush tool to make objects with the art brush; create a pattern brush from brushed objects; create and use a scatter brush.*

1

The three objects comprising a blade of grass

Colorization
Method: Tints and Shades
Key Color: Tips

The Colorization options and Tips button from the Art Brush Options dialog

The completed art brush

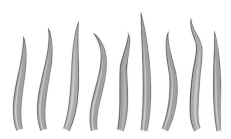

Brushed paths drawn with the Paintbrush tool

Faced with an assignment to contrast healthy and unhealthy grass and soil for a graphic to be placed on bags of organic fertilizer, Kevan Atteberry dug deep into Illustrator's Brushes panel to build his own grass, soil, and worm brushes. With the art and scatter brushes he made, Atteberry developed an easy way to create the visually complex elements of his illustration.

1 Drawing brush artwork, creating an art brush, and modifying copies of brushed paths. Creating a complex, natural-looking clump of grass was a challenge Atteberry solved by building art brushes. First, Atteberry drew a blade of grass using three objects that he overlapped. He selected the objects and dragged them into the Brushes panel. In the New Brush dialog, he selected New Art Brush and clicked OK. Then in the Art Brush Options dialog, Atteberry clicked on the Method menu in the dialog's Colorization section and chose Tints and Shades. (If you're unsure of how the Method options affect brushes, click the Tips button to display an informational dialog comparing different Methods applied to colored brush strokes.)

With the brush created, Atteberry drew several paths using the Paintbrush tool, choosing a different shade of green for each blade as he drew its path. To save time when making a large number of objects, consider duplicating paths and then editing them to make them appear different. To do this, copy and paste your paths and then apply the Scale, Rotate, and Reflect tools to vary sizes and orientations of the copies. Repeat this process until you've built a complex set of brushed paths that fills up the space you've allocated in your illustration.

2 Creating a pattern brush from brushed paths. You can take your artwork a step further by building a pattern brush from your artwork. This provides extra flexibility in case your illustration calls for your objects to be set along a wavy path or stretched to fill a space in your composition. To create a pattern brush, select your set of objects and drag them into the Brushes panel. From the New Brush dialog, pick New Pattern Brush; in the Pattern Brush Options dialog, keep the default setting of Side Tile and adjust the Colorization and Fit settings as needed. (Atteberry chose "Stretch to fit" so that the grass would stretch automatically to fit the length of the path he would draw when continuing work on the illustration.)

3 Making an art brush, drawing strokes, and covering with paths of solid and gradient fills. To show a healthy ecosystem, Atteberry drew the artwork for a worm, turned it into another art brush, and then used the Paintbrush tool to draw several paths with the worm brush. Behind the worms he drew a closed path filled with brown to make the background soil. To conceal parts of the worms, he drew brown-filled paths on a layer above the worms. For worm holes and tubes, he created dark-brown blends shaped like crescents and cylinders.

4 Making and using a scatter brush. To add a natural complexity to the brown soil, Atteberry added random particles. He first drew small shapes that he filled with light and dark browns. Then he selected the shapes and dragged them into the Brushes panel, specifying New Scatter Brush in the New Brush dialog and adjusting the settings in the Scatter Brush Options dialog. Next, with the new brush still selected, he drew a curlicue path with the Paintbrush tool, which scattered the soil particles along the path.

Brush paths that have been scaled, reflected, and rotated

2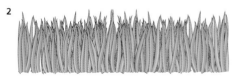

Brushed paths selected to make the pattern brush

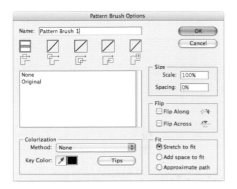

The Pattern Brush Options dialog

3

The worm artwork used to make an art brush

Path painted with the worm art brush and then partially covered by filled paths

4

Above, particle shapes used to make the scatter brush; below, the path used to paint the brush

Layers & Appearances

Layers can dramatically improve your ability to organize complicated artwork and simplify your work. Think of layers as sheets of clear acetate stacked one on top of the other so that you can keep dozens of objects—even groups of them—separate. By default new documents have one layer but you can create as many additional layers and sublayers as you wish. You can also rearrange the stacking order of the layers; lock, hide, or copy layers; and move or copy objects from one layer to another. You can use the Layers panel to select objects and groups, and you can even open a layer that allows you to view, identify and select individual paths or groups contained within a layer!

A few shortcuts will help when you're adding layers to the Layers panel (and see Tip at left). Click the Create New Layer icon to add a layer (labeled in numeric sequence) above the current layer. Hold Option/Alt when you click this icon to open Layer Options as you add the layer. To add a layer to the top of the Layers panel, hold ⌘/Ctrl when you click the Create New Layer icon. To make a new layer below the current layer and open the Layer Options, hold ⌘-Option/Ctrl-Alt when you click the Create New Layer icon (the Layer Options dialog will also open). Finally, you can easily duplicate a layer, sublayer, group, or path by dragging it to the Create New Layer icon at the bottom of the Layers panel. To delete selected layers, click on the Trash icon or drag the layers to the Trash.

Sublayers can also help you stay organized. Sublayers are contained within the layer listed above them. If you delete the *container* layer holding the sublayers, all of its sublayers will be deleted as well.

Another icon in the Layers panel is a target (the circle to the right of the layer name). See the section titled "Selecting & Targeting with the Layers Panel" later in this chapter for details about the target icon, targeting objects from the Layers panel, and to learn exactly what all this target stuff means.

Layers panel navigation

- To hide a layer, click the Eye icon. Click again to show it.
- To lock a layer, click in the column to the right of the eye (a lock displays). Click again to unlock.
- To Lock/Unlock or Show/Hide all *other* layers, Option-click/Alt-click on a Lock or Eye icon.
- To duplicate a layer, drag it to either the Create New Layer or Create New Sublayer icon.
- To select multiple contiguous layers, click one layer, then Shift-click the other. To select (or deselect) *any* multiple layers, ⌘-click/Ctrl-click layers in any order.
- Double-click any layer to open Layer Options for that layer (this works with multiple layers selected also).

Layer Options (double-click a layer name)

USING LAYER OPTIONS

You can double-click on any layer, sublayer, or named object or group in the Layers panel to access Layer Options such as the Name, Show, and/or Lock status. If you would like to know what the items are once you've renamed them, retain the name of the subcomponent. For example, you can rename a group to help organize your layer list, but keep the bracket description as part of the renaming of the layer (e.g., *floral <Group>*).

Double-click on a layer name, sublayer name, or on one of multiple selected layer/sublayer names to access the Layer Options discussed below:

- **Name the layer.** When creating complicated artwork, giving layers descriptive names keeps your job, and your brain, organized.

- **Change the layer's color.** A layer's color is visible next to its disclosure arrow, and it determines the selection color for paths, anchor points, bounding boxes, and Smart Guides. Adjust the layer color so selections stand out against artwork.

- **Template layer.** Illustrator's template layers are special layers that don't print or export. They're useful whenever you want to base new artwork on existing art. For example, you can place the existing art on a non-printing template layer, and then hand-trace over it on a regular printing layer. There are three ways to create a template layer: You can select Template from the Layers pop-up menu, double-click a layer name and enable the Template option, or enable the Template option when you first place an image into Illustrator. By default, Template layers are locked. To unlock a Template in order to adjust or edit objects, click the lock icon to the left of the layer name.

There is no restriction to how many of your layers can be template layers; see Steven Gordon's map Galleries following this chapter introduction for examples of why you might create multiple template layers.

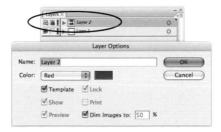

In the Layers panel, template layer names are slanted and template layers are locked by default. There is also a template icon instead of an eye icon. Placed raster images are dimmed on a template layer (can be adjusted in Layer Options).

To change the stacking order of several objects:

- Reorder the layers they are on.
- Cut the bottom objects, select the topmost object, and Paste in Front with Paste Remembers Layers *off*.
- Drag selection indicators (large square) from one layer to another.
- Shift to select multiple layers and choose Reverse Order from the Layers panel pop-up.
- Move objects within a layer using Object > Arrange: Bring to Front/Bring Forward/Send to Back/Send Backward.
- Select the objects you want to move; make a new layer (click New Layer icon) or highlight a layer into which you want to move these objects, and choose Object > Arrange > Send to Current Layer.
- If the selection is a blend, choose Object > Blend > Reverse Front to Back.

When a layer name is slanted, it's set to *not* print from within Illustrator. If the name is slanted *and* you see the Template icon, it is reliably a non-printing layer (see the "Template layer" section, on the previous page).

Note: *Template layers shouldn't be confused with Illustrator CS's Templates feature.* Templates *are a special file format ending in .ait; whereas* template layers *are simply a special kind of layer. For more about* Templates, *see the* Illustrator Basics *chapter.*

- **Show/Hide layer.** This option functions the same way as the Show/Hide toggle, which you access by clicking the Eye icon (see the Tip "Layers panel navigation" in the beginning of this chapter introduction). By default, hiding a layer sets that layer *not* to print.

- **Preview/Outline mode.** If you have objects that are easier to edit in Outline mode, or objects that are slow to redraw (such as complicated patterns, live blends, or gradients), you may want to set only those layers (or objects) to Outline mode. Toggle this option on and off directly by ⌘-clicking/Ctrl-clicking the Eye icon in the view column. Alternatively, double-click selected layers and, in Layer Options, disable Preview to set those layers to Outline.

- **Lock/Unlock layer.** This option functions the same way as the Lock/Unlock toggle, which you access by clicking the lock column of the layer (see the Tip "Layers panel navigation" at the beginning of this chapter).

- **Print.** When you print from Illustrator you can use this feature to override the default, which sets visible layers to print. If you need a quick visual clue to ensure that a layer will not print, make it into a Template layer (see the Tip "*Slanted* layer names?" at left).

- **Dim Images.** You can only dim raster images (not vector Illustrator objects) from 1% to 99% opacity.

The Layers pop-up menu

This section will look at functions unique to the Layers pop-up menu, not discussed in previous sections of this introduction.

With the ability to nest sublayers within other layers and create group objects comes the potential for confusion. It can become difficult for you to find objects when they are buried in the layer list. Use Locate Object, or Locate Layer when Show Layers Only is checked in Panel Options, to find selected objects. When you've selected two or more layers, Merge Selected is available and will place *visible* objects in the topmost layer. You can consolidate all visible items in your artwork into a single layer using the Flatten Artwork command (though be aware that you might lose effects and masks applied to the layers involved). To make a flat version in another file, unlock all layers and objects, Select > All, Copy, make a new document, and Paste (with Paste Remembers Layers disabled).

Paste Remembers Layers is a great feature: When it's enabled, pasted objects retain their layer order; when unchecked, pasted objects go into the selected layer. If the layers don't exist, Paste Remembers Layers will make them for you! This feature can be turned on and off even after the objects have been copied—so if you paste, and wish that the toggle were reversed, you can Undo, toggle the Paste Remembers Layers option, then paste again.

Collect in New Layer moves all of the selected layers into a new layer. Release to Layers (Build), or Release to Layers (Sequence), allows you to make individual object layers from a group of objects, such as a blend, a layer, or art created by using a brush. (See the *Web & Animation* chapter for applications of these options for animation.)

Reverse Order reverses the stacking order of selected layers within a container layer. Hide All Layers/Others, Outline All Layers/Others, and Lock All Layers/Others all perform actions on unselected layers or objects. And Send to Current Layer sends selected objects to your currently highlighted layer.

Panel Options customizes the layer display. This is a great help to artists who have complicated files with many layers. Show Layers Only hides the disclosure arrow so you only see the container layer thumbnail. Adding sublayers reveals the arrow, but you still can't target

New Layer...
New Sublayer...
Duplicate "Layer 1"
Delete "Layer 1"

Options for "Layer 1"...

Make Clipping Mask
Enter Isolation Mode
Exit Isolation Mode

Locate Object

Merge Selected
Flatten Artwork
Collect in New Layer

Release to Layers (Sequence)
Release to Layers (Build)
Reverse Order

Template
Hide Others
Outline Others
Lock Others

Paste Remembers Layers

Panel Options...

Layers panel pop-up menu

Go Big... or Go None

Layers panel thumbnails can be very useful when you're trying to find and select objects. But, they're sometimes difficult to see. For a closer look, set Row Size larger in Panel Options—up to 100 pixels! Or, if you have too many layers, eliminate the icons altogether.

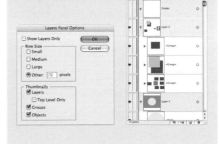

groups or individual paths in this mode. Row Size defines the size of the thumbnail for a layer. You can specify a thumbnail size from Small (no thumbnail) to Large, or use Other to customize a size up to 100 pixels. Thumbnail lets you individually set thumbnail visibility for the Layers, Top Level Only (when Layers is checked), Group, and Object.

CONTROLLING THE STACKING ORDER OF OBJECTS

Layers are crucial for organizing and building your illustration, but controlling the stacking order of objects *within* a layer is just as essential. The intuitive layers and sublayers disclose their hierarchical contents when you open the disclosure arrow. Following is a summary of the functions that will help you control the stacking order of objects within layers and sublayers.

Sublayers and the hierarchical layer structure

In addition to regular layers, there are sublayers and groups, both of which act as *containers* for objects or images. When you click on the Create New Sublayer icon, a new sublayer is added, nested inside the current layer. Artwork that you add to the sublayer will be underneath the art contained on the main layer. Clicking the Create New Layer icon with a sublayer selected will add a new sublayer above the current one. Adding subsequent layers adds the contents at the top of the stacking order or puts the artwork above the current layer.

Grouping objects together automatically creates a container "layer" named <Group>. Double-click the <Group> layer to open its options. Group layers are much like sublayers. You can target them to apply appearances that affect all the objects within the group. In some cases, such as when Pathfinder effects are applied, objects have to be grouped and the group layer must be targeted in order to apply the effect.

Note: *If you rename your <Group>, you might get confused when it doesn't behave like a regular layer. Instead, leave <Group> as a part of your new name.*

Paste in Front, Paste in Back (Edit menu)

When you choose Paste in Front or Paste in Back, if nothing is selected, Illustrator will paste the cut or copied object at the extreme front or back of the current layer. Whereas if you do have an object selected, Illustrator will paste the cut or copied object *directly* on top of or behind the selected object in the stacking order. A second and equally important aspect is that the two functions paste objects that are cut or copied into the exact same location—in relation to the *ruler origin* (*x* and *y* coordinates). This capability transfers from one document to another, ensuring perfect registration and alignment when you use Edit > Paste in Front / Back. (See the Ch02 folder on the *Wow! CD* for the "Zen lessons," including one using paste commands: 2aZen-Layers-Moving_Pasting.ai.)

Lock/Unlock All (Object menu)

In the days before it was even possible to open layers in Illustrator and select the individual items they contain, the Lock/Unlock All commands were essential. They're a little less indispensable now, but can still be very useful if you can't locate your path from within the layer contents.

When you're trying to select an object and you accidentally select an object on top of it, try locking the selected object (⌘-2/Ctrl-2 or Object > Lock) and clicking again. Repeat as necessary until you reach the correct object. When you've finished the task, choose Unlock All (⌘-Option-2/Ctrl-Alt-2) to release all the locked objects.

Hide/Show All (Object menu)

Alternatively, you can hide selected objects with Object > Hide > Selection (⌘-3/Ctrl-3). To view all hidden objects, choose Object > Show All (⌘-Option-3/Ctrl-Alt-3). **WARNING:** *Hidden objects may print if they're on visible layers. If you'll be sending your file elsewhere for printing, and if your workflow includes the Hide command, make sure to choose Object > Show All before saving your final file. And beware—Show All always unhides all objects and hidden layers!*

When is locked really locked?

Since the "Stone Age" of Illustrator, when you chose to Lock or Hide an object, it remained locked or hidden no matter what, even if the locked or hidden object was part of a group. However, since the advent of *targeting* (see the "Selecting & Targeting with the Layers Panel" section in this chapter), how you *initially* select the group determines whether you are acting on the entire group (regardless of what is locked or hidden), or merely acting on those elements in the group that are currently visible and unlocked:

- **To act upon only the current visible and unlocked objects in a group,** either Direct-Select-marquee the group, or select the <Group> in the Layers panel by clicking the space to the right of the target icon.
- **To act on all elements in a group, including those hidden and locked,** target the <Group> by clicking on its target icon in the Layers panel.

Control panel selecting

 Look for the Select Similar Objects button (and Select Similar Options menu) in the Control panel. It's a handy alternative for selecting. You'll note that the Select menu has some nifty options (Select > Same, and Select > Object).

Bring to Front/Forward, Send to Back/Backward

These commands work on objects within a layer. Bring Forward (Object > Arrange) stacks an object on top of the object directly above it; Bring to Front moves an object in front of all other objects on its layer. Similarly, Send to Back sends an object as far back as it can go in its stacking order, whereas Send Backward sends an object behind its closest neighbor.

Note: *Bring Forward/Send Backward work best with simple object groupings, and may not work as expected on complex images. If it doesn't suit your needs, expand the Layers panel and relocate your path or group.*

SELECTING & TARGETING WITH THE LAYERS PANEL

There are several ways to make selections. Click the layer's target icon or Option-click/Alt-click the layer name to select all unlocked and visible objects on the layer, including objects on sublayers and in groups. Click a sublayer's target icon to select everything on the sublayer, including other sublayers or groups. Clicking the *group's* target icon will also select all objects within that group. Shift-click the target icons to select multiple objects on different layers, including sublayers and groups. When you intend to modify the appearance of a layer, sublayer, or group, you must click on the *target* icon to make your selection first, then make your adjustments.

If you have only some (but not all) objects selected on a layer, you will see a small square to the right of the target icon. Click on the small square to select all of the objects on the layer or in the group. A larger square means that all of the objects on that layer or group are already selected. Clicking in the small space to the right of the target indicator will also select all objects on the layer, sublayer, or group.

IMPORTANT: *Be aware that if you target a top-level layer and apply strokes, fills, effects, or transparency and then copy/paste that layer into a new document, all appearance attributes that were applied to that layer will be lost in the new document, even when Paste Remembers Layers is* *enabled. Try this workaround by Jean-Claude Tremblay (which also works to maintain masks and effects applied to the layer): Since the attributes of a top-level layer are not retained and you get no warning when pasting into the new document, you need to nest the top layer into another layer and make it a sublayer. Then copy/paste this layer into the new document to retain the appearance attributes.*

APPEARANCES

Within an appearance are a collection of strokes, fills, effects, and transparency settings. An appearance can be applied to any path, object (including text), group, sublayer, or layer. The specific appearance attributes of a selection are shown in the Appearance panel. Attributes within the appearance are added to the panel in the order they are applied. Changing the order of the attributes will change the appearance. An object and its enclosing groups and layers can all have their own appearances.

To apply an appearance, make a selection or click on a target indicator (Layers panel). Then add transparency, effects, multiple fills, and/or multiple strokes (see the "Adding Fills and Strokes" section). When you've targeted a group, sublayer, or layer, strokes and fills will be applied to the individual objects within the selection, but any effects or transparency settings will be applied to the *target* (see the Tip "Selecting vs. targeting" opposite). Drag the target indicator (in the Layers panel) from one layer to another to move an appearance, or Option-drag/ Alt-drag the indicator to copy the appearance. To reuse an appearance, save it as a style in the Graphic Styles panel (for more about graphic styles see the chapter *Live Effects & Graphic Styles*).

Appearance panel

When you've selected or targeted an item, the Appearance panel displays all the attributes associated with the current selection. If there isn't a selection, the panel will display the attributes for the next object drawn. When the current target is an object, the Appearance panel always

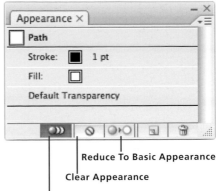

Reduce To Basic Appearance
Clear Appearance
New Art Maintains Appearance

Move or copy appearances

In the Layers panel, drag the Appearance icon circle from one object, group, or layer to another to *move* the appearance. To *copy* the appearance, hold Option/Alt as you drag.

If you can't see an appearance

If you're trying to alter an appearance, but nothing seems to be changing on the screen, check for the following:

• Your objects are selected.
• You're in Preview mode.

Appearance panel indicators

The appearance indicators for Effects and Transparency show up in the Appearance panel on layers or groups that contain elements with these attributes. See the Tip "Be a detective with files" at the end of this introduction to learn how to locate and identify effects used in any Illustrator artwork.

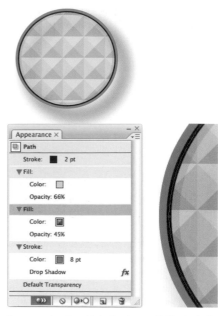

An example of multiple Strokes and Fills, including a 2-pt black stroke, a solid fill at 66% Opacity, a pattern fill at 45% Opacity, an 8-pt green stroke, and a Drop Shadow effect (see the Live Effects & Graphic Styles *chapter for more about live effects)*

New Art Has Basic Appearance

The Appearance panel's New Art Has Basic Appearance option is on by default. So, unless you disable this option (from the pop-up menu, or by clicking New Art Has Basic Appearance icon), Illustrator will not apply effects, brush strokes, transparency, blending modes, or multiple fills or strokes to new objects you create.

—*Brenda Sutherland*

Target all elements

When a group or layer is targeted, you can double-click the Contents line in the Appearance panel to target all the individual elements inside the group or layer.

—*Pierre Louveaux*

lists at least one fill, one stroke, and the object-level transparency. When the target is a group or layer, no Fill or Stroke is shown unless one has been applied (see "Adding Fills & Strokes" following) and you double-click the Contents line in the Appearance panel. "Default Transparency" means 100% opacity, Normal blending mode, Isolate Blending off, and Knockout Group off or neutral.

A basic appearance isn't always a white fill and a black stroke (as suggested by the icon). An appearance is defined as a *Basic Appearance* when it includes one fill and one stroke (with either set to None); the stroke is above the fill; there are no brushes or live effects; opacity is 100%; and blending mode is Normal (the defaults).

If the current selection has more than the *basic* attributes you can choose what attributes the next object will have. The first icon at the bottom of the panel is New Art Maintains Appearance (when disabled) and New Art Has Basic Appearance (when selected). For example, if your last object had a drop shadow but you don't want the next object to inherit this attribute, click to select New Art Has Basic Appearance and the new object will only inherit the basic attributes.

Click on the Clear Appearance icon to reduce appearance attributes to no fill, no stroke, with 100% opacity. Click on the Reduce to Basic Appearance icon to reduce the artwork's appearance to a single stroke and fill along with the default transparency. To delete an attribute, drag it to the Trash, or click it and then click the Trash. **Note:** *Keep in mind that Reduce to Basic Appearance removes all brush strokes and live effects!*

THE FINER POINTS OF APPEARANCES
Adding fills & strokes

It's not until you start adding multiple fills and strokes to an appearance that you completely understand how useful the Appearance panel is.

Select Add New Fill or Add New Stroke from the panel pop-up menu to add these attributes to the appearance profile for a selected object, or group of objects. You can also add effects and transparency attributes to each fill or stroke by first clicking on the desired fill or stroke line in the panel, and then making the adjustments in the appropriate other panel (such as the Control panel).

The Appearance panel has a stacking order similar to that of the Layers panel. Items at the top of the panel are at the top of the stacking order. You can click on items in the panel list to select them, and you can rearrange them by dragging and dropping.

There are several ways to duplicate or delete a fill, stroke, or effect. You can select the attribute in the panel list and drag it to one of the icons at the bottom of the panel. You can also select the attribute and click the appropriate icon at the bottom of the panel. Finally, you can choose the appropriate item from the pop-up menu.

Multiple fills & strokes

Create multiple line effects by adding multiple strokes to a path. Select a path, group, or layer and choose Add New Stroke from the Appearance panel pop-up menu. This adds a new stroke to the Appearance. In order to see the additional stroke on the path, you must give it different attributes from the initial stroke. Target one stroke (in the Appearance panel) and adjust the color, point size, shape, and/or transparency settings.

To create multiple fills, target an object, group, or layer and choose Add New Fill. As with multiple strokes, before you can see the effect of the added fill, it needs a different appearance. To vary the results of additional fills, apply an effect or different transparency settings.

If you're having trouble seeing the results of your multiple strokes, start with a wider stroke on the bottom (see the figures on the opposite page). To vary the results, try applying dashed lines and/or different end caps. For fills, try patterns or gradients with transparency.

See the "Basic Appearances" lesson in this chapter for an introduction to Appearances. For additional examples of art containing multiple strokes and fills, see the *Type* and *Live Effects & Graphic Styles* chapters.

Be a detective with files

When you need to modify artwork created by others (or open your own artwork created a while back) it's essential to have the Appearance panel and the Layers panel visible. This is because any number of applied effects or features (such as multiple strokes or fills, or transparency) may not be apparent. Click in the Layers panel on filled target indicators; in the Appearance panel you will see details about what has been applied. See the *Transparency* and *Live Effects & Graphic Styles* chapters for more on effects and appearances.
—*Vicki Loader*

Expandable text buttons

Want to make a text button? Type a word, then select the text object. Choose Add New Fill (in the Appearance panel menu) and drag this new fill below the Characters line. Click on the Fill line, apply the desired fill color, and then choose a shape from the Effect > Convert to Shape submenu. Set the Relative Extra Width and Extra Height how far you want the button to extend around the text, and click OK. When you edit text, the button automatically resizes itself. Yukio Miyamoto's gallery in the *Live Effects & Graphic Styles* chapter (and the *Wow! CD*) includes complex text buttons created with the Appearance panel.

Digitizing a Logo

Learning to Use a Template Layer

TOM (created for the BERTZ Design Group)

Overview: *Create a scan and place it on a template layer in Illustrator; hand-trace the template, modify the paths with the Direct Selection tool; refine lines with the Pencil tool; use basic objects for ease and speed.*

A clean, high-contrast scan of the sketch

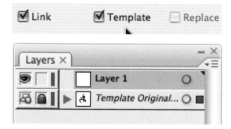

Creating the template and a drawing layer

Using the Direct Selection tool and dragging on the direction handles to adjust the path to better fit the sketch

Beginning with his scanned sketch imported as a template layer, Jack Tom used Illustrator's basic drawing tools to create this logo for the Bertz Design Group. Illustrator's Pen, Pencil and basic geometric tools, such as the Rectangle and Ellipse tools, can handle any object you need to make, creating a polished logo for any occasion.

1 Placing a scanned image as a template. Create a high-contrast copy of your sketch for the logo by scanning the image at a high resolution to provide the detail you need for hand-tracing. If you have an image-editing program such as Photoshop, you can increase contrast first, thus making your sketched lines more distinct, before placing the file in Illustrator. Save your scan as a PSD or TIFF and choose File>Open to select your scan. From the Layers panel pop-up menu, choose Template, and then create a new, empty layer for your tracing. Or create your Illustrator document first, choose File>Place, and enable Template in the Open dialog. A Template layer is placed beneath the original layer. Template layers are automatically set to be non-printing and dimmed layers.

2 Hand-tracing the template. With the template as an on-screen tracing guide, begin using the Pen tool on the empty layer for tracing the straight lines and smooth curves. Don't worry too much about the tracing being a bit off at first. You'll adjust the paths to fit the sketch more closely next. As you trace, remember to click for corners, click-drag for curves, and to hold down the Option/Alt key when dragging out a direction handle in order to create a hinged curve in the path. (See the *Zen lessons* on the *Wow! CD* for help with Bézier curves.) Once you've drawn a basic path, zoom in close and use the Direct Selection tool to adjust anchor points and direction handles. Use the Convert Anchor Point tool to switch between corners and curves, if necessary. You can simplify your view of an object by entering Outline mode. You can toggle between Outline and Preview modes for that object's layer by holding down the ⌘/Ctrl key and clicking on the visibility icon. Use ⌘-Y/Ctrl-Y to toggle the entire image between Outline and Preview modes.

3 **Drawing, and redrawing, irregular lines with the Pencil tool.** Using the mouse or a graphic tablet (such as a Wacom tablet), draw as you would with an actual pencil. Double-click the Pencil tool icon to customize settings. Create smoother lines by setting higher Fidelity and Smoothness numbers, or zoom in closer on the path while editing with the Pencil or Smooth tools. You can also select any path and start drawing close to or overlapping that path in order to redraw it (in Options specify the pixel distance from the selected path so that you can edit it instead of starting a new one). Use the Pencil tool with low settings to transform Pen tool paths into jagged lines. That will help you to express natural elements, such as the mountains in this logo.

4 **Using basic objects to help build your logo.** Illustrator includes ready-made objects to speed up drawing rectangles, ellipses, and even stars (or the sun, as in this logo). Layer these on top of each other, and add paths and filled objects drawn with the Pen or Pencil tools to finish converting your sketch to a clean illustration easy to color and/or modify to suit any purpose.

Using Option/Alt with the Pen tool to "scallop" (make a hinged curve) while you draw

Toggling between Outline and Preview mode on a single layer by holding down ⌘-D/Ctrl-D as you click on the layer's visibility icon

3

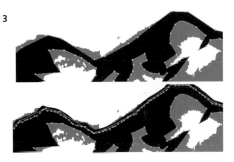

Using the Pen tool for a quick path (top), then using the Pencil tool to add a stroke expressing jagged, rough elements

4

Constructing elements quickly from geometric objects

Vector logos adapt well to B&W or color printing

Organizing Layers

Managing Custom Layers and Sublayers

Overview: *Sketch and scan a composition; set up basic, named layers in Illustrator for the objects you will create; place art into sub-layers; hand-trace the placed art; delete the temporary sublayers.*

The initial concept sketches for the illustration

The final composition for the illustration

Illustrator: STAHL / Art Director: JENNIFER MOORE

Beginning your illustration with well-organized layers and sublayers can be a lifesaver when you're constructing complex illustrations. Using these layers to isolate or combine specific elements will save you an immense amount of production time by making it easy to hide, lock, or select related objects within layers. Artist Nancy Stahl saved time and frustration when she was commissioned to design this illustration for an article in the Condé Nast Traveler magazine. She created multiple layers and sublayers to facilitate the manual tracing and arrangement of various components in the illustration.

1 Collecting and assembling source materials. Prepare your own source materials to use as drawing references and templates in Illustrator. To prepare this illustration, Stahl hand-sketched several concepts then scanned the approved composition into Adobe Photoshop where she prepared it for hand-tracing.

2 Setting up illustration layers. Before you begin to import any photos or drawings, take a few moments to set up layers. Naming and assigning a color to each layer will help you isolate and manage the key elements in your illustration. Before Stahl actually started drawing in Illustrator, she set up separate layers for the water, the sky, the railing, the steward, and the tray and ship. You can quickly name a layer while creating it by Option-clicking/Alt-clicking on the Create New Layer icon in the Layers panel. You can also name or rename an existing layer or sublayer by double-clicking on it in the Layers panel.

3 Placing art to use as a drawing reference. Click on the layer in which you plan to hand-trace your first object, then click on the Create New Sublayer icon in the Layers panel to create a sublayer for your drawing reference (Option-click/Alt-click on the icon to name your sublayer as you create it). Stahl created a sublayer that she named "JPEG Images." Use File > Place to select the scan or artwork to be placed into this sublayer. If you wish, you can enable the template option before placing the file. The sublayer should now be directly below the object layer in which you will be hand-tracing. Lock the sublayer and draw in the layer above using the Pencil, Pen, or other Drawing tools of your choice.

Using the Layers panel, Stahl repurposed the "JPEG Images" sublayer by freely moving it below each of the key element layers as she drew. To move a layer, drag and drop it to another position in the Layers panel.

4 Hand-tracing and drawing into your layers. Now you can begin drawing and hand-tracing elements in your compositional layers. Activate the layer or sublayer in which you want to draw by clicking on the layer's name. Make sure the layer or sublayer is unlocked and visible (there should be an Eye in the Visibility column and an empty box in the Lock column). It also helps to turn off the visibility of all non-essential layers before you begin working. From the Layers panel, you can lock, unlock,

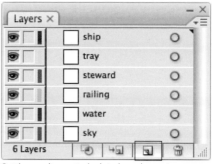

Setting up layers to isolate key elements

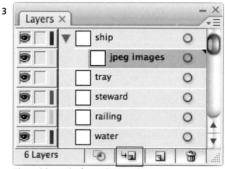

The sublayer before placing the scan

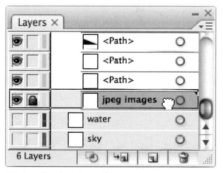

Moving the drawing reference layer

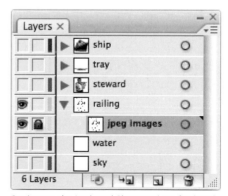

Setting up the Lock and Show options for hand-tracing an object

4

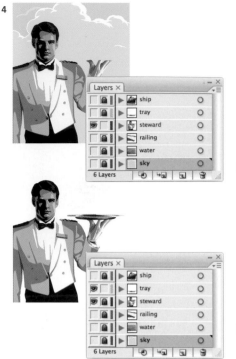

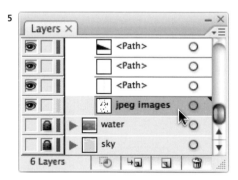

Viewing only the essential layers for each task

5

Clicking on a visible and unlocked sublayer to make it active for placing new art

6

New Layer...
New Sublayer...
Duplicate "jpeg images"
Delete "jpeg images"

Clicking on or dragging the sublayer to the Trash icon, or choosing Delete from the Layers panel pop-up menu

hide or show layers, as well as toggle between Preview and Outline modes, switch to your active layer, or add a new layer or sublayer (see the "Layers panel navigation" Tip on the first page of this chapter for helpful shortcuts in working with the Layers panel). By maneuvering in this way, Stahl could easily hand-trace a drawing reference or sketch in the layers above a locked layer.

5 Adding new placed art to a layer or sublayer. If you need to import art into an existing layer or sublayer, first make sure the layer is visible and unlocked, then make it the active layer by clicking on it. Use the Place command to bring the new scan or art into the selected layer. When Stahl needed additional drawing references she placed new art into the "JPEG Images" sublayer.

6 Deleting layers or sublayers when you are finished using them. Extra layers with placed art can take up extra disk space and increase the time it takes to save your document, so you'll want to delete them when you are done with them. When you finish using a drawing reference or template layer, first save the illustration. Then, in the Layers panel, click on the layer or sublayer you are ready to remove (Shift-click to select multiple layers) and either drag it to, or simply click on, the Trash icon in the Layers panel. Alternatively, you can choose the Delete option from the Layers panel pop-up menu. With these temporary layers deleted, use Save As to save this new version of the illustration with a meaningful new name and version number. Stahl eventually deleted all the sublayers she created as templates so that she could save her final cover illustration with all the illustration layers but without the excess template sublayers or placed pictures.

Easily changing placed art

Select the image you wish to replace and click on the name of the image that appears in the left side of the Control panel; choose Relink at the top of the resulting pop-up menu.

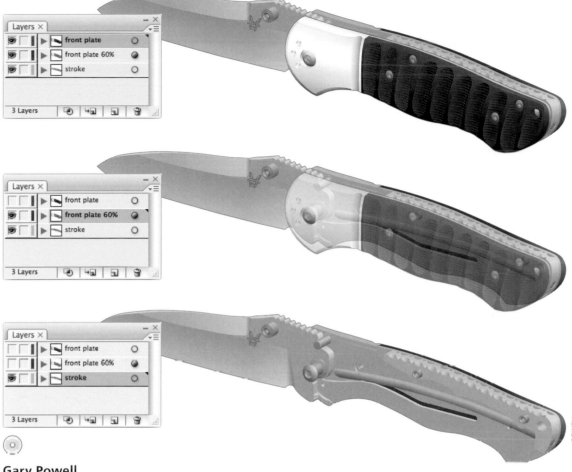

POWELL

Gary Powell

Using the same techniques as in "Organizing Layers," Gary Powell created this image for Benchmade Knife Company's training manual for product resellers. He duplicated the top layer by dragging it to the Create New Layer icon in the Links panel. He applied an Opacity value to the duplicated layer to create the transparent handle effect. When finished, he could toggle the visibility of the layers to print or export them individually.

Moving and Copying an object from one layer to another

To move a selected object to any other unlocked layer (visible or not!) open the Layers panel, grab the colored square to the right of the object's layer, and drag it to another layer (near right). To move a copy of an object, hold down the Option/Alt key while you drag (far right).

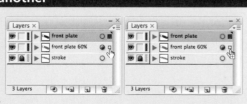

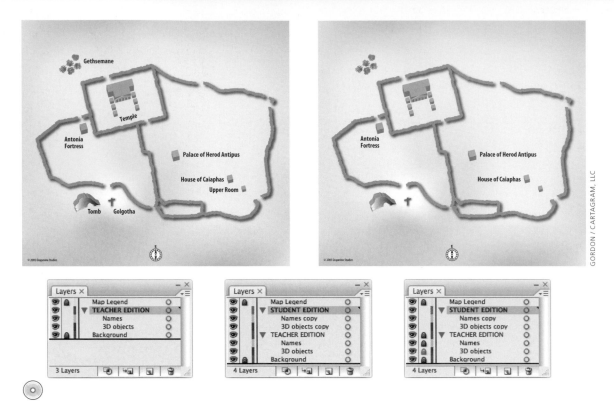

Steven Gordon / Cartagram, LLC

Steven Gordon created this map illustrating Jerusalem during New Testament times as one in a series of Bible workbook maps for Grapevine Studies. Gordon needed to design the maps for use in two versions—a detailed Teacher edition and a Student edition (in which the students would label selected map features). To simplify his work, Gordon combined both editions of each map in a single Illustrator file. He did this by first creating a layer for all of the paths and labels needed in the Teacher edition. Then, to create the Student edition, he duplicated the Teacher layer by dragging it onto the Create New Layer icon in the Layers panel. He renamed the layer and deleted the labels as required by the Student edition. Having both editions in the same file helped in making changes and corrections. When Gordon added a building, he copied and pasted the shape on the Teacher layer and then moved the copy in the Layers panel to the Student layer. When he repositioned a building, he selected the shapes on both layers and moved them simultaneously. To output each edition, Gordon first double-clicked the Student layer and chose Template from the Layer Options dialog; choosing Template both disabled the Print option and italicized the layer name, making it easy to locate. After he output the file, he repeated the process, this time turning the Teacher layer into a template layer, and returning the Student layer to its non-template condition. (Illustrator ignores non-template sublayers within a template master layer during output.)

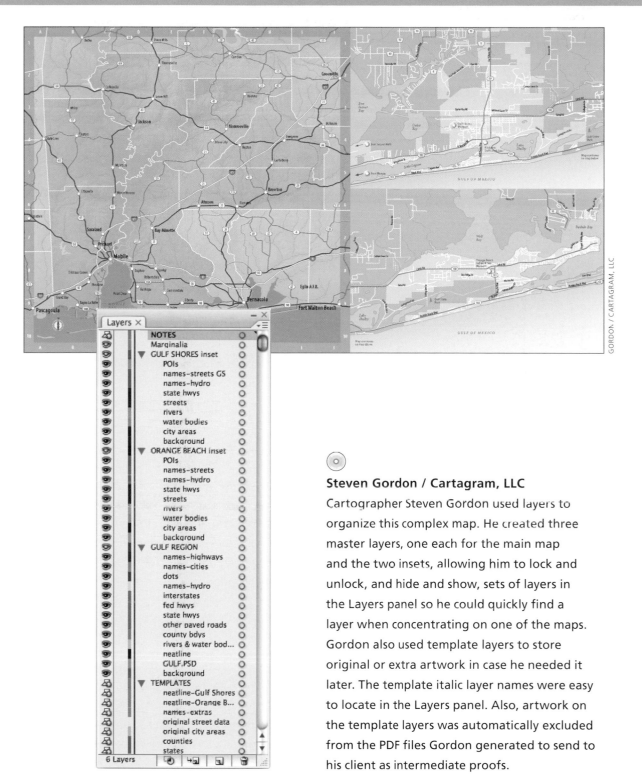

GORDON / CARTAGRAM, LLC

Steven Gordon / Cartagram, LLC

Cartographer Steven Gordon used layers to organize this complex map. He created three master layers, one each for the main map and the two insets, allowing him to lock and unlock, and hide and show, sets of layers in the Layers panel so he could quickly find a layer when concentrating on one of the maps. Gordon also used template layers to store original or extra artwork in case he needed it later. The template italic layer names were easy to locate in the Layers panel. Also, artwork on the template layers was automatically excluded from the PDF files Gordon generated to send to his client as intermediate proofs.

Nested Layers

Organizing with Layers and Sublayers

Overview: *Plan a layer structure; create layers and sublayers; refine the structure by rearranging layers and sublayers in the Layers panel's hierarchy; hide and lock layers; change the Layers panel display.*

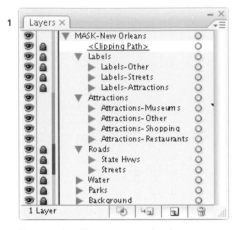

The completed layer structure for the map showing layers and two levels of sublayers (with Thumbnails disabled via Panel Options from the Layers panel's pop-up menu)

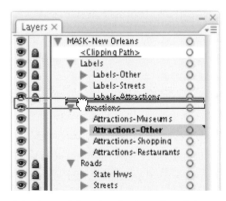

Selecting and dragging the Attractions-Other sublayer up and out of the Attractions sublayer, then, placing the Attractions-Other sublayer on the same level in the hierarchy as Attractions

Layers have always been a great way of organizing artwork. With Illustrator, you can organize your Layers panel as a nested hierarchy, making it easier to navigate and manipulate. For this map of New Orleans, created for the Metairie Hampton Inn, Steven Gordon relied on layers and sublayers to organize the map artwork.

1 Planning, then creating and moving layers and sublayers. Gordon began by planning a layer structure for the map in which layers with similar information would be nested within several "master" layers, so he could easily navigate the Layers panel and manipulate the layers and sublayers. After planning the organization of your layered artwork, open the Layers panel and begin creating layers and sublayers. (When you start a new document Illustrator automatically creates a Layer 1; it's a good habit to double-click Layer 1 to rename it.) To name a new layer or sublayer as you create it, hold Option/Alt and in the bottom of the Layers panel click on the Create New Layer icon or the Create New Sublayer icon (this creates a sublayer nested within a currently selected layer).

As you continue working, you may need to refine your organization by changing the nesting of a current layer or sublayer. To do this, drag the layer name in the Layers panel and release it over a boundary between layers. To convert a sublayer to a layer, drag its name and release it above its master layer or below the last sublayer of the master layer (watch the sublayer's bar icon to ensure that it aligns with the left side of the names field in the Layers panel before releasing it). Don't forget that if you move a layer in the Layers panel, any sublayer, group, or path it contains will move with it, affecting the hierarchy of artwork in your illustration.

2 Hiding and locking layers. As you draw, hide or lock sublayers of artwork by simply clicking on the visibility (Eye) icon or edit (Lock) icon of their master layer. Gordon organized his map so that related artwork, such as different kinds of labels, were placed on separate sublayers nested within the Names layer, and thus could be hidden or locked by hiding or locking the master Names layer.

If you click on the visibility or edit icon of a master layer, Illustrator remembers the visibility and edit status of each sublayer before locking or hiding the master layer. When Gordon clicked the visibility icon of the Names layer, sublayers that had been hidden before he hid the master layer remained hidden after he made the Names layer visible again. To make the contents of all layers and sublayers visible, Option-click/Alt-click on a visibility icon. To unlock the content of all layers and sublayers, Option-click/Alt-click on an edit icon. If you have layers hidden or locked you can also choose Show All Layers, or Unlock All Layers from the Layers panel's pop-up menu.

3 Changing the Layers panel display. You can change the Layers panel display to make the panel easier to navigate. In Layers Panel Options (from the panel pop-up) you can set custom rows and thumbnails sizes, or choose no icons at all. Double-click a layer name and change its layer color using the Color menu. Or do as Gordon did: Shift-click to select contiguous related layers (⌘-click/ Ctrl-click for non-contiguous layers) to set the same layer color in order to help identify them in the Layers panel.

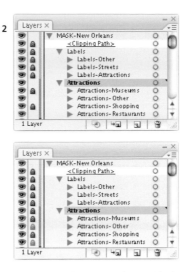

Top, the Labels "master" layer with three sublayers locked; bottom, after the master layer is locked, the three sublayers' edit icons are not dimmed, indicating that they will remain locked when the layer is unlocked

Changing the Color for the layer using the Layer Options dialog

Another way to unlock layers

A quick way to unlock all the contents of a layer: Make sure the layer itself is unlocked (the lock icon is gone) and then choose Unlock All from the Object menu.

Let Illustrator do the walking

Illustrator can automatically expand the Layers panel and scroll to a sublayer that's hidden within a collapsed layer. Just click on an object in your artwork and choose Locate Layer or Locate Object from the Layers panel's menu.

Basic Appearances

Making and Applying Appearances

Overview: *Create appearance attributes for an object; build a three-stroke appearance, save it as a style, and then draw paths and apply the style; target a layer with a drop shadow effect, create symbols in the layer, then edit layer appearance if needed.*

GORDON / CARTAGRAM, LLC

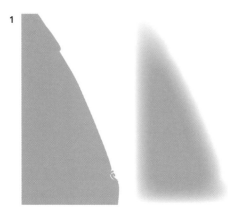

On the left, the ocean with blue fill; on the right, the water with the Inner Glow added to the appearance attribute set

Appearance panel displaying the finished set of attributes with an Inner Glow effect applied

Complexity and simplicity come together when you use Illustrator's Appearance panel to design intricate effects, develop reusable styles, and simplify production workflow. In this location map of the California coastline, cartographer Steven Gordon relied on the Appearance panel to easily build appearances and apply them to objects, groups and layers.

1 Building an appearance for a single object. Gordon developed a set of appearance attributes that applied a coastline, vignette and blue fill to a path symbolizing the Pacific Ocean. To begin building appearance attributes, open the Appearance panel and other panels you might need (Color, Swatches, Stroke, and Transparency, for example). Gordon began by drawing the outline of the water with the Pen tool and then he gave the path a dark blue fill. To create the effect that the water lightens as it approaches the shore, he applied an Inner Glow effect. To do this he opened the Appearance panel and clicked on the Fill attribute. Gordon then chose Effect > Stylize > Inner Glow. In the Inner Glow dialog, he set the Mode to Normal, Opacity to 100%, Blur to 0.25 inches (for the width of the vignette edge), and enabled the Edge option. To finish the glow, he clicked the dialog's color swatch and chose white for the glow color.

2 Creating a style for your highway paths. In the early days of Illustrator, the way you created a multi-stroked line like this "map symbol" for an interstate highway was by overlapping copies of a path and giving each copy a different stroke width. Now you can use the Appearance panel to craft a multi-stroked line that you apply to a single path. Deselect any objects still selected and reset the Appearance panel by clicking the Clear Appearance icon at the bottom of the panel (this eliminates any attributes from the last selected style or object). Next, click the Stroke attribute (it will have the None color icon) and click the Duplicate Selected Item icon to make a copy. Now, to make Gordon's interstate highway "map symbol," select the top Stroke attribute and give it a light color and a 0.5-pt width. Select the bottom attribute and choose a dark color and a 3-pt width. Because you'll use this set of appearance attributes again, open the Graphic Styles panel. With your new highway objects selected, hold Option/Alt and click the New Graphic Style icon at the bottom of the panel, name your style and click OK.

3 Assigning a style to a group. Draw the paths you want to paint with the new style you created above. Next, select all the paths you just made and Group (⌘-G/Ctrl-G). To get the three levels of strokes to merge when paths on the map cross one another, make sure Group is highlighted in the Appearance panel and apply your new interstate style.

4 Assigning appearance attributes to an entire layer. By targeting a layer, you can create a uniform look for all the objects you draw or place on that layer. Create a layer for the iconic "map symbols" and click the layer's target icon in the Layers panel. Then select Effect > Stylize > Drop Shadow. Each "map symbol" you draw or paste on that layer will be automatically painted with the drop shadow. Later, you can modify the drop shadows by clicking the layer's targeting icon and then double-clicking the Drop Shadow attribute in the Appearance panel and changing values in the pop-up Drop Shadow dialog.

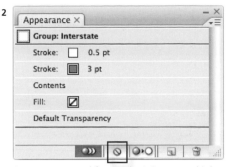

Appearance panel for Gordon's interstate highway symbol, with the Clear Appearance icon indicated

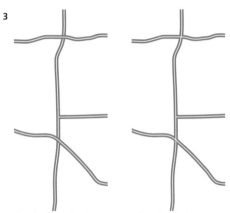

On the left, the interstates with the Style applied to the individual paths; on the right, the interstate paths were grouped before the Style was applied

Top, targeting the layer in the Layers panel; bottom, the Appearance panel showing the Drop Shadow attribute (double-click the attribute to edit Drop Shadow values)

Establishing Perspective

Using Layers and a Perspective Grid

MARIC

Advanced Technique

Overview: *Scan a sketch; create working layers using your sketch as a template; in each "guides" layer, draw a series of lines to establish perspective; convert the perspective lines to guides; construct your image using the applicable perspective guides.*

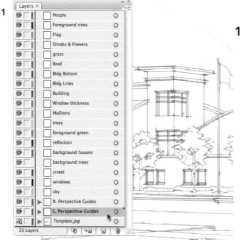

Portion of the original drawing placed on a template layer with a custom layer ready for creation of guides

Architectural renderings must be both attractive to the eye and faithful to the rules of perspective. Pete Maric was hired by the firm of ThenDesign Architecture of Willoughby, Ohio to create a realistic rendering of the proposed Charles A. Mooney PreK-8 School. Maric relied on a carefully constructed perspective grid to create a convincing scene and practiced careful layer management to keep the numerous elements of his complex illustration well organized as he worked.

1 Setting up layers. Begin by scanning a schematic drawing. After saving the scan as a JPG, TIF or PSD, place it in Illustrator and choose Template from the Layer panel's pop-up menu. Analyze your image to determine the number of vanishing points in your illustration (points along the scene's horizon where parallel lines seem to converge). Create new layers (click the Create New Layer icon in the Layers panel) for your compositional elements, and an additional layer for each of the vanishing points in your illustration.

2 Establishing the location of vanishing points. In the Layers panel, select the first layer you'll use for creating a set of perspective guides. Using your drawing as reference, find a feature that ought to be parallel with the horizon, such as a roofline and floor, or set of windows. With a high horizon, the features may actually be below the horizon line, but the vanishing point will always be directly on the line. With the Line tool, draw lines following the top and bottom of your chosen feature until the lines cross (figure A). You have now found one vanishing point. Vanishing points may need to extend beyond the borders of your artwork. Zoom out or scroll to view enough of your Artboard to see where your vanishing point lies. Now, with the Direct Selection tool, select the anchor point of a line that is opposite to its vanishing point, and swing it to the highest point (or lowest) that encompasses the objects on that plane, dragging the line out even longer if necessary (see figure B).

3 **Creating multiple perspective lines.** To create in-between lines through the same vanishing point, select both of the lines you created, then double-click the Blend tool to choose Specified Steps (for Spacing) and enter the number of lines you want. Then use Object > Blend > Make, or the keyboard shortcut, ⌘-Option-B/Ctrl-Alt-B, to create the blends (for help with the Blend tool, see the *Blends, Gradients & Mesh* chapter).

For each different vanishing point, repeat the above procedure. Remember to create each set of perspective lines on its own layer so you can work more easily with them as you proceed.

4 **Making and using the guides.** Because Illustrator can't create guides from blended objects, select them with the Selection tool and then choose Object > Expand. Next, transform the blends into guides by using View > Guides > Make Guides, or the keyboard shortcut, ⌘-5/Ctrl-5. Now begin drawing on a new layer. You may want to lock other layers containing vanishing point guides so you don't find your objects snapping to the wrong guides when you drag them into position.

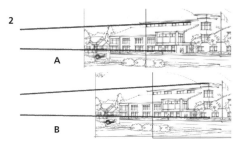

2

A

B

Dragging a perspective line to follow elements such as windows to a vanishing point, here beyond the edge of the art (top), then swinging the anchor points to the highest and lowest points, stretching the lines longer if necessary (bottom)

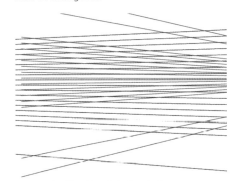

3

Using the Blend tool with Specified Steps to create multiple in-between lines from the two main bounding lines

Perspective line blends before being transformed into guides

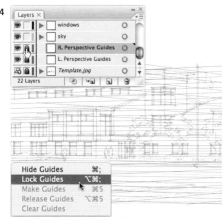

4

Turning off the "snap to" function for guides by locking the layer (left); locking guides in place by using the Lock/Unlock toggle in the View > Guides submenu

7

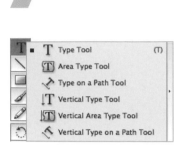

The Type tool, Area Type tool, Type on a Path tool, Vertical Type tool, Vertical Area Type tool, and Vertical Type on a Path tool. Select a Type tool and press Shift to toggle the tool between a horizontal and vertical orientation.

Selecting type by accident

If you keep accidentally selecting type when you're trying to select an object with the Selection tool, enable Type Object Selection by Path Only (Preferences > Type). With this option turned on, you won't select type objects unless you click directly on the baseline or path of the type. (If you have trouble finding the path, you can select the text object in the Layers panel by clicking the space to the right of the <Type> target icon, or marquee at least one full letter-form with a selection tool or the Lasso tool.)

Typographic controls

Most of Illustrator's default settings for type are controlled in the Type section of Preferences. However, set the unit of measurement for type in Preferences > Units & Display Performance.

Type

Two editions ago, with the release of Illustrator CS, Adobe installed a powerful, modern text engine under Illustrator's hood. That major change in functionality allowed Adobe to expand Illustrator's capabilities, and make it function more like Photoshop and InDesign —thus bringing the Creative Suite applications closer together, and allowing Illustrator users to make use of sophisticated new type features that wouldn't have been possible in the old Illustrator. Character and paragraph styles, Unicode support, and the ability to take full advantage of the subtleties of OpenType fonts are just a few of the advanced type features Illustrator users enjoy these days, thanks to that reinvention.

Of course, this step forward came with certain costs. Because Illustrator's current text engine handles type so differently, any text created prior to Illustrator CS is considered *legacy text*, and must be updated before it's editable in Illustrator CS3 (see the Tip "Legacy text," later in this intro). Also, saving type to earlier versions of Illustrator can be challenging (see "Saving and Exporting Illustrator Type," at the end of this introduction).

Although you'll probably still prefer a page layout program such as InDesign or QuarkXPress for multi-page documents like catalogs and long magazine articles, and Dreamweaver and Flash for Web page layout, this chapter will look at Illustrator's design and layout capabilities for single-page print documents.

THE SEVEN TYPE PANELS

For creating and manipulating type, Illustrator CS3 offers no less than seven panels, all accessible from the Window > Type submenu. Nested in with the Paragraph and Character panels is the OpenType panel, which gives you convenient access to the options of OpenType fonts. The Glyphs panel lets you choose quickly from a wide range of special characters. The Character Styles and Paragraph

Styles panels, nested together, are where you'll manage Illustrator's automatic text formatting capabilities. And the Tabs panel lets you manage tabs and create customized tab leaders.

The Character and Paragraph panels may first appear in a collapsed view; cycle through display options by clicking the double arrow on the Panel tab.

THE THREE TYPES OF TYPE

There are three type options in Illustrator, and all are accessible through the Type tool: *Point type*, *Area type*, and *Path type*. The flexible Type tool lets you click to create a Point type object, click-drag to create an Area type object, click on a path to create Path type (discussed a bit further on), or click within any existing type object to enter or edit text. Use the File > Open, File > Place, and Copy and Paste commands to access type created in other applications.

Select letters, words, or an entire block of text by dragging across the letters with the Type tool; or use a selection tool to select the entire text block as an *object* by clicking on or marqueeing the text baseline (the line that the type sits on).

- **Point type:** Click with the Type tool or the Vertical Type tool anywhere on the page to create Point type. Once you click, a blinking text-insertion cursor called an "I-beam" indicates that you can now type text using your keyboard. To add another line of text, press the Return or Enter key. When you're finished typing into one text object, click on the Type tool in the Toolbox to simultaneously select the current text as an object (the I-beam will disappear), and be poised to begin another text object. To edit the text click on it with the Type tool, or to select it as an object, click on it with one of the selection tools.

- **Area type:** Click and drag with the Type tool to create a rectangle, into which you can type. Once you've defined your rectangle, the I-beam awaits your typing, and the

Selecting text or objects

Once you've entered text, use the Type tool to select a text element by clicking and dragging across letters, words, or lines; double-clicking to select a word; triple-clicking to select a paragraph; or Shift-clicking to extend a selection. If the text-insertion I-beam is activated, then Select > All selects all type within that text object. Otherwise, Select > All selects *all unlocked objects* in your image.

<u>Underline</u>

~~Strikethrough~~

Illustrator makes it easy to set text as underline or strikethrough

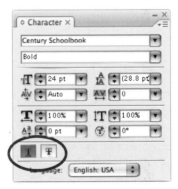

The Character panel showing the underline and strikethrough buttons

Quick Type on a Path tool

With the Type tool selected and your cursor over an object, hold down the Option/Alt key to quickly access the Type on a Path tool. Then click the edge of the object to enter type along the path rather than inside the object.

—*Jean-Claude Tremblay*

Each type object in Illustrator has an *in port* (at the upper left) and an *out port* (at the lower right). If both ports are empty, all the text is displayed and the object isn't currently linked (or *threaded*) to any other text objects. You may also see the following symbols:

• A red plus sign in the out port means the object contains *overflow text* (additional text that doesn't fit).

• An arrow in the in port means the object is threaded to a preceding text object, and text is flowing into the object.

• An arrow in the out port means the object is threaded to a subsequent text object, and text is flowing out of the object.

Area Type Options dialog

Scale text frames only

By default, Illustrator CS3's Scale tool scales both the text frame *and* its contents. To scale the text frame alone, Direct-Select it first. Then use the Scale tool, or scale it manually using the bounding box.
—*Jean-Claude Tremblay*

text automatically wraps to the next line when you type inside the confines of the rectangle.

Another way to create Area type or Vertical Area type is to construct a path (with any tools you wish) forming an object within which to place the type. Click and hold on the Type tool to access other tools, or press the Shift key to toggle between horizontal and vertical orientations of *like* tools (see the Tip "Type tool juggling" later in this chapter intro). Choose the Area Type or Vertical Area Type tool and click on the path itself to place text within the path. Distort the confining object by grabbing an anchor point with the Direct Selection tool and dragging it to a new location, or reshape the path by adjusting direction lines. The text within your Area Type object will reflow to fit the new shape of the confining object.

Illustrator's Area Type Options dialog (Type > Area Type Options) gives you precise control over a number of important aspects of Area type. You can set numerical values for the width and height of the selected Area type object. You can set precise values for Rows and Columns (i.e., you can divide a single Area type object into multiple columns or rows that will reflow as you type), and choose whether or not those values remain fixed as you scale. You can also specify Offset options, including the amount of inset (defined as the margin between the text and the bounding path) and the alignment of the first baseline of text. And finally, you can determine how text flows between rows or columns by choosing one of the Text Flow options.

To set tabs for Area type, select the text object and choose Window > Type > Tabs. The Tabs panel will open aligned with the text box. As you pan or zoom, you'll notice the Tab ruler doesn't move with the text box. Don't sweat: If you lose your alignment, just click the little Magnet button on the Tabs panel, and the panel will snap back into alignment.

One nice feature of the Tabs panel is the ability to create your own *tab leaders*. A tab leader is a repeated pattern of characters (such as dots or dashes) between a Tab and the text that follows it. Select a tab stop on the ruler in the Tabs panel, type a pattern of up to eight characters in the panel's Leader box, then hit Return or Enter. You'll see your customized Leader pattern repeated across the width of the tab.

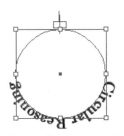

You may notice that if you try to set Path type on a circle, and the text is set to Align Center, the text will be forced to the bottom of the circle.

- **Path type:** Path type is created with the Type on a Path tool, which allows you to click on a path to flow text along its perimeter. (The path will then become unstroked and unfilled.)

    When you select a Path type object, you'll see three brackets appear: one at the beginning, one in the center, and one at the end of the Path type. The beginning and end brackets carry an in port and an out port, respectively, which can be used to thread text between objects (see the Tip "Ports illustrated"). The center bracket is used to control the positioning of the Path type. Hold your cursor over it until a small icon that looks like an upside down **T** appears. You can now drag the center bracket to reposition the type. Dragging the bracket across the path will flip the type to the other side of the path. (For example, type along the outside of a circle would flip to the inside.) Dragging the bracket forward or backward along the direction of the path will move the type in that direction.

    As with Area type, use the Direct Selection tool to reshape the confining path; the type on the path will automatically readjust to the new path shape.

    The Type on a Path Options dialog (Type > Type on a Path > Type on a Path Options) lets you set a number of Path type attributes. You can choose from five different Path Type Effects (Rainbow, Skew, 3D Ribbon, Stair Step, and Gravity); a Flip checkbox that will automatically flip type to the other side of the path; a menu that lets you set the alignment of type relative to the path; and a Spacing control that lets you adjust the spacing of type as it moves along and around a curve. (All of the Type on a Path Effects are also available directly via the Type > Type on a Path submenu.)

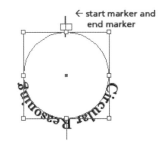

← start marker and end marker

That's because each Path type object has two handles (the start marker and the end marker) that the type is centered between. When you first draw the circle and apply the Path type to it, those two handles appear together at the top of the circle, due to the fact that the circle is a closed path.

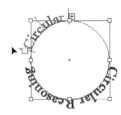

To position the text on top of the circle, all you have to do is grab the start marker handle and drag it to the 9 o'clock position, and then drag the end marker handle to the 3 o'clock position. Your text will now be centered between the two handles, on top of the circle

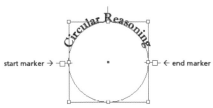

start marker →   ← end marker

Moral of the story: When you're working with center-aligned Path type, be sure to keep an eye on those start and end marker handles, and make sure they're where you need them to be.

To manually flip type on a path to the other side of the path, select the type and drag the center handle (the thin blue line perpendicular to the type) across the path, as indicated by the red arrow above. Note the tiny **T**-shaped icon that appears next to the cursor as you position it near the handle.

The same type, after dragging across the path, but before releasing the mouse. After release, the type will be in the position indicated by the blue type above the path; you can then drag the center handle from side to side to adjust the position of the text—just don't drag across the path again or you'll flip the type back. You can also flip type across a path automatically by choosing Type > Type on a Path > Type on a Path Options, enabling the Flip box (shown below), and clicking OK.

![The Type on a Path Options dialog]

The Type on a Path Options dialog

The upper text object is threaded (linked) to the lower one. The blue line connects the out port of the upper object to the in port of the lower one, showing that the two objects are threaded together; text thus flows from the first object to the second. The red plus sign in the out port of the lower object indicates that there is still more overflow text, which could flow into a third threaded object.

WORKING WITH THREADED TEXT

If a text object contains more text than it has room to display, you'll see a plus sign in the small box along its lower right side. (This box is called the *out port*; see the Tip "Ports illustrated," earlier in this chapter.) To enlarge the object to allow for more text, use the Selection tool to grab the object by a bounding side, and drag to resize it (hold down the Shift key if you want to constrain proportions as you resize).

To add a new text object that can receive overflow text, use the Selection tool to select the first text object. Next, click on the red plus sign in the out port. The cursor will change to the "loaded text" cursor, which looks like a miniature text block. Then you can click on the Artboard to create a new text object the same size and shape as the original; or drag to create a text object of any size. Either way, the new text object will be *threaded* (linked) to the original, and the text that wouldn't fit in the first object will flow into the second.

Note: *Make sure Type Object Selection by Path Only is disabled in the Type area of Preferences, or the above process won't work.*

Similarly, you can link existing text objects together by clicking the plus sign on the first object, and then clicking on the path of the object that will receive the overflow text. (Keep your eye on the cursor, which will change to indicate valid "drop" locations.) You can also link objects using a menu command: Select the first object with a Selection tool, then Shift-click to select the second object as well (or marquee both objects with the Lasso or a Selection tool). Choose Type > Threaded Text > Create, and the objects are linked.

Of course, the threads between objects can be broken as easily as they're created. If you want to disconnect one object from another, first select the object. Then double-click its in port to break the thread to a preceding object, or double-click its out port to break the thread to a subsequent object. Alternatively, you can select the object and click once on either the in port or the out port. Then click on the other end of the thread to break the link.

You can also release an object from a Text thread by selecting it, then choosing Type > Threaded Text > Release Selection. Or, if you want to remove the threading from an object while leaving text in place, select it and choose Type > Threaded Text > Remove Threading.

WRAPPING TEXT AROUND OBJECTS

Text wrapping is controlled as an object attribute and is set specifically for each object that will have text wrapped around it (known as a *wrap object*). First, make sure that the object you want to be wrapped with text is above the text you want to wrap around it in the Layers panel. Then select the wrap object and choose Object > Text Wrap > Make. The Text Wrap Options dialog will appear. Here, you'll choose the amount of offset and also have the option to choose Invert Wrap (which reverses the side of the object that text wraps around). You can also wrap text around a group of objects. In order to add a new object to the text wrapped group, open the Layers panel, click the triangle to reveal the layer content, and drag the icon for your new object into the <Group>. To release an object from text wrapping, select it and choose Object > Text Wrap > Release. To change the options for an existing wrap object, select it and choose Object > Text Wrap > Text Wrap Options.

CHARACTER AND PARAGRAPH STYLES

Illustrator's Character and Paragraph panels let you format text by changing one attribute at a time. The more powerful Character and Paragraph Styles panels take formatting to the next level by allowing you to apply multiple attributes to text simply by applying the appropriate style. (All four of these type-related panels are found under the Window > Type submenu.)

New character and paragraph styles can be either created from scratch or based on existing styles. To create a new style: Using your current type styling as a default, and with a default name (all can be changed later if you

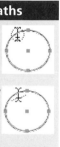

The text engine that Adobe introduced in Illustrator CS, and is refining with each release, made a lot of new features possible. But that change also meant that text is handled very differently from older versions, so *legacy text* (text created in older editions of Illustrator) needs to be updated before it can be edited in CS3. When you open a file containing legacy text, a dialog warns you that it contains text that needs to be updated. You can choose to update the text then and there by clicking Update, or wait until later by clicking OK. Text that hasn't been updated can be viewed, moved, and printed, but it can't be edited. When you select legacy text, it is displayed with an **X** through its bounding box. When you then update the legacy text, you may see the following types of changes:

- Changes to leading, tracking, and kerning
- In Area type: words overflowing, shifting between lines or to the next linked object.

You can choose to update all legacy text at any time by choosing Type > Legacy Text > Update All Legacy Text. Specific legacy text can be updated by clicking it with the Type tool. You can also preserve legacy text on a layer below the updated text for comparison.

like), click the Create New Style button in either the Character Styles or the Paragraph Styles panel. If you want to name your new style as you create it, choose New Character Style from the Character Styles panel menu, or New Paragraph Style from the Paragraph Styles panel menu. (You can also hold down the Option/Alt key while clicking the New Style button.) Type a name for your new style in the dialog that appears, and click OK—your new style will appear in the Character Styles or Paragraph Styles panel.

There are two ways to create a new style based on an existing one. Select the existing style in the Character Styles or Paragraph Styles panel, then either choose Duplicate Character Style or Duplicate Paragraph Style from the panel menu, or drag an existing style over the New Style button in the panel. Your new "cloned" style will appear in the panel.

To change the attributes of a new or existing style, double-click its name in the Character Styles or Paragraph Styles panel, or select it and choose Character Style Options or Paragraph Style Options from the panel menu. The Options dialog will let you set all your desired attributes for the style—everything from basic characteristics (such as font, size, and color), to OpenType features (see below for more about OpenType).

To apply a style to text, just select the text you want to format and click the name of the style in the Character Styles or Paragraph Styles panel. (This won't work if the type has *overrides*—extra formatting—applied, in which case you may need to remove the override by clicking a second time.)

TAKING ADVANTAGE OF OPENTYPE

One of the main reasons Adobe revamped the way Illustrator handles text was to allow users to take full advantage of the sophisticated features of OpenType fonts. (To underscore the point, Illustrator now ships with a bundle of free OpenType fonts, so you can put them to work immediately.) One great benefit of OpenType fonts is that they're platform-independent, so they can move easily between Mac and Windows.

When you use any OpenType font, Illustrator will automatically set standard ligatures as you type (see the example at right using the words *taffy* and *scuffle*). You can set options for other OpenType features by using the OpenType panel, which is nested by default with the Character and Paragraph panels, and is accessible via the menu command Window > Type > OpenType.

The OpenType panel includes two pop-up menus that let you control the style and positioning of numerals. It also has a row of buttons that let you choose whether or not to use standard ligatures (for letter pairs such as fi, fl, ff, ffi, and ffl), optional ligatures (for letter pairs such as ct and st), swashes (characters with exaggerated flourishes), titling characters (for use in uppercase titles), stylistic alternates (alternative versions of a common character), superscripted ordinals, and fractions.

If you'd like more information on what the various commands in the OpenType panel do, we've included a helpful PDF guide by InDesign expert Sandee Cohen on the *Wow! CD* (look for the file named OpenType.pdf). These pages, which are excerpted from Cohen's *InDesign CS3 Visual QuickStart Guide* from Peachpit Press, give you a primer on how to work with OpenType fonts, in the form of a handy reference table.

THE GLYPHS PANEL

Illustrator's Glyphs panel provides you with quick access to a wide variety of special characters, including any ligatures, ornaments, swashes, and fractions included in any given OpenType font. Choose Window > Type > Glyphs to display the panel. With the Type tool, click to place the insertion point where you want the special character to appear, and then double-click the character you want in the Glyphs panel to insert it in the text. In the Glyphs panel you'll find many specialty characters (like ✳ or ✿), that once required separate fonts, sitting right there in your Glyphs panel.

Character Styles panel

Paragraph Styles panel

OpenType panel

taffy scuffle
taffy scuffle

OpenType fonts automatically set standard ligatures as you type (unless you turn this feature off in the OpenType panel). In the example above, the type on the top row is set using the standard version of Adobe's Minion font. The bottom row is set using Minion Pro, one of the OpenType fonts likely installed with your Illustrator application. Minion Pro supplies the ligatures for "ff" and "ffl" (visible in the bottom row), which give the type a more sophisticated look.

Glyphs panel

Lorem ipsum dolor sit amet, consectetuer adipiscing elit. Sed at nibh. Nam ultrices erat nec pede. Vivamus est ante, aliquet vel, fermentum et, nonummy eget, ante. Morbi metus nisl, placerat ut, accumsan id, aliquet vel, nulla. Aenean scelerisque dapibus nunc. Proin augue. Vestibulum dictum. Morbi eget urna. Phasellus id augue. Nulla congue imperdiet dolor. Lorem ipsum dolor sit amet, consectetuer adipiscing elit. Sed at nibh.

Text composed using Single-line Composer

Lorem ipsum dolor sit amet, consectetuer adipiscing elit. Sed at nibh. Nam ultrices erat nec pede. Vivamus est ante, aliquet vel, fermentum et, nonummy eget, ante. Morbi metus nisl, placerat ut, accumsan id, aliquet vel, nulla. Aenean scelerisque dapibus nunc. Proin augue. Vestibulum dictum. Morbi eget urna. Phasellus id augue. Nulla congue imperdiet dolor. Lorem ipsum dolor sit amet, consectetuer adipiscing elit. Sed at nibh.

The same text composed using Every-line Composer, which automatically creates less ragged-looking text blocks with more uniform line lengths

Object rows and columns

To create rows and columns from non-type objects, select the object(s) and choose Object > Path > Split into Grid.

If you don't have the fonts...

Missing fonts? You can still open, edit, and save the file, because Illustrator remembers the fonts you were using. However, the text will not flow accurately and the file won't print correctly until you load or replace the missing fonts. Type objects that use missing fonts will be highlighted when Highlight Substituted Fonts is enabled in the Type area of Document Setup.

THE EVERY-LINE COMPOSER

Illustrator offers two composition methods for determining where line breaks occur in blocks of text: the Single-line Composer and the Every-line Composer.

The Single-line Composer (which was the only option before CS) applies hyphenation and justification settings to one line of text at a time. But this can result in uneven, ragged-looking blocks of text, so the newer Every-line Composer thinks ahead by automatically determining the best combination of line breaks across the entire run of text. The result is even-looking text blocks with minimal hyphenation and consistent line lengths and spacing, without having to fine-tune line breaks by hand. However, if you're into micromanaging your text and you want manual control over every line break, you still have the option to choose the old Single-line Composer.

To choose between composition methods, select the text to be composed and choose Adobe Every-line Composer or Adobe Single-line Composer from the Paragraph panel menu.

MORE TYPE FUNCTIONS (TYPE & WINDOW MENUS)

• **Find Font:** If you try to open a file and don't have the correct fonts loaded, Illustrator warns you, lists the missing fonts, and asks if you still want to open the file. You do need the correct fonts to print properly, so if you don't have the missing fonts, choose Find Font to locate and replace them with ones you do have.

Find Font's dialog displays the fonts used in the document in the top list; an asterisk indicates a missing font. The font type is represented by a symbol to the right of the font name. You can choose replacement fonts from ones on your system or those used in the document. To display only the font types you want to use as replacements, uncheck those you don't want to include in the list. To replace a font used in the document, select it from the top list and choose a replacement font from the bottom list. You can individually replace each occurrence of the font by clicking Change and then Find. To change every occurance at once, simply click the Change All button to replace all occurrences.

Note: *When you select a font in the top list, the first text object in the document using that font becomes selected.*

- **Type Orientation** lets you change orientation from horizontal to vertical, or vice versa, by choosing Type > Type Orientation > Horizontal or Vertical.

- **Change Case:** You can change the case of text selected with the Type tool via the new Type > Change Case submenu, which offers four choices: UPPERCASE, lowercase, Title Case, and Sentence case.

- **Fit Headline** is a quick way to open up the letter spacing of a headline across a specific distance. First, create the headline within an area, not along a path. Next, set the type in the size you wish to use. Select the headline by highlighting it, then choose Type > Fit Headline—the type will spread out to fill the area you've indicated. This works with both the Horizontal and Vertical Type tools.

- **Show Hidden Characters** reveals soft and hard returns, word spaces, and an oddly shaped infinity symbol indicating the end of text flow. Toggle it on and off by choosing Type > Show Hidden Characters.

CONVERTING TYPE TO OUTLINES

You can use the Appearance panel to apply multiple strokes to editable type (see the *Layers & Appearances* chapter for details about working with multiple strokes or fills). You can also reliably mask with live, editable type! So although there are fewer and fewer reasons to convert your type to outlines, there are still some times when converting type to outlines is your best option (see "Why convert type to outlines?" following).

As long as you've created type with fonts you have installed on your system (and can print), and you've finished experimenting with your type elements (for

The Find Font dialog

Choose text carefully!

Having access to dozens of fonts doesn't necessarily make you a type expert, any more than having a handful of pens makes you an artist. Experiment all you want, but if you need professional typographic results, consult a professional. Barbara Sudick designed this book.

Don't outline small type

If you're printing to a high-resolution imagesetter or using larger type sizes, you can successfully convert type objects to outlines. However, for several technical reasons, a *small* type object converted to outlines won't look as good on the computer screen, or print as clearly to printers of 600 dots per inch or less, as it would have if it had remained a font.

Illustrator supports multinational fonts, including Chinese, Japanese, and Korean. Check the Show Asian Options box in the Type area of Preferences to reveal Asian text options in the Character panel (if necessary, click on the double arrows on the Panel tab to fully expand it). To utilize multinational font capabilities you must have the proper fonts and language support activated on your system. Even then, some multinational options won't work with fonts that don't support the appropriate languages, including most fonts intended primarily for English and Western European languages.

Resize a text block by its bounding box handles (select it with the Selection tool) and the text will reflow. —*Sandee Cohen*

In earlier versions of Illustrator, you could set an option in the Type preferences to *greek* (gray out) text below a certain size, in order to speed up rendering. But thanks to a performance boost in CS3, greeking text would no longer save any time—so the preference has been removed. Consider it ancient Illustrator history!

example: adjusting size, leading, or kerning/tracking), you have the option to convert your live type to Illustrator objects. Your type will no longer be editable as type, but instead will be constructed of standard Illustrator Bézier curves that may include compound paths to form the "holes" in the outlined letter forms (such as the see-through centers of an **O**, **B**, or **P**).

As with all Illustrator paths, you can use the Direct Selection tool to select and edit the objects. To convert type to outlines, select all blocks of type you wish to outline (it doesn't matter if non-type objects are selected as well) and choose Type > Create Outlines. To fill the "holes" in letters with color, select the compound path and choose Object > Compound Path > Release (see the *Beyond the Basics* chapter for more about working with compound paths).

IMPORTANT: *Outlining type is not recommended for small font sizes—see the Tip "Don't outline small type" earlier in this chapter introduction.*

Why convert type to outlines?

Below are several cases where converting type to outlines may be useful:

- **So you can graphically transform or distort the individual curves and anchor points of letters or words.** Everything from the minor stretching of a word to an extreme distortion is possible. See the Galleries later in this chapter for examples. (Warp Effects and Envelopes can sometimes be used on live type for these purposes, too; see the *Live Effects & Graphic Styles* chapter.)

- **So you can maintain your letter and word spacing when exporting your type to another application.** Many programs that allow you to import Illustrator type as "live" editable text don't support the translation of your custom kerning and word spacing. Convert text to outlines before exporting Illustrator type in these instances, to maintain custom word and letter spacing.

- **So you don't have to supply the font to your client or service bureau.** Converting type can be especially useful when you need to use foreign language fonts, when your image will be printed while you're not around, or when you don't have permission to embed the fonts. If your service bureau doesn't have its own license for a font, your own license for the font may not permit you to give it to them. If this is the case, convert your fonts to outlines.

THE DOUBLE-DUTY EYEDROPPER

The Eyedropper tool allows you to copy appearance attributes from one type object to another, including stroke, fill, character, and paragraph attributes.

Illustrator's double-duty Eyedropper both picks up and applies text formatting. It has two modes: the *sampling* Eyedropper and the *applying* Eyedropper. To copy text formatting from one object to another using the Eyedropper, first select the Eyedropper from the Toolbox, and position it over an unselected type object. You'll see that the Eyedropper is in sampling mode (it angles downward to the left). When it's correctly positioned over the type object, a small **T** appears next to the Eyedropper. Click the type object to pick up its attributes.

Now position the Eyedropper over the unselected text object to which you want to apply the attributes you just sampled, and hold down the Option/Alt key. You'll see the Eyedropper switch to applying mode: it angles downward to the right, and looks full. As with the sampling Eyedropper, you'll see the small **T** when it's correctly positioned over text. Click the text to apply the attributes you sampled from the first object. (A simple click will apply the sampled attributes to the whole paragraph; you can also drag the mouse to apply the attributes only to the specific text you dragged over.)

Alternatively, you can first select the type object with appearance attributes you want to change, and then move the Eyedropper over the unselected type object from which you want to copy attributes. You'll see the small **T** when you're correctly positioned; click to sample the

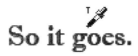

Wampeters, Foma & Granfalloons

The sampling Eyedropper, which picks up attributes, angles downward to the left. The small T next to the Eyedropper appears when the Eyedropper is correctly positioned—i.e., close enough to the text to sample its attributes by clicking.

So it goes.

As you click on text with the sampling eyedropper, "ink" appears in the eyedropper to show that it has sampled the attributes of the text.

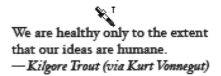

We are healthy only to the extent that our ideas are humane.
—*Kilgore Trout (via Kurt Vonnegut)*

The applying eyedropper, which appears when you press the Option/Alt key, functions like the old Paint Bucket used in previous versions of Illustrator—it applies attributes to an object. Note that the applying eyedropper angles downward to the right, and is half full of ink. As with the sampling eyedropper, the small T appears when the eyedropper is correctly positioned over text. Then just Option/Alt-click the text to apply the previously sampled attributes.

The appearance of stroked text

To add strokes to type without distorting the characters, select the type using one of the Selection tools (*not* the Type tool), then use the Appearance panel to "Add New Stroke." Move this new stroke *below* the Characters and adjust the new color and weight.

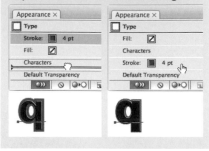

Making a new text object

Reselect the Type tool to end one text object; the next click will start a new text object. Or, deselect the current text by holding down the ⌘/Ctrl key (temporarily turning your cursor into a selection tool) and clicking outside the text block.

Making one text block of many

To join separate Area text boxes or Point type objects, select all the text objects with any selection tool and copy. Then draw a new Area text box and paste. Text will flow into the box, in the *stacking order* in which it had appeared on the page. (It doesn't matter if you select graphic elements with your text—these elements won't be pasted.) —*Sandee Cohen*

unselected object's attributes and apply them to the previously selected object.

USING THE APPEARANCE PANEL WITH TYPE

When you work with type, you work with the letter characters or with the container that holds the characters—or both. Understanding the difference between characters and their container (the "type object") will help you access and edit the right one when you style type. To help understand the difference, you'll need to watch the Appearance panel as you work.

Characters

When you click with the Type tool and enter text, you are working directly with the letter characters. In the Appearance panel, you'll see a blank Stroke and a black Fill listed underneath the Characters line in the panel. You can apply a color or pattern to a character's fill and stroke. To edit a character's fill and stroke, drag across the text with the Type tool or double-click Characters in the Appearance panel.

These are some of the things you *can't* do when working with the characters (although you can with their containers): move the stroke under the fill or the fill above the stroke; apply a live effect to the fill or stroke; apply a gradient fill; add multiple fills or strokes; or change the opacity or blending mode.

The Type "object"

All text is contained in a Point, Area, or Path type object. You are working with the type "object" when you select the text with the Selection tool and then move the object around on your page.

You can think of the type object as a group whose members are the letter characters. There are things you can do to this group that you couldn't do when working directly with the letter characters.

For example, you can add another fill (choose Add New Fill from the Appearance panel pop-up menu).

Notice that the Appearance panel changes—now there is another listing of Fill and Stroke, but this time they are positioned above the Characters line in the panel. The fill and stroke you worked with at the character level still exist. You can reveal them by double-clicking Characters in the panel. Doing so, however, brings you back to character editing; reselect the type object with the Selection tool to return to editing the type object rather than its characters.

When you add a new fill or stroke to the type object, its color or effects interact with the color of the characters. You can predict the visual results of changes to the type object and characters by knowing that all the fills and strokes applied to type are painted, with those listed at the top of the panel painted on top of those listed below (including the stroke and fill you see listed when you double-click Characters in the panel). So if you add a new fill and apply white to it, the type appears white (the white fill of the type object is stacked above the black fill of the characters).

To experiment with how this works, create two type objects in a large font size (72 pt, for example). Next, edit at the character level by dragging through one of the objects with the Type tool, and then changing the default black fill to red in the Appearance panel.

To edit at the type object level, select the other type object with the Selection tool. Add a new fill (choose Add New Fill from the Appearance panel menu); by default, the type object is filled with black, which will cover up the red fill you gave the character. With the type object still selected, click on the Swatch Libraries menu button in the lower left corner of the panel (or from the Swatches panel menu and choose Open Swatch Library > Other Library). In the pop-up menu click Swatches > Patterns > Decorative and then select Decorative_Ornament.ai. From the Decorative_Ornament panel, click on the Chinese Spirals swatch. When the type object fills with the pattern, the pattern's black objects overlay the red of the character, while its empty areas let the red show through.

The Appearance panel showing the red fill applied to the type at the Character level

The Appearance panel showing the Chinese Spirals pattern (from the Decorative_Ornaments pattern library) filling the type at the type object level

See Gordon's "Floating Type" lesson in the Transparency chapter to learn how to create transparent backgrounds for your area type objects

Typography

Typography

Typography

The original point type object at the top; in the middle, the same type object exported using Preserve Text Editability; at the bottom, the type object exported using Preserve Text Appearance

Knowing the difference between a type object and its characters rewards you in this experiment. And it will help you understand later why bad things seem to happen to good type (like the black surrounding the red spirals) so that you can make good things happen to type. Reading and working through the lessons and galleries that follow will help you master the difference between characters and their type object.

SAVING AND EXPORTING ILLUSTRATOR TYPE

While Illustrator's modern text engine has opened the door to new levels of typographic control and flexibility, sending your typography out into the world can be a tricky process. Type objects in files that you save to legacy versions of Illustrator (Version 10 and before) or as EPS files will either be broken into groups of point or path type objects, or converted to outlines. Your only control is to select File > Document Setup > Type and choose Preserve Text Editability or Preserve Text Appearance from the Export menu.

As the figures at left show, choosing Preserve Text Editability breaks the word "typography" into a group of eight separate Point type objects. By contrast, choosing Preserve Text Appearance will convert all type to outlines. In either case, your type will be severely limited for others who need to use it in legacy versions of Illustrator.

You should test bringing Illustrator CS3 type into other applications before proceeding during a critical project or urgent deadline. While you may not need to edit the type in another program, you should ensure that it imports correctly and looks as it did in Illustrator CS3.

GORDON / CARTAGRAM, LLC

Steven Gordon / Cartagram, LLC

To create this label design, Steven Gordon simulated a sunburst using the Flare tool in an Opacity Mask. He started by drawing a rectangle and filling it with a three-color gradient. He then selected the Type tool and typed "Zion" (he left the type object black so, when used later as a mask, the artwork would remain opaque). Next, Gordon clicked on the Selection tool and copied the type object. He opened the Transparency panel and chose Make Opacity Mask from the panel menu. To select the Opacity Mask and begin working in the mask, Gordon clicked on the mask thumbnail (the right thumbnail) and then clicked on Invert Mask (he left the Clip option enabled). Next,

he chose Edit > Paste in Front to paste the type object into the mask. To make the sunburst, Gordon chose the Flare tool from the Rectangle tool pop-up menu. He positioned the cursor between the **o** and **n** letters and clicked and dragged the flare to extend it outward. To fine-tune the look of the flare, he double-clicked the Flare tool icon and, in the Flare Tool Options dialog, he adjusted the controls for Diameter, Opacity, Direction, and other options. To return to working with the non-mask artwork, Gordon clicked on the artwork thumbnail (the left thumbnail) in the Transparency panel. He finished the label by applying a dark brown color to the selected type object.

Curvaceous Type

Fitting Type to Curved Paths

HUERTA

Overview: *Create artwork objects; copy object paths, then cut the paths to workable length; add text to the paths and offset the text; convert type to outlines and edit character paths.*

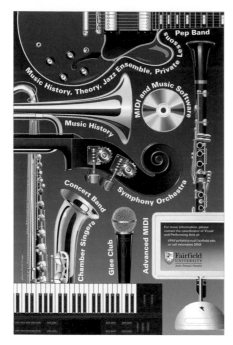

The finished poster for Fairfield University

1

The Outline view of the paths for the guitar

Using the flowing curves of musical instruments coupled with strings of text, designer Gerard Huerta captured the variety of musical studies offered by Fairfield University in this poster promoting its music program to campus and high school students. To give the type characters a more organic fit with the tight curves of some of the instruments, Huerta converted the type to outlines and then edited the shapes of the character paths.

1 Sketching and scanning the shapes, then redrawing them in Illustrator. Huerta started the poster by sketching the shapes of musical instruments by pencil. Then he scanned the drawing and placed the scan in Illustrator as a template layer. By using the Pen tool to draw the shapes, and using gradients and gradient meshes for color, Huerta built the musical instruments and then arranged them to leave space for the text he would create next.

2 Drawing paths for type and creating the type on the paths. You can draw the paths that will parallel your objects with the Pen or Pencil tool for setting type, or, like Huerta, use copies of the objects themselves. First, copy the path you want the type to parallel and paste in front (Edit > Paste in Front) so the copy directly overlays the original. Use the Scissors tool to cut the path so that it's an open-ended path instead of a closed path. Next, with the Type tool, click on the line and type the words you want on that path. Grab the type's I-beam and slide it along the path to position the text—flip it to the other side of the path if the text you typed ended up on the wrong side of the path. Make sure that the Character panel is open and your type is still selected. From the Character panel, enter a negative number in the Baseline Shift field or pick a negative number from the field's pop-up menu. Adjust the offset of the type from its path by increasing or decreasing the Baseline Shift value. Reshape the path by using the Direct Selection tool or by drawing over a section of the path with the Pencil tool.

3 Converting type to outlines, then editing character paths. Violins and guitars have sharply curved bodies that can make some letter characters look too angular and straight when positioned along the curve of the path. To correct this, Huerta changed the shapes of individual letter characters so that their strokes conformed more naturally to the curved shape of the path.

You can change character shapes by first converting the type to outlines. (Make copies of the type first in case you need to edit the type or its paths later.) To do this, select the Type on a Path object (don't select the text itself using the Type tool) and choose Type > Create Outlines. Look for characters with parallel strokes, like **m**, **n**, **h**, and **u**. Using the Direct Selection tool, move points and adjust control handles to reshape the characters. Use the Pencil tool to reshape character paths by drawing over or near a selected path. Huerta relied on the Direct Selection and Pencil tools to add curves to the straight edges of the original character shapes. He also changed the angle of some character strokes so that the characters appeared to bend with the tight curve of their paths.

Spacey characters

If you choose Auto from the Kerning field in the Character panel, Illustrator CS2 may cause letters to overlap or to be spaced too far apart on tightly curved Type on a Path objects. To fix this, you may need to manually kern letter pairs by clicking the Type tool between two characters and adjusting the Kerning value.

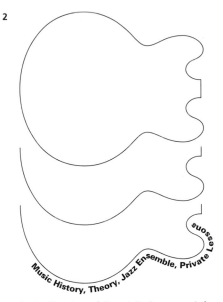

The Outline view of the original outer path for the guitar body (top); path cut from the guitar path (middle); text added to the path and then offset using a negative Baseline Shift

*On the left, the letter **T** character from the Univers font; on the right, the **T** character after Huerta edited the character's outline paths by curving the top stroke of the letter*

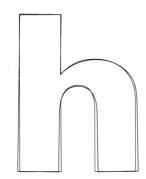

*The original letter **h** character shown here as a magenta outline; superimposed on the original letter **h** is the black outline of the **h** that Huerta edited by angling the bottoms of the vertical strokes*

Book Cover Design

Illustrator as a Stand-alone Layout Tool

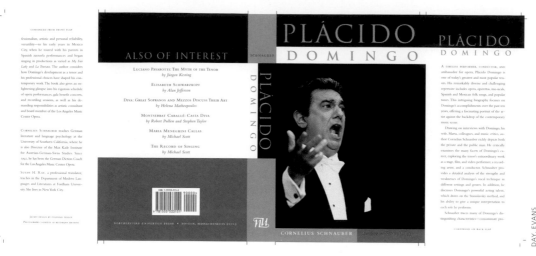

Overview: *Set your document size; place guides and crop marks; place image files and make Area type for columns and Point type for graphic typography; visually track type to fit.*

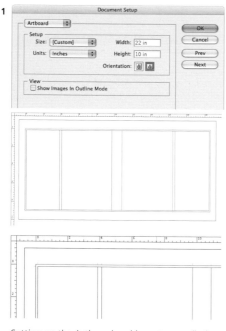

Setting up the Artboard and layout specs (below enlarged)

Page layout programs such as InDesign and QuarkXPress are essential for producing multi-page, complex documents. However, Rob Day and Virginia Evans often use Illustrator for single-page projects such as book jackets.

1 Setting up your page. Choose File > Document Setup to set up the Artboard for your design. Click on landscape or portrait page orientation and enter your Artboard size, making sure it's large enough for crop and/or registration marks (the "Size" parameter will automatically switch to "Custom"). Choose View > Show Rulers and "re-zero" your ruler origin to the upper left corner of where your page will begin (see the *Basics* chapter for more on repositioning the ruler origin), and use View > Outline/Preview to toggle between Outline and Preview modes. Although you can generate uniform grids with Preferences > Guides & Grid, for columns of varying sizes, Day and Evans numerically created two sets of rectangles: one for trims, and one for bleeds. With the Rectangle tool, click on your artboard to specify the Width and Height dimensions for the trim area. Next immediately Option-click/Alt-click on the center-point of the trim-area box to specify .25" larger in Width and Height to create a rectangle specifying a

125" bleed area. Day and Evans made trim and bleed boxes for the front, back, flaps, and spine. To place an overall trim mark, select the boxes that define the entire trim area and choose Filter > Create > Crop Marks.

2 Customizing your guides. Select your trim and bleed boxes (not the crop marks) and create Guides by choosing View > Guides > Make Guides.

3 Placing and refining the elements. Choose File > Place to select a raster image to import into your layout. Create rectangles or other objects which will define the area for columns of text. Click on the path of one of these objects with the Area Type tool. Once the text cursor is placed, you can type directly or paste text. Area Type is used in this layout for columns of type on the flaps. Alternatively, click on you page with the Type tool to create Point type, for titles, headlines, and other individual type elements. To track type visually, select a text object and use the ← or → key with Option/Alt. For help rotating or scaling (this applies to text objects as well), see the *Zen of Illustrator* chapter and the *Zen Lessons* on the *Wow! CD* (in the Ch02 The Zen of Illustrator folder in the Chapters folder).

Creating "Crop Marks" versus "Crop Area"

Every time you choose Filter > Create > Crop Marks, you'll make a set of visible (selectable) Illustrator crop marks that indicate the bounding area of your current selection. Use Object > Crop Area > Make to create *one* set of *non*-selectable crop marks that are visible in Illustrator, but invisibly mark the crop area when placed into programs such as Photoshop (see the "Software Relay" lesson in the *Illustrator & Other Programs* chapter). You can specify the area with a selected rectangle or, if nothing is selected, the crop area will be sized to the Artboard. To remove a "crop area," choose Object > Crop Area > Release, or, since there can be only one Crop Area per file, make a new selection and choose Object > Crop Area > Make.

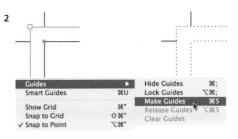
Converting trim and bleed boxes into Guides

All of the elements placed into the layout

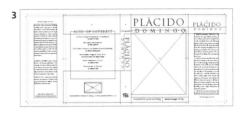
Close-ups of an Area Type object

PLÁCIDO
DOMINGO
Close-ups of Point Type objects

Tracking a line of Point Type with Arrow keys

Masking Words

Masking Images with Letter Forms

Overview: *Create text on top of a placed raster image; select all and make the text into a clipping mask for the placed image.*

1

Text using the HooskerDoo typeface (it includes the splotches), placing scanned fabric and moving it below the type using the Layers panel

2

After selecting the type and the image below, choosing Object > Clipping Mask > Make

With the clipping mask and type kept live, it's easy to change the typeface, the linked art, the type size, and the text

This "Africa" type treatment (using the HooskerDoo font) was created by Johannesburg, South Africa-based artist Ellen Papciak-Rose. Working on shoestring budgets for non-profit organizations, Papciak-Rose often scans regional textiles and crafts to incorporate into her work.

1 Creating text and placing an image. Select a typeface with sufficient weight for an image to show through (HooskerDoo includes the splotches) and create text with the Type tool. Choose File > Place, select an image, enable Link, disable Template, and click OK. In a clipping mask, the topmost selected object becomes the mask. To use your type as a mask, in the Layers panel, expand your layer and move the <Linked File > below your type.

2 Creating the clipping mask. Select the text and the image to be masked and choose Object > Clipping Mask > Make; this will group the mask and the masked objects.

3 Making changes to image and text. Select the type or image to adjust its position. To select type click on it (or along its baseline) with the Direct Selection tool; to select the image, click outside of the type, where the image is. Alternatively, you can select the text, image, or both, and click the Edit Clipping Path or Edit Contents button in the Control panel. With the image selected you can move it using the cursor keys, or apply any transformation to it using tools or the Control panel. With type selected you can change many attributes (such as size or typeface) in the Control panel, or in the Character panel (Window > Type > Character). To swap the background image, select it and click its name in the Control panel to access the Relink option, then locate the replacement file. To change the text, select it with the Type tool and retype!

Transforming Conflict, TRANSFORMiNG LIVES

The emergence of Partners in Conflict Transformation (PICOT)

SIERRA LEONE

Case study: A conflict transformation approach to peace and development work By: Richard Smith

PAPCIAK-ROSE (Photographer: Richard Smith)

Ellen Papciak-Rose

Using similar techniques as in the lesson opposite, Ellen Papciak-Rose created this cover for a 64-page book by Richard Smith (he is also the photographer). She used a cropped copy of the woman's skirt from the photo for the fabric in the words "SIERRA LEONE." Papciak-Rose chose the light blue and lime green color scheme to match the colors of the Sierra Leone flag.

Making a Typeface

Creating a Typeface from a Grid

Overview: *Create a grid and draw letter shapes; combine and cut shapes with pathfinders; use shapes to build other letters; use transparency to integrate the letters with other artwork.*

GORSKA

Illustrator's Preferences dialog

Using the Rectangular Grid Tool Options dialog to create a grid

Inspired by the Cyrillic type adorning the film posters of avant garde Russian Constructivists, and drawing on her own Eastern European heritage, Caryl Gorska designed a typeface in the course of creating this self-promotion poster. After crafting the type, Gorska developed the poster artwork and added words set in her typeface.

1 Defining the working grid for creating the alphabet. Gorska began the poster by constructing the letter characters. She drew the letters directly on-screen instead of on paper because the geometric nature of the characters benefited from Illustrator's precise measuring, drawing, and editing tools (Pen, Pencil and the Pathfinders).

You'll discover another benefit of using Illustrator when you create letter characters: grids. Why grids? A grid helps save production time and improve the character of your typeface by spreading visual consistency across varied letterforms. To make a grid, decide whether the guiding shape of your letterforms will be a square or a rectangle. If it's a square, use Illustrator's Guides & Grid tab, found within the Illustrator > Preferences dialog. Simply set the size and number of subdivisions that you want in order to create an Artboard-wide grid.

If the dominant letter shape is rectangular, then select the Rectangular Grid tool found within the Line Segment tool in the Tools panel. With the tool selected, click on the Artboard to display the Rectangular Grid Tool Options dialog. Specify the overall grid size using the Default Size fields and the proportions of the grid cells using the Horizontal and Vertical Dividers fields.

2 Drawing, and copying and pasting objects, to build the letterforms. Gorska made full use of Illustrator's tools in drawing and editing the letter characters: Pen and Pencil for drawing shapes, the Pathfinders for combining shapes or cutting letter counters (holes) from the shapes, and the Direct Selection tool for fine-tuning the control points of curves to vary letter proportions. Gorska started with basic characters like **o**, **e**, **b** and **r** that visually define the general look of the other letter characters. Once you complete several basic characters, arrange them in pairs or words to test how well they look together. Feel free to access the artwork of these characters when building other letters that are similar in structure. You can recycle shapes like stems, serifs, punctuation marks, and counters throughout the alphabet to speed up your work and make the typeface more visually consistent.

Adding a twist to her typeface, Gorska designed a second set of letterforms based on an oval shape using the same grid, complementing the rectangular shapes of the first set she created. This gave her the freedom to mix shapes when arranging the letters as words for a more eclectic look.

3 Drawing background art, composing words, and changing type opacity. To complete the poster, Gorska filled facial and geometric background shapes she drew with blends and gradients. Then she composed the words "red scare" from the letter characters she'd drawn earlier and positioned them over the artwork. She grouped the characters and changed their opacity in the Control panel to 20% to blend them visually with the artwork in the background. Setting her name against the gradient at the top of the poster, Gorska gave each yellow letter a stroke using the same red as the color well in the gradient behind the letters. This unified the appearance of the letters with the background colors in the poster.

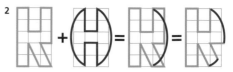

Using the parts of one letter (shown in red) in constructing another letter (shown in green)

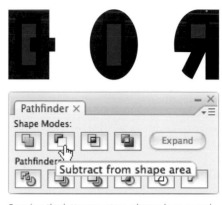

Forming the letter counters, shown here as red shapes, by punching a hole using the Pathfinder panel's Subtract from shape area Shape Mode and then its Expand button

Letters with 20% opacity applied from the Control panel

Red-stroked letters set against a gradient

Expand your repertoire

It's easy to re-create an out-of-print typeface using non-copyrighted type found in antique books, or from a royalty-free source like Dover Publications (www.doverpublications.com). Draw the fundamental shapes and copy and paste them to construct the rest of the typeface.

Brush Your Type

Applying Brushes to Letterforms

Overview: *Create, layer and blur text objects; draw paths and apply brushes; modify paths and brushes; change path transparency.*

Designed for a corporate setting where a simple, bold poster could serve as a powerful communication, San Francisco artist Michael Cronan used Illustrator's Pencil and Brush tools to blend artistry with bold type, making the simple words eye-catching and provocative.

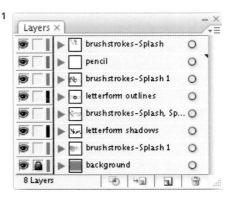

The finished illustration's Layers panel showing the separation of artwork on layers to produce the poster's visual hierarchy

1 Converting type to outlines and adding a custom blurred shadow. Cronan began the poster by typing "Now" in the font Didot Regular. Because Illustrator limits the maximum font size to 1296 points, you may need to work at a smaller size and then enlarge the illustration later. (When you enlarge, you may need to convert the type to outlines using Type > Create Outlines if your type will be larger than 1296 points.) To layer artwork you'll create later between the type and a blurred shadow of the type, first duplicate the type layer (drag the type layer and drop it on the Create New Layer icon in the Layers panel). Then, select the type objects on the duplicate layer you just created and from the Effect menu select Blur > Gaussian Blur and choose a blur radius that blurs enough without obliterating the letterforms.

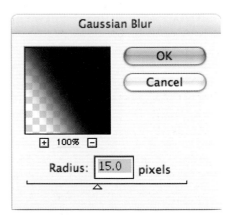

The Effect > Blur > Gaussian Blur dialog with the Radius set to a value appropriate for the smaller working size of the illustration

2 Drawing and painting paths with brushes and applying transparency to paths. Painting letterforms couldn't be easier. Using the type you created previously as a visual guide, start by simply drawing lines with the Pen or Pencil tool. Coupling the Pencil tool with a tablet (such as the Wacom tablet) makes drawing even easier and more spontaneous. For a smoother path (with fewer points and more gentle contours) use the Zoom tool to zoom out, *then* draw with the Pencil tool. Cronan mixed paths that followed the shapes of the letterforms with circles and curlicues (letter **o**) and scribbles (letter **w**).

With paths drawn, you're ready to apply brushes. Click the Brush Libraries button (in the lower left of the Brushes panel) and choose Artistic_Paintbrush. Then click on a path and select the Splash brush from the Artistic_Paintbrush panel. With the path still selected, you can refine the shape of the brushed path by selecting the Pencil tool and drawing over or near the selected path to smooth or reshape it. Use the Zoom tool to zoom in or out before you apply the Smooth or Pencil tools to give your reshaped path a smoother or more angular contour.

Because Illustrator's brushes use a path's stroke color, you can color the path before or after applying a Brush. To adjust the thickness of the brushed path, change the path's stroke weight. To change the look of all paths in the illustration painted with a brush, double-click the brush in the Brushes panel and change settings in Art Brush Options. Use the Colorization Method to control how the stroke color is applied to the brush, and adjust the Size > Width field to make the brush stroke wider or thinner.

3 Handwriting with the Pencil tool and setting transparency. Cronan completed the poster illustration by selecting the Pencil tool and drawing paths to mimic handwritten words. Be sure to experiment with the Stroke panel's Cap and Join settings to change the look of the paths. (As an alternative to the Pencil, consider using a Calligraphic brush with a small point size from the Brushes panel.) To blend the the handwriting-like white-stroked paths with the artwork below, Cronan opened the Transparency panel and reduced the Opacity to 65% for some paths and 31% for others.

2

On the left, the colored strokes of paths drawn with the Pencil tool; on the right, Splash brush applied to the same paths

Original path on the left; the same path smoothed with the Pencil tool and zoomed out on the right

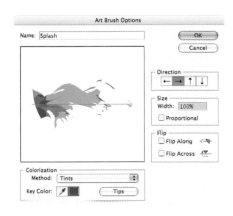

The Art Brush Options dialog showing the Splash brush

3

The Transparency panel

Crunching Type

Transforming Type with Warps & Envelopes

HAMANN

Overview: *Create and color a title using Appearances; use a warp effect to bow type; create an outline shape to "crunch" type; give the crunched type a dynamic, curved perspective effect using an envelope warp.*

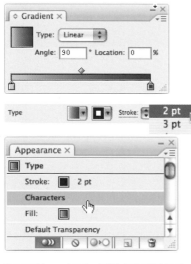

Using Add New Fill in the Appearance panel menu to add a gradient fill to the type

Warps and Envelopes are your superheroes for transforming headline type into any form you wish. No more need to convert type to outlines and laboriously move each anchor point by hand. Using Envelopes, it's literally as easy as drawing an outline and commanding the type to conform. With Warps and Envelopes, the type remains editable no matter how much you "crunch" it. Warps and Envelopes are always on hand to help rescue you from those looming deadlines!

1 Creating and coloring the E-Men title. To create the E-MEN cover title, Brad Hamann used 72-point Arial Black font, with a 2-pt black stroke. Because you can't just click on a gradient to fill type characters, he had to first select the type with a selection tool, and then choose Add New Fill from the Appearance panel menu.

2 Using a Warp effect to make the E-Men bow. There are 15 standard Warp shapes that can be turned into styles. For "E-MEN," Hamann applied Effect > Warp > Arc Lower. With Preview enabled, he used the Bend slider to bow the bottom of the letters (to 23%), then clicked OK.

Effect > Warp works in many instances, but it didn't warp his gradient fill along with the type. After applying Undo, Hamann chose Object > Envelope Distort > Envelope Options, enabled Distort Linear Gradients, and applied Object > Envelope Distort > Make with Warp, with the Arc Lower option at 23%.

3 Using a path to "crunch" type. To create the "CRUNCH!" Hamann again used the Appearance panel, this time to color "Crunch!" with a subtle gradient fill and a strong red stroke. Then, starting with a rectangle, he applied Object > Path > Add Anchor points twice, and then moved the rectangle's anchor points to form a dynamic jagged path. He then placed the path over the type, and with both the path and type selected he chose Object > Envelope Distort > Make with Top Object.

4 Using Envelope Distort > Make with Warp to create a curved perspective effect. To create a curved perspective effect, use Envelope Distort > Make with Warp to warp the "crunched" type. Because you can't nest one envelope inside another, first select your "crunched" type and choose Object > Envelope Distort > Expand. With your expanded type selected, choose Object > Envelope Distort > Make with Warp. Choose Arc in the Style pop-up menu of the Warp Options dialog, and adjust the sliders until you find the desired curved perspective look.

5 Adjusting and adding a stroke to the type. To complete the "CRUNCH!" type, in the Control panel Hamann clicked the Edit Contents button to adjust the type. In the Appearance panel, he added (in order) a yellow gradient fill, a 5-point black stroke, and a 10-point red stroke to the envelope enclosing the type to get the desired final effect.

With Effect > Warp > Arc Lower, the gradient fill remains horizontal

Using Object > Warp > Make with Warp (with Distort Linear Gradients enabled in the Envelope Options dialog), the gradient bends also

The type and path before and after applying Object > Envelope Distort > Make with Top

The released type; with Warp sliders set to 0 showing the starting envelope shape; the final Warp option settings; the resultant envelope

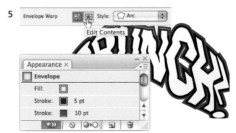

The final strokes and the finished type

Antiquing Type

Applying Scribble in an Opacity Mask

⊙

Advanced Technique

Overview: *Create a type object; copy the object, then style the text with the Roughen effect; create an Opacity Mask and paste the type object; apply the Scribble effect to the Opacity Mask; return to Outline mode.*

1

Top, the original type object with letter characters filled with black; bottom, the type object filled with a custom gradient

The Roughen dialog

Every type is unique

Your settings for one type object will look different applied to another typeface. Experiment!

When you want to re-create a hand-rendered or historical look, but don't want to stray from the fonts you're already using in a project, consider using Illustrator's Effect menu and an Opacity Mask. Ari Weinstein created this poster title for the African Art exhibit at the Bundy Museum in Binghamton, New York, by using an Opacity Mask and the Scribble effect to chip away the edges of lettering, turning contemporary type into antiqued letters.

1 Creating text, adding a new Fill, and applying the Roughen effect. Weinstein started the poster title by typing "African Art" using the font Marigold. Before taking his type any further, Weinstein clicked on the Selection tool and then chose Edit > Copy. (You'll need a copy of the type object for the Opacity Mask that you'll make later in the second step.)

Then Weinstein was ready to start styling his type. First, he made sure the type object was still selected. He then opened the Appearance panel and chose Add New Fill from the panel menu. Weinstein clicked on the new Fill attribute in the panel and applied a gradient he had built from brown colors sampled from other artwork in the poster. (For information on creating or editing gradients, refer to the *Blends, Gradients & Mesh* chapter.)

You can simulate a hand-rendered look by applying the Roughen effect. This will change the smooth, precise edges of an object to jagged or bumpy edges. To roughen your type object, make sure the Fill attribute is not selected (deselect it by clicking in an empty area of

WEINSTEIN

the Appearance panel) so that Roughen will be applied to the whole object. Then choose Effect > Distort & Transform > Roughen. In the Roughen dialog, adjust the Size, Detail, and Points controls. (Weinstein chose Size=0.5, Detail=6.5, and Points=Smooth for his type.)

Choosing the Opacity Mask in the Transparency panel

2 Pasting the type object, creating an Opacity Mask, pasting the object and applying Scribble. You can antique your type by making it look chipped or scratched. To do this, select your type object, open the Transparency panel and, from the panel menu, choose Make Opacity Mask from the panel menu. Next, click on the Opacity Mask thumbnail (the rightmost thumbnail) and make sure Clip and Invert Mask are checked. Lastly, paste the type you copied in the first step (use Paste in Front instead of Paste so this copy will overlay the original you copied).

Customizing the options in the Scribble Options dialog

Changes you make in the Opacity Mask will affect the transparency of the original type object—black artwork in the mask will punch holes in the original type. With the copy you just pasted still selected, choose Effect > Stylize > Scribble. In the Scribble Options dialog, choose one of the ready-made settings from the Settings menu, or customize the effect using the dialog's controls. Weinstein started with the Sharp setting and then changed several of its values. With the dialog's Preview enabled, he moved the Path Overlap slider to 0.04" to thin some of the chips in the edges. He also changed the Angle from the default, 30°, to 15°, so the chips aligned better with the angles in the type characters.

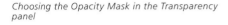

Selecting the artwork mode (instead of the Opacity mask mode) in the Transparency panel

3 Editing the type. Once you've finished with the Scribble effect, click the artwork thumbnail (the leftmost thumbnail) in the Transparency panel. If you need to edit the type—to change the text or modify kerning, for example—you'll have to do it in *both* the original type object and in the copy in the Opacity Mask. For some edits you make to the type—like scaling or rotating—you only need to work with the type object, since the Opacity Mask will be changed simultaneously with the type object.

Getting your fill

To ensure that the effects you will apply later in the Opacity Mask cut opaque holes in the artwork, make sure that the characters are filled with black. (Double-click *Characters* in the Appearance panel and check the Fill attribute.) If you then select the type object with the Selection tool and paint the object (rather than its characters) by adding a new fill in the Appearance panel, the copied type object will not adversely affect the Opacity Mask.

Olde Offset Fills

Covering a Pattern with an Offset Fill

Advanced Technique

Overview: *Create a pattern using Scribble effect; apply the pattern to letter characters; add a new fill to the text object; choke the new fill by applying a negative Offset effect; use Roughen to warp type edges.*

1

Top, black rectangle; below, with Scribble applied to fill

Scribble Options dialog

Top, Scribble effect expanded to a path; below, Thick Pencil brush applied to scribble pattern path

ye Olde Inne

COHEN

Filling lettering with patterns is a simple way of turning familiar fonts into fresh designs. Sometimes, though, you want a pattern to fill only part of each letter character. Finding a way to block patterns from the center of letter strokes was a challenge that Sandee Cohen, AKA VectorBabe, solved in creating this logo.

1 Creating and expanding a pattern, applying a brush, saving the pattern as a swatch. Breaking the edges of type is the key to making font lettering look aged. Illustrator's Scribble effect is a perfect tool for replacing the solid fill of letter characters with an irregular pattern. Cohen started by drawing a rectangle and filling it with black. With the rectangle selected, she chose Effect > Stylize > Scribble. In the Scribble Options dialog, Cohen customized the default values until she was satisfied with the loose drawing style the effect produced.

You can further customize the scribbled object by turning it into a path and applying a brush to it. To do this, make sure the scribble rectangle is selected and then choose Object > Expand Appearance. This converts the Scribble effect in the rectangle into a path. Cohen applied the Pencil-Thick brush (from Brush Libraries > Artistic_ChalkCharcoalPencil) to the expanded scribbled path.

In order to use the scribble object with the type you'll create, convert your brushed scribble object into a pattern swatch by dragging it to the Swatches panel.

2 Creating the type and filling it with the scribble pattern. Once your pattern is made, you're ready to create your text. First, open the Appearance panel—this will help you see whether you're editing the characters or their type object as you perform the following steps. Select the Type tool from the Toolbox, click on the Artboard, and type your text (Cohen used 72-pt Caslon). Select the characters by dragging through the text with the Type tool; the text will have a black fill. Then select the Fill attribute in the Appearance panel and select your scribble pattern from the Swatches panel.

3 **Adding a new fill, applying the Offset effect and using the Roughen effect.** Cohen needed a way of covering up the scribble pattern in the centers of the letters. Using the Offset effect, she created a fill that covered part of the lettering underneath. To do this, first select the type object by clicking on it with the Selection tool. Now, create a new fill by choosing Add New Fill from the Appearance panel menu. The new fill, by default, will be colored black and will completely cover the pattern that filled the letters. With the new fill selected, choose Effect > Path > Offset Path and, from the pop-up Offset Path dialog, enter a negative value in the Offset field. Be sure that the Preview box is enabled so you can gauge the visual effect of the number you enter in the Offset field. (Cohen used -1 pt for Offset.)

Complete the aging of your type by applying Roughen to the type object's fill to warp its edges. Select the type object with the Selection tool and choose Effect > Distort & Transform > Roughen. Because Cohen used a font with thin character strokes and serifs, she entered a small value for Size (0.4 pt), and selected Absolute, to be sure that the edges were not overly distorted.

A pattern of change

Pattern swatches are global. If you edit or create a pattern, simply drag the artwork with the Option/Alt key depressed and drop it on the swatch in the Swatches panel. The pattern filling your type will automatically change to the new pattern.

2

Top, the type with default black fill; right, the black fill replaced by the pattern

3

Offset Path effect applied to the new fill (shown here filled with gray instead of black), and the Offset Path dialog

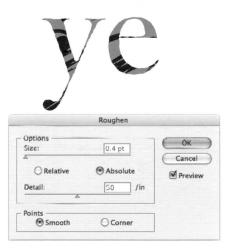

Roughen effect applied to the new fill (shown here in gray), and the Roughen dialog

Enlargement of two letters

Type Subtraction

Applying Live Subtract from Shape on Type

Advanced Technique

Overview: *Create several interleaved groups of shapes; create type objects and a shape; subtract the shape from the type using the Pathfinder panel.*

Left, the three groups of wave shapes made from one group (top); right, their combination in the final form used in the logo

Rotate by center

When you double-click the Rotate tool, Illustrator automatically sets the rotation centerpoint at the exact center of the selected artwork. This means your copy precisely overlays the original on the Artboard.

For a conference on protecting the world's rivers, Innosanto Nagara of Design Action designed a logo that could appear in applications as diverse as posters, report covers, and t-shirts—and stand out against a variety of backgrounds, including a solid black square and a photograph. Illustrator's Pathfinder effect subtracted Nagara's wave shapes, leaving a gap between the logo type that would remain invisible against different backgrounds.

1 Creating a wave shape, rotating and copying it, and reflecting and copying it. Nagara designed the logo as two components: the conference title, "Rivers For Life," split into two lines, and the interleaving colored waves that separated them. To re-create Nagara's design, begin by drawing a set of curved blue shapes. Instead of drawing a second set of green waves, select the blue wave shapes you just drew with the Selection tool, and then double-click the Rotate tool. In the Rotate dialog, enter 180° in the Angle field and then click the Copy button. With the copy still selected, change its fill color from blue to green.

With the set of green waves still selected, complete the interleaving of blue and green waves by creating a third set of wave shapes. Use the Reflect tool this time (you can access this tool by pressing the mouse button down on the Rotate tool icon in Illustrator's tool panel). In the Reflect dialog, set the reflection axis to Horizontal and click the Copy button. Then change the fill of the wave shapes to blue, producing a blue-to-green-to-blue series of interleaving wave shapes.

2 Creating two type objects, drawing a subtracting shape, then applying the Pathfinder effect. Suggesting the action of waves, Nagara decided to use a flowing wave shape to cut into the top and bottom edges of the logo's lettering. To ensure that the wave shape allows the different backgrounds to appear, you'll need to cut into the lettering with your shapes and not simply paste the shape in front of the type to visually block it.

After typing the two lines of type as separate type objects, Nagara drew a new wave shape with the Pen tool and copied it so he could use it later with the second line of type. He moved the wave shape over the type until it blocked the lettering the way he wanted.

Then he selected the type object and the wave shape and, from the Shape Modes section of the Pathfinder panel, he clicked the Subtract from shape area icon.

To maintain the separate colors in "FOR" and "LIFE," Nagara selected the first word and chose Paste in Front to overlay the wave shape in front of that second line of lettering. Selecting that word and the wave, he clicked Subtract from shape area to cut the wave shape from the object. He then repeated the sequence for the other word.

3 Selecting the subtracting and modifying the subtracting shape. When you apply one of the Pathfinder's Shape Modes to artwork, the result is a compound path in which the top object (in Nagara's case, the wave shape that subtracts from the type object below it) remains "live" and editable. You can select and modify the subtracting shape with the Direct Selection tool, or redraw with the Pencil tool if you'd like. This is especially useful when the uneven contours and counters (holes) of a line of lettering require you to tweak the subtracting shape. If you use the same object more than once, as Nagara did, you can tweak each one to make them appear a little different, giving greater spontaneity to the finished artwork.

2

Type with the wave shape that will subtract from the type

The wave placed on top of the top type object and the resulting cut in the type

Top shows the wave pasted above word "FOR" and then after then applying the Subtract from shape area from the Pathfinder panel; bottom shows these steps repeated for the word "LIFE"

The Pathfinder panel and the Subtract from shape area icon (the Subtract function remains "live" unless the Expand button is pressed)

3

Using the Direct Selection tool to select the subtracting shape to modify its points

Avoiding strokes

When working with a compound shape, remember that selecting the subtracting shape and applying a stroke will not change how much that shape cuts into the object below it. Adding a stroke or increasing its width will affect the bottom object—when that object is type, a stroke will change how the letter characters look.

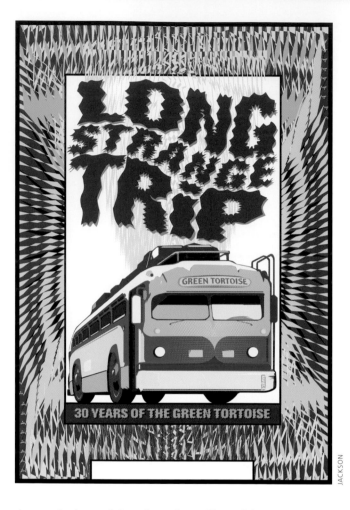

JACKSON

Lance Jackson / *San Francisco Chronicle*

For the wonderful type "LONG STRANGE TRiP" in this poster for the cross-country "Green Tortoise" bus, illustrator Lance Jackson used a combination of many effects. Starting with the typeface Akzident ExtraBold, Jackson created three text blocks (one for each word) and chose a bright red fill. Combining so many effects creates unique results because of variables such as type size, kerning, and the ordering of effects, so just experiment. You can keep your type live or outline it (⌘-Shift-O/Ctrl-Shift-O). If you outline your text, you must then select it and choose Object > Compound Path > Make so it operates as one unit (see the *Beyond*

the Basics chapter for more on compound paths). To emulate Jackson's effects using live effects, keep your type live and select one word at a time; then choose Effects > Distort & Transform > Zig Zag (do this to each of the words separately so you can vary the amount of Zig Zag you're applying). Next, make a green Live Effects offset version of the type so that if you change your type, the offset changes as well. Select all three words and group (⌘-G/Ctrl-G). From the Appearance panel pop-up menu, choose Add New Fill and choose a darker green color. Now drag that green fill below the word "Contents" in the Appearance panel. Next, choose Effects > Distort & Transform > Transform and enter a small Move for Horizontal and Vertical (enable Preview) to offset the green version. Now select Group in the Appearance panel and start experimenting. Try applying Effects > Distort & Transform > Twist. From here, add additional live effects, or remove Twist and start again. See how this differs from Effects > Warp > Twist (see *Live Effects & Graphic Styles* for more about multiple fills and live effects). For the psychedelic border effects, Jackson used techniques similar to those in his gallery in the *Blends, Gradients & Mesh* chapter.

"W" Blend tool   "G" Gradient tool   "U" Mesh tool

The speed of the blend

To control the speed of the blend, create the blend and set the number of blend steps. This creates the blend spine, which is editable just like any other Illustrator path. Using the Convert Anchor Point tool, pull out control handles from the anchor point at each end of the blend spine. By extending or shortening the control handles along the spine, the speed of the blend is controlled. —*Derek Mah*

Automatically updating colors

Changing a spot or global color definition (see the *Drawing & Coloring* chapter) automatically updates blends and gradients containing that color. Blends between tints of the same spot color (or a spot color and white) update when changes are made to that color, even if the blend isn't "live." (See David Cater's "Mini Cooper" Gallery in the *Advanced Techniques* chapter for a practical application of this technique.) —*ThoughtForm Design*

Blends, Gradients & Mesh

To create shading and modeling with fills and colors, it's important to learn how to work with blends, gradients, and mesh. In the history of Adobe Illustrator, blends came first, then gradients, then gradient mesh. Each can be both simple and very complex. So, we intermingle them in the lessons and galleries, even though we discuss these features "chronologically" in the introduction.

BLENDS

Think of blends as a way to "morph" one object's shape and/or color into another. You can create blends between multiple objects, and even gradients or compound paths such as letters. Blends are *live*, which means you can edit the key objects' shape, color, size, location, or rotation, and the resulting *in-between* objects will automatically update. You can also distribute a blend along a custom path (see details later in this chapter).

Note: *Complex blends, especially gradient-to-gradient blends, require a lot of RAM when drawing to the screen.*

The simplest way to create a blend is to select the objects you wish to blend and choose Object > Blend > Make. The number of steps you'll have in between each object is based on either the default options for the tool, or the last settings of the Blend Options (discussed in the following section). Adjust settings for a selected blend by selecting the blend, then double-clicking the Blend tool (or via Objects > Blend > Blend Options). This feature has improved in recent editions of Illustrator and is now the most predictable method for blending, so you'll probably want to use it for most of your blends.

Another way to create blends between individual paths is to *point map* using the Blend tool. In the past, the Blend tool was used to achieve smooth transitions between blended objects. However, now that it's been modified, it's probably best to use it for special morphing or twirling effects. To use the *point map* technique, begin by clicking on an anchor point of one object, and then on an anchor point of another object. Continue clicking on anchor points of any object you want to include in the blend. You can also click anywhere on the path of an object to achieve random blending effects.

When a blend first appears, it's selected and grouped. If you Undo immediately, the blend will be deleted, but your source objects remain selected so you can blend again. To modify a key object before or after making a blend, Direct-Select the key object first, then use any editing tool (including the Pencil, Smooth, and Path Eraser tools) to make your changes.

Blend Options

To specify Blend Options as you blend, use the Blend tool (see the *point map* directions in the previous section) and press the Option/Alt key as you click the second point. The Blend Options dialog will appear, allowing you to change any settings before making the blend. To adjust options on a completed blend, select it and double-click the Blend tool (or Object > Blend > Blend Options). Opening Blend Options without a blend selected sets the default for creating blends *in this work session*; these Options reset each time you restart the program.

- **Specified Steps** specifies the number of steps between each pair of key objects. Using fewer steps results in clearly distinguishable objects, while a larger number of steps results in an almost airbrushed effect.

- **Specified Distance** places a specified distance between the objects of the blend.

- **Smooth Color** allows Illustrator to automatically calculate the ideal number of steps between key objects in a blend, in order to achieve the smoothest color transition. If objects are the same color, or are gradients or patterns, the calculation will equally distribute the objects within the area of the blend, based on their size.

To blend or not to blend...

In addition to blending between individual paths, or groups of objects, you can blend between symbols (see the *Brushes & Symbols* chapter for more on symbols), Live Paint objects, or between Point type objects. Some of the objects you *can't* include in a blend are meshes, raster images, and type objects that aren't Point type. When blending between objects containing brushes, effects, and other complex appearances, Illustrator blends affect options, which can help you create interesting animations (see the *Web & Animation* chapter for more on exporting animations).—*Teri Petit*

Efficient Blending

To make a blend follow a specific path, just select a manually drawn path (with no fill or stroke) and any objects you want to blend. Once you make the blend (Object > Blend > Make), the path becomes the spine of the blended objects. —*Jean-Claude Tremblay*

To insert objects into a blend

Group-Select a key object and Option/Alt-drag to insert a new key object (the blend will reflow). You can also insert new objects by entering Isolation mode (see previous chapter) or by dragging them into the blend in the Layers panel.

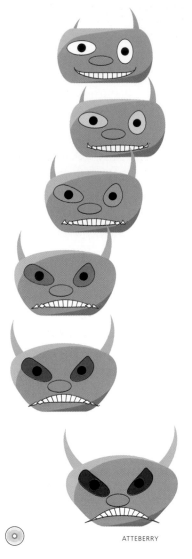

ATTEBERRY

*Groups of objects blended into each other using the Align to Path orientation, Specified Distance, and the "spines" edited into **S** curves (for more about blends see "KevanAtteberry-blends.ai" on the* Wow! CD*)*

• **Orientation** determines whether the individual blend objects rotate as they follow the path's curves. Align to Path (the default, first icon) allows blend objects to rotate as they follow the path. Align to Page (the second icon) prevents objects from rotating as they're distributed along the path's curve (objects stay "upright" as they blend along the curve).

Blends along a path

There are two ways to make blends follow a curved path. The first way is to Direct-Select the *spine* of a blend (the path automatically created by the blend) and then use the Add/Delete Anchor Point tools, or any of the following tools, to curve or edit the path: the Direct Selection, Lasso, Convert Anchor Point, Pencil, Smooth, or even the Path Eraser tool. As you edit the spine of the blend, Illustrator automatically redraws the blend objects to align to the edited spine.

Secondly, you can also replace the spine with a customized path: Select both the customized path and the blend, and choose Object > Blend > Replace Spine. This command moves the blend to its new spine.

You can also blend between pairs of grouped objects. If you're not getting the results you expect, try creating your first set of objects and grouping them (⌘-G/Ctrl-G). Now copy and paste a duplicate set (or Option/Alt and drag to create a copy of your group). Select the two sets of grouped objects and blend choosing Specified Steps as the blend option. Once the objects are blended, you can rotate and scale them, and use the Direct Selection tool to edit the objects or the spine. (To experiment with a pair of grouped blends in this way, find the figures at left on the *Wow! CD* as "KevanAtteberry-blends.ai.")

Reversing, releasing, and expanding blends

Once you've created and selected a blend, you can do any of the following:

• **Reverse** the order of objects on the spine by choosing Object > Blend > Reverse Spine.

- **Release** a blend (Object > Blend > Release) if you wish to remove the blended objects between key objects and maintain the spine of the blend (be forewarned—you may lose grouping information!).

- **Expand** a blend to turn it into a group of separate, editable objects. Choose Object > Blend > Expand.

GRADIENTS

Gradients are color transitions. To open the Gradient panel, double-click the Gradient tool icon on the Toolbox, or choose Window > Gradient. Gradients can be either radial (circular from the center) or linear.

To apply a gradient to an object, select the object and click on a gradient swatch in the Swatches panel. To view only gradient swatches, click on the gradient icon at the bottom of the Swatches panel.

To start adjusting or creating a new gradient, click on the gradient preview in the Gradient panel. Only after clicking on the preview will you see the color stops and midpoints. Make your own gradients by adding and/or adjusting the stops (pointers representing colors) along the lower edge of the gradient preview; adjust the midpoint between the color stops by sliding the diamond shapes along the top of the preview.

You can adjust the length, direction, and centerpoint location of a selected gradient. In addition, you can apply a gradient to multiple selected objects across a unified blend by clicking and dragging with the Gradient tool (see lessons in this chapter for detailed examples of how to use the gradient tool). *Hint: A special feature of the Gradient panel is that, even if it's tabbed or docked with other panels, you can expand its height and width to get a better view of the Gradient bar; just grab the lower right corner of the Gradient panel and resize it as you wish.*

To create the illusion of a gradient within a stroke, convert the stroke to a filled object (Object > Path > Outline Stroke). You can use this method to create a "trap" for gradients.

How long can a gradient be?
Click and drag with the Gradient tool anywhere in your image window; you don't need to stay within the objects themselves.

Reset gradients to defaults
After you select an object that has an altered gradient angle (or highlight), new objects you draw will have the same settings. To "re-zero" gradient settings, Deselect All and fill with None by pressing the "/" key. For linear gradients, you can type a zero in the Angle field. Or, you can use the Gradient panel to switch between the Radial type and the Linear type and then back again to reset a custom angle without removing or relocating color stops.

Adding color to your gradient
- Drag a swatch from the Color or Swatches panel to the gradient slider until you see a vertical line indicating where the new color stop will be added.
- If the Fill is a solid color, you can drag color from the Fill icon at the bottom of the Toolbox.
- Hold down the Option/Alt key to drag a copy of a color stop.
- Option/Alt-drag one stop over another to *swap* their colors.
- Click the lower edge of a gradient to add a new stop.

PAIDRICK

The amazing work with mesh only starts in this chapter—don't miss the additional mesh artwork in the Advanced Techniques *chapter—above is a detail of an Ann Paidrick illustration.*

Adding rows and columns

To add new rows and columns to your mesh, click on the mesh object with the Mesh tool (U). To add a new mesh row, click on a column mesh line. To add a new mesh column, click on a row.

Adding color to the mesh

When adding a new mesh point, the color currently selected in the Swatches panel will be applied to the new point. If you want the new mesh point to remain the color currently applied to the mesh object, hold the Shift key while adding a new point.

Moving rows and columns

When moving a mesh point, both the row and column mesh lines intersecting that point will move with it. To move a row or column mesh line independently, without moving the other, hold the Shift key while you drag a line. If you drag up or down, only the row line moves; if you drag left or right, only the column line moves.

To turn a gradient into a grouped, masked blend, use Object > Expand (see the *Advanced Techniques* chapter for more on masks and masked blends).

GRADIENT MESH

In this book you'll find many amazing photorealistic images created using gradient mesh. A *mesh object* is an object on which multiple colors can flow in different directions, with smooth transitions between specially defined *mesh points*. You can transform a solid or gradient-filled object into mesh (you can't transform compound paths into mesh). Once transformed, the object will always be a mesh object, so be certain that you work with a copy of the original if it's difficult to re-create.

Transform solid filled objects into gradient mesh objects either by choosing Object > Create Gradient Mesh (so you can specify details on the mesh construction) or by clicking on the object with the Mesh tool. To transform a gradient-filled object, select Object > Expand and enable the Gradient Mesh option.

Use the Mesh tool to add lines and points to the mesh. Select individual points, or groups of points, within the mesh using the Direct Selection tool or the Mesh tool in order to move, color, or delete them. For details on working with gradient meshes (including the Warning Tip about printing mesh objects), see Galleries and lessons later in this chapter, as well as the *Advanced Techniques* chapter. **Hint:** *Instead of applying a mesh to a complex path, try to first create the mesh from a simpler path outline, then mask the mesh with the more complex path.*

Get back your (mesh) shape!

When you convert a path to a mesh, it's no longer a path, but a mesh object. To extract an editable path from a mesh, select the mesh object, choose Object > Path > Offset Path, enter 0, and press OK. If there are too many points in your new path, try using Object > Path > Simplify (for more on Simplify see the *Drawing & Coloring* intro). —*Pierre Louveaux*

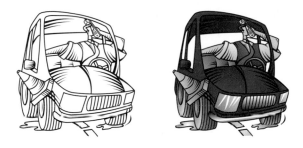

WEBB

Tim Webb

Tim Webb used just a few features of Illustrator to create his Victory Climb and Road lessons illustrations. The crisp woodcut appearance is a result of bold line work layered above gradient fills. Webb began by drawing the image with the Pen tool. Webb then created his color palette by importing colors from a swatch library into the Swatches panel. He then double-clicked the Gradient tool icon to open the Gradient panel and created gradients by dragging colors from the Swatches panel onto the stops of the Gradient panel. (For more detail on creating a gradient, see the gradients section of the introduction to this chapter.)

After he created and saved the gradients in the Swatches panel, Webb drew closed paths and filled them with either a linear or a radial gradient, varying the direction and length of the gradient in order to give volume to the image. The woodcut appearance was created by blending between two triangular shapes on a curved path. Webb created custom art brushes to make the small rocks and the raindrops.

Simplest of Mesh

Filling a Shape with a Gradient Mesh

Overview: *Draw paths; select paths and fill with colors; select a shape and click with the Mesh tool; choose a color for the mesh highlight point; copy and paste, and scale and rotate copies to compose the illustration.*

1

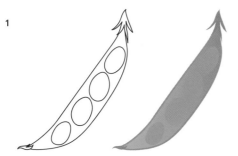

Left, the paths drawn for the soybean pod; right, the paths filled with two shades of green

2

Left, the Preview View of a gradient mesh; right, the Outline View of the selected mesh

3

The three pods (original is on the left and the two scaled and rotated copies are on the right)

For her book for the Japanese market, *Adobe Illustrator CS*, which she co-authored with Yukio Miyamoto, artist Nobuko Miyamoto found that creating a gradient mesh was easier and made a more shapely and editable gradient than creating a radial gradient with the Gradient tool.

1 Drawing and coloring the pod. Miyamoto began by drawing the vine and a soybean pod with its four beans. She filled the pod with a green gradient and then filled the bean shapes with a medium green. Use a color that contrasts with the colors around it for shapes that you'll paint later with a gradient mesh—this ensures that the mesh will not appear to fade into surrounding artwork.

2 Coloring the beans with gradient mesh. To create the gradient mesh for each bean, Miyamoto chose the Mesh tool, selected a light green for the highlight color, and then clicked on the unselected shape. When you click with the Mesh tool, Illustrator will automatically create a highlight point at the spot you clicked inside the shape. With the mesh still selected, you can change the highlight color by selecting another color from the Color or Swatches panel. If you want to move the highlight point, click on it with the Mesh tool and move it.

3 Copying, pasting, scaling and rotating. Miyamoto completed the illustration by copying and pasting the pod twice, and then scaling and rotating each copy before arranging the three soybean pods and vine.

GORDON / CARTAGRAM, LLC

Steven Gordon / Cartagram, LLC

Large areas of solid color can be a necessary but boring fact of life for cartographers. With Illustrator's Mesh tool, however, they needn't stay boring for very long. In this location map, Gordon turned a solid green background into a natural-looking backdrop for his map. To create the background, Gordon first drew a rectangle and filled it with a solid green color. With the rectangle still selected, he chose Object > Create Gradient Mesh. In the Create Gradient Mesh dialog, he entered 4 in the Rows and Columns fields, and left the Appearance menu set on the default setting of Flat. This created a mesh with editable points along the edges and inside the rectangle. Next, Gordon chose the Mesh tool and clicked on several of the points in the selected mesh. For each point inside the rectangle he clicked on, Gordon changed the original green color to a lighter yellow-green using the Color panel. For the mesh points on the edges of the rectangle Gordon clicked on, he changed the color to a darker blue-green.

Unified Gradients

Redirecting Fills with the Gradient Tool

picturedance.com ©joly

Overview: *Fill objects with gradients; use the Gradient tool to adjust fill length and angle, and unify fills across multiple objects.*

1

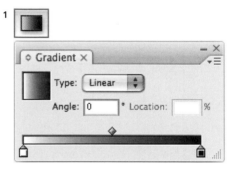

The Gradient tool (top), and the Gradient panel (bottom)

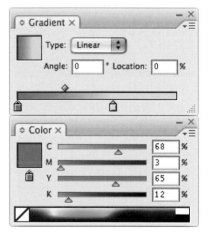

The Gradient panel customized for the flippers; when you select a gradient slider, the slider color appears in the Color panel for editing

Gradient applied to the flippers using the Gradient panel

The Gradient tool complements the Gradient panel by providing more ways to edit gradient fills, and by stretching and unifying gradients across multiple paths. For this *Sunset* magazine illustration, Dave Joly used the Gradient panel to apply initial gradients, and then used the Gradient tool to customize gradients and unify them across multiple paths, as seen in the clouds and fish scales.

1 Applying and editing gradients. The Gradient tool can edit gradients, but it can't create them. To apply an initial gradient to the flippers, Joly selected them, opened the Gradient panel, and clicked the gradient icon at the top left corner of the Gradient panel. To edit gradient colors, Joly clicked on each gradient slider and either mixed a new color in the Color panel or Option-clicked/Alt-clicked a color swatch on the Swatches panel. He dragged the far right Gradient slider to the left to extend the ending gradient color. You can add sliders by clicking under the gradient bar, and you can drag the diamonds above the slider bar to adjust the rate of change between gradient sliders.

2 Editing a gradient using the Gradient tool. To set a new gradient length and angle, select a path and drag the Gradient tool over it. You can start and stop dragging the Gradient tool anywhere inside or outside the selected path. To constrain a linear gradient's angle to 45-degree increments, hold down the Shift key as you drag. To edit a radial gradient, you can click the Gradient tool to reposition the center, or click and drag if you want to change both the center and the radius of the radial gradient.

3 Unifying gradients with the Gradient tool. Joly first selected two clouds and applied the same gradient to both. He then dragged the Gradient tool all the way from the left edge of the left cloud to the right edge of the right cloud. The length and angle of the unified gradient spanned both clouds as if they were one object.

As you drag, the Info panel displays the cursor position and the gradient distance, size, and angle. The Gradient panel displays the final gradient angle until you deselect the paths.

4 Editing a unified gradient. To edit the length and angle of the unified gradient across the fish scales, Joly selected all of the scales and then dragged the Gradient tool across them until he achieved the effect he wanted.

While you can also edit a unified gradient by using the Gradient panel, the Gradient tool provides additional flexibility because you can drag it to position the starting and ending points of the gradient outside the paths that make up the gradient.

Selecting unified gradients more easily

To simplify selection of all of the paths in a unified gradient, combine the paths into a group, a compound path, or a compound shape. That way, clicking any part of the group or combined shape selects the entire unified gradient. Or, while all your unified gradient objects are still selected, choose Select > Save Selection to save and name the selection.

2

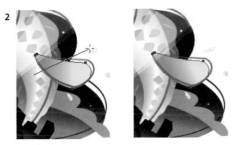

Changing a gradient's angle by dragging the Gradient tool over a selected flipper

3

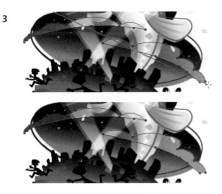

Dragging the Gradient tool across two clouds (top), so that the unified gradient starts in the left cloud and ends in the right cloud (bottom)

◇ Info ×			
+	X : 485 px	⌐⌐	W : 334 px
	Y : 584 px		H : -73 px
	D : 341.884 px		∠ : -12.329°

The Info panel provides numeric feedback as you drag the Gradient tool

4

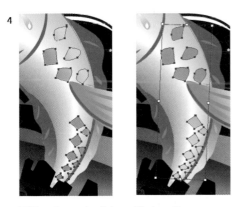

Editing the angle of the unified gradient across all selected fish scales, from a horizontal angle (left) to a vertical angle (right)

Gleaming Gold
Simulating Shining Metal with Gradients

Overview: *Create the look of gold with gradients; create depth by offsetting paths and adding bevels; create custom-shaped gradients with blends.*

1

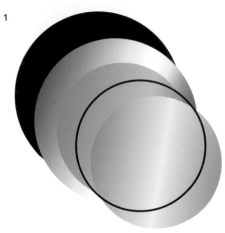

The coin paths pulled apart to show their fills

FERSTER (Client: Intuit, Inc., Product: Quickbooks 2005) (Creative Director: Riccardo Spina)

This logo for the popular Intuit QuickBooks line of business accounting software is used for everything from packaging to marketing materials, in print and online. It was originally designed in Illustrator and Photoshop, but the original file size was so large that Gary Ferster was asked to re-create the logo as a smaller file. Ferster's efficiently rebuilt version of the logo, created exclusively in Illustrator, takes up 93% less disk space than the original. To suggest the gleam of gold, Ferster applied gradients or blends depending on which technique was most appropriate for various parts of the illustration.

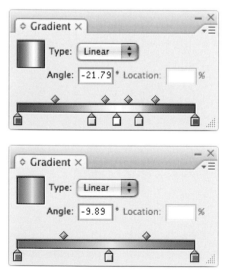

The Gradient panels for the coin edge (top) and the coin center (bottom)

1 Adding shiny highlights to the coin. Ferster built the coin as a set of concentric circles, each with a different fill. The outer golden band is a large circle filled with a customized linear gradient, and the center is another circle with a similar gradient. The outermost black outline is a circle filled with black, placed just behind and made slightly larger than the outer golden circle.

By default, gradients have one starting and ending color slider. To create the metallic gleam, Ferster customized the gradients by clicking below the gradient bar to add sliders, and then applied lighter colors to the middle sliders. The outer circle uses five sliders.

2 Creating the dollar sign. Just as he did for the coin circles, Ferster created depth for the dollar sign by stacking filled paths. He started from the smaller path (the raised surface of the dollar sign). He selected the path, chose Object > Path > Offset Path, entered a positive value to create a larger duplicate (Ferster entered 5 pt), and clicked OK. The new offset path became the base of the dollar sign. With the new outer path selected, he chose the Offset Path command again, but this time entered 2 pt to create the outer border of the dollar sign.

3 Making the gleaming bevels. Ferster created bevels by cutting up copies of the inner and outer paths. He drew lines to bisect the paths at their corners, selected the lines and both dollar sign paths, and then clicked the Divide button in the Pathfinder panel. The Divide button converts all enclosed areas into separate closed paths. Ferster used the Direct Selection tool to delete line remnants but kept all closed bevel paths. He applied no stroke and linear gradients to the bevel paths. Ferster refined the gradient angles and colors with the Gradient panel because he prefers its precision compared to the Gradient tool.

Ferster also applied a radial gradient fill to the clock hub and linear gradient fills to the clock hands. He built the bar chart by applying linear gradient fills to rectangles edited for perspective by dragging points and segments with the Direct Selection tool. The sides of the bars are filled with linear gradients. For the bar tops, Ferster applied linear gradients that used three gradient sliders.

4 Adding shadows and highlight blends to the man. Ferster wanted to add airbrush-like shadows and highlights to the human figure. The shape of this shading was too organic for linear or radial gradients, so Ferster created custom-shaped blends. For each blend, he drew a base path filled with the color of the man's body, and a smaller path filled with either a highlight or shadow color. Ferster selected both paths and then chose Object > Blend > Make to blend the fills.

2

Using Offset Path to create a larger duplicate

3
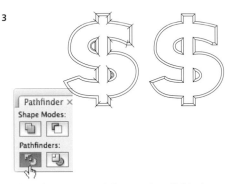
Lines drawn over path intersections (left), then using the Divide button to slice along paths to create closed paths (right) for the bevels

The completed dollar sign and its gradient-filled components (left to right): The original path, offset base path, and filled bevels (pulled apart)

4
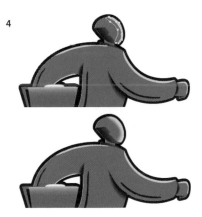
Before (top) and after (bottom) applying a blend to paths forming the highlight on his head

Custom Radials

Distorting Radial Fills & Recoloring Radials

Overview: *Swap colors of a gradient; fill circular-oval objects with radial gradients; distort the circles to squash the gradient; scale a solid filled object up and fill it with a radial gradient; vertically scale it back down to squash the fill; select and recolor gradients.*

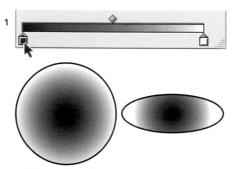

Holding Option/Alt when dragging one stop over another to swap the colors, then filling a circle and oval with a radial gradient

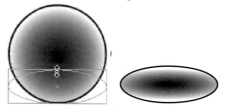

Filling a circle with a radial gradient, then squashing it using the bounding box to squash the radial fill as well

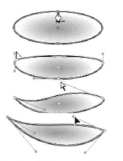

Reshaping the filled oval using path editing tools

Fill an oval with a radial gradient, and you get a circular gradient within an oval. Illustrator expert Daniel Pelavin cleverly fits a radial gradient snugly within an oval frame using a trick of scaling his object up, and down again.

For the PC Magazine awards for Technical Excellence, artist Pelavin designed the type, then created the reflective surfaces of the medal by filling the objects with a series of linear gradients. Pelavin set custom angles for the linear gradients and used the Gradient fill tool to adjust the length and position of some of the fills. In order to create the illusion of volume in the outer half of the leaf (that repeats to form the wreath), Pelavin made a circular radial fill snugly fit within the elongated oval-shaped leaf contour. To create the gold version of the award, Pelavin updated each of his gradients using his gold color scheme.

1 **Squashing your circles and radials.** This first method is best used with objects that don't require much editing beyond the initial shape of an oval. It's quicker to get the squashed results, but it's more editing work afterwards.

You'll first distort a circle to most closely fit your needs. Start by creating a circle using the Oval tool. Either click with the tool on your page and specify the same number for Height and Width, or drag to make an oval while holding Shift. Now open the Gradient panel and click on the black-and-white radial (circular) gradient. To reverse the gradient (or swap any gradient color with another), hold Option/Alt and drag-and-drop one stop over another. Next create a long oval; notice how the gradient doesn't fit the contour. With the Selection tool, click on the circle. Grab one of the handles of the bounding box and squash and stretch the circle. You'll see that the radial gradient distorts to match the contour.

In order to now make your oval fit a leaf shape (for instance), you now have to use the path editing tools to customize the path. As necessary, add and delete points, convert anchor points from curves to corners, and change the length and angle of the points and direction handles using the Direct Selection tool.

2 Vertically scaling your objects to squash the radial fills. Pelavin chooses to draw his objects first, and then he forces the radial gradients to fit his shapes. He drew the outer shape of his leaf with the Pen tool and gave it a solid fill (the stroke has been added so the gradients are easier to see). Then, double-clicking the Scale tool, Pelavin specified a 400% Vertical scale, 100% Horizontal. Next he chose a radial gradient from the Swatches panel and double-clicked the Scale tool again, to reverse the scaling with a 25% Vertical scaling (again 100% for Horizontal).

With his radial contour on the outer leaf, Pelavin finished the leaf cluster with a linear gradient-filled inner leaf, duplicated the leaf, and then placed a stroked outline of the combined leaves behind the filled objects.

3 Creating other color schemes. Using a copy of the silver award, Pelavin remade each of the gradients using shades of gold. He began by creating three custom global colors: light, medium and dark gold. For each gradient variation, he selected one object with that fill and chose Select > Same > Fill Color. With that fill selected, in the Gradient panel he then dragged one of his new gold color swatches onto a gradient stop, or onto the gradient itself to add a new stop. (See the *Drawing & Coloring* chapter for more on global colors, and "Distort Filter Flora," step 4, for how to recolor gradients using Live Color.)

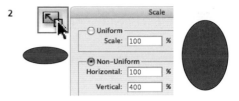

2

Scaling a solid-filled object up vertically by 400% by double-clicking the Scale tool

Filling the scaled oval with a radial gradient, then vertically scaling it back down by 25%

Pelavin's leaf object vertically scaled up by 400%, filled with a radial gradient, then vertically scaled down by 25%

From left to right: Pelavin's actual squashed radial fill (shown outlined), with a linear fill (shown outlined), then combined, and with finishing outline (behind the filled objects)

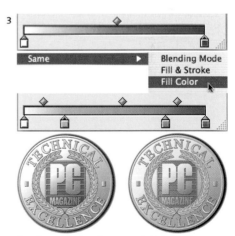

3

Starting with the silver award, Pelavin chose each gradient, used Select > Same > Fill Color and then customized that gradient using his new global gold colors

Zosia Rostomian / The Sharper Image®

Zosia Rostomian made complex combinations of stacked gradient and solid filled objects to render this Sharper Image® product illustration. Some of the many objects she stacked to make the phone are shown in the detail to the right (the bottom-most object is on the left). To apply a gradient to a selected object, she double-clicked on the Gradient tool, opened the Gradient panel (left detail), then selected either Linear or Radial for the Type. She expanded the height and width of the panel to get a better view of the gradient. Rostomian clicked under the Gradient bar to add more stops and moved them to make adjustments.

To change the midpoint between the stops, she moved the diamond-shaped stops on top. With the gradient-filled object still selected she opened the Swatches panel and clicked the New Swatch icon, named the gradient, and clicked OK. Before she continued drawing, she Deselected All (Select > Deselect, or ⌘-Option-A/Ctrl-Alt-A) and changed the fill to None so the next object she drew would not have the same fill attribute as the previous one. She repeated this process for each object that required a different gradient. She adjusted the length and angle of the gradient fill for some objects by clicking and dragging across them with the Gradient tool.

ROSTOMIAN

Zosia Rostomian / The Sharper Image®

Blending between grouped objects was an ideal technique to use for this Sharper Image® product illustration of a laptop desk. Zosia Rostomian placed a product photo on a layer below her drawing to use as a template. To make the ridged area, she drew the initial ridged line with two 1-pt strokes in a light and dark gray (shown above). She grouped the two strokes (⌘-G/Crl-G), selected that group, and Option-clicked/Alt-clicked as she dragged to make a copy. Rostomian Direct selected the first set of grouped strokes, chose the Blend tool, and pressed the Option/Alt key to open the Blend Options dialog. She set the Spacing to Specified Steps, entered 12, clicked OK, then clicked on the second set of strokes to make the blend and complete the ridged lines. To draw the dotted pattern, Rostomian first created one dot with layered circles and then grouped them. The first row is made of two separate dot objects. She copied and pasted other dots into two columns (highlighted in blue, above). To make one row of dots she Direct-selected one dot, then selected the Blend tool. She clicked on another dot, pressed the Option/Alt key, entered the number of Specified Steps needed to fill in the row, clicked OK, then clicked on the other dot. Since Rostomian was working directly over a template, she knew how many dots were needed in the row and entered that amount in Specified Steps. Each row of dots was blended separately with a different number of Specified Steps.

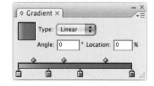

Christiane Beauregard

Christiane Beauregard created subtle color transitions throughout this illustration with linear and radial gradients. Beauregard drew each shape with the Pen tool, and as she progressed, created the gradient to fill the shape. She clicked on the gradient preview in the Gradient panel, selected the type of gradient (linear or radial), and added custom colors to the color stops and midpoints. (Two gradients Beauregard used are shown above.) She adjusted the length and direction of the gradient fills within the shapes by using the Gradient tool.

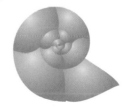

Christiane Beauregard

Using the same coloring technique as in the Fall illustration (opposite page), Christiane Beauregard created the shell (detail right) with separate shapes filled with the same radial gradient. With the shape selected, she clicked and dragged with the Gradient tool from the beginning to the end point of the area and changed the angle of the gradient to give each shape its specific highlight. She created a luminosity in the depths of the sea by varying the opacities in the gradient-filled shapes. Beauregard clicked on the word Opacity in the Control panel and reduced the Opacity of the shapes. She overlapped some of these shapes to enhance the sea's depth.

STANKIEWICZ

Steven Stankiewicz

Steven Stankiewicz uses a technique he calls "blends to blends" to smooth one colorful blend with another in his illustrations. To create a butterfly wing, he first drew the wing shape and its spots with the Pen tool and then colored each object. For the wing blend, he copied the wing object, pasted it in front, and scaled it smaller with the Scale tool. After selecting the original and the copy, he used the Blend tool to click on an anchor point on the original wing and Option-clicked on the corresponding point of the copied (smaller) wing. From the pop-up Blend Options dialog, Stankiewicz chose the Smooth Color option. Then he performed the same steps to create blends for each of the wing spots. Stankiewicz decided to smooth the color transition

between each wing spot blend and the wing blend behind it. To accomplish this, he chose the Direct Selection tool and selected the outermost object in one of the wing spot blends; then he Shift-selected the innermost object of the wing blend behind it. With both objects selected, Stankiewicz clicked points on both objects that were in roughly the same position on each object. As a result, a new blend was created that smoothly bridged the blend of a wing spot with the blend of the wing behind it.

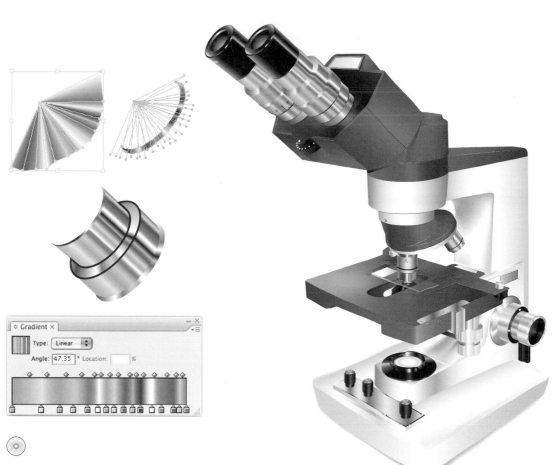

SIMONSON

Rick Simonson

For his remarkable feat of photorealism with this illustration of a microscope, Rick Simonson used blends and gradients to mimic reflections in metal. To make some of the metal sections that reflected multiple colors, he began by drawing with the Line tool. After drawing a line, he selected one end with the Direct Selection tool and left the other anchor point unselected. He dragged on the selected point, adding the Option/Alt key to duplicate the line in the start of a fan shape—the unselected anchor remaining in place. He repeated adding new lines at varying distances from each other, and coloring them, until he had enough lines to equal all the color changes in the reflection. He then selected all the lines and chose the Blend tool with Smooth Color selected in the tool's Options. With the keyboard shortcut ⌘-Option-B/Ctrl-Alt-B, he created a blend object from the lines. Next Simonson drew the object he required for a part of the microscope on top of his newly blended object. With both objects selected, he chose Object > Clipping Mask > Make (⌘-7/Ctrl-7). For other complex reflections, Simonson created gradients with multiple color stops that colored the objects to match up with those made from the blends.

Shaping Blends

Controlling Shaped-Blend Transitions

ATTEBERRY

Overview: *Prepare your base objects; create modified copies of the base objects to create simple blends; further modify top objects in blends to create special blending effects; add finishing details.*

Atteberry's original drawing and the version he made using Live Trace

After drawing base objects, reflecting copies of the base objects that don't cross the center line

A manufacturer of theme park prizes commissioned illustrator Kevan Atteberry to create this logo to be printed on basketballs. After digitizing his initial line drawing, Atteberry colors his images with shape-to-shape blends, which he prefers over the less precise gradients, and more laborious gradient mesh. Creating shaped blends is a necessary skill to master before you can go on to the more complex techniques of masking shaped blends in the *Advanced Techniques* chapter.

1 Creating your base objects and setting options. Since his dragon is symmetrical, Atteberry drew half the face in ink on paper, scanned it in black and white at 600dpi and opened it in Illustrator. After applying Object > Live Trace, he chose Object >Expand, then selected and deleted the white objects (see the *Beyond the Basics* chapter for more details about working with Live Trace). Then he dragged out a vertical guide from the ruler to the face's center. Using the Reflect tool he clicked on the guide, then Option-Shift/Alt-Shift-clicked on another point of the guide to reflect a copy on the other side of the guide. With the line drawing complete, he locked the layer containing the line work, and created layers underneath to create his base, solid-colored objects with the Pen and Pencil tools. For objects that didn't cross the center line, Atteberry made one version and reflected a copy to the other side. To prepare for blending, double-click the Blend tool to set Smooth Color for Blend Options.

2 **Making simple, smooth blends.** For each of his blends, Atteberry begins by selecting the base object and copying. Then using Edit > Paste in Front (⌘-F/Ctrl-F), he modifies the top object and blends between the two. The modifications often include scaling the top copy of the object smaller, shifting the location of the object, or sometimes modifying the outline itself. In the example shown (the dragon's right cheek), Atteberry redrew the top object's path using the Pencil tool. Selecting both objects he chose Object > Blends > Make. Even though the top object contains many more points, the blend is still smooth.

3 **Shaping blends for special effects.** Sometimes smooth blending isn't the effect that you want. Atteberry achieves many different effects by altering the top object in the blend. Sometimes he wants to create an irregular shape (the dragon's eyebrow shown), other times he wants to create feathering or shaped effects. He uses the Direct Selection and Pencil tools, as well as the Free Transform tool and other transformation tools, to substantially modify the top shape. Although he generally just distorts the object and moves around the positioning of points, he does sometimes add new ones (using the Add Anchor Point Tool or redrawing with the Pencil). After applying the blend, because it's live, Atteberry continues to adjust the positioning and shape of the top object with all the tools at his disposal until he achieves the desired effect.

4 **Adding finishing details.** After adding the blends to his images, Atteberry adds finishing details with solid-filled, gradient-filled, and stroked small accents. For this image, Atteberry even filled the line work with a gradient. The menacing teeth are on a layer above the line work.

2

Modifying a copy of the bottom object to create smooth blend transitions

3

Modifying the top object in blends to achieve special blending effects

4

The dragon with copied and modified versions in place, and after creating all of the blends

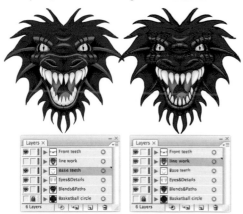

The final dragon with blends and details and then with the line work (still just in black) on a layer above (the front teeth are on the top layer)

Rolling Mesh

Converting Gradients to Mesh and Editing

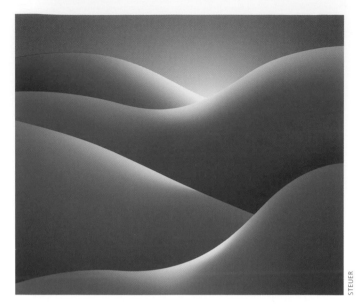

Overview: *Draw shapes and fill with linear gradients; expand gradient-filled objects into gradient meshes; use various tools to edit mesh points and colors.*

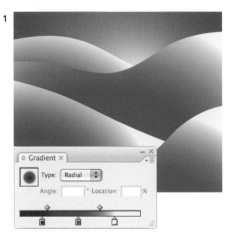

The hills shown filled with radial gradients—although there is some sense of light, it isn't possible to make the radial gradient follow the contours of the hills

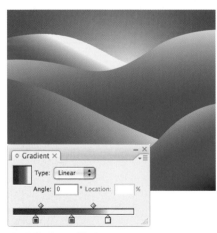

The hills shown filled with linear gradients, which are easier to edit than radial gradients when converted to gradient meshes

For many images, gradients can be useful for showing the gradual change of light to shadow (if you need to learn more about creating and applying gradient fills, first see "Unified Gradients" earlier in this chapter). For these rolling hills, artist Sharon Steuer expanded linear gradients into gradient mesh objects so she could better control the curves and contours of the color transitions.

1 Drawing shapes and then filling them with linear gradients. Begin your illustration by creating closed objects with any of the drawing tools. After completing the objects, select each object with the Selection tool and Fill it with a linear gradient fill. For each linear gradient, adjust the angle and length of the gradient transition with the Gradient tool until you can best approximate the desired lighting effect. Steuer created four hill-shaped objects with the Pen tool, filled them with the same linear gradient, then customized each with the Gradient tool. **Note:** *Although in some objects radial gradients might look better before you convert them, linear gradients create gradient mesh objects that are much easier to edit!*

2 Expanding linear gradients into gradient meshes. To create a more natural lighting of the hills, Steuer converted the linear gradients into mesh objects so the color transitions could follow the contours of the hills. To accomplish this, select all the gradient-filled objects that you wish to convert and choose Object > Expand. In the Expand dialog, make sure Fill is checked and specify Expand Gradient to Gradient Mesh. Then click OK. Illustrator converts each linear gradient into a rectangle rotated to the angle matching the linear gradient's angle; each mesh rectangle is masked by the original object (see the *Advanced Techniques* chapter for help with masks).

3 Editing meshes. You can use several tools to edit gradient mesh objects (use the Object > Lock/Unlock All toggle to isolate objects as you work). The Mesh tool combines the functionality of the Direct Selection tool with the ability to add mesh lines. With the Mesh tool, click *exactly on* a mesh anchor point to select or move that point or its direction handles. Or, click *anywhere* within a mesh, except on an anchor point, to add a new mesh point and gridline. You can also use the Add Anchor Point tool (click and hold to choose it from the Pen tool pop-up) to add a point without a gridline. To delete a selected anchor point, press the Delete key; if that point is a mesh point, the gridlines will be deleted as well.

Select points within the mesh using either the Mesh tool or the Lasso tool, using the Direct Selection tool to move multiple selected points. Move individual anchor points and adjust direction handles with the Mesh tool in order to reshape your gradient mesh gridlines. In this way, the color and tonal transitions of the gradient will match the contour of the mesh object. Recolor selected areas of the mesh by selecting points, then choosing a new color.

If you click in the area *between* mesh points with the Eyedropper tool while holding Option/Alt you'll add the Fill color to the four nearest mesh points.

By using these tools and editing techniques, Steuer was able to create hills with color and light variations that suggest the subtlety of natural light upon organic forms.

2

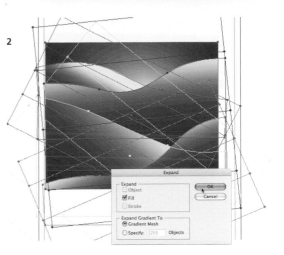

After Expanding the gradients into gradient mesh objects

3

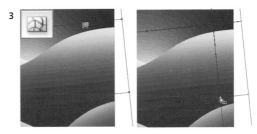

Using the Mesh tool to add a mesh line, then moving the mesh point with the Direct Selection tool

Using the Add Anchor Point tool, using the Lasso to select a point, moving selected point (or points) with the Direct Selection tool

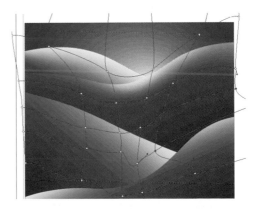

The final rearmost hill, shown after making mesh adjustments

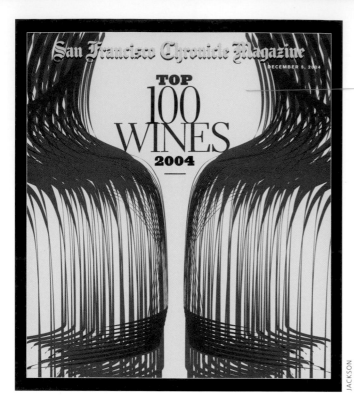

JACKSON

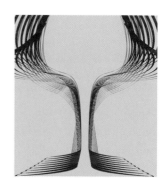

Lance Jackson / *San Francisco Chronicle Magazine*

For this *San Francisco Chronicle Magazine* cover, staff illustrator Lance Jackson made artistic use of blended brush strokes. Jackson customized a calligraphic brush and chose the Brush tool. Then with a pressure-sensitive tablet, he drew a simple, elegant, gestural silhouette evoking a wine goblet. Using a variety of tools, Jackson modified a copy of this silhouette. Selecting the original and modified strokes, he chose Object > Blend > Make (although you can blend live brush strokes, Jackson prefers to expand them first by using Object > Expand). While still selecting the blend he double-clicked the Blend tool to access Blend Options where he adjusted the number of Specified Steps. Next Jackson expanded the blend using Object > Blend > Expand (the expanded blend is automatically grouped). He then adjusted the position and shape of each blend object, and recolored the grouping. By copying these expanded groups, Jackson created new silhouettes, modifying colors and strokes. He created one side of the glass and used the Reflect tool to create the other silhouette by reflecting along the Vertical axis.

GORSKA

Caryl Gorska

Gradient fills with transparencies colorize this pencil sketch based on Les Usines by Fernand Léger. Caryl Gorska placed the black and white pencil sketch on a bottom layer and selected Filter > Colors > Adjust Colors to give the sketch an overall ocher hue (shown above). On a layer above the sketch Gorska drew the geometric shapes with the Pen tool. She filled the shapes with a variety of linear and radial gradients that shared the same five colors Gorska designated in the Swatches panel. With the Gradient panel open, Gorska dragged the colors from the Swatches panel to the gradient sliders and adjusted the stops. She applied the individual gradients to the shapes with the Gradient tool. Gorska adjusted the opacity ranging from 30% to 70% in the Transparency panel where she wanted the texture to show through the gradient. To further darken some areas she applied the blending mode of Multiply. The detailed image in the upper left shows the variety of gradients in the drawing without the texture of the pencil sketch underneath. For more about Transparency and Blending modes see the *Transparency* chapter.

Transparent Blend

Drawing Semiopaque Haze Effects

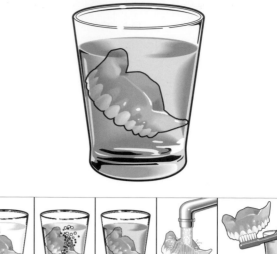

Advanced Technique

Overview: *Create blends that simulate colored water; apply a blending mode that allows objects in the water to be partially obscured.*

The main outlines of the dentures and tonal contours, drawn with the Pen tool (right)

Two denture paths before (left) and after (center) applying a blend using the Blend command

All denture paths before applying blends (left) and after applying blends (right)

The Blend tool provides complete control over both color and shape transitions. Scott Crouse drew these five-step instructions for a package of denture cleaning tablets. (The large glass above is a detail of step 3, and the final version includes captions.) Crouse used the Blend tool to model the complex surface of the dentures, and to show how the cleaning tablets color the water over time.

1 Drawing the dentures. Crouse used the drawing tools to hand-trace the dentures from an imported photo. To set up his sophisticated shading effects, Crouse precisely drew pairs of paths marking the key contours where specific gray tones start and end. Each pair of paths would become the starting and ending paths for a blend. For each pair, he first drew a larger path with a fill matching the overall color of the gums or teeth, and then in front of that path he drew a smaller path with the shape and fill color of a highlight or shadow on that surface.

2 Creating the denture blends. Crouse applied a blend to each pair of paths he drew earlier. To blend two paths, select them and choose Object > Blend > Make. The completed blend creates a smooth transition between paths.

3 Creating the effect of light through water. Like glass, water picks up and distorts ambient light and the colors and shadows from surrounding objects. Crouse found blends to be useful here too. As with the dentures, Crouse drew pairs of paths for blends, again shaping the paths in terms of light and dark. Crouse filled each pair's larger path with 8% to 20% black and each pair's smaller path with white, then blended each pair of paths.

4 Submerging the dentures. Crouse positioned the dentures in the glass. Next, he selected the water blends and chose Object > Arrange > Bring to Front to move them in front of the dentures. While the water blends were still selected, Crouse clicked Opacity in the Control panel to change the blending mode from Normal to Multiply. Applying Multiply to the blends partially darkened the dentures so that they appeared to be submerged.

5 Showing the change in water color. Steps 2 and 3 of Crouse's illustration had to show how the cleaning solution turns green as the cleaning tablets dissolve. The packaging was not printed in full color, so the concept had to be illustrated in grayscale. To duplicate the glass and dentures, Crouse selected and then Opt/Alt-dragged them, creating a copy. To color the water, he used the Direct Selection tool to select the gray-filled paths of each water blend, and used the Color panel to darken their gray fills to 40% black. When you change the attributes of a path used in a blend, the entire blend updates.

For his steps 2 and 3, Crouse also added a filled path to darken the water behind the dentures and blends. He also used the Ellipse tool to draw the cleaning tablet and bubbles in step two.

3

Paths making up the glass (left) and the same paths filled (right)

Paths added to create light and water effects with blends (selected at left) and after applying a blend to each pair of paths (right)

4

Blends selected (left), and then transparent after applying Multiply blending mode (right)

5

Steps 1 to 3 of the directions (top) and the changes at each step (bottom); selected paths that were darkened (bottom left), and the larger path added to darken the background (bottom center and bottom right)

When blends are better than gradients

While gradients are quick and easy to set up, they are only available as simple linear and radial forms. A great advantage of blends is that they follow the shape of the paths you draw, allowing complex modeling.

Molding Mesh

Forming Bottles Using Gradient Mesh

Advanced Technique

Overview: *Create a basic rectangle; add mesh lines; use the Scale tool to move points in tandem; use the Direct Selection tool to edit paths; color the mesh; add finishing details.*

Making a basic rectangle, adding mesh points where the shape will be contoured, using the Scale tool to move groups of points inward

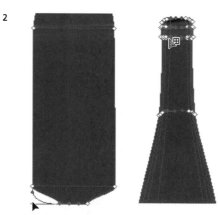

Using the Direct Selection tool to round curves, and adding new grid lines by clicking with the Gradient Mesh tool

Yukio Miyamoto is one of the world's experts in creating objects using the Gradient Mesh tool. This wonderful collection of bottles was created for the book and CD that he and his wife Nabuko Miyamoto write and produce; published in Japan, the *Adobe Illustrator CS* book is an amazing compendium of Illustrator techniques.

1 **Creating mesh from rectangles.** To create his complex mesh objects, Miyamoto begins with a colored rectangle. Then using the Gradient Mesh tool, he clicks on the rectangle to create basic horizontal mesh lines where he intends to modify the exterior shape of the object.

   To narrow the bottle neck, Miyamoto then used the Direct Selection tool to select the anchor points at the top of the bottle. With these points selected he switched to the Scale tool. By default the Scale tool is centered on the object, so he grabbed one of the selected points and holding the Shift key, dragged towards the center of the bottle, narrowing the neck symmetrically. He also selected the bottom two points and dragged the points inward. (For details on radically modifying rectangle mesh objects see "Modeling Mesh" in the *Advanced Techniques* chapter.)

2 **Shaping mesh objects.** To continue to transform your rectangle into a rounded bottle, you'll next modify the corner points along the edge into curves. Using the Convert Anchor Point tool (hidden under the Pen tool) and the Direct Selection tool, select anchor points, smooth

anchor points and modify the corners to rounded curves. Miyamoto smoothed curves at the bottom of the bottle, holding Shift to constrain the path curves.

With the new shape contour established, Miyamoto used the Gradient Mesh tool to click within the bottle to establish vertical mesh lines, aligned with the new curve at the bottom of the bottle.

3 **Modifying the mesh lines to create distortion, shadows and highlights.** Light reflects and refracts on glass bottles. Once the basic inner and outer topography of the bottle is in place, Miyamoto uses the Direct Selection tool to modify the mesh lines within the bottle to mimic the affects of light. Using the Direct Selection tool, select points and groups of points to adjust their position. Click on anchor points to activate their direction handles so you can modify the length and angle of the curves.

Once your mesh lines are in place, you can select individual or groups of points, or click in areas between points and adjust colors using the Color panel sliders. You can also click on a color swatch in the Swatches panel, or pick up colors from another object by clicking in on the color you want with the Eyedropper tool. Miyamoto used a photographic reference to help him decide where to place lights and darks.

4 **Creating finishing details.** Although Gradient Mesh objects are an astoundingly flexible and powerful drawing tool, sometimes it's necessary to create details in layers above the mesh object. To make selections and isolated viewings of the various objects easier, create new layers for your detail objects above your mesh objects. For the blue bottle (in a layer above the mesh), Miyamoto created a few punctuations of color and light using objects drawn with the Pen tool, and filled with solid colors or custom gradients. For his beer bottle Miyamoto created type shapes, for the small milk bottle he added additional rim colors, and for the green wine bottle he added more reflections and a raised inner bottom.

3

Coloring the bottle

The finished blue bottle mesh in outline, hidden, and in Preview with details on a layer above

4

The final bottles shown with the mesh layer in Outline mode, and the finishing details (mostly gradient-filled objects) in Preview mode

9

Transparency

You're introducing transparency whenever you apply an opacity percentage, a blending mode, an Opacity Mask from the Transparency or Control panels, and whenever you apply certain kinds of effects (such as shadows, feathers, and glows) or styles that include those features. It's easy to apply transparent effects to your artwork without actually understanding what takes place "under the hood." However, some knowledge about how transparency works will help you later when you print or export art that uses transparency.

If the concepts of *Appearances* or *Targeting* are new to you, it's very important that you start first with the "Appearances" section of the *Layers & Appearances* chapter. By the time you've arrived here at the *Transparency* chapter, the assumption is that you have a basic knowlege of fills, strokes, and layers in particular. If you find you become confused while reading this chapter, it may help to first revisit the *Drawing & Coloring* and *Layers & Appearances* chapters.

BASIC TRANSPARENCY

Although the Artboard may look white, Illustrator treats it as transparent. To visually distinguish the transparent areas from the non-transparent ones, choose View > Show Transparency Grid. To change the size and colors of the transparency grid, select File > Document Setup > Transparency. You can enable Simulate Colored Paper if you'll be printing on a colored stock (click on the top swatch next to Grid Size to open the color picker and select a "paper" color). Both Transparency Grid and paper color are non-printing attributes that are only visible in on-screen preview once you click OK to exit the dialog.

The term *transparency* refers to any Blending Mode other than Normal and to any opacity setting that is less than 100%. Opacity Masks or effects, such as Feather or Drop Shadow, use these settings as well. As a result, when

Use transparency with...

- **Fills**—apply an opacity, a blend mode, or an effect that utilizes transparency (e.g., Inner Glow).
- **Strokes**—just as with fills, apply an opacity, a blend mode, or an effect that utilizes transparency (e.g., Outer Glow).
- **Brush Strokes**—create scatter brushes, art brushes, and pattern brushes from transparent artwork, or make brush strokes (including calligraphic brush strokes) transparent by applying an opacity, blend mode, or effect that utilizes transparency.
- **Text**—apply transparency to selected text characters and/or the entire text object.
- **Charts**—apply transparency to the entire chart or the elements that make up the chart.
- **Groups**—select or target the <Group> and apply an opacity, a blend mode, or an effect that utilizes transparency (such as Feather). When you select an entire group, you will automatically be targeting the group.
- **Layers**—target the layer and apply an opacity, a blend mode, or an effect that utilizes transparency. —*Sandee Cohen and Pierre Louveaux*

you apply Opacity Masks or effects, you're using Illustrator's transparency features.

It can be tricky to print or export correctly when working with transparency. To make this easier, Illustrator has a few tools to help you control how transparency will translate when you print or export.

Opacity and Blending modes

To apply transparency, select or target an object, layer or group in the Layers panel, then choose a Blending Mode or reduce the Opacity slider in the Transparency or Control panels. An object or group is completely opaque when its opacity is set to 100%. It is completely see-through, or invisible, when its opacity is 0%.

Blending modes control how the colors of objects, groups, or layers interact with one another. Blending modes will yield different results in RGB and CMYK. As in Photoshop, the blending modes show no effect when they're over the *transparent* Artboard. To see the effect of blending modes, you need to add a color-filled or white-filled element behind your transparent object or group.

OPACITY MASKS

Opacity masks allow the dark and light areas in one object to be used as a mask for other objects. Black within the mask indicates areas of the masked artwork that will be completely transparent. White within the mask represents areas of the masked artwork that will be fully opaque and visible. Grays allow a range of transparency. (This works exactly like Photoshop *layer masks*.)

The easiest way to create an Opacity Mask is to first create the artwork you want to mask. Next, place the object, group, or raster image you want to use as the mask on top of it. Select the artwork and the masking element, and choose Make Opacity Mask from the Transparency panel pop-up menu. Illustrator automatically makes the topmost object or group the Opacity Mask.

You may want to start with an empty mask and draw into it—in effect, painting your objects into visibility. To

Transparency is cumulative

The ultimate apprearance of transparency is determined by the combination of objects, groups, sublayers, and container layers. **Note:** *To clear all effects for the multiple levels, you must target each level in the Layers panel and click the Clear Appearance icon.*

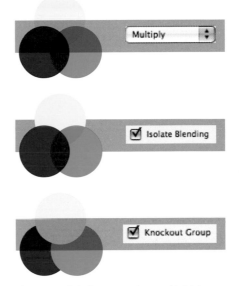

The group of circles at top shows a Multiply blending mode applied to each individual circle; middle shows after enabling Isolate Blending to confine the blending mode to objects within the group; bottom shows after enabling Knockout Group to keep objects within the group from applying their blending mode to each other

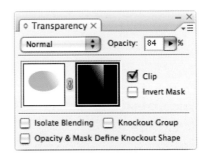

The Transparency panel with all options shown (choose Show Options from the Transparency panel menu)

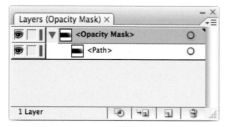

Objects being masked by an Opacity Mask are indicated by a dashed line in the Layers panel

Opacity Masks are indicated with < (less than), and > (greater than) symbols in the Layers panel if you click on the Opacity Mask thumbnail in the Transparency panel

create an empty mask, start by targeting a single object, group, or layer. Since the default behavior of new Opacity Masks is clipping (with a black background), you'll need to turn off the "New Opacity Masks Are Clipping" option in the Transparency panel menu or your targeted artwork will completely disappear when you first create the empty mask. Next, choose Show Thumbnails from the Transparency panel menu, and double-click in the right thumbnail area. This creates an empty mask and puts you in mask-editing mode; the Layers panel changes to show the Opacity Mask. Use your drawing and editing tools to create your mask. (For instance, if you create an object filled with a gradient, you'll see your artwork through the dark areas of the gradient.) While the Opacity Mask thumbnail is selected, you won't be able to select or edit anything else in your document because Illustrator puts you into a kind of isolation mode. To exit this mask-editing (isolation) mode, you must click the artwork thumbnail in the Transparency panel (the artwork thumbnail is on the left; the Opacity Mask is on the right).

A few hints can help you with Opacity Masks. First, Opacity Masks are converted to grayscale, behind the scenes, when a mask is created (even though the Opacity Mask thumbnail still appears in color). The gray values between white and black simply determine how opaque or transparent the masked object is—light areas of the mask will be more opaque and dark areas will be more transparent. In addition, if you select Invert Mask, you'll reverse the effect of dark and light values on the opacity—dark areas of the mask will be more opaque and light areas will be more transparent. To identify which elements have been masked by an Opacity Mask, look for the dashed underline in the Layers panel.

The link icon in the Transparency panel indicates that the position of the Opacity Mask stays associated with the position of the object, group, or layer it is masking. Unlinking allows you to move the artwork without moving the mask. The content of the mask can be selected and edited just like any other object. You can transform or apply a blending mode and/or an opacity percentage to each individual object within the mask.

Option-click/Alt-click on an Opacity Mask thumbnail in the Transparency panel to hide the document's contents and display only the masking element in its grayscale values. Shift-click the Opacity Mask thumbnail to disable the Opacity Mask.

For more on Opacity masks, see the "Opacity Masks 101" and "Opacity Collage" lessons in this chapter, and lessons and galleries in the *Advanced Techniques* chapter.

Knockout controls

Choose Show Options from the Transparency panel pop-up menu to display the checkboxes that control how transparency is applied to groups and multiple objects. You can also click on the word Opacity in the Control panel to show these settings.

With a group or layer targeted, check the Knockout Group option to keep individual objects of the group or layer from applying their transparency settings to each other where they overlap. This is particularly useful for blends containing one or more transparent objects. For this reason, Illustrator automatically enables the Knockout Group option for all newly created blends.

If you enable Isolate Blending for a selected group, then the transparency settings of the objects inside the group only affect how those objects interact with each other, and transparency isn't applied to objects underneath the group.

The final checkbox, Opacity & Mask Define Knockout Shape, is used in very specific situations to limit the knockout of a color to the area defined by the opacity and the mask. To see any effect, you must use this option on a transparent object inside a knockout group.

This option is most useful on raster images and feathered edges. It's automatically enabled for Drop Shadow, Blur, Feather, and Photoshop effects. If it weren't, putting objects with these effects in knockout groups would produce unwanted results: The entire rectangular

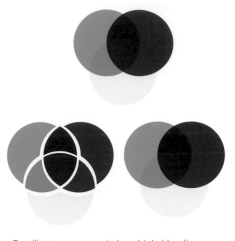

Top (live transparency): A multiply blending mode applied to each individual circle; Bottom Left (flattened transparency, exploded view): Flattening the three circles results in seven separate regions; Bottom right (flattened transparency, non-exploded view): The final printed circles appear the same as the original non-flattened version

The Flattener Preview panel with all options showing (choose Show Options from the panel menu), including the Flattening Preset settings in the center of the panel. Click the Refresh button at the top of the panel, and the current document will be displayed in the preview area at the bottom of the screen. The section "Using the Flattener Preview panel" explains how to use this preview to highlight areas of your art that flattening will affect.

bounding box of Drop Shadows, Blurs, and Photoshop effects would knock out, as would the unfeathered outline of Feathered objects.

THE ART OF FLATTENING

PostScript printing devices and file formats such as EPS can only reproduce transparent artwork in "flattened" form. Illustrator's flattening process is applied temporarily if you print, and permanently if you save in a format that doesn't support transparency natively (transparency was first introduced in Illustrator 9). Flattening occurs when areas of transparent overlap are converted into opaque pieces that look the same. Some of your objects may be split into many separate objects, while others may be rasterized.

Using the Flattener Preview panel

Illustrator's Flattener Preview panel (Window > Flattener Preview) lets you see how flattening will affect your art. The Flattener Preview panel lets you highlight areas of your artwork that will be affected when you flatten it, so you can see the effect of various settings and adjust them accordingly.

To begin, choose a preview mode from the panel menu: either Quick Preview (which gives you the fastest preview, but excludes the All Rasterized Regions option in the Highlight menu) or Detailed Preview (which enables All Rasterized Regions). Then choose an option from the Overprint menu: Preserve, to retain overprinting; Simulate, to imitate the appearance of printing to separations; or Discard, to prevent any Overprint Fill or Overprint Stroke settings that have been set in the Attributes panel from appearing on the composite.

Now you're ready to choose a flattening preset from the Preset menu (or create a new one), as described later in the "Working with Flattener Presets" section. When you've done that, click the Refresh button at the top of the panel, which will update the display in the panel's preview area according to the settings you've chosen.

At this point, you can use the panel's Highlight menu to highlight areas that will be affected by the flattening process. You can choose from a variety of options—from All Affected Objects to specifics such as Outlined Strokes or Outlined Text. You'll see the areas in question flagged in red in the preview pane. See *Illustrator Help* for more details about the various Highlight Options, and other aspects of using the Flattener Preview panel.

The Flatten Transparency dialog (Object > Flatten Transparency) and the Advanced section of the Print dialog both let you change transparency and flattening settings. The Transparency Flattener Presets dialog (Edit > Transparency Flattener Presets) also gives you quick access to your presets (this is discussed further in the "Working with Flattener Presets" section following this one), allowing you to edit existing custom presets and create new ones.

Here are the flattening options you can adjust:

- **Name** lets you name settings to be saved as a preset.
- **Raster/Vector Balance** lets you control the degree to which your artwork is rasterized (discussed in greater detail in the "Setting Raster/Vector Balance" section a little further on in this chapter).
- **Line Art and Text Resolution** sets the resolution for vector objects that will be rasterized when flattening.
- **Gradient and Mesh Resolution** lets you set the resolution for gradient and mesh objects that will be rasterized in the course of flattening.
- **Convert All Text to Outlines** keeps the width of text consistent during flattening by converting all type objects to outlines and discarding glyph information.
- **Convert All Strokes to Outlines** ensures that the width of objects stays consistent during flattening by converting all strokes to simple filled paths.
- **Clip Complex Regions** reduces stitching artifacts by making sure that the boundaries between vector artwork and rasterized artwork fall along object paths.
- **Preserve Alpha Transparency** (Flatten Transparency dialog only) preserves the alpha transparency of flattened

The Advanced section of the Print dialog (choose File > Print, then select Advanced in the menu just above the preview)

The Flatten Transparency dialog (Object > Flatten Transparency)

The Transparency Flattener Presets dialog (Edit > Transparency Flattener Presets)

The Transparency Flattener Preset Options (New) dialog that results when you click the New button in the Transparency Flattener Presets dialog (above)

Click the Custom button in the Advanced section of the Print dialog to display the Custom Transparency Flattener Options dialog, where you can create a new custom preset

The Flattener Preview panel's Highlight pop-up

The Flattener Preview panel with artwork highlighted in red in its preview area, after choosing All Affected Objects from the Highlight menu

objects, which can be useful if you are exporting to SWF or SVG.

• **Preserve Overprints and Spot Colors** (Flatten Transparency dialog only) preserves spot colors and overprinting for objects that aren't involved in transparency.

To access these settings in the Flattener Preview panel, open the panel and choose Show Options from the panel menu. In the Flatten Transparency dialog, you can select any existing preset as a starting point and then make changes in the dialog. In the Advanced section of the Print dialog, choose any existing Preset from the Presets menu and click the Custom button to change the settings. See *Illustrator Help* for more details about Illustrator's flattening options.

Working with Flattener Presets

Once you've adjusted any of the settings in the Flattner Preview panel, you can save the results as a preset, so you won't have to create them from scratch the next time you want to apply the same flattening settings (or create a slight variation).

Illustrator comes with three default presets to get you started: High Resolution (for final press output and high-quality proofs such as color separations), Medium Resolution (for desktop proofs and print-demand-documents to be printed on PostScript color printers), and Low Resolution (for quick proofs to be printed on black-and-white desktop printers). You can't edit these default presets, but you can use them as a starting point, making changes and saving them as your own custom presets.

You can create and save your own custom flattening presets in any of the four following ways:

• **Using the Flattener Preview panel:** Select an existing preset from the Preset menu. Make your changes to its settings in the panel (choose Show Options from the panel pop-up menu if they aren't visible), and then choose Save Transparency Flattener Preset from the panel menu. Give your new preset a name and click OK. (If the existing preset you chose isn't one of the predefined default presets, you can also choose to apply your changes as an edit to that preset by choosing Redefine Preset.)

- **Using the Object > Flatten Transparency dialog:** Choose an existing preset from the Presets drop-down menu, adjust the settings in the box, and click Save Preset to name and save your new settings.
- **Using the Edit > Transparency Flattener Presets dialog:** Click the New button to create and name a new preset; click the Edit button to make changes to an existing (non-default) preset.
- **Using the Advanced section of the Print dialog:** Under the Overprint and Transparency Flattener Options heading, click the Custom button next to the Preset drop-down menu to create a custom preset. Click the Save Preset button at the bottom of the Print dialog to name and save your settings into a new print preset. This option will not save a separate Transparency Flattener Preset.

To apply flattening presets when you're ready to print or export, choose an existing preset (or create a new custom preset) in the Advanced section of the Print dialog.

Setting Raster/Vector Balance

The Raster/Vector Balance setting (one of the flattening settings mentioned in "The Art of Flattening" earlier in this chapter) determines how much art is rasterized and how much remains vector. In case you're unfamiliar with the terms, raster art is made up of pixels, while vectors are discrete objects. These days, most programs contain aspects of both vectors and rasters, but Photoshop is primarily raster and Illustrator primarily vector.

By default, Illustrator's Raster/Vector Balance setting is 100—which results in the greatest possible amount of art remaining in vector form. At the highest setting, the file contains the most vector objects and may produce longer print times. As you move the slider to the left, toward zero, Illustrator tries to convert vectors (like pure Illustrator files) to rasters (like Photoshop files). At a setting of zero, Illustrator converts *all* art to raster. Usually, you get the best results using the all-vector

Object > Flatten Transparency > Save Preset

More than one way to preview

Keep in mind that the Flattener Preview panel isn't intended for precise viewing of spot colors, overprints, or blending modes. Instead, use Overprint Preview mode to preview how those features will appear upon output.

Flattener Preview tools

To magnify the preview in the Flattener Preview panel, click anywhere on it with the default Zoom (magnifying glass) tool. To zoom back out, press the Option-Alt key as you click. To change the Zoom tool to the Hand tool so you can move the preview around, just hold down the spacebar and drag anywhere on the preview.

Resolution of live effects

The Flattener Preview panel can't help you fix everything that affects the output of your file. For instance, if you've applied a live effect with a specific resolution, in order to increase its resolution you'll need to reapply your effect at the resolution you desire (see the *Live Effects & Graphic Styles* chapter for more on applying live effects).

The Illustrator Save Adobe PDF dialog, showing the different PDF versions you can choose (File > Save/Save As, then choose Adobe PDF from the Format menu and click Save)

setting of 100, but if this takes too long to print, try the all-raster setting of 0. In some cases, when transparent effects are very complex, this might be the best choice. Generally, the in-between settings create awful results.

Because objects are always flattened to a white background, you might see color shifts after you flatten your artwork. To preview the way your artwork would look if flattened, you can turn on Simulate Paper (Document Setup > Transparency) or Overprint Preview (in the View menu), and you can use the Flattener Preview panel to highlight the areas that would be affected.

Using the Appearance and Layers panels

Although Transparency can be tracked using the Flattener Preview panel, it is virtually impossible to decipher exactly what level and type of transparency has been applied to individual objects and groups without referring to the Appearance and Layers panels. This is because you can apply transparency to individual strokes and fills, objects, sub-groups, groups, sub-layers, and layers. For example, you can apply a blending mode to an object, then group it with several other objects and apply an opacity level to that group. Later, you might even apply another blending mode or change the opacity of the layer containing that group.

To determine the level and type of the applied transparency, you'll first need to detect the location of the applied transparency. With the Appearance panel visible, use the Direct or Group Selection tool to click on an object within a group where you suspect that transparency has been applied. Looking at the Appearance panel will indicate whether transparency has been applied to the base object, or its fills and/or strokes; but the presence of the Transparency icons on the panel for the group and/or layer will show that cumulative transparency has been applied. Once you've determined the location of the transparency, you can use the Layers panel to locate active target icons, and look in the Appearance panel to find the type of applied transparency or effect.

FISHAUF

Louis Fishauf / Reactor Art + Design

Louis Fishauf created the holiday glow that radiates from his mischievous Santa by using Illustrator's Gaussian Blur effect, the Transparency panel, and one of a set of custom art brushes. Fishauf created the background by drawing a large circle with a purple radial gradient and applied a 25-pixel radius Gaussian Blur. He selected the Star tool and drew a shape. He then selected Blur > Gaussian from the Effect menu, setting the Opacity to 25%. To create the illusion that the orbiting streak fades into the distance behind Santa, and to add a sense of depth to the entire image, Fishauf applied an art brush he created with short tapered ends to a 0.36-pt white stroke. He then integrated the streak into the image by giving it an opacity of 34% with the Lighten

mode. As for St. Nick, Fishauf constructed the globe-like body, legs, arms, head, and hat from gradient-filled objects. He then made copies of these and pasted them behind the original set of objects, applying to each a white Fill and white Stroke ranging from 5 points to 7.26 points. A Gaussian Blur was applied to these objects, along with a uniform opacity of 68%. The gift box, computer, and Christmas tree each received individual glows. Fishauf added even more visual interest by adding a Drop Shadow to Santa's face and beard. Santa's list was created from a set of white Strokes, behind which Fishauf pasted a white-filled shape with an Opacity set to 50%, and a second copy of the shape with a gradient fill set to Lighten mode for a subtle modeled effect.

Transparent Color

Customizing Transparent Brushes & Layers

Overview: *Create customized Calligraphic brushes; set Paintbrush Tool preferences; assign basic Transparency to individual strokes and layers; use selections to easily choose brush styles; use layers to organize different types of strokes.*

1

Customize the settings for each new Calligraphic brush using the Brush Options window

Four custom Calligraphic brushes in List view (from the Brushes panel pop-up menu)

Adjusting the Opacity slider to preset the default opacity for the next brush; for quick and convenient access to the Opacity setting, use the Opacity slider in the Control panel

Illustrator provides an extremely forgiving way to create transparent "watercolor-like" marks. Unlike traditional media, or even digital tools such as Adobe Photoshop or Corel Painter, individual marks can be easily altered after the fact. In painting "Cyclamen in winter," artist Sharon Steuer used a few custom Calligraphic brushes, Transparency settings to adjust the appearance of overlapping marks, and Layers to control whether marks would be made above or below previous ones.

1 Creating custom Calligraphic brushes and setting the Opacity. You'll first customize a few brushes so you can better control the size of the marks you make. If you have a pressure-sensitive tablet, you can customize brushes so they respond to your touch. To make the first brush, start a new file, then open the Brushes panel and click the New Brush icon at the bottom of the panel. Select New Calligraphic Brush, and click OK. In the resulting Calligraphic Brush Options window, experiment with various settings, then click OK and make a stroke to test the brush. For her first custom brush, Steuer chose a Pressure setting for Diameter (9 pt with a 9-pt Random Variation), set the Angle to 60° and the Roundness to 60% with both Fixed, and clicked OK. For greater stroke variation, try choosing Pressure or Random options (pressure settings are unavailable and don't work unless you have a pressure-sensitive graphics tablet installed). To create additional brush variations, drag a custom brush over the New Brush icon in the Brushes panel and double-click the desired brush to adjust the settings.

To set the defaults for your next brush stroke and to paint in transparent color, first choose a Calligraphic brush and stroke color, then set the Opacity setting in the Control panel. To set opacity, click and hold the triangle to the right of the Opacity field to reveal the Opacity slider, which you can adjust. Alternatively, you can click on the word "Opacity" in the Control panel, which temporarily reveals the Transparency panel, or you can adjust the opacity and other transparency settings in the floating Transparency panel.

2 Setting Paintbrush Tool Preferences. In addition to creating your initial custom brushes, you'll need to set the Paintbrush Tool Preferences so you can freely make overlapping brush strokes. Double-click on the Paintbrush tool, then disable the Options "Fill new brush strokes" (so your brush strokes will be stroked and not filled) and "Keep Selected" (so new strokes won't redraw the last drawn stroke). With the "Keep Selected" option disabled, you can still repaint a stroke by selecting it first with a selection tool, then drawing a corrected mark within the distance specified in the Within field of the Paintbrush Tool Preferences dialog. To create accurate marks, Steuer set the Fidelity to .5 pixels and the Smoothness to 0%. If you want Illustrator to smooth your marks, experiment with higher settings.

3 Painting and using the last selected object to determine the next brush style. For this step to work, you must turn off the New Art Has Basic Appearance feature (it's on by default); toggle it on/off in the Appearance panel. One of the wonderful aspects of working with Illustrator is that your last selected object determines the appearance for the next object you paint. To see how this works, select

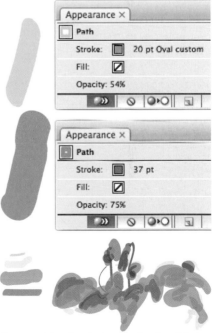

2 · Setting the Paintbrush Tool Preferences to prevent new brush strokes from filling and to prevent redraw of marks already made

3 · To make sure that any settings are maintained after each completed stroke, turn off the New Art Has Basic Appearance feature

Steuer continually selects a previously painted stroke so the appearance settings from that selection are remembered for the next stroke. Working this way allows her to quickly change brushes and colors as she paints

4

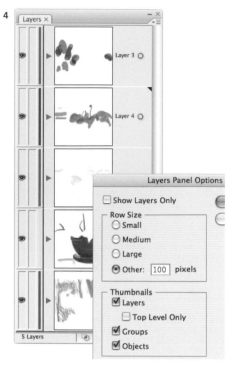

By changing the size of the thumbnails in the Layers panel (from the Layers panel pop-up), it's easier for Steuer to identify each kind of stroke and what layer it's on

5

Steuer selected the layer containing a batch of flowers and experimented with different Blending Modes and Opacity settings until she was satisfied with their appearance

one of your brushes and start to paint. Notice that the brush, stroke color, and opacity you choose will continue to apply after you complete each stroke. By selecting a specific stroke that's similar to the one you want to create next, you can minimize the time it takes to customize your next brush stroke.

4 Using layers to organize different types of strokes. To organize your artwork, keep sets of similar brush strokes in their own layers. When you are ready to make more strokes, create a new layer for them (click the New Layer icon). If you want the new set of strokes to be underneath a previous set, drag that layer below the layer containing the previous strokes. By keeping your layers organized in this way, you can use layer thumbnails to easily identify different strokes and manage the placement of new strokes. You can use layers to hide, lock, delete, and select groups of similar strokes efficiently.

Since Illustrator remembers the layer of the last selected object, your brush strokes will remain conveniently organized into separate layers. For instance, say you select a petal, then deselect it by clicking outside of the object itself (or ⌘-Shift-A/Ctrl-Shift-A): The next stroke you make will be placed at the top of the same layer. If you want the new stroke to be placed on a different layer, first select the desired layer, then begin painting.

5 Assigning Opacity and Blending Modes to selected layers. Once you have organized different types of brush strokes into separate layers, you have the opportunity to globally adjust the Opacity and Blending Mode on entire layers. For example, after creating a batch of flowers on one layer, Steuer wanted them to appear brighter, so she changed the Blending Mode and Opacity for the entire layer by first clicking that layer's targeting circle (this selects and targets all objects within a layer, allowing any transparency settings to be applied to the entire layer). After changing the Blending Mode from Normal to Color Burn, she reduced the opacity to 55%.

Sharon Steuer (Film by Frank Jacoby)

Artist Sharon Steuer created an opening sequence test for filmmaker Frank Jacoby's short film "Le Kiosk" by combining calligraphic brushwork with the opening still of the film. Working in RGB, she placed a TIF still (captured from Apple's Final Cut video editing program) into Illustrator as a Template. After copying brush marks containing custom "pressure sensitive" calligraphic brushes from another file, she pasted these marks into a layer above her template, automatically placing the brushes into the Brushes panel. Steuer mixed a sienna brown color, saved it as a swatch, and named it "Kiosk." Using the Control panel, she set the Blending mode to Multiply, reduced the Opacity to 80% and drew the outline of the kiosk. In new layers below the kiosk outline, she drew the background and foreground elements. Steuer selected all the marks in one of the layers (by clicking the space to the right of the layer target icon) and then created new colors for the brush marks on that layer by Option/Alt clicking the New Swatch icon. In the resulting Swatch Options dialog she enabled Preview to see the results as she mixed a new color. By enabling Global, she could easily change the color to automatically update the color (and the marks with that color). To create the transition from drawing to opening video, Steuer duplicated the template layer (by dragging it over the New Layer icon), double-clicked it to disable the Template option, and moved it above the drawing layers. After experimenting, she set this layer to Hard Light at 40%, then duplicated the layer and saved the file. Using File > Export, Steuer saved each of five stages (building from line drawing to full image) as a TIF, and then imported them all into Final Cut.

Basic Highlights

Making Highlights with Transparent Blends

STEUER

Overview: *Create your basic objects and a light-colored highlight shape; use blends to make the highlights; scale the highlights to fit.*

1

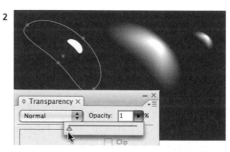

The original objects (locked in the Layers panel) shown with the basic highlight shape

2

The highlight objects before blending (the outer object is set to 0% Opaque in the Transparency panel); after blending in 22 steps; the blend shown at actual size

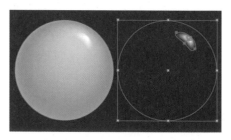

The final blend in place and shown in a "registration" circle for easy scaling on other bubbles

Using transparency, highlights are now as simple as creating a blend in the correct highlight shape. If you'd like help creating smooth contoured blends, see the *Blends, Gradients & Mesh* chapter.

1 Creating your basic objects and determining your basic highlight shape and color. Artist Sharon Steuer created this "Bubbles" image using overlaying transparent radial gradients (to see how she created the hill, see "Rolling Mesh" in the *Blends, Gradients & Mesh* chapter). She modified an oval with the Direct Selection tool to create her basic highlight shape. After creating your main objects, make a light-colored highlight object on top. Use the Layers panel to lock everything except the highlighted object (see the *Layers* chapter for help).

2 Creating the highlight. Select the highlight shape, copy it, choose Edit > Paste in Back, then Object > Lock. Now, select and shrink the front copy (for scaling help see the *Zen* chapter). Choose Object > Unlock All, then set the Opacity of this selected larger object to 0% in the Transparency panel. Select both objects, then with the Blend tool, click on one anchor point of the larger object, then Option/Alt-click on the corresponding anchor point of the smaller object and specify the number of blend steps (Steuer chose 22 steps). Steuer scaled copies of her highlight blend (with a "registration circle") for each bubble.

CASSELL / 1185 DESIGN

Peter Cassell / 1185 Design

Peter Cassell's European cityscape, commissioned for an Adobe Illustrator packaging illustration, was built with mists he created using a gradient mesh as an Opacity Mask. After drawing the rough shapes of reflections in the water, Cassell drew a rectangle in a layer above the water and filled the rectangle with white. He copied the rectangle, pasted it in front, filled it with black, and then selected Object > Create Gradient Mesh to turn it into an 18 x 15 mesh. He edited the mesh by selecting mesh points with the Direct Selection tool and filling the points with gray values varying from 30%

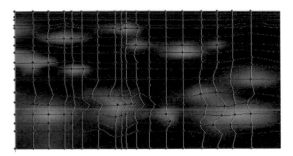

to 50% black. To shape a mist, he selected and moved mesh points. To mask the white rectangle with the gradient mesh above it, Cassell selected the mesh and the rectangle and chose Make Opacity Mask from the Transparency panel's pop-up menu.

Opacity Masks 101

Transparency Masks for Blending Objects

Overview: *Create a simple mask and apply it to an object; refine transparency by adding controlled masking with a precise Opacity Mask; choose Opacity Mask options.*

1

Drawing the object that will become the glow around the match, and the gradient-filled object that will become the object's Opacity Mask

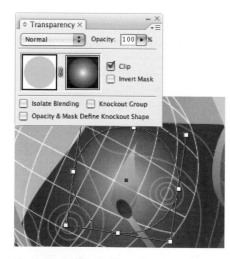

The semitransparent object after adding a gradient-filled Opacity Mask

Christiane Beauregard's illustrations often depend upon the intertwining and overlapping of objects to convey connections between ideas and elements. She frequently uses transparency to express those connections in a direct, visual manner, and depends upon Opacity Masks to control more precisely the extent of the transparency than the Opacity setting allows. In "Global Warming," Beauregard used Opacity Masks to immerse her objects in their surroundings.

1 Creating and applying a Opacity Mask. Beauregard expressed one aspect of global warming by showing her subject holding a match to the globe. To create the glow, she first drew a circle filled with a yellow-orange. Next she drew a circle directly on top and fully covering the first circle so that transparency would carry to the very edges of the glow. She filled it with the White, Black Radial gradient. She selected both circles, opened the Transparency panel's pop-up menu, and chose Make Opacity Mask. This automatically placed the top object (the gradient-filled circle) in the right thumbnail pane to make the mask. The glow is fully visible where the mask is white, transparent where it's gray, and invisible where it's black. You can use colored artwork for the masking object, but the mask only uses the luminosity values of the hues.

2 **Combining transparency with a precisely constructed Opacity Mask.** For several objects, Beauregard used both transparency (to blend objects with the objects below), and an opacity mask for localized, typically gradated, transparency. She created the effect of the fish's tail fading into the water by drawing a separate object filled with white for the tip of the tail. So that the mask would align precisely with its path, she copied the tail path and used Paste in Front (⌘-F/Ctrl-F) to create the mask object. This time she filled the mask with the White, Black linear gradient, using the Gradient tool to adjust it so that it faded to black at the tip. With both objects selected, she chose Make Opacity Mask to place the gradient-filled path into the Transparency panel's mask pane. She could further adjust the opacity of the masked object using the Opacity slider in the Transparency panel, or even toggle the mask on and off by Shift-clicking the mask pane.

3 **Clipping and non-clipping masks.** Because Beauregard's masks typically are either contoured to the objects they mask, or are larger than the object, she doesn't normally bother to alter the default setting of New Opacity Masks Are Clipping, since clipping will not clip off any portion of the masked object. If the masking object is the exact same size or larger, and in the same position, a clipping mask affects transparency only. If the mask is smaller than the object being masked, enabling the option will clip the object. At any time, she can change a mask's clipping behavior with the Clip checkbox, and choose to invert the mask then as well, if an object is inadvertently being clipped or the transparency needs to be reversed.

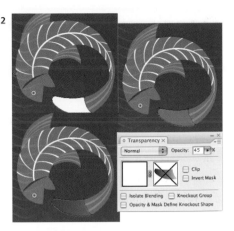

2

Original object, copied and pasted into mask; mask disabled (above right) and enabled (below), with object's Opacity lowered

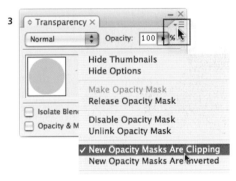

3

Choosing default settings for creating Opacity Masks through the Transparency panel pop-up menu

Objects that make masks

Opacity Masks can be made from any artwork, whether comprised of a single object or several. These objects can be distorted, filtered, stroked or otherwise manipulated like any normal object. They can even have their own Opacity Masks. However, only the luminosity values of the masking object will determine the masked object's transparency.

Floating Type

Type Objects with Transparency & Effects

⊙

Overview: *Create an area type object, key in text; add a new fill attribute in the Appearance panel; convert the fill to a shape; change transparency and add an Effect.*

GORDON / CARTAGRAM, LLC

1

Top, the Selection tool (at right selected); bottom, the Type tool in the Toolbox (right selected)

BRYCE CANYON
Navajo Loop (Sunset Point)
1.3 miles (2.2 km) / 521 ft (159 m)
Moderate Hike: 1 to 2 hours
Attractions: Thors Hammer,
Two Bridges, Wall Street

The type object after clicking with the Selection tool (the background photograph has been hidden in this view)

2

Appearance ×
☐ Type
   Stroke: ▨
   Characters
   Fill: ☐
   Default Transparency

The Appearance panel after selecting the fill attribute and applying white to it

Using the Convert to Shape effect, you can create an area type object with transparency and effects that will save you from making and manipulating two objects (a type object and a rectangle with transparency and effects below it). For a virtual guide to Bryce Canyon National Park, Steven Gordon created a transparent area type object with a hard-edged drop shadow that provided information for each of the Park's most popular hiking trails.

1 Making the area type object. Start by selecting the Type tool, dragging it to create an area type object, and then keying in your text. When you have finished typing, click on the Selection tool (the solid arrow icon) in the Toolbox. This deselects the text characters while selecting the type object, preparing the object (rather than the characters) for editing in the next step.

2 Creating a new fill and converting to a shape. Open the Appearance panel and select Add New Fill from the panel menu. Drag the new Fill attribute below Characters in the panel. The Fill attribute will be automatically deselected when you move it in the panel so you'll need to click on it again to select it. Next, apply a light color to it (Gordon chose white from the Swatches panel). Now choose Effect > Convert to Shape > Rectangle. In the Shape Options dialog, control the size of the rectangle around your type object by modifying the two Relative options (Extra Width and Extra Height). To make the shape wrap more tightly around his area type object, Gordon keyed in 0 inches for the Extra Width and Extra Height options.

3 Adjusting transparency and adding a drop shadow effect. Gordon designed each trail information box to incorporate transparency and a drop shadow, so its text would float above, but not obscure, the background photograph. To adjust the transparency of the shape you converted in the previous step, first ensure that the type object's Fill or Rectangle attribute is selected in the Appearance panel. (If either attribute is not selected, then the transparency changes that you're about to make will also affect the text characters.) Open the Transparency panel and adjust the transparency slider, or key in a value (Gordon chose 65% for transparency).

Instead of creating a soft drop shadow, Gordon opted to make a hard-edged shadow. To create this shadow, make sure the Fill attribute is still selected in the Appearance panel. Choose Effect > Stylize > Drop Shadow and in the Drop Shadow dialog set Color to black, Blur to 0, and then adjust the X Offset and Y Offset sliders so the shadow is positioned as far down and to the right as you wish.

4 Editing the area type object. As you continue working, you may decide to resize the type object you originally created when you dragged with the Type tool. (This is different from editing the Shape Options dialog values to change the size of the transparent rectangle around the type object, as you did previously.) To resize the object, choose the Direct Selection tool and click on the edge of the type object you want to resize, then drag the side of the object inward to make it smaller, or outward to enlarge it. Because the transparent drop shadow shape was formed using the Convert to Shape effect, it is "live" and will automatically resize as you resize the type object.

Similarly, if you edit the text by adding or deleting words, the type object will resize, causing your transparent drop shadow shape to resize automatically.

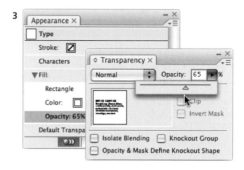

The Shape Options dialog with the Relative options edited

3

Left, the Appearance panel with the transparency attribute selected; right, the Transparency panel

The Drop Shadow dialog

4

The Direct Selection cursor when it nears the edge of an area type object

Getting an edge

It can be hard to click the edge of a type object that has a drop shadow. To easily find the edge, choose View > Outline. Now the selectable edge will display as a black line. Alternatively, turn on Smart Guides (View menu).

Glass and Chrome

Highlights and Shadows with Transparency

Advanced Technique

Overview: *Apply transparency to white to simulate a glass highlight, and reinforce overall lighting by combining the Multiply blending mode with an underlying gradient.*

Kelley's hand-tracing without the reflected highlights and shadows, shown in Outline mode (left) and Preview mode (right)

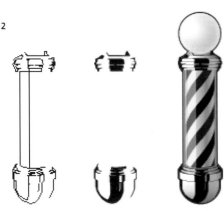

The glass highlight and chrome reflection shapes shown in Outline mode (left), Preview mode (center), and in position over the finished barber pole (right)

The transparency and blending modes in Illustrator can greatly enhance the look of glass and chrome reflections. Andrea Kelley created this barber pole illustration for a business card designed by Jodie Stowe. To heighten the realism of the barber pole, Kelley used Illustrator's transparency features to reproduce the long, clean highlights that appear when glass and chrome reflect ambient lighting and surrounding objects. The finished business card was die-cut along the barber pole edge to set it apart from other business cards. You can use this technique by Kelley to create convincing glass and chrome highlights.

1 Placing the template image and tracing the pole. Kelley was given a JPEG image of the original barber pole art, which was a useful reference for getting the alternating blue and red stripes just right as they wrapped around the pole. She placed the JPEG image as a template and then used the Pen tool and other drawing tools to hand-trace the objects making up the barber pole. To draw the perfectly round, white light globe on top of the pole, Kelley Shift-dragged the Ellipse tool. At this point, the chrome and glass reflections hadn't been traced yet.

2 Tracing the reflections. Next, Kelley traced the reflections—the highlight in the glass cylinder, and the dark reflections in the chrome at the bottom of the barber pole. Kelley recognized that the highlight was vertically continuous throughout the glass and chrome, so she made sure to position and align her highlight and reflection paths accordingly. She filled the glass highlight with white, and filled the dark chrome reflections with black.

To model the lighting on the frosted light globe, Kelley applied a radial gradient between white and warm gray (Kelley used 12.8% C, 12.8% Y, 16% M, 18% K), and also added a slight Inner Glow effect. To add a shine to the chrome base, Kelley applied a linear gradient between the same light gray as above, and a medium gray (16% C, 16% Y, 20% M, 16% K).

3 Applying transparency to the highlight shape. To reveal the objects under the glass highlight, Kelley selected the highlight and used the Transparency panel to apply an Opacity value of 50%.

4 Unifying the lighting. Kelley reinforced the overall lighting by combining the Multiply blending mode with a gradient to create a soft, vertical shadow along the entire right side of the pole. Kelley first needed to create a separate path for the entire perimeter of the barber pole. She duplicated the pole and, with the paths still selected, she clicked the Add to Shape Area button in the Pathfinder panel to make the shapes behave as a single object. She applied a light, linear gradient to the new object.

Kelley wanted to reproduce how various pole and reflection paths would be affected to different degrees by the shadow. To control this, Kelley first positioned the gradient behind the other paths by choosing Object > Arrange > Send to Back. Kelley then applied the Multiply blending mode to pole and reflection paths so that their fills and strokes were darkened by the shadow. She created the variations she wanted by varying the Opacity values of different paths. To emphasize the overall barber pole outline, Kelley applied a 7.5-pt black stroke to a duplicate of the perimeter path, and positioned the duplicate path behind the rest of the drawing.

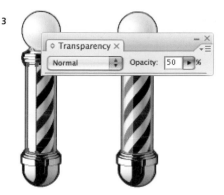

3

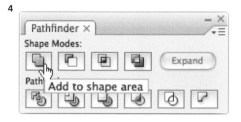

The glass highlight selected (left), and the same highlight deselected after applying 50% opacity with the Transparency panel (right)

4

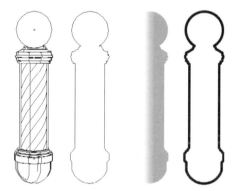

Kelley unified the lighting by uniting the pole's paths (left) with the Pathfinder panel, and filling the new path (second from left) with a linear gradient (third from left); a duplicate with a heavy stroke (right) strengthens the outline

The Multiply blending mode was applied to the barber pole objects so that the unifying background gradient could show through

Transparent Kite

Revealing Hidden Details with Opacity

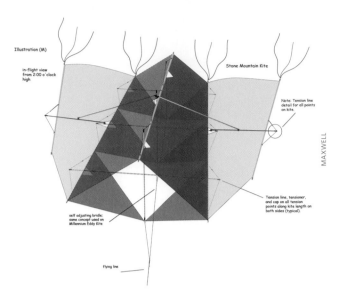

Advanced Technique

Overview: *Apply transparency to gradient fills as an alternative to the traditional cutaway view; adjust opacity levels for different effects.*

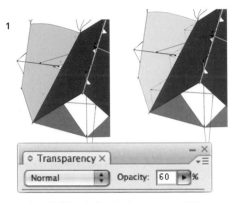

Before (left) and after (right) applying 60% opacity to left wing to reveal underlying trusses

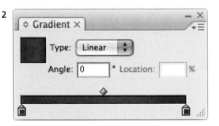

Gradient panel for the top sails

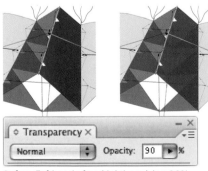

Before (left) and after (right) applying 90% opacity to top right sail

Eden Maxwell illustrated Bobby Stanfield's innovative Stone Mountain kite for a project commissioned by Encyclopedia Britannica. In 1986, this kite design set a record by staying aloft for over 25 hours. Maxwell used Illustrator's transparency features to reveal the underlying structure of the kite and to simulate the sheer, semitransparent quality of the kite fabric.

1 Applying a transparent fill to the beige wings. Maxwell applied a beige color to the wings (0% C, 25% M, 41% Y, 0% K). He wanted the truss system to be visible behind the wings, so with the left wing path selected, he set Opacity to 60%. He set the right wing Opacity to 65%.

2 Applying a transparent fill to the top sails and keels. Maxwell filled the kite's top sails with a gradient from blue (91% C, 1% M, 10% Y, 39% K), to orange (0% C, 71% M, 73% Y, 19% K). To reveal the underlying structure and simulate translucent fabrics seen at different angles, he applied 60% opacity to the top left sail and 90% opacity to the top right sail. You can specify an Opacity value in the Control panel; for more opacity options use the Transparency panel.

Finally, Maxwell applied 65% opacity to the triangular keels under the kite.

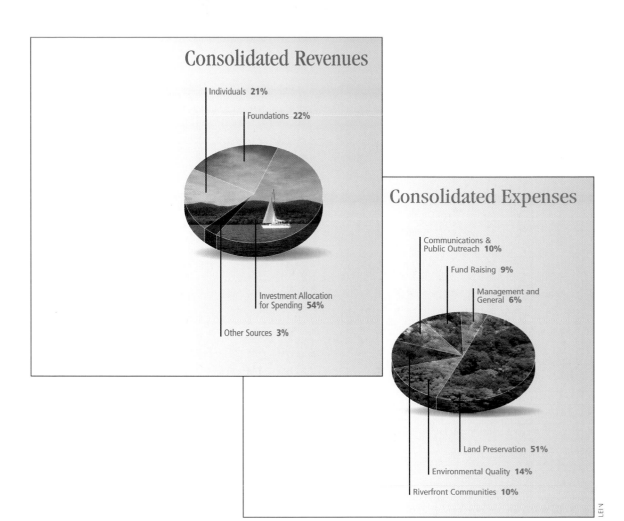

Consolidated Revenues

Individuals **21%**

Foundations **22%**

Investment Allocation
for Spending **54%**

Other Sources **3%**

Consolidated Expenses

Communications &
Public Outreach **10%**

Fund Raising **9%**

Management and
General **6%**

Land Preservation **51%**

Environmental Quality **14%**

Riverfront Communities **10%**

LEIN

Adam Z Lein

Adam Z Lein incorporated images of New York's Hudson Valley in this pie chart for an annual report of the environmental organization, Scenic Hudson. Lein used Microsoft Excel and Excel's Chart Wizard to turn data into a chart tilted in a perspective view. Lein used the Acrobat PDF maker to create a PDF of the graph. When he opened it in Illustrator, the graph retained all of the shapes as vector objects. Lein then placed a photographic image on a layer below the pie chart artwork, and used the Control panel to change the blending mode from Normal to Soft Light. Lein controlled the varying tints and shades of the underlying image by applying gradients and shades of gray to each pie piece. To fit the image inside the pie chart, Lein created a clipping mask in the shape of the pie chart. (See the *Advanced Techniques* chapter for more about clipping masks.) He then placed the charts in his page layout program where he added the text and data points.

Tinting a Scan
Adding a Color to a Grayscale Image

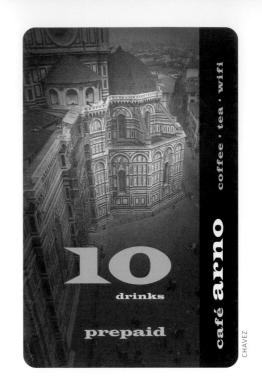

Advanced Technique

Overview: *Prepare a grayscale image; import the image into Illustrator; colorize the image; trim the artwork to the required shape; add a vignette.*

The original scanned image

The layout (left) and the image placed in the layout, initially on top of the design (right)

Conrad Chavez created this concept for a prepaid coffee card that can use different background photographs. To preserve design flexibility, Chavez imported a grayscale version of the image and added color in Illustrator so that he could change the image color at any time.

1 Scanning and preparing the image. Chavez started by scanning a photograph and saving it as a grayscale image. Save the image in a format Illustrator can place, such as a TIFF or Photoshop file. If your original image is in color, you must first convert the image to grayscale in a program like Photoshop. Color images can't be tinted in Illustrator.

2 Importing the image. Chavez chose File > Place to import the image. In the Place dialog, he disabled the Template and Replace checkboxes. He then positioned the image on the layout.

You can also use Adobe Bridge to browse a folder of images, then import the images you want by dragging them from Bridge to the Illustrator document window.

3 Colorizing the image. Chavez selected the image, clicked the Fill box in the Toolbox, and then clicked a solid color swatch in the Swatches panel to tint the image. He had already applied the dark brown swatch to other elements in the design, unifying the composition.

If applying a color doesn't change the image, make sure the Fill box is active and that the image was saved as a true grayscale image, not as an RGB or CMYK image.

4 Visualizing a trim. To preview the composition as it would appear after trimming, Chavez drew a rounded-corner rectangle at the trim size. With the rectangle in front of both the background image and the dark vertical rectangle, he selected all three objects and chose Object > Clipping Mask > Make, which created a clipping group.

5 Adding a vignette. Chavez created a vignette to better distinguish the foreground and background. He drew a new rectangle the size of the Artboard and used the Gradient panel to apply a radial gradient. He changed the gradient's default black slider to the same dark color swatch applied to the image. In the Control panel, he clicked Opacity and then chose Multiply from the pop-up menu to blend the gradient with the image under it.

The vignette needed to be behind all objects except the scan. In the Layers panel, Chavez not only dragged the vignette further back in the stack but also into the clipping group, so that the vignette could be visualized within the temporary clipping group.

6 Editing the vignette. Chavez decided to refine the composition by editing the vignette. He selected the vignette in the Layers panel and clicked the Gradient tool over the building to reposition the gradient center there. He dragged the Gradient panel sliders to widen both the light center and the dark edge of the gradient. Finally, to restore the bleed required for the press, Chavez selected the clipping group and chose Object > Clipping Mask > Release, and then he deleted his temporary clipping path.

3

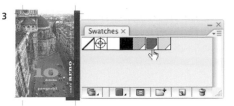

Colorizing the image (left) by selecting it and then clicking the dark brown solid color swatch on the Swatches panel (right)

4

Rounded-corner rectangle indicating final trim (left) and after clipping artwork to it (right)

5

Applying a radial gradient to the new rectangle (left), applying the Multiply blending mode to the rectangle (right), and after dragging the vignette path into the clipping group (right)

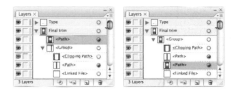

Layers panel before (left) and after (right) dragging the vignette into the clipping group

6

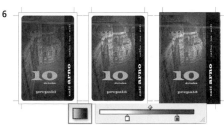

Before (top left) and after (top right) gradient edits: moving the radial gradient center with the Gradient tool (bottom left) and editing the Gradient panel's slider positions (bottom right); ready for prepress with mask deleted (top right)

Blending Elements

Using Transparency to Blend and Unify

Advanced Technique

Overview: *Prepare images in Photoshop to integrate in Illustrator; use Multiply and Opacity to blend; make Backgrounds transparent.*

JENNINGS

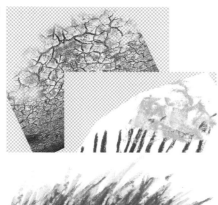

1

Using a photo or hand drawing for texture, prepared in Photoshop for use in Illustrator—here two are shown with Photoshop's Transparency grid, while the fire is completely opaque

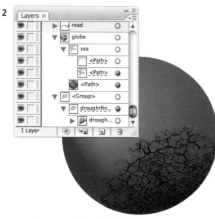

2

Layering a gradient-filled globe above a grayscale photo, and then setting the globe's Blending Mode to Multiply to add texture

When David Jennings was hired to make an illustration about environmental issues for Climate Concern UK, he wanted to use contrasting textures to highlight negative influences on the global climate. He used Photoshop for some of the textural elements, but because most of the details would be vector, he used Illustrator for blending all the objects, raster and vector, into one coherent whole.

1 Preparing images to place in Illustrator. Jennings began the project by using pastels on paper to hand-draw smoke, clouds, trees and fire. He scanned them into Photoshop and adjusted color in preparation for placing them in Illustrator later on. He also adjusted a grayscale image of cracked earth that would serve to depict drought once he blended it with the globe in Illustrator. With these files ready and saved as PSD images, he turned to Illustrator to build the illustration.

2 Using Multiply and reduced opacity to blend textures and add shading. Now in Illustrator, Jennings drew a circle for the planet and filled it with a brown radial gradient. He created a layer below the planet and chose File > Place to bring in the earth texture. After scaling and rotating the image, he changed the globe's Blending Mode in the Transparency panel from Normal to Multiply. This caused the values of the texture darker than the gradient to show through the globe, while the brown gradient replaced the photo's lighter values.

Using mainly the the Pen tool, Jennings began drawing manmade and solid natural elements—the cars and planes, the factory and housing, the human and polar bear. To create shading he added darker objects on top of the originals, switching the Blending Mode to Multiply and/or changing Opacity in the Transparency panel to alter the appearance of the objects below. If he needed the shading to be even darker than the color he had already chosen, he used Multiply to deepen the colors. If the color was a bit too dark, he lowered the opacity. To create the shadow for the factory, he not only used Multiply to deepen the colors below his shadow shape, but he also chose Gaussian Blur as a Live Effect to add even more transparency and softness to the shadow's edges.

3 Making transparent backgrounds for Photoshop images. Jennings now needed to add the textured, natural elements he had prepared in Photoshop. He knew that Multiply mode drops out the white backgrounds often imported with raster images, so he placed the cloud, trees and smoke images, scaled and transformed them to fit, and then selected Multiply to merge them seamlessly with the objects below. For the fire, however, Jennings needed both transparency within the fire image itself and opacity when he placed it over the tree layer. If he used Multiply, then the fire, being lighter than the trees, would seem to disappear. In this instance, Jennings painted a transparency mask for the fire in Photoshop, which Illustrator recognized and preserved upon import. (See the *Illustrator & Other Programs* chapter for more about working with Photoshop and Illustrator.)

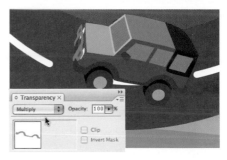
Adding shading with an object in Multiply mode

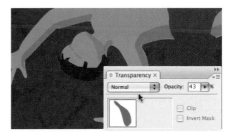
Adjusting Opacity to precisely determine degree of shading and depth

Using Blending Mode > Multiply and also applying Effect > Blur > Gaussian Blur, creates transparent shadows

3

Trees and tree trunks set to Multiply drop their white background against the globe, but the lighter-colored fire requires transparency painted into a mask in Photoshop

Opacity Collage

Combining Objects using Transparency

Advanced Technique

Overview: *Apply an opacity mask; experiment with blending modes; shade with a gradient mesh.*

The heart path, doily image, and currency image

Before and after using a gradient as an opacity mask for the currency image; the Transparency panel when the masked result is selected

Sharon Steuer created this Valentine's Day card using type, vector graphics with applied effects, and imported bitmap images. Steuer created this project for a Valentine's Day feature article on creativepro.com. She started from a hand-drawn heart and images of currency and a lace doily. Illustrator lends itself to Steuer's process of continuous experimentation by making it easy to copy objects or layers, vary their appearance, and hide or show different combinations of objects or layers.

1 Setting up the main elements. Steuer chose File > Place to import the image of scanned currency. Steuer also placed a scan of a doily with a blue background, and chose Object > Arrange > Send to Back to position the doily behind the currency. Next, Steuer used the Pen tool to draw a heart shape, and gave it a red outline stroke.

2 Masking an image with opacity. Steuer used an opacity mask to fade the currency image vertically. In an opacity mask, black areas are transparent, white areas are opaque, and gray areas are semitransparent. To create the mask, she drew a rectangle and filled it with a black-to-white gradient. She positioned the rectangle over the currency image, selected both objects, and chose Make Opacity Mask from the Transparency panel menu.

3 Varying the heart outline. To add texture and visual interest, Steuer created playful variations on the heart outline. She first chose Edit > Copy, then Edit > Paste in Front to duplicate the heart outline. Her experiments led her to enlarge the heart outline and choose Effect > Stylize > Scribble. She also applied a thicker stroke weight and a shade of red. Steuer also used the Ellipse tool to draw a circle that echoed the doily shape. She stylized the circle using the same technique she used for the heart outline, but with a bluish gray color instead of red.

4 Experimenting with blending modes. With the main elements in place, Steuer experimented with integrating the design elements. She tried different opacity values and blending modes to adjust the color and tone relationships among objects and layers.

While opacity applies an overall level of transparency, blending modes change the tone and color relationships between areas that overlap. For example, the Overlay mode increases the contrast between light and dark overlapping areas, and the Color mode applies an object's hue and saturation to underlying areas. Steuer used the Transparency panel to change the blending mode and opacity for the layer or objects she selected. If a blending mode created a stronger effect than she wanted, she adjusted the opacity of the layer or object.

When you apply appearance attributes, the object or layer's target circle in the Layers panel becomes shaded. This makes it easy to identify objects and layers for which attributes like Opacity and Blending Mode have changed. Simply click an object's target indicator in the Layers panel, and then look at the Appearance panel to see the appearance settings for the object.

3

The red heart and blue circle over the composed elements, before and after applying the Scribble effect first to the heart and then to the circle

4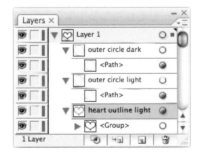

The blending mode pop-up menu and Opacity value in the Transparency panel

Shaded circles indicate objects or layers with appearance changes such as blending modes, opacity, and effects

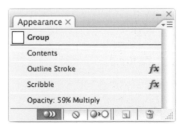

The Appearance panel for a selected heart outline displays effects and transparency settings

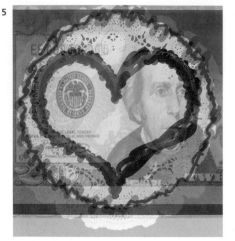

5

The composition after adjusting blending modes and opacity values

6

The heart with a custom gradient fill, and after expanding the gradient fill into a masked gradient mesh and adding a mesh point

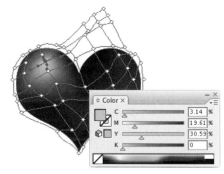

Changing the color of a mesh point on the edited gradient mesh

7

Detail of the type and the underlying hand-drawn shadow

5 Creating variations. Steuer felt the illustration needed a bit more depth and impact. She duplicated the heart outline, changed the Scribble effect settings (by double-clicking the Scribble effect in the Appearance panel when the heart outline was selected), and changed the blending mode. In the completed piece, one heart outline uses the Multiply blend mode at 59% opacity, the other heart outline uses the Color Burn blend mode at 100%, and their Scribble settings are different. Steuer created similar variations of the currency and the doily.

6 Shading with a gradient mesh. To achieve the surface modeling she wanted, Steuer decided to use a gradient mesh to shade a duplicate of the heart. Using the Gradient panel, Steuer created a custom linear gradient. She applied it as a fill to the duplicate heart outline, and used the Gradient tool to adjust the gradient's endpoints and angle. She then chose Object > Expand to convert the gradient fill into a gradient mesh. The heart outline became a clipping mask with the rectangular gradient mesh inside it. The expanded mesh rectangle is rotated because the original gradient fill was at an angle. Steuer shaped the mesh by adding mesh points with the Mesh tool, adjusting mesh point colors using the Color panel, and using the Direct Selection tool to move the mesh points and edit their direction lines.

7 Finishing up with type. Steuer used the Type tool to add the line of text "Money can't buy me love…" below the heart. She added a scribbled type shadow by hand with a graphics tablet, and tried different blending modes and opacity settings for the shadow before settling on the Saturation blending mode at 25% opacity.

Faster access to a clipping mask and its contents

When a clipping mask is selected in Illustrator CS3, two new buttons appear at the left end of the Control panel: Edit Clipping Path and Edit Contents. Click them for direct access to a clipping mask's path or contents.

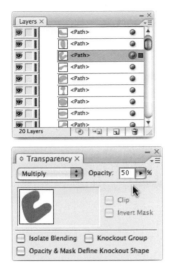

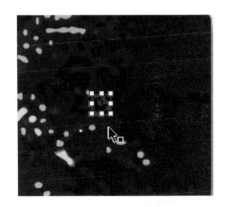

HESS (Parker photo by Milton H. Greene, ©2007 Joshua Greene, www.archiveimages.com)

Kurt Hess

As an exercise to refine his technique, Kurt Hess created this portrait of Suzy Parker, based on a 1952 photo. Hess located the owner of the copyright of the original image, who generously granted permission for the illustration to be published here with the photo credit by Milton H. Greene (©2007 Joshua Greene, www.archiveimages.com). He used the Watercolor filter in Photoshop to add important contrast to the image, and then, layer by layer, he built a convincing portrait in Illustrator. Hess began by creating a palette of global colors that he would use as he traced areas in the photograph onto separate layers, using both Pen and Pencil tools. He created the illusion of depth by overlapping individual objects depicting tonal values. He then adjusted their settings in the Transparency panel—using Multiply, Overlay or Screen for contrast control, while fine-tuning Opacity as well. This method permitted Hess to return to each object and readjust the settings as often as needed until the shading was exactly what he wanted. Further, using a global palette made it easy to refine the colors later to create a glowing rendition of "Suzy."

Peter Cassell / 1185 Design

As a kind of artwork not normally associated with Illustrator's hard-edged vector tools, Peter Cassell's fluffy cumulus clouds comprised one of the packaging illustrations created for an Adobe Illustrator box (see Cassell's cityscape Gallery later in this chapter). Cassell began by placing a photographic image on a template layer in Illustrator. Next, he created a gradient mesh with the maximum number of rows and columns (50). To color the clouds, he first chose View > Outline (so he could see the cloud image in a layer below the mesh). Next, he selected the Direct Selection tool, clicked on a mesh point, selected the Eyedropper tool, and then clicked in the cloud image to sample its color. He repeated this process to color the rest of the mesh to match the cloud image. To reshape parts of the grid to follow the contours of the clouds, Cassell clicked mesh points with the Mesh tool and dragged them. Where he

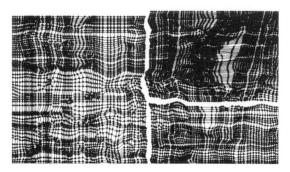

needed more detail, Cassell added rows and columns to the mesh by clicking on a mesh line or in an empty space in the mesh with the Mesh tool. As the composition became unwieldy with detail, Cassell selected overlapping sections of the mesh and copied and pasted each section into a separate file. Once he finished with a section, Cassell copied and pasted it into the final, composite file. He was careful not to adjust mesh points where sections overlapped, so he could maintain a seamless appearance where the separate sections he had worked on overlapped.

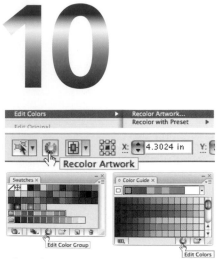

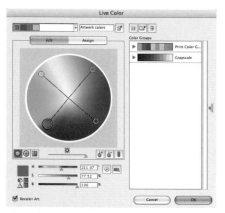

Live Color

Hue, or color, is relative. Individual hues are perceived differently when juxtaposed with other hues. Illustrator's new Live Color feature lets you begin to examine color relationships in a way that has not been possible before with other software applications. You can quickly explore new color combinations, find an exact color faster, and determine which hues work well together based on scientific color theory and predefined color harmony rules. Live Color provides a tool set you can use to mix and adjust color in new ways, as well as the capability to extract color from artwork and create color groups. (See the *Drawing & Coloring* chapter introduction for a discussion of the Color, Swatches, and Color Guide panels, as well as a few lessons that include Live Color features.)

Live Color is not just a single panel or feature. Instead, it's an interactive color exploration environment comprised of various interfaces and tools that work together. In fact, it's difficult to find anything at all labeled Live Color. The name doesn't exist in the Window menu or in the Control panel or in the Color panel. In fact, there's only a single dialog assigned that name, even though there are many ways to get to it.

While it's true the way Live Color works can be intimidating, this chapter and its lessons should help you add at least a few Live Color features and functions to your artistic arsenal.

SETTING UP A LIVE COLOR WORKSPACE

Several components make up the feature set Adobe named Live Color. The Color panel, Color Guide panel, Swatches panel, kuler panel (more on this panel later), and the Live Color dialog are all integral to working with this environment.

To work with Live Color most effectively, you'll want to have the Color, Color Guide, and Swatches panels (and perhaps the kuler panel) visible simultaneously; you'll

Edit > Edit Colors > Recolor Artwork (top); Recolor Artwork in the Control panel; Edit Color Group button in the Swatches panel; and the Edit Colors button in the Color Guide panel—all ways to enter Live Color

The only place the name Live Color can be found is on this dialog (Edit mode shown)

Live Color swatches & brushes

If you use Live Color to edit objects styled with patterns, brushes or gradients, Live Color will style your objects with new swatches and/or brushes, and these new styles will be automatically added and saved into the Swatches and/ or Brushes panel. (See the "Distort Filter Flora" in the *Drawing & Coloring* chapter for an example.)

need all the artwork you are recoloring available as well. With all color panels visible, you can generate and save color groups, drag and drop color between panels, and also see how each panel changes contextually. For help with arranging panels and customizing your workspace, see the "Workspaces" section in the *Illustrator Basics* chapter. To load preconfigured workspaces optimized for Live Color, see the "Trading spaces" tip in the *Illustrator Basics* chapter.

Mix, store, and explore

Essentially, the Color panel can be thought of as your color mixing tool. Imagine the Swatches panel as a kind of color filing cabinet to store and organize the hues you've mixed. The Color Guide panel can be considered a color laboratory—a place to study and seek inspiration. The kuler panel is an environment for sharing color ideas (more on this concept later in the chapter).

RECOLORING ARTWORK

Live Color can be used to recolor artwork methodically or completely at random. You can access the Recolor Artwork function (the Live Color dialog) from a number of different places, depending on what you have selected, and what you want to do. As long as you have objects selected containing at least two different colors, clicking the Recolor Artwork button in the Control panel will open the Live Color dialog, starting out with the colors from your selected art (selection edges will automatically be hidden). If you enter the Live Color dialog via another path (such as from the Color Guide's Recolor Artwork button), your image might initially appear with assigned new colors. If that's not what you intended, click the "Get colors from selected art" button to reload the original colors and reveal them once again in your artwork.

Live Color dialog highlights

At the very top left of the Live Color dialog is the Active Colors field. Clicking the arrow to the right will drop

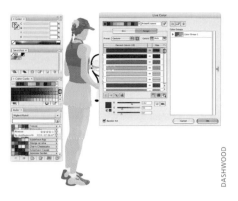

To work with Live Color effectively, you'll want to be able to see all your color-related panels and the artwork you're recoloring simultaneously; selection edges are automatically hidden when you enter Live Color

Powerful Live Color

One of the many powerful capabilities of Live Color is the ability to globally change the colors of almost any kind of colored object in your Illustrator artwork. Colors in envelopes, meshes, symbols, brushes, patterns, raster effects (but not RGB/CMYK raster images), and in multiple fill and stroke objects can all be easily recolored with the Live Color dialog!

—*Jean-Claude Tremblay*

Recolor Artwork button

There are many ways to enter Live Color, but probably the most predictable, quickest way to get to the Live Color dialog is from the Control panel. If you have one or more objects selected with at least two distinct colors, then you'll see the Recolor Artwork button in the Control panel—just click it.

Active Colors appear in the upper left field of
the Live Color dialog; Active Colors can be colors
from your selected artwork or colors from a Harmony Rule or Color Group you've chosen; you
can rename and create new Color Groups here;
circled in red is the "Get colors from selected
art" button

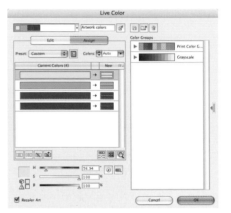

The Live Color dialog viewed in Assign mode;
each color bar represents a color in your selected art objects

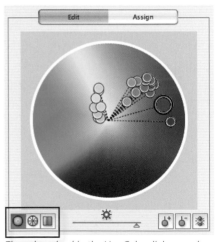

The color wheel in the LIve Color dialog can be
viewed as smooth, segmented, or as bars (by
using the buttons circled in red); each circle or
"marker" represents a color in your selected artwork; the large marker is the current base color
Live Color is using

down a menu showing several of Adobe's "Harmony Rules." Color harmonies are hues that work well together or appear harmonious. Live Color can use the specific color combination you choose as a "rule" to recolor artwork. When you select one of these rules, you change the Active Colors to a new, unlabeled "Color Group." You can enter a new name in the field and then save this group by clicking the New Color Group button. This will add your new color group to the Color Groups section in the Live Color dialog. Clicking on any of your saved color groups will load those colors in the Active Colors field.

The Color Groups section lists any color groups you saved in your Swatches panel before you entered Live Color, and also any color groups you created using Live Color. Keep in mind that deleting and creating new color groups in the Live Color dialog will delete and add color groups in your Swatches panel, so don't click the trash icon unless you're positive you want to delete that color group from your document entirely. If you create color groups you want to save during a Live Color session, but don't want to apply any changes to your artwork, disable the Recolor Art checkbox and click OK. If you click Cancel instead, all the work you did creating (or deleting) new color groups will be canceled.

Just below the Active Colors are two main tabs—Edit and Assign. If the Assign tab is inactive when you enter Live Color, it means that you don't have any artwork selected (you probably clicked the Edit Colors button in the Color Guide panel). If Assign isn't available, click Cancel, select artwork, then re-enter Live Color.

The Assign tab displays a row of long horizontal color bars, with each long bar representing one of the colors in the artwork currently selected. To the right of each long color bar is a right-pointing arrow indicating a smaller color swatch that's initially the same color as the larger bar. This small swatch, under the column heading "New," is where you can load or mix a replacement color. Clicking on the right-pointing arrow transforms it into a straight line, and protects that color from change.

With the Edit tab active, you'll see a color wheel with lines (in default view). Attached to the lines are small circles called markers. Each marker represents one of the colors in the objects currently selected. Depending on whether the Lock icon is enabled or disabled, you can move the markers around on the color wheel individually (unlocked) or in unison (locked) to adjust the color in your art. In addition to the default "smooth" Color Wheel, you can also click the icons to display a segmented color wheel, or color bars (see the "Night Into Day" lesson, later in this chapter, for a practical example of using the color bars view).

In addition to dragging markers around on the color wheel, you can use the sliders and controls just below the color wheel to adjust the various aspects of color (hue, saturation, and value). You can work in the standard color modes (RGB, CMYK, and so on) to adjust individual colors of your artwork, or you can Global Adjust all colors at once. As you adjust individual colors with the sliders, notice that the color marker you selected moves on the color wheel as you move a slider. (For practical examples of Edit and Assign mode functions, see the lessons later in this chapter.)

Limiting and reducing colors

Perhaps the most significant benefit of Live Color is the ability to reduce and limit colors to a predefined set of colors in order to recolor your artwork. You can limit color usage to a swatch library, such as one of the Pantone Color Books; you can use a Harmony Rule; or you can choose a recoloring Preset. You can even use your own custom Color Groups as the limiting color set.

When you select one of the 23 color "rules" that exist under the Harmony Rules menu, Live Color does its job and delivers hues in harmonious existence with your base color, i.e., harmonious in the tradition of color theory. (For a more in-depth experience of Adobe's Color Rules, see the "Color Guide" section and the lesson "Color Guidance" in the *Drawing & Coloring* chapter.)

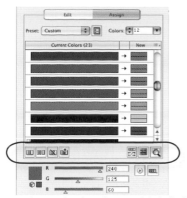

In Assign mode, these buttons (circled) allow for merging, separating, excluding, and adding new color rows. You can also randomly change color order, saturation, and brightness, and find a particular color in your artwork.

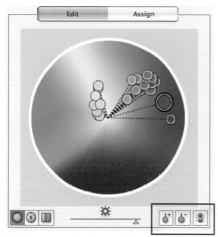

The buttons on the lower right will add and delete markers and link or unlink them

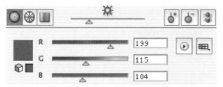

In Edit mode, these color adjustment tools appear just below the color wheel. Hue, saturation, and value (brightness) can be tweaked here.

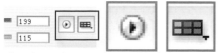

The color modes menu button (the left button) specifies the mode of the color adjustment sliders; the swatch libraries button (the right button) lets you limit your color group to a particular swatch library

The Color Reduction Options button (under the Assign tab in Live Color)

The Color Reduction Options button opens this dialog

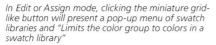

In Edit or Assign mode, clicking the miniature grid-like button will present a pop-up menu of swatch libraries and "Limits the color group to colors in a swatch library"

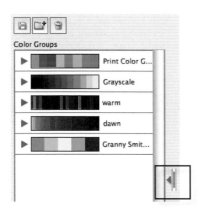

Click the arrow tab (circled in red) to hide and show the Color Group storage area of the Live Color dialog. All Color Groups that exist in your Swatches panel will show here. Create new, change, and delete Color Groups with the buttons directly above the storage area.

In Assign mode, click the Color Reduction Options button (to the right of Presets) in order to bring up the Recolor Options dialog. Limit to Library in this dialog allows you to choose a specific Swatch Library to limit your color choices. In Edit or Assign mode, you can click the small grid-like icon to the right of the sliders named "Limits the color group to colors in a swatch library." The color wheel will be noticeably different when limited to a swatch library. In Assign mode, New colors will be populated exclusively with hues from the chosen swatch library, replacing all original colors with what it determines are the closest match.

Occasionally, designers and illustrators are asked to produce artwork that will print in only one, two, or three colors. That's what Live Color's Presets are all about. You can map your artwork's multiple original colors to one or two hues you've specifically defined. Live Color can be a huge timesaver for reducing colors. In Assign mode, choose Preset > 1 Color Job (or 2 Color Job, and so on) and then select a Swatch Library (most likely Pantone if you're going to press) from which you'll specify the replacement color(s). Live Color will use tints and shades of the replacement color to transpose colors from your original art. (See the "Recoloring Black" lesson in this chapter for an example of using Presets.)

You may wish to use a very specific set of colors like team colors or specific "designer" hues for the season. In that case, you'll want to first create and save a Color Group (or groups) in the Swatches panel. Then, when you open Live Color, your Color Groups will be in the storage area, ready to recolor your artwork.

The kuler panel

You'll need an active Internet connection and an open mind in order to use the kuler panel. (In fact, your internet connection must be active even before launching Illustrator so the kuler panel will be able to communicate with its server.) Kuler is a web-hosted application from Adobe Labs designed for color exploration, inspiration, experimentation, and sharing. RSS feeds deliver the Most Popular, Highest Rated, and Newest color themes to the kuler panel (which is built entirely in Adobe Flash). You can even enjoy kuler without Illustrator. Go to http://kuler.adobe.com to find the kuler Web application.

Kuler lets you create your own color schemes and share them with others, or search or browse other users' schemes. You can download colors directly from the kuler panel; they'll be added to your Swatches panel ready to fuel your Live Color flights of fancy. For more about kuler, also see the "Exchanging swatches" section in the *Drawing & Coloring* chapter and the kuler *Wow! Appendix* excerpted from *Real World Adobe Illustrator CS3* by Mordy Golding (Peachpit Press).

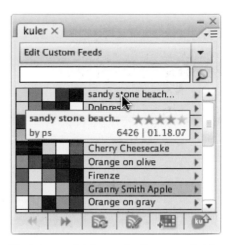

The kuler panel delivers color themes created by many different users. (But, the limit is five color swatches per theme)

LIVE COLOR, NOT MAGIC COLOR

Much of Live Color simply serves to automate and enhance color experimentation. The aforementioned recoloring methods in Live Color are not in any way intended to be failsafe scientific processes. Obviously, using a Harmony Rule will not automatically deliver spectacularly colored artwork. But, Harmony Rules will help you quickly find colors considered harmonious with your base color (in the tradition of color theory). You may or may not find these suggestions harmonious for each of your projects. The bottom line is: Live Color allows you to explore coloring possibilities quickly and easily and perhaps find some inspiration along the way.

Studying and applying (rather than just reading) the lessons that follow in this chapter is the best way to internalize working with Live Color. It's also a great way to discover how Live Color might enhance your Illustrator workflow. Also (even though it's a brand-spanking new feature), there are already some fabulous resources available that offer very comprehensive descriptions, explanations, and practical applications of Live Color features and tools. If you're looking for more help with Live Color, see http://www.adobe.com/designcenter/video_workshop or Mordy Golding's *Real World Adobe Illustrator CS3*.

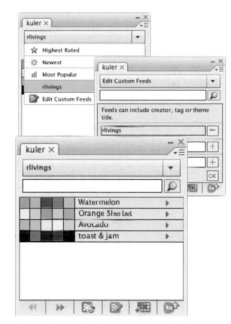

Choose Highest Rated, Newest, or Most Popular kuler RSS feeds to find the colors you like, or create your own Custom Feeds

Buttons at the bottom of the kuler panel

Recolor Artwork

Creating Color Schemes with Live Color

Overview: *Use the Color Guide panel to create color groups based on rules; add groups of swatches to Live Color while launching the dialog; manipulate several colors at once and allow for serendipity in Live Color.*

1

The original fine art piece called "Ahava," meaning "Love"

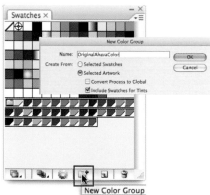

Saving the colors in the original artwork by creating a New Color Group from the selection

When you need to change colors in your artwork, you will want to look at the newest color features in Illustrator. The Color Guide panel can jumpstart your ideas for new color schemes, as well as help you create color groups, while features in Live Color can help you inject spontaneity into a makeover. Ari Weinstein found this to be true when he changed the colors of his original fine art print to those that would reflect the warmth of a greeting card and work well on a new background.

1 Using the Color Guide panel and creating new color groups in the Swatches panel. Weinstein began altering his original file by deleting the background watercolor wash and substituting a layer filled with a cream color. He selected all the lettering for placement on a new layer, so the background wouldn't be affected. With the lettering still selected, Weinstein opened the Swatches panel and clicked on the New Color Group button to name and save the original artwork swatches. He deselected the artwork and selected the red swatch he had used for the English lettering and opened the Color Guide panel. This way the red was set as the base color for the Color Guide panel to use. Clicking on the Harmony Rules arrow, Weinstein looked at the several color schemes that could be based on the swatch color he had just selected, and applied as a harmony "rule." He decided he liked Analogous 2, and clicked on the "Save color group to Swatches panel" button, which automatically named the group "Color Group 1." After reselecting the artwork, Weinstein selected Color Group 1 and clicked on the Edit or Apply Color Groups button on the Swatches panel. Live Color opens to the Edit tab with all the color groups listed in the Color Group storage, but the selected group (or groups) is at the top of the list with the topmost group previewed in the artwork. (If you enter Live Color from the Recolor Artwork button on the Control panel instead, no color group will be automatically previewed in the artwork, which you might prefer before choosing a color group.)

2 Editing the colors and allowing a measure of randomness to keep color edits lively. Clicking on the Assign tab, Weinstein noted that the colors in the artwork were combined (reduced) to the number of colors in Color Group 1. Weinstein then clicked on one color bar at a time in the "New" column, adjusting the HSB sliders to taste. Mainly he chose to increase saturation, making the artwork brighter and warmer. When using the sliders made it difficult to adjust a color, he double-clicked on the Color Picker swatch beside the sliders to open the Color Picker. These controls are much bigger and allow more room in which to make very fine changes. Finally, Weinstein inserted some randomness in the color assignments by dragging the small color bars from one row to another in the Current Colors column. (Alternatively, you can click on the "Randomly change color order" button.) The artwork updated in real time, showing the changes as he dragged. When he saw what he liked, he clicked OK to exit the dialog and apply his color edits.

With the major changes complete, Weinstein made a few final changes to color by the time-honored method of painstakingly selecting individual sections and manually adjusting the colors in the Color panel.

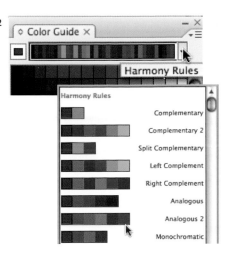

Selecting the Harmony Rules drop-down list and choosing a color rule based on a selected color

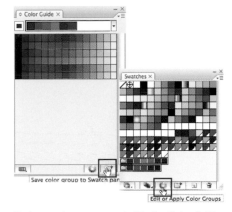

Saving a color group created in the Color Guide panel to the Swatches panel, then selecting a group or groups for use in Live Color

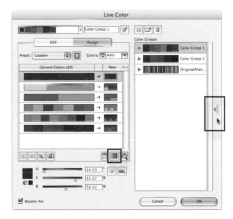

Reducing and grouping colors by assigning a saved color group from the Color Groups panel

Fashionable Colors

Applying Spot Colors with Live Color

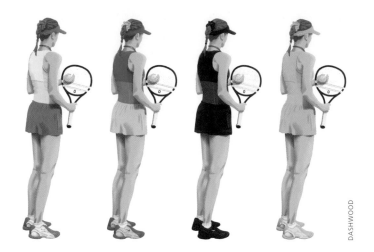

DASHWOOD

Overview: *Apply colors with Live Paint; duplicate images; use Live Color to create Spot colors; Merge colors in Live Color.*

1

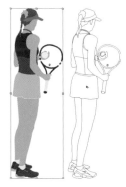

Option-drag/Alt-drag to create duplicates of your image on the Artboard

Enter Live Color by clicking on the Recolor Artwork button in the Control panel

2

Access color books inside of Live Color using the flyout menu

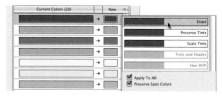

Choose Exact from the new Color flyout menu to avoid getting tints of Spot Colors

To create these seasonal apparel color changes for an interactive series of instructional materials, Andrew Dashwood used Live Color to Preview and Assign multiple color variations.

1 Preparing for Live Color. Dashwood began by drawing the tennis player's outline, using the Pen tool to make closed paths. To prepare paths for future recoloring, first block out a basic color scheme by clicking on paths and choosing colors, or use the Live Paint Bucket to convert your figure to a Live Paint object and fill colors with it. Choose the colors first for the parts of the drawing that will not change, in this case, the hair, skin and tennis racket. Then, choose a random color for each piece of apparel and footwear. You'll find it easier to experiment with color combinations if you begin with a wider variety of colors than you anticipate using in your final image. It's not possible to divide colors inside of the Live Color dialog, but it is very easy to merge them together.

Create duplicates of your artwork so you'll be able to apply different color changes to each of the versions. Select your artwork, hold Option-Shift/Alt-Shift, and drag it sideways. Then let go of your mouse to create a duplicate of your art. Use ⌘-/Ctrl-D to create additional duplicates. Select an image and click on the Recolor Artwork button in the Control panel to enter the Live Color dialog.

2 Working with Live Color and Spot Colors. Once you enter the Live Color dialog, make sure the Assign tab is active; once it is, you'll be able to change the colors in your image. Since most clients will want you to restrict colors to a specific palette of colors, you can load a color book or custom library by clicking on the Swatch Libraries drop-down menu button at the bottom of the dialog. Next, navigate and select the range of colors you want to use. Spot, process, and global swatches will all work equally well; their names will be displayed in the Color panel when you return to the Artboard and select them. To avoid creating tints of spot colors, click the drop-down menu next to the color you are working with and then select Exact.

Using Live Color you can choose to protect colors you don't want to change (such as the skin tone, hair, and tennis racket colors). To protect a color from change, click the arrow to the right of its Current Color icon. The arrow toggles to a straight line, protecting that Current Color from changing to a New Color (click again to toggle protection off). To begin changing the colors, click on the Edit tab. If you chose a custom color book, the color wheel will be divided to display only those colors. Make sure the Link Color Harmony button is unlocked on the color wheel, so that moving one of the color values on the color won't affect the others. Once you find a tonal range that suites your image well, click on the Link Color Harmony button to enable the lock option. Once the lock is enabled, you can then drag the linked colors around the wheel to experiment with different color combinations.

3 Reducing Colors. To merge two or more Current Colors into a single New Color in a predictable way, click on the Assign tab at the top of the dialog, select one Current Color, and then drag onto another one. The color bar in the Current Colors will be divided in two and an arrow to the right of it will show you the changed effect. Once you've created a color scheme you like, click OK to exit the Live Color dialog and apply your changes.

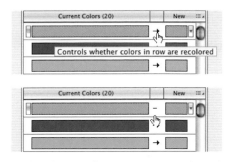

Click on the arrow between a Current Color and New Color to prevent the original color from being modified

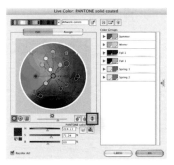

The color wheel when limited to a color book; Link Harmony Color button highlighted in red

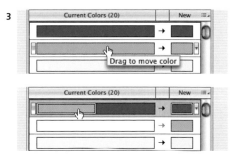

Assign the same New Color to two or more Current Colors by dragging them into one another

Recoloring Black
Using Live Color to Replace Blacks

PINABEL (client: La Ville De Montreal)

Overview: *Work with Live Color's Recolor Options dialog; limit color choices to a Swatch library; choose the right settings to ensure the appropriate colors change; protect specific colors from change.*

The original artwork

Default settings for Recolor Options and how they affect the assignment of color in Live Color's main dialog

Illustrator's Live Color dialog provides exciting ways to experiment with color changes, but there are times when you'll get unexpected results if you don't know how to control it. After Laurent Pinabel gave Jean-Claude Tremblay this poster and flyer artwork for printing, a last-minute client request required changing the process black to a Pantone metallic silver spot color. Knowing the ins and outs of Live Color made it possible for Tremblay to edit only the black objects without having to select them manually, while protecting the gold and white colors.

1 Opening Live Color and changing default settings in the Recolor Options dialog. Tremblay began by selecting the entire graphic. This ensured that he quickly captured all tints and shades of any color, should there be more than one for each. He clicked the Recolor Artwork button on the Control panel to enter Live Color. With default settings, Black and White are protected colors in Live Color (meaning new colors will not be assigned to them), so there will not be a color bar for Black in the New column of the dialog. Tremblay clicked the Color Reduction Options button to open the Recolor Options dialog. This dialog helps set up colors to suit the type of document being worked on before they are edited in the main Live Color dialog. While Tremblay worked in the Recolor Options dialog, the main Live Color dialog updated to reflect his current settings in the Recolor Options dialog.

If the Recolor Options settings are changed out of sequence, Live Color might not update properly.

Therefore, Tremblay began adjusting the settings at the top and worked his way down. With only two spot colors used for printing, he first chose Preset: 2 color job. This opens the Limit To Library dialog where he selected Color Book > Pantone metallic coated. In the Live Color dialog, swatch colors were updated, with Black still below the gold. For Live Color to work properly in a 2-color job when you're only changing one of the protected colors (Black, White or Grays), you must move that color to the top of the Current Colors column. Tremblay clicked the Color Reduction Options button and chose Sort: Lightness - dark to light, and disabled Preserve: Black. The Live Color dialog updated by placing Black at the top.

Tremblay also wanted to make certain that if the artwork had any tints of the Black in it, these would be replaced by a single metallic color. He chose Exact for the Colorize Method and unchecked Combine Tints since he only wanted one color to replace any black found in the artwork. If he had wanted to keep tints of a process color while exchanging it for another process color (a CMYK black to a CMYK purple, for instance), he would have kept the default setting of Scale Tints for the Colorize Method, and kept Combine Tints checked. (For a more complete explanation, search for *Colorize Method* in Adobe Illustrator Help.) Tremblay clicked OK to close the Recolor Options dialog. When settings have been changed, some settings in Recolor Options will be remembered, while others will return to their default. It's a good idea to look in the Recolor Options dialog when Live Color is launched to see that the settings are appropriate for the current job.

2 Protecting a color from change and assigning a new color. Back on the Assign tab, Tremblay clicked on the arrow connecting the gold color bars to eliminate gold from any further change. He double-clicked on the color bar in the New column to the right of the Black's arrow, and chose 877 C from the Color Picker. Clicking on the color swatch also would bring up the same Color Picker.

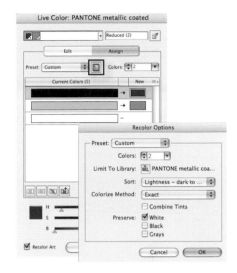

Settings made in random sequence, or not made at all, causing the Live Color dialog to fail to update properly

Correct settings for a 2 color job (set via the Color Reduction Options button) changing a protected color (Black), with Live Color updating to reflect the new assignment and Swatch Library colors replacing original colors

The Live Color dialog with all Recolor Options settings in place, gold protected from change and a metallic silver being exchanged for Black

Night Into Day

Recoloring a Complex Composition

Advanced Technique

Overview: *Simplify selections for color edits; switch views in Live Color for greater manageability; isolate values within a hue in Live Color to control color changes.*

1

The original nighttime Palms image

Select All makes it difficult to isolate color for editing, but selecting just a few layers simplifies viewing and editing in Live Color, which hides selection edges

Complex illustrations often contain many colors inside a large variety of objects, including colors in gradients and gradient mesh. Using Live Color, you can edit all of these at once, but in order to make using Live Color practical for handling large numbers of color, Sharon Steuer found methods for selecting and viewing colors in "bite-size" chunks. There are myriad ways to approach editing in Live Color, but she chose to focus on restricting selections. She then used Live Color's different ways of viewing selections to isolate the colors she wanted to change.

1 Making targeted selections to reduce complexity in Live Color. When Steuer decided to produce a daytime version of her Palms art, instead of having to rework the many gradients and mesh objects in her illustration individually, she decided to use Live Color so that she could make compositional color changes quickly. At first she selected the entire image, but this resulted in selecting so many colors that finding any individual color was impractical. Instead she decided to hide the foreground layers containing the main subject (the palms and grasses), working on just the background layers of sky, sand and water. She clicked on the Recolor Artwork button on the Control bar to enter Live Color.

2 Using the Color Bars and Color Wheel views effectively to target and edit colors. In Live Color, Steuer clicked on the Edit button. The default smooth color wheel view showed far too many markers to distinguish just the values she wanted, so she switched to a linear view by clicking on the "Display color bars" button. Now the values among the blues were much easier to select. Steuer clicked on the darkest value she could find in order to change the shadow of night into a shaft of sunlight. By clicking on the color bar she highlighted the color easily, but now Steuer had to decide which color mode to use. If she clicked on the arrow to the right of the sliders, Steuer could choose to work in any standard color mode, select Tint for working with Spot colors, or check Global Adjust to ignore hue selections and globally change all the colors by the same amount. Steuer decided to use the default HSB mode, since changing just the Saturation and Brightness sliders would create a very pale blue "shaft of light."

After creating color for the shaft of light, Steuer wanted to change the hue of all the blues, including those in the shaft of light. To shift the hues without changing the overall range of brightness or saturation, she clicked back on the "Display smooth color wheel" button and then enabled the "Link harmony colors" button. The icon now displayed an unbroken link so that any marker Steuer moved on the color wheel would move all others in tandem, thus preserving the relationship between separate hues. She slid the "chain" of markers to a slightly more turquoise blue. Since the "moon" was almost completely neutral, it wasn't noticeably affected. She disabled the link to allow for individual hue changes later on.

3 Using the magnifier on the Assign tab to target very specific colors. Steuer now wanted to lighten those blues that were still too dark, but she found they were difficult to distinguish with certainty on either the color wheel or on the color bars. Steuer returned to the Assign tab and clicked on the "magnifier" button (labeled "Click on colors above to find them in the artwork"). Clicking with the "magnifier" on a color bar isolates that color in the image. The rest of the image is dimmed, or "screened back."

2

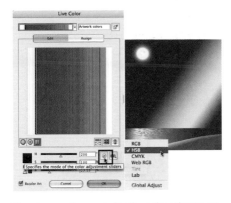

Choosing "Display color bars" to make it easier to find, select, and edit values within a gradient

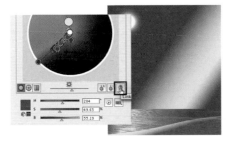

Choosing a color mode for the color adjustment sliders

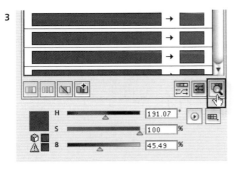

Linking colors and sliding linked markers on the smooth color wheel to adjust hue

3

Getting ready to isolate a color by clicking on the "magnifier" button ("Click on colors above to find them in the artwork" button)

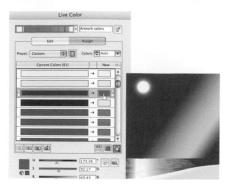

Finding the dark blue that fills the sky and water, isolating it from all other colors in the image by using the magnifier button on the Assign tab

Lightening the sky and water and restoring visibility to all the layers except the stars

4

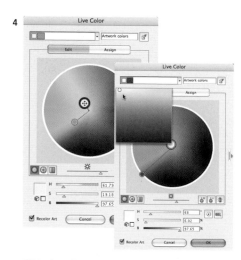

Click-dragging on a smooth color wheel's marker makes it easy to change hue along with saturation and brightness, whereas Control-clicking/right-clicking on the marker restricts changes on a pop-up color picker to saturation and brightness only.

Steuer scrolled through the list of colors, looking for the darkest of blues to lighten up. Clicking on any dark blue permitted her to see where that particular color was used in the image. When the image displayed the original dark blue of the sky and water and nothing else, she knew she had the right color bar selected. With the main area that needed to be lightened now targeted for change, Steuer switched back to the Edit tab and used the Saturation and Brightness sliders once again to lighten and brighten the sky and water for a daytime appearance. She made certain that the Recolor Artwork option was enabled (so her edits would be applied to the image), then she clicked OK to exit the Live Color dialog.

4 Live Color controls editing color for restricted changes in the newly created sun. Steuer restored the visibility to all the layers except those containing the stars. Looking at the new sun, she decided the glow was too cool for a bright sunny day. She selected just the "moon" layer (not the "moon mesh") and reentered Live Color. With so few colors, it would be easy to select just the yellow marker on the smooth color wheel. However, sliding the marker manually by clicking and dragging on it can change the hue itself, even with very small movements. Steuer decided to Control-click/right-click the yellow marker instead. This brought up a restricted color picker for that particular hue, which allowed more precision than dragging on the sliders would have, while also preserving the hue. The color representation of the swatch also made it easy for Steuer to pick out a slightly more saturated, but not much darker, yellow. The moon now looked like a sun with a gentle, warm glow around it, completing the night-into-day transformation.

Modifier keys alter the editing interface

A Control-click/right-click on a color marker or color bar pops up a hue-limited color picker, protecting the hue from changing. A double-click brings up the Color Picker to allow a full range of changes to your color.

Brenda Sutherland

Brenda Sutherland created the original logo for a micro-brewery. With the advent of Live Color, she realized she could easily create color variations to accompany the different micro-brews. Because the original coloring is very complex, she divided the logo into three sections — the text portion, the center of the logo and the outer circle. The inner circle alone has two gradient fills and multiple strokes, which only Live Color can handle easily. She selected the Text layer and saved the artwork colors to the Swatches panel. She repeated this for both the center and outer circles. Sutherland placed copies of the logo on their own layers. She selected just the outer circle on one layer and opened Live Color. There she chose the Edit tab and moved the markers on the smooth color wheel until she found a scheme she liked. She saved the colors as a new color group, then clicked

OK to apply the color scheme and return to the main image. Sutherland repeated this process for the other two areas in the logo, and again to create two more color schemes.

Reducing Color

Going Monochromatic with Live Color

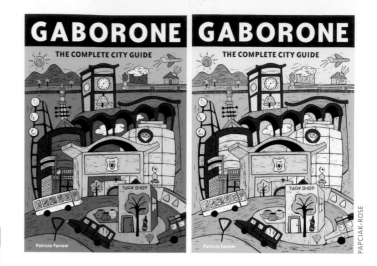

PAPCIAK-ROSE

Advanced Technique

Overview: *Place color groups in the Swatches panel; reduce colors in a grayscale conversion; make a modified color version using the grayscale values and Global Adjust sliders.*

Why Live Color for Grayscale?

With automatic grayscale conversions such as Edit > Edit Colors > Convert to Grayscale, you can't make many decisions about how your image is converted. However, using a grayscale color group and Live Color you can control replacing color with grayscale values to achieve optimal contrast.

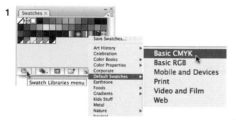

Finding the Grayscale color group in the Default Swatches library

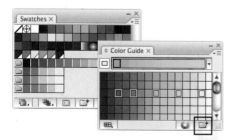

Saving color groups to the Swatches panel; using the Color Guide panel to generate monochromatic palettes

Designers and artists frequently need to reduce the number of colors they used in original artwork in order to feature the same piece in another venue. In this book cover for *Gaborone: The Complete City Guide* by Patricia Farrow, South African illustrator Ellen Papciak-Rose used a full range of bright colors. Using Live Color's remarkable ability to combine and replace colors, you can control the way colors are reduced in number to make subtle or exaggerated changes. Live Color allows you to experiment or to make specific color changes, such as converting color to grayscale, protecting accent colors if desired, and even to create color-tinted versions of your newly converted grayscale image.

1 Placing Color Groups in the Swatches panel for a monochromatic scheme. Before you can convert colors in your image, you need to make sure that your file contains the color groups that you'll be applying to your image. In this case, your file should contain a grayscale color group, and at least one hue-based monochromatic color group. New documents contain a grayscale color group in the Swatches panel. If your image hasn't been saved with the grayscale color group, open the Swatches Libraries button and select Default CMYK (or RGB) from the menu. For the monochromatic color group, select a swatch or use the Color panel to create a color that will become the base in the Color Guide for your color group. Select a series of tints and shades and click on the "Save color group to Swatch panel" button. Four or five swatches for the tints and shades (the same number that the Harmony Rules include in a group) are normally enough for a grayscale conversion. Once you've created the color groups you like and saved them to the Swatches panel, select your artwork and click on the Recolor Artwork button on the Control panel.

2 Reducing colors in Live Color for a monochromatic scheme. When Live Color opens, scroll through the list on the Assign tab until you come to any colors you want to protect from change, such as the red, black, and white of the "Gaborone" image. If any of these colors has an arrow between its color bars, click on it to toggle protection on. To create a satisfactory grayscale conversion, click on the Grayscale color group in the color group storage area, then begin dragging color bars in the Current Colors column from one row to another, combining and changing the value of the gray that has been assigned to each color. Watch the live update in the image as you experiment with combining colors in order to arrive at good contrast. If you now want to "tint" this grayscale, make sure the grays don't exceed the number of swatches in your color group and proceed with Step 3; otherwise, if you want to keep the grayscale conversion, stop here and, with Recolor Art enabled, click OK to apply the change.

3 Using your grayscale conversion to generate "tints." While your grayscale color conversion is still in Live Color, you can now tint your image using the monochromatic color groups you created. Click on a color group to preview the color scheme in the image. If you wish to make adjustments to the selected color scheme, click on the Edit tab, and use the color adjustment sliders (such as Global Adjust, used here) or drag linked color markers. If you find a scheme you want, click the New Color Group icon to add it to your list. Once you like the results, with Recolor Art enabled, click OK to apply the change.

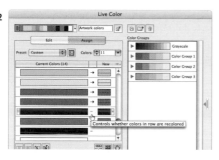

2

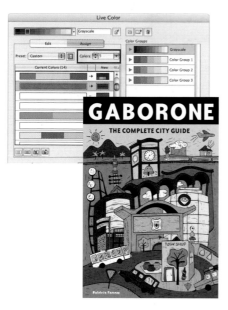

Protecting colors from change in Live Color

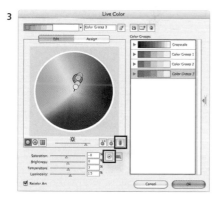

Reducing colors for grayscale by dragging color bars together in combinations that get assigned to the same values and/or hues

3

Choosing a monochromatic color scheme to "tint" the grayscale conversion, and modifying the colors on the Edit tab using color adjustment sliders or dragging markers on the color wheel

A Live Workflow

Moving From Photograph to Illustration

Advanced Technique

Overview: *Use default settings in Live Trace on a photograph; duplicate the tracing and adjust Live Trace settings for each object; change the values for the Global swatches; use Live Paint to adjust outlines; edit tones with Live Color.*

Running Live Trace from the Control panel with default settings

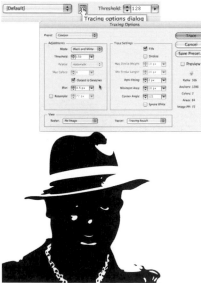

Increasing Thresholds using the Tracing Options dialog results in silhouette with saved swatches

To create Chris Daddy, Brenda Sutherland developed a method for using Live Trace with Live Paint that allowed her to maximize control over the process. By duplicating and adjusting tracing objects, she was able to build dark to light variations, creating a custom posterization effect, rather than depending upon the values in the photograph to create the tones. She edited the tones in Live Color to complete the transition from photograph to illustration.

1 Starting the Live Trace portrait. Sutherland began her illustration with the portrait of Chris Daddy isolated on a transparent background. On the Control panel, she clicked on the Live Trace button, which traced the portrait with the default Black and White settings. She then selected the traced object and clicked on the Tracing options dialog button. Sutherland turned on Preview and increased the Threshold setting until the image was almost a silhouette. To prevent the paths from becoming overly complex, she added a small amount of Blur and increased the Corner Angle to a fairly large amount. In order to create global swatches, she checked Output to Swatches and clicked on Trace to apply the new settings. Next Sutherland copied the tracing three times by dragging the sublayer to the Create New Layer icon in the Layers panel. She renamed the sublayers for ease of use.

2 Creating the posterized effect with four tracing layers. In order to see the change in Threshold as she adjusted it, Sutherland locked "Tracing" and turned off the visibility icon on "Tracing 3" and "Tracing 4." She selected "Tracing 2," the first copy she had made, and again clicked on the Tracing options dialog button. She enabled Preview and Ignore White. Because new swatches aren't generated when Live Trace settings are adjusted, and Illustrator still sees "Tracing 2" as a copy of "Tracing" instead of a new tracing, she temporarily disabled Output to Swatches. She then immediately enabled it again to force Live Trace to create a new Global swatch that would be associated with this tracing. (Illustrator automatically names the swatch it ouputs as "Tracing 2" in the Swatches panel, and Live Trace treats "Tracing 2" as an independent object.) Then, in order to see the Threshold adjustment she was about to make to "Tracing 2," she changed the Vector setting to Outlines with Tracing and adjusted the Threshold to a smaller amount than the first. Until she saw new tonal values applied to the tracings, she had to rely on the outlines to show the separation of tones. However, by keeping the objects live, she could later adjust the Threshold settings while viewing the separate tones once she had edited the values of the Global swatches. Sutherland clicked Trace to apply the new settings and repeated these steps for the last two tracings, each time decreasing the Threshold amount.

3 Using Global Swatches to color the tracings and adjusting the outlines. With Global swatches now assigned to each of the tracings, Sutherland double-clicked on the first Black Global swatch that had been added to the Swatches panel (called "Tracing" or

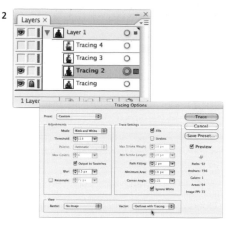

Duplicating the original tracing, setting up visibility for adjusting Threshold settings and creating new swatches for every tracing object

Four tracings made with different Threshold settings, Vector set to Outlines with Tracing, and a Black swatch output for each object.

After changing the tones for three of the four Black swatches

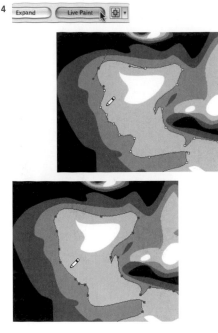

"Tracing 1"), and changed the Black to a pale gray. She then changed the second and third Black swatches in the panel to successively darker grays and left the last Black ("Tracing 4") alone. Now she could see the four-color shading of the portrait, and further adjust the Threshold for the tracing objects to achieve a better balance.

Selcting and smoothing paths on a Live Paint object with the Pencil tool

4 Creating a Live Paint object to gain control over Live Trace outlines. Sutherland wanted to be able to adjust some of the outlines without worrying about creating gaps between filled objects, which could happen if she expanded the Live Trace objects and then altered some of the paths. Live Paint adjusts fills as the paths are adjusted. She selected all the tracing objects and clicked the Live Paint button on the Control panel. She didn't merge the new Live Paint objects at first because Live Paint's performance is better with less complex objects. She selected paths with the Direct Selection tool that weren't pleasing and used the Pencil tool to redraw and smooth some areas. When done, she selected Merge Live Paint from the Control panel. This reduced her objects to a single Live Paint object, but still kept the object "live" enough that she could easily edit the paths later on.

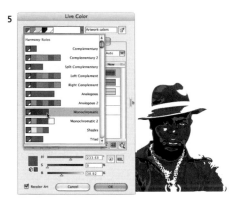

After choosing the Monochromatic Harmony Rule

5 Editing Global Swatches using Live Color. With her Live Paint object still selected, Sutherland clicked on the Recolor Artwork button on the Control panel. When the dialog opened, she clicked on the Harmony Rules arrow next to the swatches and selected Monochromatic from the drop-down list. (The Monochromatic Harmony Rule locks the Harmony link on the Edit tab automatically, holding the markers in a single "line" to restrict changes as you drag to the same Hue setting for all the markers.) The assigned colors didn't match the tones she had established in the portrait, but she could change that easily. She clicked on the Color Reduction Options button to open the Recolor Options dialog and disabled Preserve: Black in order to permit Black to be colorized. She clicked OK and returned to the Assign tab. The tonal values were

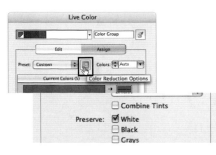

Disabling Preserve: Black, permitting it to be colorized with the other shades of gray

still misassigned, with lighter values being assigned to the original dark values. To correct this, Sutherland dragged the color bars in the New column from one row to another until the darkest values were in one row, the next darkest in another, and so on. She used the HSB sliders to change the Brightness levels to the range of values she wanted, making sure both Hue and Saturation were identical for each tone. These preliminary adjustments made it easier to visualize the relationship between the values when she switched to the Edit tab.

When she had the Brightness variances approximately correct, she clicked on the Edit button and carefully dragged the color markers on the smooth color wheel until she found a monochromatic color scheme that she liked. She could still change Saturation by dragging a marker closer to or further away from the center of the wheel, or by double-clicking on the marker to open the Color Picker. She could use the Brightness slider to change overall brightness, or use the B slider for individual markers. Each time she found a harmony she liked, she saved it as a Color Group in the color group storage. (See the Night Into Day lesson for more on the editing features in Live Color.) After experimenting, Sutherland chose a harmony of blues for Chris Daddy. She looked to see that Recolor Artwork was enabled and clicked OK to apply the colors.

To create the background, Sutherland repeated this entire process on another layer—again using Live Trace, converting to Live Paint and using Live Color—to turn the city scene from photograph to illustration, harmonizing color and style with the portrait.

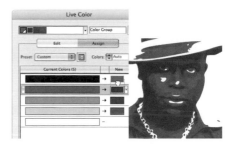

Dragging color bars in the New column up or down to reorder the assignment of values

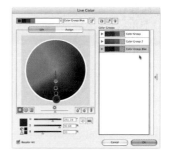

Choosing a monochromatic color scheme and creating and saving several color groups

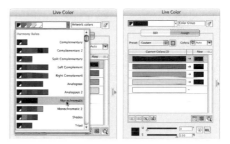

When to use Expand before Live Paint

When you create several tracings of the same subject and then convert them to Live Paint, occasionally a color will flood the image because the objects bleed off the edge. Undo and click Expand on the Control panel. This turns the tracing into paths which Live Paint can then identify and fill individually.

Too Many Blacks?

Too many blacks, as in the illustration above, is caused in this case by Preserve: Black already disabled when you open Live Color and try to select a Harmony Rule. To fix it, open the Recolor Options dialog, enable Preserve: Black, close the dialog and select your Harmony Rule. Now you can open Recolor Options again and disable Preserve: Black if you want Black to be an editable color.

Live Effects & Graphic Styles

11

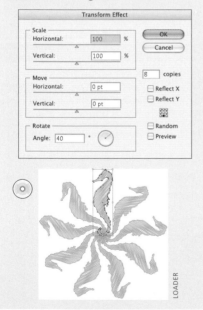

LOADER

These days Illustrator boasts a formidable array of live effects—from the warps and envelopes to 3D, Gaussian Blur, and Scribble . A few of the more robust live effects reside in their own chapters: Live Trace and Live Paint are in *Beyond the Basics*, and 3D is in the *Live 3D Effects* chapter. This chapter will focus on bringing you up to speed on working with all of Illustrator's other effects, and creating and working with Graphic Styles

EFFECTS VS. FILTERS

You may find yourself looking at the Filter and Effect menus and wondering what the difference is. Good question! Essentially, filters permanently change your artwork, whereas effects are live. They alter the look of your work but can be easily edited or removed at any time. When an effect is applied to an object, group, or layer, it displays as an attribute in the Appearance panel. The effect's position in the panel indicates which element it will modify.

The Effect menu is divided into two sections. The effects in the upper section (labeled Illustrator Effects) are mostly for use with vector images. Those in the lower section (labeled Photoshop Effects) are for use with raster images. Although none of the effects let you save or export presets of settings that you like from within their dialogs, you *can* save any set of effect attributes that you like as a Graphic Style. To save your set of effects as a Graphic Style, just drag the thumbnail in the Appearance panel to the Graphic Styles panel (for more about Graphic Styles, see the final section of this chapter intro, as well as the Lessons and Galleries that follow it).

RASTER EFFECTS

In the New Document dialog, when you choose a profile from the New Document Profile drop-down menu, Illustrator automatically selects a default resolution for your raster effects based on the profile you've chosen. For instance, if you choose the Print profile Illustrator will set a document raster effects setting of 300 ppi, and for a Web profile it sets it to 72 ppi. Once your document has been created, you can always view or change the document raster effects resolution by choosing Effect > Document Raster Effects Setting.

There's an important distinction between the raster effects that originated in Photoshop (and were then added in the bottom part of Illustrator's Effect menu, such as Gaussian Blur), and the raster effects developed specifically for Illustrator, such as Feather, Glow, and Drop Shadow. The Photoshop effects specify their options in pixels, whereas the native Illustrator effects specify their distances in ruler units. So if you apply a Gaussian Blur at 3 pixels, it looks much more blurry when the resolution is 72 ppi compared to 288 ppi. On the other hand, if you have a drop shadow with a 3-pt blur, it automatically adjusts to the resolution, and just covers more pixels at a higher resolution. For this reason, if you have Photoshop effects applied and you change the Document Raster Effects resolution, you may need to adjust the specific effect options, like Blur Distance, as well. (This process should be familiar to anyone who has changed the resolution of a Photoshop document containing Layer effects.)

Our output expert Jean-Claude advises that you should never send a file to be printed without setting the desired high resolution yourself and proofing it. Illustrator files created with raster effects might need adjustments, and you cannot trust that those who haven't seen your art will know how it should look, or that they know how to make adjustments to the file.

SCRIBBLE EFFECT

The Scribble Effect (Effect > Stylize > Scribble) lets you quickly create a variety of scribble effects—from loose and *scribbly* to a tight crosshatch. Scribble effects can be applied to the fill and/or stroke of an object depending on what you have targeted in the Appearance panel when you apply the effect.

Applying effects

Once you have applied an effect to an object, double-click the effect in the Appearance panel to change the values. If you reselect the effect from the Effect menu, you'll apply a second instance of the effect to the object, rather than change it. (In the case of 3D, avoid applying two 3D effects to a single object. Understanding what you can do in the various 3D dialogs will help you avoid that; see the Tip "3D—Three dialogs" in the next chapter.)

Flare—tool or effect?

The Flare tool turns up in Ted Alspach's Gallery later in this chapter. That's because although the Flare tool isn't technically an effect, it behaves like one—you can select and re-edit your Flare tool work using the Flare Tool Options dialog (double-click the Flare tool to open it).

Keep spot colors with effects!

You can use and preserve spot colors as spot colors, even with live effects such as Drop Shadow, Gaussian Blur, and Feather applied! To take advantage of this, make certain that the "Preserve spot colors when possible" option is enabled in Effect > Document Raster Effects Settings.

—*Jean-Claude Tremblay*

The Scribble Options dialog

The Scribble effect can be applied to the stroke, the fill, or both the stroke and the fill of an object

The Scribble effect can be applied to the stroke, the fill, or both the stroke and the fill of an object

African Art
WEINSTEIN

ye Olde Inne
COHEN

For more lessons with Scribble, see Ari Weinstein's "Antiquing Type" and Sandee Cohen's "Olde Offset Fills" lessons in the Type chapter

Crosshatching using Scribble

You don't have to duplicate a shape to create a crosshatch effect using Scribble. Instead, after applying Scribble to the object's fill (and after selecting your object), choose Add New Fill from the Appearance panel menu. Then choose Effect > Stylize > Scribble, and for the Angle setting, add 90° to the angle. —*Mike Schwabauer*

The Scribble Options dialog is divided into three sections. The Settings menu contains a fixed number of Scribble presets. Use the Angle slider to control the overall direction of the Scribble lines. A setting of 0° causes the Scribble lines to run left to right; 90° makes them run up and down. Use the Path Overlap slider to control how much the scribble stays inside or extends outside of a path boundary. In the Line Options section of the Scribble dialog, use the Stroke Width control to specify how fat or thin you want the scribble line to be. Use the Curviness slider to set how Angular or Loopy the ends of each scribble stroke should be. Use the Spacing slider to specify how tight or loose you want your strokes to be. Use the Variation sliders to further control how each attribute is applied: For a very regular machine-made look, set the slider to None, and for a more freehand and natural look move the slider toward Wide.

By combining other effects, or applying brushstrokes to your scribbles, you can create an almost infinite variety of looks. Use them as fills or masks to transform type; or save them as graphic styles to apply to other artwork.

WARPS AND ENVELOPING

Illustrator's Warp Effects and Envelope tool are robust and very powerful, offering much more than just simple transformations. Warps and envelopes may look similar at first, but there's an important difference between them. Warps are applied as live *effects*—meaning they can be applied to objects, groups, or layers. Create them by choosing from the predefined options in the Warp dialogs; you can save them within a graphic style. Envelopes, on the other hand, are also live, but rather than effects, they're actual *objects* that contain artwork. You can edit or customize the envelope shape, and Illustrator will conform the contents of the envelope to the contour.

Warps

Applying a warp is actually quite simple. Target an object, group, or layer and choose Effect > Warp > Arc. It doesn't matter which warp effect you choose, because you'll be presented with the Warp Options dialog where you can choose from any of the 15 different warps. While the warp effects are "canned" in the sense that you can't make adjustments to the effects directly, you can control how a warp appears by changing the Bend value, as well as the Horizontal and Vertical Distortion values.

Once you've applied a warp, you can edit it by opening the Appearance panel and double-clicking on the warp icon. Like all effects, a warp can be applied to just the fill, or just the stroke—and if you edit the artwork, the warp updates as well. Since warps are effects, you can include them in a graphic style, which can then be applied to other artwork. (For more about graphic styles see "Graphic Styles in Illustrator" later in this chapter intro.)

Envelopes

While warp effects do a nice job of distorting artwork, Illustrator envelopes provide a higher level of control.

There are three ways to apply envelopes. The simplest way is to create a shape you want to use as your envelope. Make sure it's at the top of the stacking order—above the art you want to place inside the envelope. Then, with the artwork and your created shape both selected, choose Object > Envelope Distort > Make with Top Object. Illustrator will create a special kind of object: an envelope. This object you created becomes an envelope container, which appears in the Layers panel as <Envelope>. You can edit the path of the envelope with any transformation or editing tools; the artwork inside will update to conform to the shape. To edit the contents of the envelope, click the Edit Contents button in the Control panel or choose Object > Envelope Distort > Edit Contents. If you then look at the Layers panel, you'll notice that the <Envelope> now has a disclosure triangle that reveals the contents of the envelope—the artwork you placed. You can edit the artwork directly or even drag other paths into the <Envelope> in the Layers panel. To again edit the envelope itself, choose Object > Envelope Distort > Edit Envelope.

Add a bounding rectangle

Since warps start at the bounding box of objects, when using inside a group or layer, it is often useful to draw a large square/rectangle with no stroke or fill as the definer of the bounding box. This allows the possibility to add to a group/layer with a warp without seeing too much rewarping. This is also true for envelopes.
—*Jean-Claude Tremblay*

Editing envelopes

Remember that you can edit the contents of any envelope by selecting the envelope path and then either clicking the Edit Contents button in the Control panel, or choosing Object > Envelope Distort > Edit Contents. See Sandee Cohen's "Warps & Envelopes" lesson later in this chapter for examples of combining meshes with envelopes to create realistic shading effects.)
—*Mordy Golding*

Four's company

"Stylize" is listed twice in the Filter menu and twice in the Effect menu. The Filter > Stylize commands change the paths of the objects to which you apply them. The Effect > Stylize commands produce "live" effects, altering the appearance of objects, but leaving the paths unchanged and available for editing.

The three Envelope buttons in the Control panel, from left to right: Edit Envelope, Edit Contents, and Envelope Options

Envelope distort options

If your artwork contains pattern fills or linear gradients, you can employ envelopes to distort them by choosing Object > Envelope Distort > Envelope Options and checking the appropriate items in the dialog. —*Mordy Golding*

Smart people use Smart Guides

Smart Guides can be quite helpful when you work with Warps or Envelopes, as it may become difficult to edit artwork that has an appearance applied to it. With Smart Guides turned on, Illustrator will highlight the art for you, making it easier to identify where the actual artwork is (and not the appearance). Make use of the ⌘-U/Ctrl-U keyboard shortcut to turn Smart Guides on and off. —*Mordy Golding*

Photoshop effects don't scale

Keep in mind that Photoshop effects won't scale along with an object—not even if you have the Scale Strokes & Effects option enabled in your Preferences. —*Jean-Claude Tremblay*

There are two other types of envelopes, and they're closely related. Both types use meshes to provide even more distortion control. One of them is called Make with Warp and it's found in the Object > Envelope Distort submenu. This technique starts off by displaying the Warp dialog. When you choose a warp and click OK, Illustrator converts that warp to an envelope mesh. You can then edit individual mesh points with the Direct Selection tool to distort not only the outer edges of the envelope shape, but also the way art is distorted within the envelope itself. To provide even more control, use the Mesh tool to add more mesh points as desired.

Another way to create an envelope is to start from a rectangular mesh. Select artwork and choose Object > Envelope Distort > Make with Mesh. After you've chosen how many mesh points you want, Illustrator will create an envelope mesh. Use the Direct Selection tool to edit the points and use the Mesh tool to add mesh points.

EFFECT PATHFINDERS

The effects listed in the Effect > Pathfinder menu are effect versions of the Pathfinders described in the *Beyond the Basics* chapter. To apply a Pathfinder effect, you should either group the objects, making sure that the group is also targeted, or target the layer with the objects (which applies the effect to *all* objects on that layer). Then, select Effect > Pathfinder and choose an effect. If you don't do one of those two things, before applying the effect to a non-group, you might not see a visible result.

Pathfinder Effects vs. Compound Shapes

With live Pathfinder effects, you create a container (group or layer) and then apply one effect (Add, Subtract, Intersect, or Exclude) to the container. But in a compound shape, *each component* independently specifies whether it adds to, subtracts from, intersects with, or excludes from the components below it.

When you're using more than one or two shape modes, you'll find it simpler to work with compound shapes. One of the great benefits compound shapes have over Pathfinder effects is that compound shapes behave much more reliably when the objects being combined aren't simple.

Compound shapes can be exported live in Photoshop files, or copied in Illustrator and pasted into Photoshop as shape layers. See the *Drawing & Coloring* chapter for more about Pathfinders and compound shapes.

GRAPHIC STYLES IN ILLUSTRATOR

If you think that you'll want to apply an appearance more than once, whether it's a simple stroke and fill, or a complex combination of effects, save it as a graphic style in the Graphic Styles panel. A *graphic style* is simply a combination of one or more appearance attributes that can be applied to objects (including text objects), groups, and layers. See the *Layers & Appearances* chapter to learn the basics of working with appearances.

To save a set of appearance attributes as a graphic style, in the Appearance panel (with or without an object selected), select the desired appearance attributes, and then either click the New Graphic Style icon in the Graphic Styles panel or drag the appearance thumbnail from the Appearance panel to the Graphic Styles panel.

To apply a graphic style, simply select an object, or target a group or layer, and click on a style in the Graphic Styles panel. You can also sample a style from another object using the Eyedropper. You can also drag a style from the Graphic Styles panel directly onto an object.

To separate a graphic style from the object to which it's applied, click on the Break Link to Graphic Style icon at the bottom of the panel, or select the item from the Graphic Styles panel menu. You might want to do this when you are replacing a graphic style and don't want to change all the objects using the current graphic style to the updated or replaced version. Select two or more styles in the Graphic Styles panel, and choose Merge Graphic Styles from the panel menu to combine appearance attributes into a new style.

Pathfinder Group Alert

Even if you already grouped your objects, you may still get the following warning when you apply an Effect menu Pathfinder Effect:

> ⚠ Pathfinder effects should usually be applied to groups, layers, or type objects. This may not have any effect on the current selection.
>
> ☐ Don't show again   [Cancel]   [OK]

This happens if you Direct-Select the objects and miss some of their points, causing the objects to get targeted. To fix this, target the <Group> the objects are in, then apply the Pathfinder effect.

Load graphic styles easily

The quickest way to load Graphic Styles installed by Illustrator, or custom saved styles, is by using the handy Graphic Styles Libraries Menu button in the lower left corner of the Graphic Styles panel.
—*Jean-Claude Tremblay*

Replacing graphic styles

To replace a saved appearance in the Graphic Styles panel with a new set of attributes, Option-drag/Alt-drag the thumbnail from the Appearance panel (or an object from the Artboard), to the Graphic Styles panel and drop it onto the highlighted graphic style. To replace the currently selected graphic style, make adjustments and choose Redefine Graphic Style from the Appearance panel menu. The applied styles will update.

Scratchboard Art

Combining Strokes, Fills, Effects, & Styles

Overview: *Apply multiple strokes and fills to simple objects; offset strokes; apply effects to strokes and fills; create and apply graphic styles.*

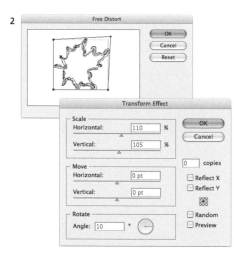

The original scratchboard art consists of simple primitive shapes

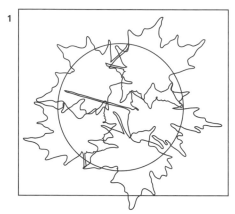

To offset a path's Stroke from its Fill, select the Stroke in the Appearance panel and apply Free Distort and Transform from the Effect >Distort & Transform menu

Sandee Cohen, author and consultant, discovered a way to simulate scratchboard art in Illustrator. Artist Gary Powell created a variation of Cohen's technique using an assortment of Art Brushes, multiple strokes and fills, and effects, which he then combined and saved as graphic styles. Once a series of effects is saved as a graphic style, you can easily apply that graphic style to multiple objects to create or quickly modify a design theme. Art directors may find this method helpful for unifying and stylizing illustrations created by a number of different artists.

1 **Applying Art Brushes and Fills.** To create a natural-looking stroke, Powell applied an assortment of Art Brushes to simple primitive objects. He used Waves, Weave, Dry Brush, and Fire Ash Brushes (on the *Wow! CD*), then he applied solid fills to each object. Select a simple object, then click on your choice of Art Brush in the Brushes panel or in a Brush Library. (For more on Art Brushes, see the *Brushes & Symbols* chapter.)

2 **Offsetting a stroke.** To develop a loose, sketchlike look, Powell offset some of the strokes from their fills. To do this, select a stroke in the Appearance panel and

apply either Effect > Distort & Transform > Free Distort, or Effect > Distort & Transform > Transform to manually or numerically adjust the position of the stroke so that it separates from the fill. This gives the stroke the appearance of a different shape without permanently changing the path. (You can further reshape the stroke by double-clicking the Transform attribute in the Appearance panel and adjusting the offset of the Stroke attribute.)

3 Adding more strokes and fills to a path. To add to the sketchlike look of the square background, Powell applied additional strokes to the path. First, he chose the Stroke attribute in the Appearance panel and clicked the Duplicate Selected Item icon at the bottom of the panel. With the new Stroke copy selected, he changed the choice of Art brush. He also double-clicked the stroke's Distort & Transform effect in the Appearance panel and changed the settings to move the Stroke copy's position. Powell repeated this until he had as many strokes as he liked.

To create the scratchboard look in the leaves, Powell applied additional fills and effects to each of them. First, he chose the Fill attribute in the Appearance panel and duplicated it. With the new Fill copy selected, he changed the color and applied Effect > Stylize > Scribble. (You can apply as many fills and effects to a path as you like, then drag and drop to change their stacking order.)

4 Working with graphic styles. To automate the styling of future illustrations, Powell used the Appearance and Graphic Styles panels to create a library of graphic styles. Whenever you create a set of strokes and fills you like, click the New Graphic Style icon in the Graphic Styles panel to create a new graphic style swatch.

Once Powell assembled a palette of graphic style swatches, he altered the look and feel of the artwork by applying a variety of graphic styles to selected paths. The use of graphic styles allows an artist or designer to create a variety of themes in a graphic style library and then apply them selectively to illustrations or design elements.

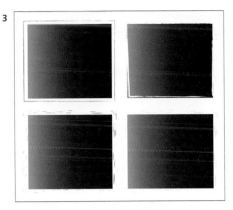

The individual strokes that Powell combined to create multiple strokes for the background

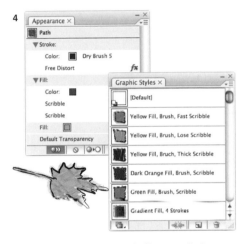

Multiple Strokes, Fills and Effects applied to an object shown in the Appearance panel; appearance attributes saved in the Graphic Styles panel by clicking the New Graphic Style icon

Applying different graphic styles to objects can give the same artwork several different looks and create a cohesive look throughout a project or series

Warps & Envelopes

Using Warping and Enveloping Effects

Overview: *Group clip art for use with Warp; apply Warp; save Warp effect as a graphic style; apply Envelope using a shaped path; add a shading effect using a mesh.*

1

Making sure that the flag artwork is grouped.
Note: *The Appearance panel shows information for the currently targeted (not just selected or highlighted) object in the Layers panel.*

The Flag Warp applied to a not-fully-grouped flag artwork. The stripes are grouped, but the stars and the union (blue field) are separate objects.

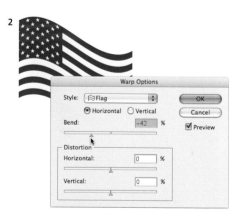

2

With Preview enabled, experiment with the Warp Options settings

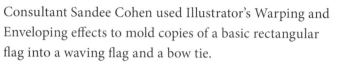

Consultant Sandee Cohen used Illustrator's Warping and Enveloping effects to mold copies of a basic rectangular flag into a waving flag and a bow tie.

Warps are the easier of the two methods to understand and use. Simply choose one of the 15 preset shapes from the Warp menu and adjust the shape using the sliders in the Warp Options dialog.

Envelopes let you use any path, warp preset, or mesh object to shape and mold your artwork into almost any form imaginable. You can further manipulate the shape using the envelope's anchor points. Be aware that although Warps and Envelopes leave original artwork unchanged, only Warps can be saved as graphic styles.

1 Grouping clip art for use with Warp effects. Cohen started with a standard United States flag from a clip art collection. First, she made sure that the flag artwork was a grouped object by selecting the flag artwork (which also targets it in the Layers panel) and checking its description in the Appearance panel. If the artwork is not a grouped object, then the effects will not be applied to the artwork as a whole, but rather to each of the paths individually (as shown in the sidebar).

2 Making a copy of the flag artwork and applying a Warp effect. Next, Cohen made a duplicate copy of the flag by selecting it and, holding down Option/Alt, dragging it to a position below the original. While the duplicate was still selected, Cohen chose Effect > Warp > Flag to bring up the Warp dialog. She enabled the Preview checkbox in the Warp dialog so she could preview the effect her settings would have on the artwork. Cohen set the Horizontal Bend slider to –42% to create the first stage of her waving flag effect, and clicked OK to apply the Warp. She then applied a second Warp effect to the flag artwork, to complete her waving flag. With the artwork still selected, she chose Effect > Warp > Arc and, with Preview enabled, set the Horizontal Bend slider to 40%. **Note:** *In the Warp dialog, you have access to the full library of Warp shapes no matter which warp you chose from the Effect > Warp menu. Simply click and drag on the style pop-up menu in the Warp dialog to access any of the Warp shapes. As long as Preview is enabled, you can then experiment with each Warp shape and settings to see how each will affect your artwork before you apply one.*

To remove a Warp effect, in the Layers panel target your artwork. Then, in the Appearance panel, select the Warp and either click on, or drag your selection to, the Trash.

3 Saving your Warp effect as a graphic style. Once you are pleased with a particular Warp effect or effects that you have achieved, you can easily save the effects as a graphic style for application to other artwork. Begin by targeting the artwork that you applied your warp(s) and other effects to in the Layers panel. Then Option-click/Alt-click on the New Graphic Style button at the bottom of the Graphic Styles panel to create and name your new graphic style. If the appearance you save as a graphic style has no fill or strokes, the thumbnail for the graphic style you created will be blank. When this happens, choose either the Small or the Large List View (from the Graphic Styles panel pop-up menu) to view the graphic styles by name. To apply a graphic style, simply target the object, group, or layer, and then click on the graphic style in the Graphic Styles panel.

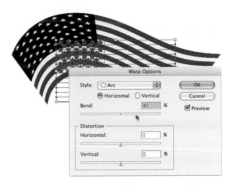
Applying a second Warp effect. Because Warps are live effects, the original flag artwork (seen here as an outline in light blue because the artwork is still selected) remains unchanged.

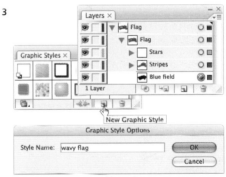
Removing Warp effects from the artwork by highlighting the effects in the Appearance panel, and then clicking on the Trash button to delete them

To create a new graphic style, target your artwork, then Option-click/Alt-click the New Graphic Style button, and give your new graphic style a name

Applying a Warp effect graphic style to a grouped object

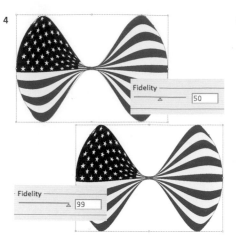

4

With Envelope Options fidelity set too low, red color in the lower right corner of the upper figure spills outside the bow tie shape. When the fidelity is set to 99% the artwork conforms much more closely to the envelope shape.

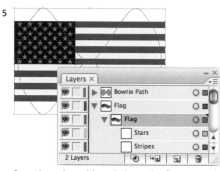

5

Bow tie path positioned above the flag artwork, and selected, just before making the envelope

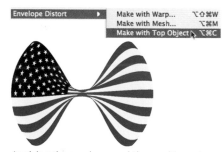

Applying the envelope, and the resulting artwork

6

Using Edit > Paste in Front to create a duplicate positioned directly over the original artwork

4 Using Envelope Options to maximize Envelope fidelity. Envelopes are more versatile in the ways you can shape and manipulate them, but sometimes (especially when the shape you use to create the envelope is kinked or makes sharp changes in direction) the artwork may not conform tightly to the envelope. To minimize this problem, set the Object > Envelope Distort > Envelope Options Fidelity to 99%. Note: Setting Fidelity to 100% creates many more intermediate points along the deformed path, and is usually not necessary.

Cohen used an Envelope to give her flag the shape of a bow tie, and added some shading using a mesh.

5 Applying Envelope using a shaped Path. Cohen added points to a circle and then distorted it into a bow-tie-shaped path. To apply a shaped path of your own, place it above your flag artwork, select both the flag and your shaped path, and choose Object > Envelope Distort > Make with Top Object.

6 Adding a shading effect with a mesh. Next, Cohen added a shading effect by using a mesh object on top of her bow tie flag. Begin by creating a duplicate of the bow tie flag (Edit > Copy), then paste it in front of the first one using Edit > Paste in Front to exactly align it over the original. With the duplicate still selected, choose Object > Envelope Distort > Reset with Mesh. In the Reset Envelope Mesh dialog, make sure that Maintain Envelope Shape and Preview are both enabled. Increase the number of Rows and Columns until you are satisfied with the mesh grid in terms of how you intend to shade it. For her mesh, Cohen used 6 rows and 6 columns. Click OK, and with the mesh artwork still selected, choose Envelope > Distort > Release to free the mesh from the flag. Delete the flag artwork and keep the mesh object. When a mesh object is released from an envelope, it is filled with 20% black. Select the mesh object, then, with the Lasso or the Direct Selection tool, select points on the mesh grid and change their fill to a shadow color. Cohen selected interior grid points and gave them a value of white until she was satisfied with the mesh's shading.

Note: *Multiple contiguous points and large areas in the mesh are most easily selected using the Lasso tool.*

To see the effect of the shading on the original bow tie flag beneath the mesh, Cohen (with the mesh selected) set the Blending Mode in the Transparency panel to Multiply. This applied the Blending mode only to the selected mesh object, and not the whole layer.

Finally, using the same enveloping and mesh techniques described above, Cohen created a center for the bow tie using a copy of some of the stripes and an elongated rounded rectangle path.

Creating a mesh object using a duplicate of the bow tie flag envelope artwork

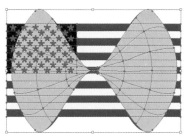

Using Envelope > Distort > Release to free the mesh from the flag artwork

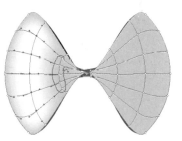

Using the Lasso to select multiple mesh points

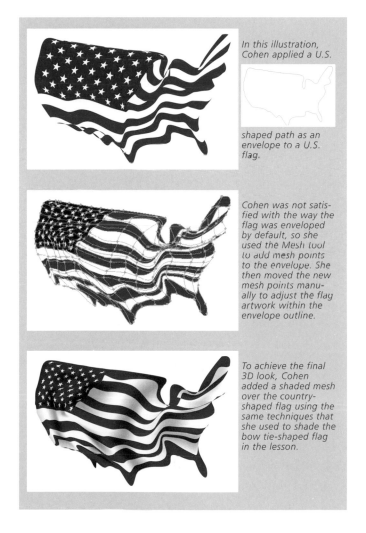

In this illustration, Cohen applied a U.S. shaped path as an envelope to a U.S. flag.

Cohen was not satisfied with the way the flag was enveloped by default, so she used the Mesh tool to add mesh points to the envelope. She then moved the new mesh points manually to adjust the flag artwork within the envelope outline.

To achieve the final 3D look, Cohen added a shaded mesh over the country-shaped flag using the same techniques that she used to shade the bow tie-shaped flag in the lesson.

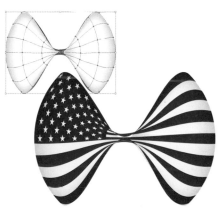

Before and after applying a blending mode of Multiply to the shaded mesh object

Scribble Basics

Applying Scribble Effects to Artwork

Overview: *Apply default Scribble effect settings; choose from preset Scribble styles; make custom adjustments to Scribble settings.*

STEAD

Hiding edges to see the effect

Applying a Scribble effect can generate a complex set of edges that make it difficult to view the artwork underneath. Get into the habit of hiding the edges of your selection before trying out an effect. Use the ⌘-H/Ctrl-H keyboard shortcut to toggle the visibility of the edges on and off.

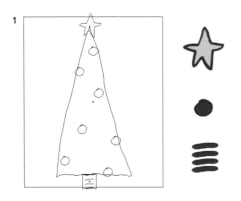

Shown here in Outline mode, Stead created her first tree by drawing with the brush tool

Judy Stead's evergreen tree began simply, but with the help of Illustrator's Scribble effect, it evolved into an eye-catching Christmas card. Here, you will learn how to apply the Scribble effect to your artwork, how to make use of the preset Scribble styles, and how to make custom adjustments to the effect in order to add excitement and energy to your art.

1 Creating the base art and the variations. Stead began by using the Brush tool to create a simple, filled shape for the tree. She used a 5-pt round Calligraphic brush to create the star, and applied a red stroke and a yellow fill to the path. She drew the ornament using the same brush and stroke with a magenta fill. Stead copied and pasted this shape several times to decorate her tree. She created the base of the tree using a 12-pt oval Calligraphic brush to draw a single horizontal stroke. She then made three copies and grouped them against a white rectangle.

Stead decided that her card would contain three variations of the first tree, so she copied and pasted them into position and gave each one a different color scheme. Beginning with the first variation, she selected the red background rectangle. She chose Effects > Stylize > Scribble, after first hiding the selection edges of her art (⌘-H) in order to observe the results more clearly. When the Scribble Options menu appeared, Stead clicked Preview. Satisfied with the Default settings, she clicked OK. These settings applied the appearance of a loose, continuous stroke to her solid red rectangle.

2 Using the Scribble presets. For her next variation, Stead first selected the light green tree and chose the Scribble style set entitled Sketch. She decided to leave the Sketch settings as they were and clicked OK. Then she selected the magenta background. After applying the Scribble style set entitled Sharp, she opened up the denseness of the effect's strokes by using the slider to change the Spacing value from 3 pt to 5 pt. The Scribble Options dialog also contains sliders to control the Stroke Width, the general Curviness of the strokes, and the degree of Variation or evenness of the effect.

3 Further Scribble settings. For the final variation, Stead selected the green background and chose Swash from Settings in the Scribble Options. Using the circular Angle slider, she changed the preset angle of the strokes from 0 to –30 degrees. Stead then selected all the tree ornaments and applied a final Scribble effect using Dense from the Settings pop-up in Scribble Options. Stead was able to go back and readjust all her settings, as needed, by clicking the instance of the effect in each object's Appearance panel. As a final touch, Stead selected the solid red tree and sent it backward (Object > Arrange > Send Backward) so that the green Swash scribble effect would overlay the tree and provide an interesting texture.

2

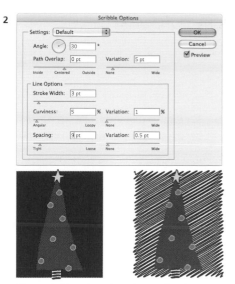

After switching the color scheme, Stead selected the red background, hid the edges, and applied a Custom Scribble (Effects menu)

For the light green Christmas tree, Stead chose the Sketch Settings from the Scribble Options

In Scribble Options Stead applied the Sharp settings to the background, changing spacing setting from 3 pt to 5 pt for a looser appearance

3

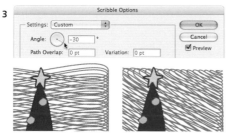

In Scribble Options, Stead applied Swash (from Settings) to the green background of the final tree art, and changed the Angle slider (which then changed the "Settings" to Custom)

Mike Schwabauer

To create this banner for a benefit performance, Mike Schwabauer made extensive use of Live Effects, and the Transparency and Appearance panels. He started by drawing a rectangle and filling it with gradient. For the main text, he chose a bold font (Impact) that could stand up to the effects he planned to apply. He set the Stroke to 1.5 pt with White as the color, and the Fill to either red or green. He typed the text for each color on a separate layer, and manually kerned and adjusted the leading in the Character panel. To give the stroke dimension, he targeted it in the Appearance panel and added a small Drop Shadow from the Effect > Stylize menu. He then targeted Fill and set the Transparency Blending Mode to Multiply.

He reduced the opacity slightly. Schwabauer selected New Fill from the pop-up menu, and then dragged it below the original Fill. He set White as the color and set the Blending Mode in the Transparency panel to Screen. He set the Opacity to 50%. He chose Effect > Stylize > Scribble and adjusted the settings to taste. To soften the scribbles, he used a small amount of Gaussian Blur (Effect > Blur > Gaussian Blur). Schwabauer chose Duplicate Item from the Appearance panel's menu. On the duplicate, he double-clicked on the *fx* icon beside Scribble to open the dialog, and adjusted the angle setting to form the crosshatch. For the type at the bottom, he used Helvetica Black and added a drop shadow to give it an embossed look.

Yukio Miyamoto

Illlustrator Yukio Miyamoto, well-known for his photorealistic illustrations with gradient mesh and author of several books on Illustrator in Japanese, has recently produced the *Illustrator Appearance Book* (with DVD), currently available only in Japanese. He used Live Effects and multiple Fills, among other features. He has kindly given us some examples for the *Wow! CD*. He has saved these as Graphic Styles that can be applied to type with a click of the mouse. They can be modified through the Appearance panel, and the type is live (see the inset for examples of changing Appearance attributes and text for the "Gold" button).

Miyamoto plans to produce an English version of the book. You can see several of his Graphic Styles at http://venus.oracchi.com/Illustrator/appearance/appearance.html.

BENFANTI

Russell Benfanti

If you look closely you'll see that Russell Benfanti's lush illustrations are actually constructed of fairly simple shapes. He calls his use of color "an exercise in restraint"; he consciously limits his palettes to only a few colors per image. Using these simple shapes, rich colors, and fine attention to detail, Benfanti creates his depth of field by applying Effect > Blur > Gaussian Blur in varying degrees to objects in the foreground and background (the version at right shows the Gaussian Blurs removed). He also incorporates complex gradients shaped by masks (see Benfanti's lesson "Masking Details" in the *Advanced Techniques*

chapter). He often provides a raster version of his image to the client (using File > Export > Photoshop) to minimize the opportunity for printing error.

Ted Alspach

Ted Alspach initially experimented with Effects and the Flare tool to create an interesting desktop background, but ultimately ended up with a striking image he then made it into a large wall hanging. He created this effect with multiple fills applied to a single textured rectangle. Working in RGB mode, Alspach filled a rectangle with a multicolored gradient (center figure, left). He applied Effect > Pixelate > Color Halftone, and entered a Pixel Max. Radius of 8 (center). Alspach then applied Effect > Pixelate > Crystallize, and adjusted the cell size slider to 40 (center figure, right). He made two copies of this rectangle by selecting Duplicate Item in the Appearance panel pop-up. He made adjustments to the duplicated rectangles by selecting the Fill appearance attribute in the Appearance panel. Using the Gradient tool, Alspach applied gradients of varying colors and angles. He double-clicked on the effects (Crystallize and Color Halftone) and changed the values for the Max. Radius and Screen Angles. Alspach also adjusted the Opacity (between 20% and 80%) and applied Soft Light, Multiply, and Color Burn blending modes. To make the flare, he selected the Flare tool, clicked and dragged to set the halo and click-dragged again to set the distance and direction of the rings while using the arrow keys to adjust the number of rings (bottom figure). Alspach made another copy of the rectangle and applied a blue gradient fill. He positioned this copy as the topmost fill and masked the flare to fit the image.

ALSPACH

MACADANGDANG

 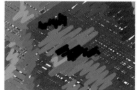

Todd Macadangdang

Todd Macadangdang used the Scribble effect to turn this photo into an artistic crosshatch sketch. He started by adjusting the colors and posterizing the photograph in Photoshop, using adjustment layers. Macadangdang then placed the image in Illustrator and drew filled objects based on the posterized areas. Starting with the smallest, front-most area, he clicked on the area with the Eyedropper tool to set the Fill color (with Stroke of None), then hand-traced over it using the Pencil tool. He repeated this process, working his way toward the largest, rearmost areas, using Object > Arrange > Send Backward as he went along to keep the shapes in the correct visual stacking order. He then applied the Scribble effect to each traced area. To give his image a greater depth, he used fatter, looser Scribble strokes (with Settings such as Childlike, Loose, or Snarl) for the front-most areas, and smaller, denser strokes (with the Angle setting rotated 90°) for the larger, rearmost crosshatched areas.

Steven Gordon / Cartagram, LLC

When you mix Illustrator's brushes with live effects, you can transform the lettering of a font into art that looks hand-rendered with traditional pens and brushes. To begin this map title, Steven Gordon typed "Yakima" and then chose a calligraphic font, Zapfino, at 72 points. In the Character panel, he adjusted kerning to tighten the space between several pairs of letter characters. With the text object selected and the Appearance panel open, Gordon chose Add New Fill from the panel's Options menu and gave the new fill a dark magenta color. He duplicated the fill by clicking on the Duplicate Selected Item icon at the bottom of the panel, and then gave the duplicate a pale blue color. Lastly, he clicked on a brush in the Brushes panel and chose the Dry Ink brush. He selected a dark blue color for the brush. Because the brush strokes were too large for the lettering effect he wanted, Gordon double-clicked the brush name in the Appearance panel, resized its width to 60% of the default size, and clicked to apply it to existing objects. To further customize the title, Gordon selected the pale blue fill in the Appearance panel, offset the fill and distorted the fill's edges using the Transform and Roughen commands from the Effect > Distort and Transform menu. He also reduced opacity by moving the Opacity slider in the Transparency panel to 35%. To finish, Gordon selected the bottom fill and applied the Roughen command from the Effect > Distort and Transform menu to tightly erode the fill's edges.

Extruding an object using the Effect > 3D > Extrude & Bevel dialog—the two-dimensional object on the left was extruded to create the three-dimensional covered bridge

Live 3D Effects

3D effects are much like the other live effects, except… they're 3D. If "live effects" or graphic styles are new concepts to you, please look at the intros to the *Live Effects & Graphics Styles* and *Layers & Appearances* chapters.

Illustrator offers you the power to transform any two-dimensional (2D) shape, including type, into a shape that looks three-dimensional (3D). As you're working in Illustrator's 3D effect dialogs, you can change your 3D shape's perspective, rotate it, and add lighting and surface attributes. And because you're working with a live effect, you can edit the source object at any time and observe the resultant change in the 3D shape immediately. You can also rotate a 2D shape in 3D space and change its perspective. Finally, Illustrator lets you map artwork, in the form of a symbol, onto any of your 3D object's surfaces.

To begin, think of Illustrator's horizontal ruler as the X axis and the vertical ruler as the Y axis. Now imagine a third dimension that extends back into space, perpendicular to the flat surface of your monitor. This is the Z axis. There are two ways to create a 3D shape using 3D effects. The first method is by extruding a 2D object back into space along the Z axis, and the second is by revolving a 2D object around its Y axis, up to 360°.

Once you apply a 3D effect to an object, it will show up in the Appearance panel. As with other appearance attributes, you can edit the effect, change the position of the effect in the panel's stacking order, and duplicate or delete the effect. You can also save 3D effects as reusable graphic styles so that you can apply the same effect to a batch of objects. Once the style has been applied, you can modify any of the style parameters by double-clicking the parameter in the Appearance panel.

EXTRUDING AN OBJECT

To extrude a 2D object, begin by creating an open or closed path. Your path can contain a stroke, a fill, or both.

2D or not 2D...?

Although Illustrator's 3D effect does a terrific job of rendering objects that look fully three-dimensional, you should bear in mind that Illustrator's 3D objects are only *truly* three-dimensional while you're working with them in a 3D effect dialog. As soon as you're done tweaking your object and you click OK to close the dialog, the object's three-dimensional qualities are "frozen"—almost as if Illustrator had taken a snapshot of the object—until the next time you edit it in a 3D dialog again. On the page, it's technically an impressive 2D rendering of a 3D object that can only be worked with in two-dimensional ways. But because the effect is live, you can work with the object in 3D again any time you want, by selecting the object and then double-clicking the 3D effect listed in the Appearance panel.

If your shape contains a fill, it's best to begin with a solid color. (See Tip "Solid advice on 3D colors" following.) With your path selected, choose Extrude & Bevel from the Effect>3D submenu. The top half of the 3D Extrude & Bevel Options dialog contains rotation and perspective options that we'll examine a bit later, but for the moment we'll concentrate on the lower portion of the dialog. Choose the depth to which you'd like your 2D object extruded by entering a point size in the Extrude Depth field or by dragging the pop-up slider. Choosing to add a cap to your object will give it a solid appearance (the end will be "capped off"), while choosing to turn the cap option off will result in a hollowed-out-looking object (see figures at right).

You also have the option to add a beveled edge to your extruded object. Illustrator offers you ten different styles of bevels to choose from, and a dialog in which to enter the height of the bevel. You can choose between a bevel that will be added to the original object (Bevel Extent Out), or a bevel that will be carved out from the original shape (Bevel Extent In). These options result in objects that appear radically different from each other (see the second pair of figures at right).

Note: *When you apply bevels to some objects (like stars), you might generate the error, "Bevel self-intersection may have occurred" when you click "Preview"—this may or may not actually mean that there is a problem.*

Remember that because you're working with a live effect, any changes you make to the original 2D source shape will immediately update the 3D object. The original shapes of the vector paths will be highlighted when you select the 3D shape—you can easily edit them just as you would any other path. You can always edit the settings you've entered for a particular 3D effect by double-clicking it in the Appearance panel.

REVOLVING AN OBJECT

You can also create a 3D object from a 2D path (either open or closed) by revolving it around its Y (vertical)

Customized bevels!

All the 3D Bevels Shapes are located inside a file called "Bevels.ai" (within the folders Adobe Illustrator CS3 > Plug-ins > Bevels.ai). Each bevel path is saved as a Symbol inside this document, so to add a custom bevel, draw a new path, drag it to the Symbols panel, name it and, resave the file.
—*Jean-Claude Tremblay*

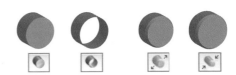

Left to right: Turn cap on for solid, Turn cap off for hollow, Bevel Extent Out, Bevel Extent In

3D—Three dialogs

There are three different 3D effects, and some features overlap. So before you apply 3D to an object, first decide which effect best accomplishes your goals. If all you need to do is rotate or change the perspective of an object, use Rotate. If you want to map a symbol to the object, use either Revolve or Extrude & Bevel (you can still rotate an object from these as well). —*Brenda Sutherland*

HAMANN

Revolving an object using the Effect>3D> Revolve dialog—the 2D shape on the left was revolved to create the 3D object on the right

You can rotate objects in three dimensions by using the Effect >3D >Rotate dialog (or the upper halves of the Revolve and the Extrude & Bevel dialogs). The star on the left was rotated in 3D to create the star on the right.

HAMANN

Another example of rotating an object in three dimensions

3D effect—pass it on

Although in this book we generally recommend working with the New Art Has Basic Appearance setting turned off, you might want to turn it on when working with 3D effects. Otherwise, any new paths that you create subsequent to applying 3D effects to an object will also have the same appearance set, unless you first clear the appearance set from the panel, or click on the default fill and stroke icon in the Tools panel. On the other hand, if you *want* your next object to have the same 3D effects as the one you just created, leave New Art Has Basic Appearance turned off.

axis. Solid strokes work just as well as filled objects. Once you've selected your path, choose Effect >3D >Revolve. In the 3D Revolve Options dialog you can set the number of degrees you wish to revolve the object by entering a value from 1 to 360 in the Angle text field, or by dragging the slider. An object that is revolved 360° will appear solid. An object revolved less than 360° will appear to have a wedge carved out of it. You can also choose to offset the rotation from the object's edge. This will result in a 3D shape that appears to be carved out in the center. And finally, as with extruded shapes, because the 3D options you've chosen are live effects, any changes you make to your original source object will immediately change the look of the 3D shape you've revolved.

ROTATING AN OBJECT IN 3D SPACE

You can rotate both 2D and 3D objects by choosing Effects >3D >Rotate. The 3D Rotate Options dialog contains a cube representing the planes that your shape can be rotated through. You can choose a preset angle of rotation from the Position menu, or enter values between –180 and 180 in the X, Y and Z text fields. (The Rotate controls also appear in the upper half of both the Extrude & Bevel and the Revolve Options boxes.)

If you'd like to manually rotate your object around one of its three axes, simply click on the edge of one of the faces of the white cube and drag. The edges of each plane are highlighted in a corresponding color that tells you through which of the object's three planes you're rotating it. Red represents the object's X axis, a green highlight represents the object's Y axis, and blue edges represent the object's Z axis. The object's rotation is constrained within the plane of that particular axis. Remember, to constrain the rotation you must be dragging an edge of the cube. Notice the numbers changing in the corresponding text field as you drag. If you wish to rotate your object relative to all three axes at once, click directly on a surface of the cube and drag, or click in the black area behind the cube and drag. Values in all three text fields will change. And if you simply want to rotate your object, click-and-drag inside the circle, but outside the cube itself.

Changing the perspective of an object

You can change the visible perspective of your object by entering a number between 0 and 160 in the perspective text field, or by dragging the slider. A smaller value simulates the look of a telephoto camera lens, while a larger value will simulate a wide-angle camera lens, with more of an "exploded" perspective.

APPLYING SURFACE SHADING TO 3D OBJECTS

Illustrator allows you a variety of choices in the kind of shading you apply to your 3D object. These range from dull and unshaded matte surfaces to glossy and highlighted surfaces that look like plastic. And because you can also choose how you light your object, the possible variations are limitless.

The surface shading option appears as part of both the 3D Extrude & Bevel and the 3D Revolve Option dialogs. Choosing Wireframe as your shading option will result in a transparent object whose contours are overlaid with a set of outlines describing the object's geometry. The next choice is No Shading, which will result in a flat-looking shape with no discernible surfaces. Choosing the Diffused Shading option results in your object having a soft light cast on its surfaces, while choosing the Plastic Shading option will make your object look as if it's molded out of shiny, reflective plastic.

If you choose either the Diffused Shading or Plastic Shading options, you can further refine the look of your object by adjusting the direction and intensity of the light source illuminating your object. By clicking the More Options button, the dialog will enlarge and you'll be able to make changes to the Light Intensity, Ambient Light level, Highlight Intensity, Highlight Size, and number of Blend Steps. The default for Blend Steps is quite low (25 out of a maximum of 256)—see the Tip "Not enough steps…" at the right. You can also choose a custom

Solid advice on 3D colors

You'll get best results using solid fill colors for 3D objects. Gradients and pattern fills don't produce reliable results.

For the smoothest 3D

When creating profile objects that you will extrude, revolve, or rotate into 3D, your goal should be to draw the objects with as few anchor points as possible. Since each anchor point will produce an additional surface, the more points that you have, the more irregular your form might appear. Also, extra surfaces might create potential problems you'll encounter when mapping artwork onto the surfaces later.

—Jean-Claude Tremblay

Making 3D can be slow…

Depending on processor speed and RAM, 3D effects can be slow.

Not enough steps…

If you click on the More Options button, you'll get the opportunity to adjust Surface and Shading Color options. The default setting for Blend Steps is 25—not nearly enough steps to create smooth color transitions from light to shaded areas. Since the maximum setting of 256 is smooth but slows you down, experiment to find the best resolution-to-speed setting for each image.

GOLDING

Mordy Golding used the Map Art feature to wrap the label art (above left) around the bottle (shown in detail, above right)—to create the bottle he used the 3D Revolve effect with a custom Surface Shading (for more about this art see the Mordy Golding Gallery later in this chapter)

Mapping—don't get lost!

Here are some tips to help you avoid confusion about the surface to which you're mapping symbols:

- Remember that you need to choose a surface in the dialog. Select by clicking the Arrow keys to view each surface.
- When clicking through the various surfaces, it's sometimes easier to identify the surface you want by the red highlight on the object itself, rather than by the flattened proxy in the mapping dialog.
- Even the red highlight can fool you. If the symbol isn't mapping to a selected surface, it may be because it's being mapped to the *inside* of the surface.
- A stroke will add more surfaces to an object.
- A stroke can obscure mapped art on a side surface.

—Brenda Sutherland

Shading Color to add a color cast to the shaded surfaces. If you want to maintain a spot color assigned to your Extruded object during output, then enable the Preserve Spot Colors checkbox. However, be aware that Preserve Spot Colors removes custom shading and resets your Shading Color to Black. If you choose Preserve Spot Colors, you should turn on Overprint Preview (View menu) so you can see your shading and color accurately.

MAPPING ART ONTO AN OBJECT

One of the most exciting aspects of the 3D effect is the ability to map artwork onto the surfaces of your 2D or 3D shape (as with the label on Mordy Golding's wine bottle at left). The key is to first define the art that you wish to map onto a surface as a symbol; select the artwork you want to map and drag it to the Symbols panel. For some images, you'll want to define a number of symbols. For instance, in Mordy's wine bottle, the label was one symbol and the printing on the cork was a separate symbol.

Once you've made your artwork into symbols, you can map the symbols onto your 3D objects from the Extrude & Bevel, Revolve, or Rotate Options dialogs. In any of these 3D options boxes you simply click on the Map Art button, then choose one of the available symbols from the menu. You can specify which of your object's surfaces the artwork will map onto by clicking on the left and right Arrow keys. The selected surface will appear in the window; then you can either scale the art by dragging the handles on the bounding box or make the art expand to cover the entire surface by clicking the Scale to Fit button. Note that as you click through the different surfaces, the selected surface will be highlighted with a red outline in your document window. Your currently visible surfaces will appear in light gray in the Map Art dialog, and surfaces that are currently hidden will appear dark. (See the "Quick Box Art" lesson later in this chapter for an example of mapping 3D surfaces with custom symbols.)
Note: *To see artwork mapped onto the side surfaces of your object, make sure that the object has a stroke of None!*

SHOULAK

Joseph Shoulak

This tower of Tupperware (left) accompanied a San Francisco Chronicle story about the history of the Tupperware container. Shoulak created each container by using the 3D features in Illustrator (see his lesson later in this chapter). The round containers were made by drawing a 2D path of a container's profile, then applying the Effect > 3D > Revolve command to revolve the path 360° (above). He created the square containers by applying the Effect > 3D > Extrude & Bevel command to 2D paths. When a container used complex surfaces or multiple colors, Shoulak assembled it from multiple components. As he arranged the tower on the Artboard, he drew shadows and used the Control panel to adjust opacity.

Quick & Easy 3D

Simple 3D Techniques

GORDON / CARTAGRAM, LLC

Overview: *Draw or modify 2D artwork, prepare artwork for 3D; apply 3D Effect; expand artwork and edit objects to complete visual effects.*

Steven Gordon was hired to design a set of contemporary map symbols for Digital Wisdom, Inc. that would be sold as a clip-art set of map symbol artwork and Illustrator symbols (www.map-symbol.com). To make this set stand out from other map symbol sets and fonts, Gordon explored Illustrator's new 3D Effect and found that it made it easy to turn the ordinary into the unusual.

1

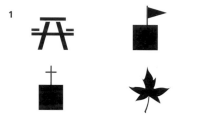

Some of the standard map symbols that Gordon modified for the map symbol set

Left, the original tent artwork objects; center, the white triangle selected; right, the tent after subtracting the white triangle from the black triangle and changing the fill color to green

1 Drawing artwork, visualizing 3D appearance, and using editing tools to prepare for 3D. Gordon started with some standard map symbol clip-art. For the camping symbol, he modified the tent artwork by removing the bottom horizontal object and applying a light green fill to the remaining triangle. When visualizing how the object would look in 3D, Gordon realized that the white and green triangles would both be rendered as 3D objects; instead he needed the white triangle to form a hole in the green triangle that would become the tent. He selected the white and green triangles and clicked the Subtract from Shape Area icon in the Pathfinder panel to punch a hole in the green triangle.

As you prepare artwork for the 3D Effect, refer to the *Beyond the Basics* chapter to review techniques for making compound shapes by combining or cutting objects (as Gordon did to make the tent opening), and for making compound paths (which may yield different results than applying a 3D Effect to separate artwork objects). Also, change stroke attributes for caps, joins, and miter limits to round off path intersections in the 3D rendering you'll create in the next step.

Single-axis movements in 3D

In the 3D Extrude & Bevel Options dialog, you click on a *side* of the cube and drag to rotate artwork using the X, Y, or Z axis. If you want to move the artwork by just one axis, click instead on a white *edge* of the cube and then drag.

---

2 Applying 3D Effect, modifying Position controls to extrude and rotate objects, and creating a Style. When you finish creating your artwork, make sure it is selected, and then from the Effect menu, select 3D > Extrude & Bevel. In the 3D Extrude & Bevel Options dialog, enable the Preview checkbox to see what your artwork will look like using the dialog's default settings.

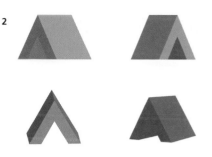

2

You can change the artwork's rotation by clicking on the three-dimensional cube in the Position pane of the dialog and dragging until the artwork moves to an orientation you like. You can also fine-tune the position by keying in values in the X, Y, and Z axes rotation fields.

Artwork in preview mode for several adjustments of the Position cube in the 3D Extrude & Bevel Options dialog

To change the amount or depth of the extrusion, use the Extrude Depth slider in the Extrude & Bevel pane of the dialog. To give the tent less depth than the default setting (50 pt), Gordon dragged the slider to extrude by 40 pt. To simulate perspective, drag the Perspective slider to adjust the amount of perspective from none/isometric (0°) to very steep (160°). Gordon used 135° for his artwork. When you are satisfied with your artwork's appearance, click OK to render the object.

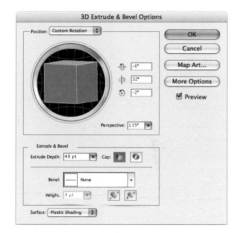

Gordon converted the 3D appearance he had created for the tent into a reusable style. Refer to the *Live Effects & Graphic Styles* chapter for instructions on creating and modifying graphic styles. You can use a style for other artwork, as way of providing a uniform 3D appearance for several objects, or as a starting point for creating a new 3D appearance for an object.

The 3D Extrude & Bevel Options dialog with the settings Gordon used for the final version of the tent symbol

3 Editing the artwork after using the 3D Effect. After applying the 3D Effect to the tent artwork, Gordon decided to make color and shape changes to the artwork. To edit shapes or change colors of objects in the 3D artwork, you must first expand the appearance by choosing Object > Expand Appearance. (Note: this will remove the "live" editability of the artwork; it's safer to work with a copy of the artwork instead of the original.) Once expanded, ungroup the artwork (Object > Ungroup) and select and edit its paths.

3

Left, the tent artwork after expanding the 3D artwork (Object > Expand Appearance); right, shapes after filling with different colors

Selecting and modifying one of the shapes to create the interior floor of the tent

3D Effects

Extruding, Revolving, and Rotating Paths

Overview: *Create basic paths working with a custom template layer; extrude, revolve, and rotate paths; map artwork onto shapes.*

1

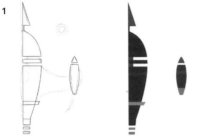

The original pencil drawing, placed as a template, and the vector shapes drawn over them

2

The original group of paths, selected and revolved as a group with the same settings

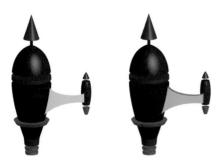

The wing shape drawn to follow the contour of the hull and then extruded and rotated slightly

To complete this illustration, Brad Hamann created a set of basic paths and applied a series of live 3D effects to them. He then added lighting and mapped artwork to the components.

1 Planning ahead. Because he would be rotating his shapes, Hamann needed to draw only one side of the symmetrical space cruiser. Working over a pencil drawing he had scanned in Photoshop and placed on a designated template layer, he drew one closed shape for the hull. He divided it into sections using the Pathfinder tool so he could color each part differently. He filled the paths with solid color and no stroke. When revolved, a filled path with no stroke will present the fill color as its surface color. A stroked shape that is revolved uses the stroke color as its surface color, regardless of fill color.

2 Applying the 3D Revolve effect to a group of shapes and extruding the wings. Hamann chose to revolve the group of shapes that make up the ship's hull all at the same time, because they shared the same left-side vertical rotation line. He also revolved the three shapes making up the rocket-shaped wing end as a group, using the same settings. Once the shapes were revolved, Hamann selected and moved each shape into its proper position within the group, using the Bring to Front command. He deleted the two inner green circles, because they would be invisible within the 3D model anyway.

For the wings Hamann then drew a flat shape for the right wing that followed the contour of the 3D hull and chose Effect > 3D > Extrude & Bevel. He selected an extrusion depth and rotational angle for the wing that would be visually consistent with the hull.

3 **Mapping artwork.** Hamann decided to map a star pattern, which he had previously saved as a symbol, onto the wing to liven up the look of the spaceship. He was able to return to the 3D Effects settings window by selecting the wing and clicking the Effect setting from the Appearance panel. He then clicked the Map Art button to access the Map Art window, which presented an outline of the first of the six surfaces available on the wing for mapping. Hamann chose his star pattern from the menu of available symbols. He scaled the pattern using the handles on the bounding box and then clicked OK. At this time, he also changed the wing color from green to red. Finally, Hamann selected the wing and the rocket at its end, and reflected and copied the wing to the opposite side of the spacecraft. He made a slight adjustment to the rotational angle of the new wing's Y-axis to account for its new position.

4 **Ready for takeoff.** Hamann completed his rocket ship by creating a porthole from a circular path to which he applied a 5.5-pt ochre-colored stroke. He then extruded the path and applied a rounded bevel. A blue gradient filled path, and a Gaussian Blur was applied, which completed the porthole.

3
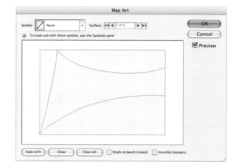
Clicking in the wing's Appearance panel to return to the 3D Effects settings window

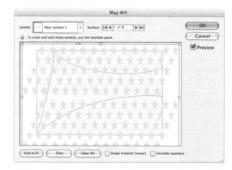
The Map Art window showing the first of the wing's surfaces available for art mapping

After selecting the star pattern from the Symbol menu, the pattern was scaled and positioned onto the wing outline

4

Hamann applied a rounded bevel to a circular path he had extruded to create the porthole

3D Logo Object

Revolving a Simple Path into a 3D Object

GILBERT

Overview: *Draw a cross-section; use the 3D Revolve feature to build a 3D object from the cross-section.*

1

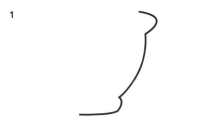

The cross-section path for the mortar, shown here with a black stroke for clarity; the actual path has a very light black fill and no stroke

2

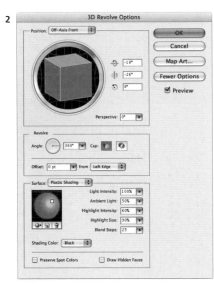

3D Revolve Options dialog with settings for the final mortar bowl

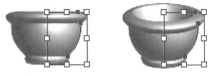

The mortar with all rotation angles set to 0° (left), and at the default angles (right)

When Reggie Gilbert redesigned this logo for an herbal extract company, he decided to draw the mortar and pestle as 3D objects. Gilbert used the 2D basic shape tools and gradient fills to easily draw the pestle, but for the more complex mortar, he used the 3D Revolve feature.

1 Drawing the cross-section of the mortar. Gilbert drew a path for the cross-section of the mortar and applied a white fill to it. He didn't need to draw more than that, because in the next step he formed the whole mortar by revolving the path in 3D. Because 3D is a live effect, you can edit the path later and the 3D result will update, so you don't need to be concerned about drawing the cross-section path perfectly the first time.

2 Applying the 3D Revolve effect. With the cross-section selected, Gilbert chose Effect > 3D > Revolve. In the Revolve section of the 3D Revolve Options dialog, he entered 360° for Angle, which swept the cross-section around in a full circle. The Offset option showed that by default, the center of the revolution was the path's left edge. The Surface settings shaded the mortar, using the fill color Gilbert applied to the original path (clicking the More Options button reveals Surface settings). You can rotate a 3D object by dragging the proxy cube in the 3D Revolve Options dialog or by entering rotation angles next to the cube. Gilbert used the default values for the rotation angles and the Surface settings.

© HALLMARK LICENSING, INC.

Mike Schwabauer / Hallmark Cards

To announce a company blood drive, artist Mike Schwabauer produced this illustration that was emailed as a low-resolution graphic and printed as a sign. For the background flag, Schwabauer started with flat, rectangular flag artwork. He selected the Free Transform tool to rotate and scale the flag. Then he chose Object > Envelope Distort > Make with Warp. In the Warp Options dialog, he selected Flag from the Style menu. Schwabauer modified the default settings for the Flag style. When he had the look he wanted, he clicked OK. To fade the flag, he drew a rectangle large enough to cover the flag and filled it with a black-to-white gradient. After selecting the rectangle and the flag, he opened the Transparency panel and chose Make Opacity Mask from the panel menu. For the blood drop, Schwabauer drew half of the blood drop shape. Then he chose Effect > 3D > Revolve and customized the

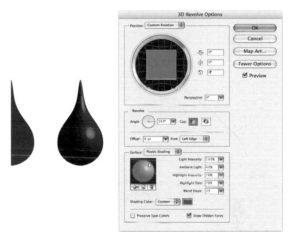

settings in the 3D Revolve Options dialog. After clicking OK, he changed the object's transparency in the Transparency panel to 93% to make the drop look more like a liquid. To complete the blood drop, Schwabauer selected the blood drop object and chose Effect > Stylize > Drop Shadow. In the Drop Shadow dialog, he set Mode to Multiply, Opacity to 50%, Blur to 0.12 inches, and Offset to –0.5" (X) and 0.2" (Y).

Assembling in 3D

Building 3D Objects from Multiple Paths

SHOULAK

Overview: *Draw 2D paths with rounded corners; use the 3D Extrude & Bevel effect to create 3D objects from the 2D paths; arrange the 3D objects to build a more complex 3D object.*

Joseph Shoulak drew this plastic container as part of a larger illustration for a San Francisco Chronicle story about a Tupperware documentary film. Shoulak cleverly rendered complex plastic forms in Illustrator by stacking and aligning paths that were extruded and rotated using the 3D features in Illustrator.

1 Drawing the 2D paths. The container is like a beveled box with non-beveled lips that extend where the white base and blue lid meet. These attributes led Shoulak to draw four paths for extrusion: the white container body, the white lip, the blue lip, and the blue body. The need for four shapes will become evident when they are later extruded in 3D.

The Rectangle and Rounded Rectangle tools (highlighted) in the toolbox, and the Round Corners dialog for adding round corners to rectangles that don't already have them

Seen from the top, the container consists of rectangles with round corners. To create them precisely, draw with the Rectangle tool; the rectangle for the blue top is 136 pt by 170 pt. Then choose Effect > Stylize > Round Corners and enter a Radius value of 12 pt. Alternatively, you can use the Rounded Rectangle tool, adjusting the corner radius by pressing the Up or Down arrow keys before releasing the mouse button.

These four paths will eventually form the entire container

The 3D effects in Illustrator pick up the fill and stroke colors applied to paths. Shoulak filled the rectangles with the blue and white colors of the container body and lid. He set the stroke color to None, because a stroke color would have colored the sides of the objects.

2 Extruding the 2D paths into 3D. Shoulak selected the blue container lid and chose Effect > 3D > Extrude & Bevel. He entered an Extrude Depth of 40 points. Shoulak also applied a bevel by choosing the Classic style and entering a Height of 4 points. He also adjusted the 3D rotation angles (X axis: 77, Y axis: 35, Z axis: -10). When he was satisfied, he clicked OK.

For the other three paths, Shoulak used the same rotation angles, but slightly different extrusion and bevel settings. For the thin blue lip path, he entered an Extrude Depth of 10 points with no bevel. For the thin white lip, Shoulak entered an Extrude Depth of 5 points with no bevel. For the white container base, he used an Extrude Depth of 45 pts with a 4-pt Classic bevel.

Enable the Preview checkbox to see your changes interactively, but be aware that previewing 3D effects can take time. Because a 3D effect is live, you can edit it by selecting the object using the effect, then double-clicking the effect name in the Appearance panel. If selecting 3D objects becomes a challenge, you can select objects using the Layers panel, or working in Outline view. (3D objects in Outline view appear without the 3D effects.)

3 Assembling the objects. To complete the illustration, Shoulak repositioned the four 3D objects into their final arrangement. He used the Control panel to center all four objects horizontally. Then he moved each path up or down until they fit together perfectly.

There are several ways to keep objects along a vertical axis as you move them. You can Shift-drag an object, drag an object vertically with View > Smart Guides enabled, press the up or down arrow keys to nudge the object, or enter a value into just the Y value in the Control panel or Transform panel.

While you can rotate individual 3D objects by using the 3D Extrude & Bevel dialog, you can't position 3D objects relative to each other in 3D space. 3D objects on the Artboard behave like 2D page objects—you can position them only on the Artboard's 2D space.

2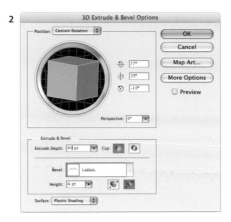

The 3D Extrude & Bevel dialog settings for the larger blue lid piece

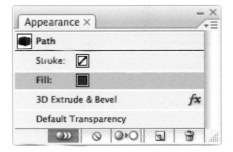

The four paths after applying extrusion settings

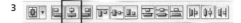

Appearance panel showing applied 3D effect

3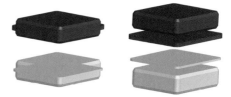

The Control panel with the Horizontal Align Center button highlighted; Align buttons appear when multiple objects are selected

The four extruded paths after horizontal centering (left) and after repositioning them vertically (right), closing in on their final positions

Quick Box Art

Converting 2D Artwork to 3D Packages

Overview: *Start with a 2D package drawing; create symbols from package sides, use 3D Extrude and Bevel to rotate a box in perspective; map side art to each surface.*

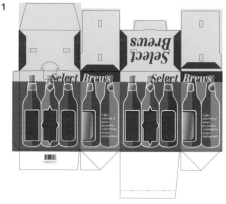

The prepress-ready flat box drawing

The three required sides separated from the main drawing

Gary Moss designed this easy-to-carry box for assorted beer bottles. The client requested a rendering of the finished box for a catalog. Moss used the 3D Extrude & Bevel effect to simulate the final three-dimensional box and to quickly map the box sides to their surfaces.

1 **Drawing the flat box.** Moss created a design sketch in Illustrator. Then using an Illustrator file provided by the box manufacturer, he applied precise dimensions to his sketch to meet the printing specifications, including all necessary sides, folds, bleeds, and die cuts.

2 **Separating the sides.** Moss created a copy of the flat box drawing, then used the Selection and Direct Selection tools to delete everything except the three sides that would be visible in the simulated box. For the 3D box, he wouldn't need the bleeds that extended beyond the actual edge of a side, so Moss trimmed them back, resizing the bleed paths to meet the actual box edge.

3 Creating symbols from the sides. Moss planned to use the 3D Extrude & Bevel feature to map the art to the sides of the box; this feature requires each side to be made into an Illustrator symbol first. If you're not using other symbols, you can delete them to reduce panel clutter: In the Symbols panel, choose Select All Unused, and click the Delete Symbol button. To create a symbol, select the objects making up one side and click the New Symbol icon in the Symbols panel. Repeat for each side.

In Illustrator, a symbol is normally used to creatively reuse an object many times. Mapping art in the 3D Extrude & Bevel feature is a special use of symbols.

4 Creating the 3D form. Moss drew a rectangle the size of the box front. With the rectangle selected, he chose Effect > 3D > Extrude & Bevel. He set the Extrude Depth to 120 points (the side panel width). He adjusted the rotation angles (X axis: -20, Y axis: 30, Z axis: -10), and to add slight linear perspective, he set Perspective to 19°.

5 Mapping the art. To apply art to each box surface, Moss used the Map Art feature in the 3D Extrude & Bevel dialog. Click the Map Art button, click the arrows to select next and previous surfaces (the current surface highlights in red on the Artboard), and select the desired symbol. Click the Scale to Fit button to size the art to the surface, or use the handles to position, rotate, or size the art manually. It may be simpler to create the symbols at the proper orientation and size, as shown in step 3.

If mapped art doesn't preview, it may be mapped to the non-visible surface of a side. When viewing non-mapped surfaces in the Map Art dialog, a light gray surface faces you, while a dark gray surface faces away.

6 Finishing the illustration. Although the 3D Extrude & Bevel dialog provides lighting controls (click More Options to see them), Moss wanted to add more creative lighting and shading effects by hand in Photoshop. In Photoshop, choose File > Open to open an Illustrator file.

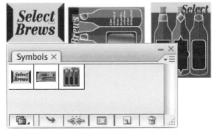

3

Symbols created from each side of the bottle box, after deleting all unused symbols

4

3D Extrude & Bevel dialog (top), the 2D front side before (bottom left) and after (bottom right) applying 3D extrusion

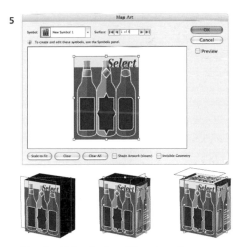

5

Map Art dialog (top) and the art on the Artboard (bottom) as each side is mapped

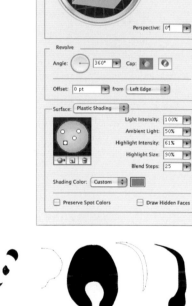

WAI

Trina Wai

Trina Wai created her playful panda by taking
full advantage of Illustrator's 3D Revolve and
3D Extrude and Bevel effects. She started with
a series of very simple flat shapes and ended
with a truly organic look. Wai began by drawing an open path for one side of the panda's
head. Choosing Effect > 3D > Revolve, she
rotated the path 360° along its left edge. To
create the soft shiny reflections of the panda's
fur, Wai specified plastic shading as the surface
type and added additional light sources using
the New Light button. The bamboo stalk was
also revolved from a simple open path, then
rotated and grouped with a set of flat leaf
shapes. Wai then extruded the main body parts
by selecting 3D Extrude and Bevel. Each shape
received its own extrusion depth ranging from
150 pt for the legs and body, 37.5 pt for the
ears, 30 pt for the nose and 7 pt for the areas

surrounding the eyes. Each shape also received
a rounded bevel and plastic shading lit with a
single light source. The small eyes were created
using a blend between a large black circle and
a smaller gray circle.

GOLDING / ADOBE SYSTEMS, INC.

3D Revolve Options

Position: Off-Axis Front

OK
Cancel
Map Art...
Fewer Options
☑ Preview

-18°
-26°
8°

Perspective: 0°

Revolve

Angle: 360° Cap:

Offset: 0 pt from Left Edge

Surface: Plastic Shading

Light Intensity: 100%
Ambient Light: 50%
Highlight Intensity: 61%
Highlight Size: 50%
Blend Steps: 50

Shading Color: Custom

☐ Preserve Spot Colors   ☐ Draw Hidden Faces

Mordy Golding

To demonstrate the 3D effect of Illustrator for
Adobe Systems, Inc., Mordy Golding created a
wine label and then dragged the label to the
Symbols panel (so he could use it next to create
the 3D rendering). He drew a half-bottle shape
and selected Effect > 3D > Revolve. In the 3D
Revolve Options dialog, Golding enabled the
Preview checkbox and then clicked on the Map
Art button. From the Map Art dialog's Symbol
menu, he selected the wine label symbol he
had created previously. Back in the 3D Revolve
Options dialog, Golding adjusted the preview
cube, changing the rotation angles until he
was satisfied with the look of the bottle. He
finished the effect by adding lights, using the
New Light icon in the Surface panel of the
dialog; this created the cascading highlights
on the bottle. After creating the cork, using
the same technique as he used for the bottle,
Golding selected the bottle, moved it above
the cork, and changed its opacity to 94% in the
Transparency panel.

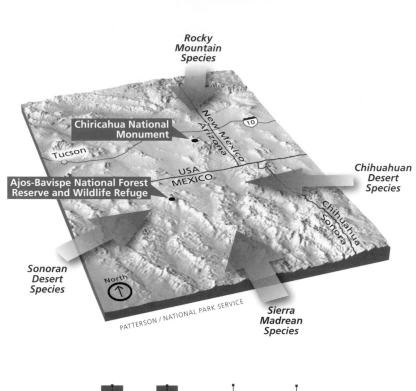

Tom Patterson / National Park Service

Cartographer Tom Patterson used Illustrator's 3D effect to show species movement across the Sonoran Desert. Patterson drew a straight path with the Pen tool and chose a 20-pt stroke. To turn the path into an arrow, he chose Effect > Stylize > Add Arrowheads. In the Add Arrowheads dialog, he selected an arrowhead design (11) and specified 25% for Scale. Next, Patterson chose Effect > 3D > Rotate and in the 3D Rotate Options dialog, he enabled the Preview and dragged the three-dimensional cube in the Position pane to adjust the spatial orientation of the arrow. When the arrow looked right, he clicked OK. To fill the arrow, Patterson first chose Object > Group to change the arrow from an object to a group. Then he selected Add New Fill from the Appearance panel menu and applied a custom gradient to the new fill. He repeated these steps to create the other three arrows. To finish, Patterson targeted the layer containing the arrows and changed opacity to 80% in the Transparency panel; he also added a drop shadow (Effect > Stylize > Drop Shadow) to the layer.

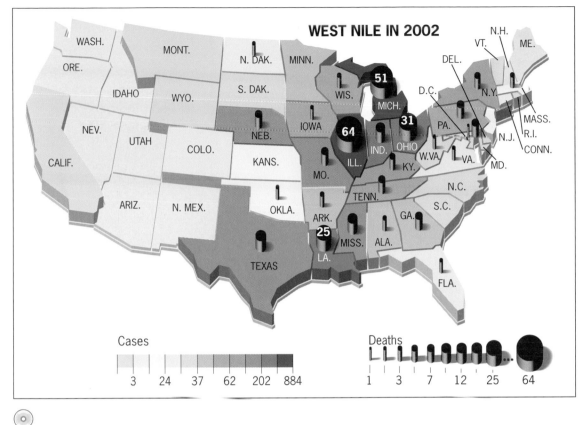

LERTOLA

Joe Lertola / *TIME*

Joe Lertola of *TIME* Magazine relied on the 3D Effect (Effect > 3D > Extrude & Bevel) to turn an otherwise flat map into an eye-catching 3D thematic map. After drawing all the artwork, Lertola created groups for the gray states and the colored states. To give each group a different height, he applied the 3D Effect to each group, but specified a different Extrude Depth value in the 3D Extrude & Bevel Options dialog for each group (6 pt for the gray states and 24 pt for the colored states). Lertola completed the effect by adding a second light (he clicked on the New Light icon in the Surface panel) to change the position of the highlight and shadow of each group.

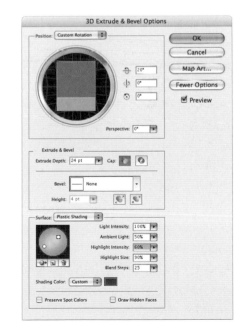

Ted Alspach

Ted Alspach creates a new version of his comic strip "Board2Pieces" twice a week (plus a large-format bimonthly strip). When creating the whole concept for the strip, he understood he would need to create his characters and their positions and expressions consistently and quickly. To have time to concentrate on the written content instead of repetitive drawing, Alspach chose to use 3D objects for their live, editable effects, and a full Symbols panel of facial expressions to control his characters' appearance frame to frame. Early in the process he determined an extrusion amount for each character, using 3D's ability to rotate the character without the need to redraw the basic figure. Next he created a variety of facial expressions that would allow his characters to respond to each other. Alspach saved even more time by creating some characters that could share facial expressions. He saved all these expressions as symbols in order to be able to use 3D's ability to map symbols as art to a selected surface on the 3D object. (For more on creating symbols, see the *Brushes & Symbols* chapter.) Now, instead of laboriously drawing

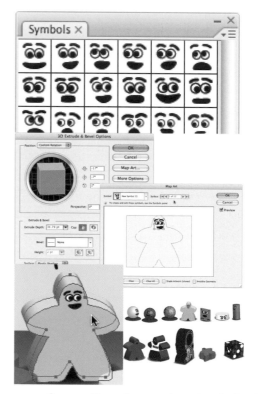

every frame, Alspach can select the desired character and place it where he needs it in the frame. He can then double-click on the effects icon in the Appearance panel to modify the figure's position, and remap its facial expression using a library of symbols, which leaves him a lot more time for writing.

HAMM

Michael Hamm

For this personal digital assistant (PDA) concept, Michael Hamm used 3D features and custom guides. He drew a rounded rectangle then chose Effect > 3D > Extrude & Bevel to specify 3D values. Hamm selected No Shading from the Surface pop-up menu in the 3D Extrude & Bevel dialog because he wanted to shade the PDA manually. When the perspective looked good (top right), he expanded a copy of the case (Object > Expand Appearance) and applied meshes and blends to shade each side. When creating additional 3D objects like the buttons,

Hamm matched them to the case perspective by copying the 3D rotation values or the Appearance from the original unexpanded 3D case, which he kept on a hidden layer. Hamm aligned objects using a layer of hand-drawn perspective guides (bottom right). He used the Rectangular Grid tool (bottom left) to draw the LCD pixel grid, and used the Free Transform tool to apply perspective (grid detail at bottom center). To combine the grid with the screen, Hamm applied 50% opacity and the Color Dodge blending mode to the grid.

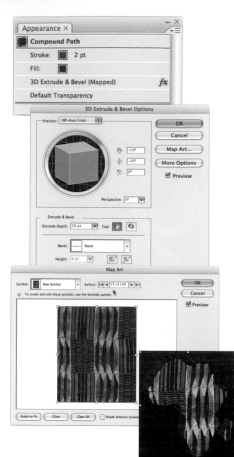

JOGIE

Mohammed Jogie

Mohammed Jogie created this bookcover for the African Peer Review Mechanism, an arm of NEPAD, for an annual progress report on Ghana. He purchased and photographed some of the objects and created the pattern for the map of Africa based on fabrics he bought. The fabric is Kente cloth, entirely hand-woven by Ghanaian weavers, which he obtained from the African art market in Johannesburg. He saved the fabric pattern as a symbol, a step necessary to map art to a 3D object. Jogie next created the flat, 2D object to represent Africa and Madagascar. He used a red Fill and a 2-point Stroke to give the extruded edge the color and detail

he wanted. He selected his "Africa" object and chose Effect > 3D > Extrude and Bevel. He set an amount for the extrusion, set the Cap to produce a solid edge, and rotated the object to the position he wanted, using the Preview to judge the effect. Jogie then chose Map Art and selected the surfaces he wanted to display the fabric. After mapping the fabric pattern, he clicked OK to exit the mapping dialog, and OK again to exit and apply the 3D effect. He used other illusions of depth, such as gradients within Opacity Masks and drop shadows, to complement the 3D structure of the map, and used a copy of the 3D map for the reflection.

SHARIF

Robert Sharif

Robert Sharif used the power of Illustrator's 3D Extrude & Bevel effect to transform and combine a set of flat shapes into a stunningly realistic rendering of a classic Fender electric guitar. Robert chose Off-Axis-Front as the position for each shape he wanted to extrude, including the red guitar body, the wooden neck/headstock, and a grouped set of shapes containing the fingerboard, frets, and dot-shaped position markers. Because each extrusion shared the same position, the extruded pieces all lined up. Robert varied the value of the extrude depth for each piece, from a deeper extrusion for the body (25 pt), to a shallower extrusion for the white face plate (0.65 pt). Robert also chose to add a variety of bevels to various parts of the guitar, including rounded bevels to the body and neck, and a classic bevel to the control knobs. The three white pickups, the fret board, and other square edged parts were extruded with the Bevel set to None. To create the soft highlights on the guitar body, Robert used the Plastic Shading

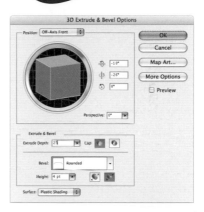

rendering style. The 3D Extrude & Bevel effect was also used to create the screw heads for the tuning pegs, whose shafts were created using 3D Revolve. The tuning peg handles and other parts of the guitar were made using gradient-filled shapes.

Advanced Techniques

Choose Clipping Mask >Make from the Object menu or use the Make/Release Clipping Mask button on the Layers panel (right)

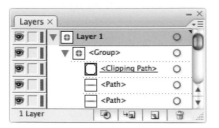

Choosing Object >Clipping Mask >Make puts all of the masked objects into a group with the clipping path at the top of the group

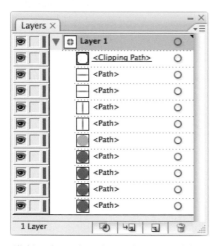

Clicking the Make/Release Clipping Mask button at the bottom of the panel turns the first item within the highlighted group or layer into a clipping path, without creating a new group

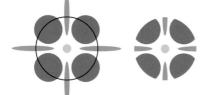

Before masking (left), the circle is positioned as the topmost object in the stacking order, so it will become the clipping path when the Clipping Mask is created (right)

The organized whole is more than the sum of its parts. Combining tools and techniques in Illustrator can yield *Wow!* results. In this chapter we'll look at such synergy.

Please keep in mind that this chapter will be quite daunting unless you're comfortable with what has been covered in previous chapters. If you're having trouble following the lessons in this chapter, then please revisit layers and stacking order (see the *Layers & Appearances* chapter), blends and gradients (the *Blends, Gradients & Mesh* chapter), and compound shapes and Pathfinders (the *Beyond the Basics* chapter).

Although this chapter contains a variety of techniques, this introduction focuses on creating and working with Clipping Masks. Masks control what portion of an object or image is visible, and what portion is hidden. Illustrator features two kinds of masks: Clipping Masks and Opacity Masks. Since Opacity Masks are made using the Transparency panel, see the *Transparency* chapter for details on creating and working with Opacity Masks.

CLIPPING MASKS

All of the objects involved in a mask are organized in one of two ways depending on how you choose to make your mask. One method collects all selected objects into a group. The other method allows you to keep your layer structure and uses the master "container" layer (see the Layers panel illustrations at left). With any kind of clipping mask, the topmost object of that group is the *clipping path*; this clips (hides) portions of the other objects in the group that extend beyond the clipping mask boundaries. Regardless of the attributes assigned to this top object, once you create the mask, it will become an unfilled and unstroked clipping path (but, keep reading to see how you can apply a stroke and fill to the new clipping path)

In the Layers panel, there are two indicators of an active Clipping Mask. First, your <u><Clipping Path></u> will be underlined and will remain underlined even if you rename it. Second, with an active Clipping Mask, you'll see dotted lines, instead of the standard solid lines. between the clipped items in the Layers panel.

To make a Clipping Mask from an object, you must first create that object. Make sure it's above the objects to be clipped, then create the Clipping Mask using one of two options. Use either the Make/Release Clipping Mask button on the Layers panel, or the Object > Clipping Mask > Make command. Each has its inherent advantages and disadvantages. The Object menu command gathers all the objects into a new group as it masks, allowing you to have multiple masked objects within a layer. It also gives you the ability to freely move masked objects within a layer structure without breaking the mask. However, if you have a carefully planned layer structure, it will be lost when everything is grouped. In contrast, the Layers panel command maintains your layer structure as it masks, but you can't have separately masked objects within a layer without building sublayers or grouping them first. This makes it difficult to move masked objects as a unit.

After you've created a Clipping Mask, you can edit the masking object, as well as the objects within the mask, using the Lasso, Direct Selection, or any path-editing tools. You can also use the new Edit Clipping Path or Edit Contents buttons in the Control panel or Object > Clipping Mask > Edit Mask (or Object > Clipping Mask > Edit Content). Further, you can add a stroke (it will appear as if it's in front of all masked objects) and fill (it appears as if it's behind all masked objects) after it's been made into a mask. And, as the magical tip on the next page says, you can even move it in the stacking order of the group or container and still keep its masking effect.

Masking technique #1: The Layers panel options

To mask unwanted areas of art within a *container* (meaning any group, sublayer, or layer), first create an object to use as your mask—make sure it's the topmost object in your container. Next, highlight that object's *container*

Clipping Mask icon disabled

In the Layers panel, you must select the *container* (layer, sublayer, or group) that holds your intended clipping object before you can apply a Clipping Mask. Also, in order for the button to be enabled, the top item inside the highlighted container must be something that can be turned into a clipping path.

The new Edit Clipping Path (left) and the Edit Contents (right) buttons appear in the Control panel when an object using a mask is selected

Compound Path & Shape masks

When creating masking objects, use Compound Paths to combine simple objects. Use Compound Shapes for more control over the "holes" in overlapping objects or to combine more complex objects.

You can add a stroke and fill to a mask (right)

Alignment bug fix

When aligning or distributing content that is masked, Illustrator now considers the shape of the mask as the basis for alignment or distribution. Previous versions of Illustrator problematically used the shape of the underlying objects (and not the mask).

When a placed image is selected, the Mask button shows in the Control panel

PAPCIAK-ROSE

See the Type chapter for masking with live type

and click the Make/Release Clipping Mask button on the Layers panel. The result: The topmost object, *within* the highlighted container, becomes the clipping path, and all elements within that container extending beyond the clipping path are hidden (for details on using complex objects as a mask, see the section below: "Using type, compound paths or shapes as a mask").

Once you've created a Clipping Mask, you can move objects up or down within the container (layer, sublayer, or group) to change the stacking order. However, if you move items outside of the Clipping Mask container, they will no longer be masked. Moving the clipping path itself outside of its container releases the mask completely. To release a Clipping Mask without reordering objects or layers, select it and choose Object > Clipping Mask > Release.

Masking technique #2: The Object menu command

You can also create masks for objects using the Object menu command. Use this method when you want to confine the Clipping Mask to a specific object or group of objects that need to be easily duplicated or relocated. Since this method modifies your layer structure, don't use it if you need to maintain objects on specific layers.

As before, start by creating an object or compound object that will become your Clipping Mask. Make sure that it's the topmost object, then select it and *all* the objects you want to be masked (the topmost object will become the mask). Now, choose Object > Clipping Mask > Make. When you use this method, all the objects, including the new clipping path, will move to the layer that contains your topmost object and will be collected into a new <Group>. This will restrict the masking effect to only those objects within the group; you can easily use the Selection tool to select the entire clipping group. If you expand the <Group> in the Layers panel (by clicking the expansion triangle), you'll be able to move objects into or out of the clipping group, or move objects up or down within the group to change the stacking order. (Don't miss the Tip "Magical Clipping Path" at left.)

Mask button

If you use File > Place to place an image, when the placed image is selected, you can instantly create a clipping path for the image by clicking the Mask buttton in the Control panel. However, masking is not immediately apparent because the clipping path has the same dimensions as the placed image's bounding box. Make sure the Edit Clipping Path button (in the Control panel) is enabled and then adjust the clipping path to shape the mask that is "cropping" your image.

Using type, compound paths or shapes as a mask

You can use editable type as a mask to give the appearance that the type is filled with any image or group of objects. Select the type and the image or objects with which you want to fill the text. Make sure the type is on top, then choose Object > Clipping Mask > Make.

To use separate type characters as a single Clipping Mask, you have to first make them into a Compound Shape or Compound Path. You can make a Compound Shape from either outlined or live (i.e., non-outlined) text. You can make a Compound Path only from outlined text (not live text). Once you've made a Compound Path or Shape of your separate type elements, you can use it as a mask. (See Tip "Compound Paths or Shapes?" in the *Beyond the Basics* chapter. And see the *Type* chapter for examples of masking with type.)

Opening legacy documents that contain masks

Prior to Illustrator 9, if you selected objects on different layers and chose Make Mask, you'd create a "layer-mask" that would hide all objects between the selected objects, with the topmost object becoming your mask. If you open one of these files in the current version of Illustrator, you'll see that all your layers are now contained within a new container layer we call a "master layer." If you want to mask across layers, you must manually create your own "master layer" into which you'll place everything you want to mask (see Tip "Collect in New Layer" at right).

Figuring out if it's a mask

- <Clipping Path> in the Layers panel will be underlined if it's a mask (even if you've renamed it), and the background color for the icon will be gray.
- Object > Clipping Mask > Release being enabled means a mask is affecting your selection.
- An Opacity Mask has a dotted underline in the Layers panel.
- Select > Object > Clipping Masks can help you find masks within a document as long as they aren't inside linked files (such as EPS or PDF).

Mask error message

If you get the message, "Selection cannot contain objects within different groups unless the entire group is selected," the objects you've chosen to mask are a subset of a group. To create a mask with these objects, Cut or Copy your selected objects, then Paste in Front (⌘-F/Ctrl-F). Now you'll be able to apply Object > Clipping Mask > Make.

Collect in New Layer

To collect selected layers into one "master layer" Shift-click to select contiguous layers, or ⌘-click/Ctrl-click to select noncontiguous layers and choose Collect in New Layer from the Layers menu.

Masking Details

Using Masks to Contour & Hide Elements

BENFANTI

Advanced Technique

Overview: *Create basic elements; make basic masks; mask compound path objects with Live Effects; make compound paths to act as masks; create an overall cropping mask.*

1

Making radial gradients for a grape shapes, drawing and combining basic objects

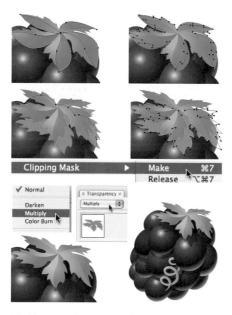

Masking to make two-toned leaves; making shadows by masking and setting the fills to Multiply mode; the final grapes with masking and shadows throughout

To be a true Illustrator expert, you must master a range of masking techniques. Russell Benfanti's lush and masterful illustrations are filled with masks. This lesson looks at four applications of masking in Illustrator.

1 Contouring masks for detail and shadows. First create your basic objects using any tools, including blends and gradient mesh. Benfanti used ovals filled with radial gradients customized using the Gradient tool, so that the blue would appear as a reflection on the bottom edge.

In a layer above his grapes, Benfanti drew a two-toned leaf. He began by drawing the outline shape, filled it with a radial gradient, and copied it. Then he quickly drew teardrop shaped wedges extending beyond the leaf-shapes, filled with a darker green gradient. With the leaf shape still on the Clipboard, he used Paste In Front (⌘-F/Ctrl-F). Next, selecting *all* the leaf objects, he chose Object > Clipping Mask > Make (⌘-7/Ctrl-7).

To create the shadow for the leaf, he used Paste In Back (⌘-B/Ctrl-B) to paste another copy of the leaf underneath. He then shifted the position of this "shadow" down and to the right, and gave it a medium blue solid fill. To fit that object within the silhouette of the grapes (not extend beyond it), he needed to make a contouring object that matched the silhouette of the grapes. Selecting the grapes, he copied and used Paste In Front. In the Pathfinder panel he held Option/Alt and clicked the first Add to Shape icon to permanently unite the grapes into one simple contouring-outline object.

Masking objects must be above the objects they mask, so move your grape-contour object above the "shadow" using the Layers panel. With the grapes contour above the blue leaf, Benfanti selected both and made a new clipping mask (⌘-7/Ctrl-7). To make the shadow more realistic, he selected only the blue leaf object and from the Control panel Opacity pop-up, he changed the blending mode from Normal to Multiply (you can change the blending mode before applying the mask). Benfanti also created shadows for individual grapes and the stem curl.

2 Masking roughened compound paths. To make the watermelon stripes, Benfanti drew arcs over the oval using the same gradient as the oval, and chose Object > Compound Path > Make, unifying the color. He then used the Gradient and Color panels to make the colors of the arc gradient warmer and lighter. To ripple the selected arcs he chose Effect > Distort & Transform > Roughen, and used Preview to decide on Size: 2%, Relative, Detail: 5.53/in, and Corner. He used a copy of the melon oval as a mask so the arcs stay within the contour.

3 Using compound paths to mask. You can use multiple objects to act as one masking object by first making the selected objects into a compound path. For Benfanti's orange sections, he created the overall shapes and the inner textures. Next he drew section wedges, selected them all and chose Object > Compound Path > Make. Selecting the textures of the orange with this compound path, he used ⌘-7 (Ctrl-7) to section the orange. Before adding the finishing details, he selected the compound path mask object, and applied a darker orange gradient that shows through as a background.

4 Cropping the image with a layer mask. Benfanti placed all layers within one enclosing layer. Loose in that enclosing layer he created a rectangle that would define the cropping area. Finally, he clicked the master layer to highlight it, and then the Make Clipping Mask icon.

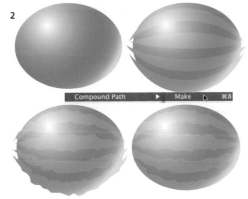

The original oval, making arcs and combining them into a compound path, applying Roughen, and masking with a copy of the original oval

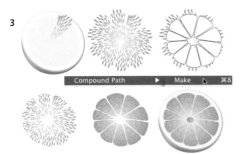

Making the basic orange elements; making wedge objects into one compound path; using the compound path as a mask; finishing details

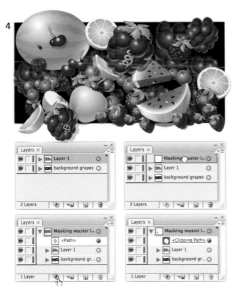

The final illustration before cropping the margins and the original Layers panel; after making a new layer, dragging the two original layers into it, clicking the Create Layer Mask icon and the final panel showing the clipping mask

Mask Upon Mask

Creating Reflections with Many Masks

Advanced Technique

Overview: *Create an arc blend; widen the blend; fade the blend; apply a compound-path clipping mask; add a custom gradient; create final refraction and fading details.*

1

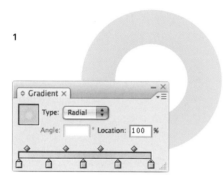

Creating a compound path and filling the duplicate with a custom radial gradient

2

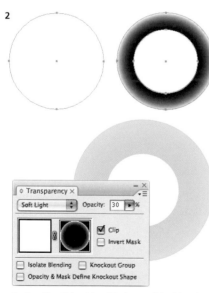

Fading the disk with a black-to-white blend on top of a white circle, making the blend into an Opacity Mask over the white circle, then placing this Opacity Mask over background disk and applying Soft Light mode at 30% opacity

Linotype commissioned Frank Jonen to create a new icon suite for the Linotype Library GmbH font collections (Bad Homburg, Germany, www.linotype.com). Jonen used many masking techniques to achieve the rainbow reflections and glare for the logo (center above) representing Linotype's line of "standard" fonts (the gold logo is above left, and the platinum logo is above right).

1 Creating a disk gradient. Create a circle defining an outer disk shape by holding Shift when you drag with the Ellipse tool. Next, holding Option-Shift/Alt-Shift, from the center of your previous circle, draw a second circle to define the center hole area. Now select both circles and choose Object > Compound Path > Make to cut the first hole from the second, like a donut. With his disk created, Jonen filled the compound path with a custom, muted-color radial gradient. Keeping the compound path selected, he adjusted the colors and stops until the colors transitioned where he wanted them (see the *Blends, Gradients & Mesh* chapter for help with gradients).

2 Fading the disk. To make the disk vary in tonality, Jonen created a "fader" using an Opacity Mask. After turning on Smart Guides (View menu), with the Ellipse tool, he held Option-Shift/Alt-Shift and dragged from the current circle's center to create a new circle slightly smaller than the outer disk, and filled it with white (no stroke). After copying this white circle, he pasted a copy on top (⌘-F/ Ctrl-F) and then swapped the fill and stroke (Shift-X) so it had a white stroke and no fill. Jonen then created a smaller black-stroked circle from the same center (not as small as the CD hole). Selecting the two stroked circles (if you have trouble selecting, expand the Layers panel to view the <Path> objects and Shift-click to the right of the target icons to select both stroked <Path> objects), he then chose Object>Blend>Make. Unlocking the white-filled circle underneath, Jonen selected it along with the new blend. From the Transparency panel pop-up he chose Make Opacity Mask, then he set the blending mode to Soft Light, reduced the Opacity to 30%, and made sure to enable Clip.

3 Creating arc blends. Blends are probably the best way to create arcs of color. To re-create Jonen's blend, you'll blend between five different colored lines. On a new layer above, draw the first line from the circle center point beyond the edge of the outer disk, and give it a 1-pt bluish stroke (make sure Opacity is 100% and Blending Mode is Normal). Hide the disk layers. Make the second line by selecting the top anchor point of the line with the Direct Selection tool, grab it and swing it up about 15° and press down the Option/Alt key, holding until after you release the mouse. Color this line Cyan, then repeat the duplication process above (varying the distance) to create the third (green), fourth (yellow), and fifth (red) lines. Before you blend these lines together, select the outer two (bluish-purple and red) and copy (you'll need these lines on the Clipboard for the next step). Next, double-click the Blend tool to set Blend Options as Smooth Color. Finally, select all the lines and choose Object>Blends>Make.

4 Widening the end colors. To prepare the rainbow to fade along the edges, Jonen created wider versions of the outer colors. To do this, choose Paste in Front (⌘-F/ Ctrl-F) to paste the copied lines in perfect registration with the blend. In the Layers panel, make a new layer above the blend and move the lines into that new layer by dragging their selection indicators. Now hide the blend layer, showing just your copied lines. Starting with the bluish line, expand it with the Pen tool into a triangular wedge-shape: Start with the upper anchor point to

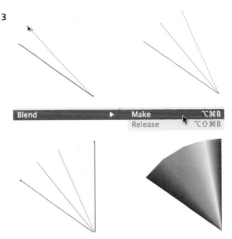

3

Drawing a first line then swinging copies up and recoloring, making a Smooth Color blend

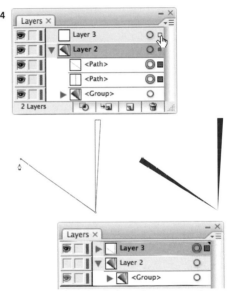

4

Copying and pasting in front the outer strokes, widening the copies

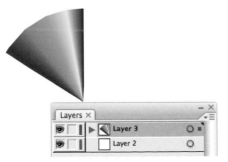

Showing the rainbow blend underneath, grouping the wider shapes with the blend objects

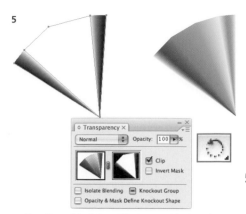

5

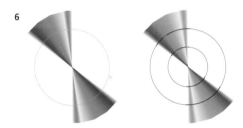

Creating a black-to-white larger object and applying it as an Opacity Mask for the rainbow and using the Rotate tool to make a copy

6

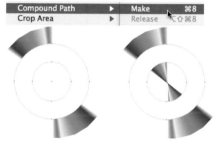

Drawing two circles centered on the rainbow center point with the Ellipse tool

| Compound Path | ▶ | Make | ⌘8 |
| Crop Area | ▶ | Release | ⌥⇧⌘8 |

Selecting the two circles to make a compound path

| Clipping Mask | ▶ | Make | ⌘7 |
| Compound Path | ▶ | Release | ⌥⌘7 |

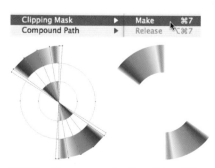

Selecting the compound path and the rainbow and choosing Object > Clipping Mask > Make

continue the line, then click to create a perpendicular segment that extends out wider than the blend below. Then click the Swap Fill and Stroke icon in the Toolbox (or press Shift-X), so that the new triangular color object is filled, not stroked with that blue color. Repeat this for the red line. Show the rainbow layers, Select All (⌘-A/Ctrl-A), and Group (⌘-G/Ctrl-G).

5 Fading the rainbow with an Opacity Mask and duplicating it. To fade the rainbow along the edges, Jonen used three objects to create an Opacity Mask. On a new layer above, he created a small black-to-white blend along the edge of the rainbow. Drawing a black line outside of and slightly longer than the rainbow, he held Option/Alt while moving the upper anchor point (as he did in making the lines in step 3), and changed the stroke copy to white. Selecting and blending these strokes, he then created a mirror version of this blend on the other side of the rainbow (you can re-create this blend, or use the Reflect tool to reflect a copy). Lastly, with the Pen tool, Jonen drew a white-filled triangle covering the remainder of the rainbow, overlapping into the white of the blends. After grouping the black-and-white objects, Jonen selected the rainbow and black-and-white groups, opened the Transparency panel, and chose Make Opacity Mask from the pop-up menu. To create a copy of the rainbow, with the Rotate tool hold Option/Alt and click on the rainbow-blend point, enter 180°, and click Copy.

6 Masking the rainbows with a copy of the compound path. Next, mask the rainbows with a copy of the background disk. One way to copy the disk is to expand the layer containing the background disk objects and locate <Compound Path>. Enable the view icon if it's still hidden, and click on the right side of the panel to select it. Now click the New Layer icon, and drag the selection indicator for the <Compound Path> to the new layer while holding Option/Alt. Since you're going to make these circles into a mask, it doesn't matter that the circles are filled; creating the mask removes all styling. To apply this compound path as a mask, select it along with the rainbows, and choose Object>Clipping Mask>Make (if you have trouble isolating objects, use the Layers panel to lock or hide objects that are in the way).

7 Fading the rainbow with more masks. Jonen changed the blending mode for both rainbow objects to Overlay. Then, selecting each rainbow group separately, he reduced its opacity—60% for the top group, and 50% for the bottom rainbow group.

8 Creating a bright "reflection." To create a lighter "reflection," Jonen created an Opacity Mask applied to a white disk. Starting from the circle centerpoint, he drew a black line, a center white line, and an outer black line. Selecting the three lines, he chose Object>Blend>Make. After rotating a copy of this blend across the circle (hold Option/Alt, click on the circle centerpoint, enter 180°, and click Copy), and grouped these blends to form a "butterfly" <Group>. Selecting the donut-shaped compound path in the Layers panel, Jonen copied, and then selected the butterfly blends. Using ⌘-B (Ctrl-B), he pasted a copy of the compound path directly behind the butterfly objects. Giving this compound path a white fill and no stroke, he selected it and the butterfly objects and chose Make Opacity Mask (with Clip enabled).

9 Making glare. Lastly, Jonen created a crescent-shaped glare on half the disk. You can make a crescent by drawing two circles, one slightly larger than the outer disk, and one smaller than the hole. With the Pen tool, draw two arcs defining the ends of the crescent. Then select all and click the Divide Pathfinder icon. After deselecting, Direct Select and delete the excess objects. Selecting his crescent, Jonen set a white fill (no stroke), copied, and used ⌘-F (Ctrl-F). He applied a radial gradient fill (gray to black) to this upper crescent, selected both, chose Make Opacity Mask, and reduced the opacity to 50%.

7

Moving the rainbow blends on top, Jonen changed the blending mode to Overlay and reduced the opacity (60% for the top rainbow and 50% for the bottom one)

8

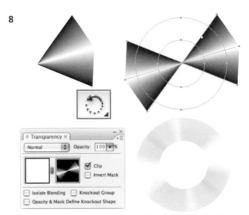

Creating a black-to-white-to-black blend, duplicating it to form a "butterfly" shape; then applying this as an Opacity Mask over a copy of the compound-path disk object (filled white)

9

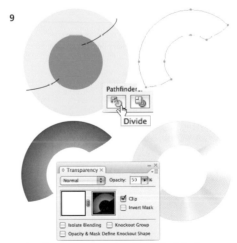

Creating a crescent using Divide Pathfinder on a pair of circles with paths defining the cut lines; filling one crescent with white and a copy with a radial gradient, making an Opacity Mask and reducing opacity to 50%

Glowing Starshine

Drawing Stars with Gradients and Strokes

Advanced Technique

Overview: *Create a star shape on top of a circle and adjust the shape using the Direct Selection tool; add a glow by applying a radial gradient to the star and circle shapes.*

1

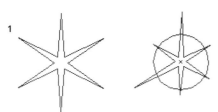

The original star, and the modified star positioned over a circle

2

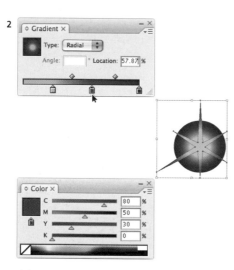

Color panel displaying color for selected slider on the Gradient panel with star shape selected

Gradient-filled shapes on the sky background

Illumination is the key to creating a realistic nighttime sky. This technique by Kenneth Batelman will help you create glowing lights of all sizes, simply and directly.

1 Drawing a big star. Batelman used the Ellipse tool to create a circle, and then the Star tool to draw a star on top of the circle. To make the star shape more interesting, he repositioned some of the star points using the Direct Selection tool.

2 Applying a radial gradient. To make the star glow, Batelman applied a radial gradient to the star. The gradient slider at the edge matches the sky color (he used 100% C, 80% M, 60% Y, and 20% K), and the slider at the center is the star glow at its brightest (he used 30% C, 5% M, 0% Y, and 0% K). Batelman added a third gradient slider between the original two, set to an intermediate color (he used 80% C, 50% Y, 30% M, 0% K). Applying the same radial gradient to the circle adds a halo effect to the star (for more on creating and storing gradients see the *Blends, Gradients & Mesh* chapter). To keep the star and glow together, he selected the star and circle and chose Object > Group (⌘-G/Ctrl-G).

Batelman created the small stars by overlapping specialized dashed strokes; see the Gallery opposite for details on this technique.

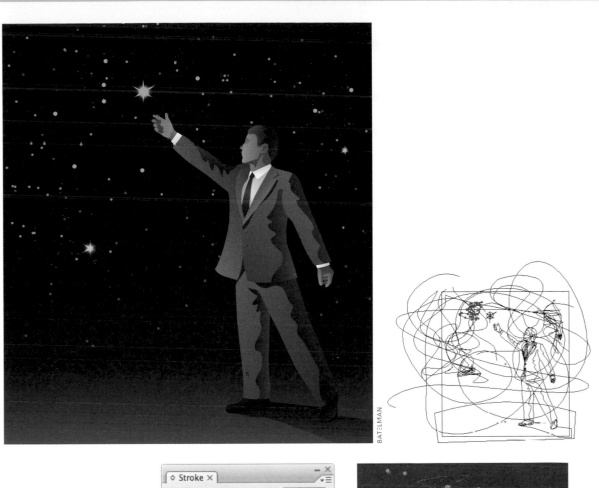

Kenneth Batelman

Batelman blanketed his sky with small stars by using dashed-line paths drawn with the Pencil tool. He created dots along the path by entering a Dash value of 0. For the Gap value, Batelman entered a value between 20 and 90 points. He chose the rounded options for both the cap and join so that the dots would be circular instead of square, and then set Weight values ranging from .85 to 2.5 points. By overlapping multiple paths with varying weights and dash gap values, Batelman's "dashes" appear to be points of light that vary in size and spacing. The Stroke panel settings shown above left are for the path of small stars selected above right.

WEIMER

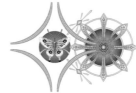

Alan James Weimer

Alan James Weimer constructed this pattern tile (detail right) using the steps described in the "Intricate Patterns" lesson in the *Drawing and Coloring* chapter. Once he had filled the tile elements with gradients and blends, Weimer Option/Alt-dragged the tile to the right to form the first row. To create the repeating pattern, Weimer diagonally Option/Alt-dragged copies of the first tile row onto a grid of guidelines to create a row above and a row below the first row. To crop the pattern into the square, he drew a square on the same layer as the tiled design, and at the bottom of the Layers panel, he clicked the Make/Release Clipping Mask icon. On a layer above the mask, he added a border composed of blended, stroked rectangles for the sides and created the corner medallions with blended, stroked concentric circles. He then added a gradient-filled circle to the center of the medallion. For the background, Weimer used a solid fill beneath a layer of radial gradients which are positioned underneath the butterflies.

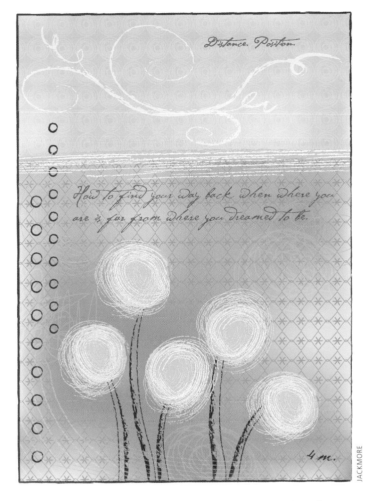

JACKMORE

Lisa Jackmore

Lisa Jackmore combined layers of patterns, brushes, and gradient mesh, to create texture in this interpretation of a page in her sketchbook. For each gradient mesh background, she filled a rectangle with a solid fill and added mesh points with the Mesh tool. Jackmore kept most of the mesh points near the edges of the rectangle, and filled them with a light color to achieve a faded appearance. She created two patterns to layer above the mesh. For the circle pattern, she drew several concentric circles with the Ellipse tool, grouped them, and applied the Pencil Art brush. She selected the Twirl tool, and while holding Shift-Option/Shift-Alt, she click-dragged on the Artboard, and sized the diameter of the Twirl to fit over the circles. Then she clicked on the circles with the Twirl tool until she was happy with the amount of twirl. She grouped the objects and dragged them to the Swatches panel. To make the diamond pattern, Jackmore used a combination of Rectangle, Ellipse, and Rotate tools. She then grouped the objects and dragged them to the Swatches panel. Jackmore colored the pattern the same base color as the gradient mesh background so the pattern disappears in the dark areas. She then added more details to the background, and made the flowers with custom brushes she created. (For details about how she made some of these brushes, refer to her galleries in the *Brushes & Symbols* chapter). Jackmore also used several default brushes from the Artistic_ChalkCharcoalPencil library. Finally, she created a clipping mask to contain the brush marks that extended beyond the rectangle.

AUBÉ

Jean Aubé

For his "Nuit De Terreur" poster, Jean Aubé began by using the Pen tool to trace the outline of a photograph he took of a friend. He added a gradient fill and applied Effect > Stylize > Outer Glow. For the overall lighting, he created a background with a radial gradient, positioning the center between the hands. He then drew a circle for the moon. He made a tiny blue circle to represent a star and saved it as a symbol. Using the Symbol Sprayer, he sprayed the "stars" on two layers for depth. He expanded the symbols in order to delete unwanted extras. He set "Nuit de Terreur" as a block of type, then converted the type to outlines. Aubé chose Object > Envelope Distort > Make with Mesh to distort the type. He set the other blocks of type separately. On a layer behind the stars and type he created spooky swirls by drawing many ovals, and then used Pathfinder operations on the ovals until he had broken them down to strands. He selected and deleted portions of the strands that remained. Finally he arranged, grouped and filled them with a single linear gradient. He made the ovals appear ghostly by placing them in Overlay Mode and applying Outer Glow to them.

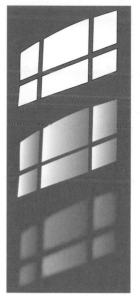

GILBERT

Reggie Gilbert

To create his photorealistic fire station, illustrator Reggie Gilbert laid his bricks like a master. He began by creating five different rectangles and customizing a gradient for each using the Gradient panel. Then creating one solid-colored brick on an angle, duplicated that brick, and moved the duplicate along that angle, a distance away. Selecting the two angled bricks he double-clicked the Blend tool to set Blend Options to Specified Steps for Spacing, and entered 8. Gilbert then chose Object > Blend > Make to create the blend, then Object > Expand to break the blend into 10 separate objects. He next used the Direct Selection tool to select individual bricks to move them slightly out of alignment, giving the line of bricks a more organic look. Then he again selected each of the angled bricks and this time use the Eye-dropper tool to click on one of the pre-made gradients to fill it with that gradient. With

this line of bricks complete, he grouped them (⌘-G/Ctrl-G) and starting with the blended line of bricks, he'd customize a new line. By creating each line of bricks with deliberate randomness Gilbert avoids the appearance of repeating patterns in the bricks. To create the windows (shown against blue at top), he drew the objects, grouped them, then filled them with a custom light-to-slightly-darker gradient in the hue of the objects that behind the glass. In the Layers panel he targeted the <Group>, and in the Control panel he reduced the opacity and applied Effect > Stylize > Feather (for the windows shown above he used 40% Opacity and 9 pt Feather).

"Red Chrome"   Copyright © 2005 Chris Nielsen

NIELSEN

"Red Chrome"   Copyright © 2005 Chris Nielsen

Chris Nielsen

Drawing with the Pen tool and using Path-finder's Divide mode, Chris Nielsen created a series of shapes with increasing complexity to create photo realism. Nielsen began by placing an original photograph on a bottom layer to use as a guide for both shape and color values. Using the Pen tool he drew the larger shapes first (such as the pipe shown above). He continued to draw shapes to define the object by first drawing all the dark red shapes, then those having a lighter value. Once the lines of the pipe were drawn for several values (such as dark red and light red), he selected all the

paths, and from the Pathfinder panel selected Divide. Nielsen continued to draw more shapes to further define the area and repeated the process of using Pathfinder and Divide to break down the areas into increasingly smaller shapes. (The pipe detail shows steps 1, 2, 7 and the final 11th step.) Nielsen then filled the shapes with colors sampled from the underlying photograph using the Eyedropper tool. If you look closely, you can see a reflection of Nielsen (taking the photograph) in the round chrome shape directly below the red pipe.

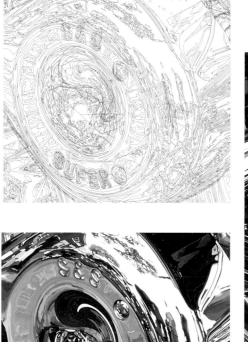

"Super Stock"

Copyright © 2005 Chris Nielsen

NIELSEN

Chris Nielsen

Chris Nielsen created another stunning image using the same drawing technique described on the opposite page. Nielsen likes to begin drawing an area of the photograph that contains a large object, such as a gas tank, or big pipe. Working over a template layer that contained his original photograph, he first drew the outline of a large object with the Pen tool. Then he drew paths for each area where the color value changed within that object. He selected the paths and applied Effect > Pathfinder > Divide. He continued in this manner until there were enough shapes to define the object. This was a particularly challenging motorcycle to draw because there are only slight variations in one overall color. Nielsen filled each individual object with a custom color chosen from the Swatches panel. In all of his motorcycle illustrations, the reflection of Nielsen taking the photograph is visible—here it's shown in the magnified detail on the left.

BRAD NEAL / THOMAS • BRADLEY ILLUSTRATION & DESIGN

Brad Neal

Brad Neal combined an attention to detail with Illustrator's wide range of drawing and rendering tools to create this photo-realistic image of a Ford Taurus stock car. Beginning with a contour shape filled with a flat color, Neal overlaid a series of custom blends to replicate the subtle modeling of the car's surface. Neal simulated the grill work at the front of the car by overlaying a series of four dashed stroked paths. The racing logos on the side of the car were drawn by hand, grouped, and positioned using the Shear tool. The Taurus, Valvoline, and Goodyear logos were fitted to the contour of the body with the help of the Envelope Distort tool. To achieve the realistic look of the front right wheel, Neal created custom blends with outer edges that blended smoothly into the flat color of the underlying shapes. Neal created a drop shadow for the car using a carefully controlled blend. This blend had an inner path that contained a solid black fill that blended to white as it approached the outer edge.

CATER (©INMOTION 2003)

David Cater

David Cater created this Mini Cooper image for reproduction on T-shirts, posters, and note cards. Knowing that different clients would want the car in a variety of colors, he started by creating two spot color swatches for the mid and shadow tones of the car. He then used those two spot colors (global process colors would also work) to create the handful of gradients he used to fill each of the approximately 1,500 shapes he used to create the car. Because he was careful to color only the body panels using gradients created from those two colors, he was later able to easily change the color of the car by simply double-clicking on each of the two color swatches and using the CMYK sliders to redefine the colors. Although he could have used blends more extensively (he only used a few for the cowlings along the front and side of the car), Cater found it faster and easier to use simple, gradient-filled shapes.

Modeling Mesh

Shaping and Forming Mesh Objects

Advanced Technique

Overview: *Create an outline for smoke; create a simple rectangular mesh; bend the mesh using the Rotate and Direct Selection tools; align the mesh to your outline; add columns to lend a 3D effect; color your mesh; use the Screen Blend mode to make the smoke transparent.*

1

Create an outline of the desired final smoke form

Smoke outline locked in a layer, with the starting mesh above

Ivan Torres molded a mesh as though it were a piece of clay to form the smoke in his art piece "Meshsmith." One of the highlights of this lesson is Torres's use of the Rotate tool to bend *portions* of a mesh (as opposed to using it to rotate *whole* objects).

1 Setting up your artwork. Start by using the Pen or Pencil tool to create an outline of a smoke form. Lock the smoke outline in a layer, then place a rectangle at the base of the smoke. Convert the rectangle to a mesh, using the Object > Create Gradient Mesh command, with 1 column and 3 rows. Keep your starting mesh simple; it is easier to add rows as needed later.

2 Making the rough bends. Make your first big bend using the Rotate tool. Start by Direct-Selecting all but the bottom two points of the mesh. Next with the Rotate tool click on the inside of the first curve of the smoke outline to place the center for rotation, and then grab the top of your mesh rectangle and drag it around the center of rotation to form the first curve (see images at right).

At each bend or pinch in the smoke, you will need a row in order to make the next bend. If an existing row of your mesh is nearby, Direct-Select it and move it over the bend or pinch. To add a row, click with the Mesh tool on the edge of the mesh outline, at the bend or pinch. Once you have placed or added a mesh row at a bend or pinch, leave those points out of the next selection as you work your way up the smoke. Repeat this step until you reach the top of your smoke outline.

3 Aligning and straightening the mesh rows. Once you have the mesh roughly aligned, zoom in at each pinch and bend where you placed a mesh row and make it straight and perpendicular to the curve. Straightening out the mesh rows is essential for your final smoke to look correct and work smoothly.

4 Aligning the mesh curves with the smoke. With the Direct Selection tool, start at the bottom and click a section of the mesh curve. Adjust the direction handles so they align with the smoke outline. You may have to go back and forth between the next and previous sections of the curves in order to properly adjust the sides of the mesh to fit the smoke outline.

5 Adding columns to lend a 3D effect. The final 3D form of the mesh will be defined by where the highlight and shadow colors are placed on the mesh. If you were to draw evenly spaced columns around the actual smoke and photograph it, the columns in the photograph would appear to be closer together near the edges of the smoke outline and farther apart in the middle of column. To create this

2

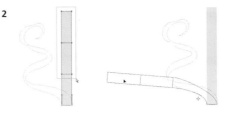

Selecting top portion of mesh. After clicking on inside of the first curve to set the rotation point (blue crosshair in lower right), clicking the top of the rectangle, and dragging to left and down

Working up the smoke, rotating the mesh at each major bend; placing mesh rows at pinches and using the Direct Selection tool to adjust

3

Aligning the rows with the pinches in the outline, making them straight and perpendicular to the sides of the curve

4

Starting from the bottom, using the Bézier handles to align the curves of the mesh to the outline of the smoke

5

Adding columns to the smoke mesh using the Gradient tool and spacing them closer at the edges to create a rounded 3D look

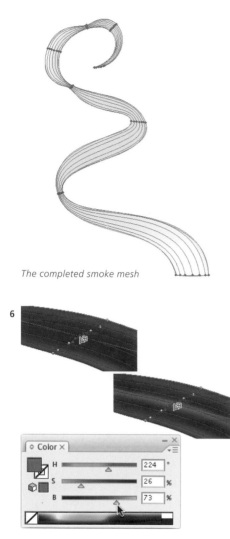

The completed smoke mesh

Creating a highlight at a mesh point

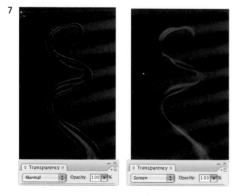

The smoke before and after setting the Blend Mode to Screen on the Transparency panel

3D effect, use the Mesh tool to add a first column by clicking on the center of the bottom edge of the smoke. Next, add two more columns close to each outside edge of the smoke. Then, place two columns between the center and the next closest columns on each side—not exactly in between, but closer to the outside edge.

Because of your careful work in steps 3 and 4 above, your new columns will be parallel to—and flow smoothly through—the pinches and bends of your smoke outline.

6 Coloring the mesh. Torres chose a dark blue color for his smoke (if you want to use a different color you will have to adjust the color choices in the steps below). To help you see where the mesh points are as you work, turn on Smart Guides from the View menu, or ⌘-U/Ctrl-U. In order to make the selection line color interfere less with the mesh color as you work, use a dark shade of blue for the layer color (choose Dark Blue from the Layer Options Color menu). Also, learn to use the single-key navigation shortcuts to quickly switch between the Mesh (U), Eyedropper (I), and Direct Selection (A) tools.

Start by adding a middle blue value to the whole mesh. Next, from the Color panel pop-up menu, choose HSB, and then use the Brightness ("B") slider to create lighter highlight or darker shadow tints of your starting color. At the center of where highlight or shadow areas should be (either on a point, mesh line, or between the mesh lines), click with the Direct Selection tool and choose a color or swatch, or pick up a color using the Eyedropper tool. If you add a point with the Mesh tool it will remain selected, so you can easily adjust the fill color using the HSB sliders. For final tweaking of the highlights and shadows, use the Direct Selection tool or Lasso tool to select areas, and then make adjustments using the HSB sliders.

7 Making the smoke transparent. Select your smoke and on the Transparency panel, experiment with various combinations of the Screen Blend mode and Opacity settings until you get the desired effect.

MIYAMOTO

Yukio Miyamoto

The "Molding Mesh" lesson in the *Blends, Gradients & Mesh* chapter shows how Yukio Miyamoto created these amazing mesh bottles. To create the reflections in this version, Miyamoto used the Reflect tool to reflect a copy of the bottles along the base of the bottles. He next pulled a horizontal guide from the ruler to align with the end of the table top. For each of the reflections, he targeted the mesh and in the Transparency panel he reduced the opacity to 80%. To make the reflections fade, he used Path> Offset Path and entered 0 as the Offset. He filled this outline with a white-to-gray gradient, and then used the Gradient tool to run from white at the guideline to gray at the bottle bottom. To make certain that the reflection stopped abruptly at the table edge,

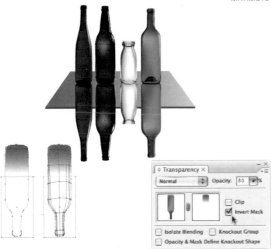

he grouped each gradient bottle with a white rectangle covering the neck half of the bottle, and ending at the guideline. He then selected each pair of gray and mesh bottle objects, chose Make Opacity Mask from the Transparency panel pop-up, and enabled the Invert Mask option.

Chapter 13 *Advanced Techniques* **367**

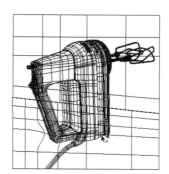

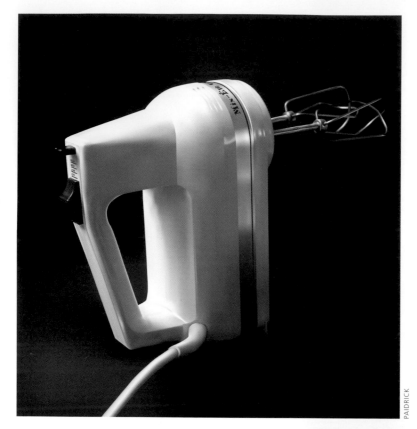

PAIDRICK

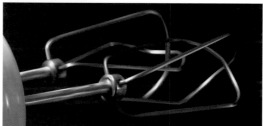

Ann Paidrick

Using an original photograph as a template, Ann Paidrick made gradient mesh objects to re-create this mixer with incredible precision. Focusing on one section at a time (such as the beaters, handle, or the cord), she drew rectangular paths with the Pen tool based on the relative size and shape of each object. She filled the rectangles with a base color sampled from the photograph, then changed the object into a mesh (Object > Create Gradient Mesh). In the Create Gradient Mesh dialog, she specified one row, one column, and a flat appearance. She added more rows and columns with the

Mesh tool and adjusted the points to form the contour she desired. She continued to sample color from the photograph to color the mesh points. To further define the mesh, she also added individual points with the Add Anchor Point tool, then adjusted those points with the Direct Selection tool. See "Molding Mesh" in the *Blends, Gradients & Mesh* chapter for a lesson on contouring mesh.

PAIDRICK

Ann Paidrick

In addition to the technique used in the drawing opposite, Ann Paidrick used symbols to enhance the realistic appearance of this glass of iced tea (panel detail at right). To make the tiny bubbles at the top of the tea, she created blended circles of various sizes and colors to make a symbol set. (See the *Brushes & Symbols* chapter for more about symbols.) Paidrick created numerous complex gradient mesh shapes to complete the amazing level of detail

in the objects. Some of these gradient mesh shapes are shown in the cookie detail above (shown in outline view).

CROUSE

Scott Crouse

Scott Crouse required the flexibility of a vector drawing and the realism of a photograph for use in a variety of mediums (various sizes of signs and banners). He created this fishing lure with a combination of blends and solid filled paths. Crouse made the realistic head, beads of water, and the shadows with blended shapes. He layered vibrant solid filled shapes to construct the tail. Crouse used the contrast of the filled shapes next to the blended objects to emphasize the fine detail in this vivid illustration.

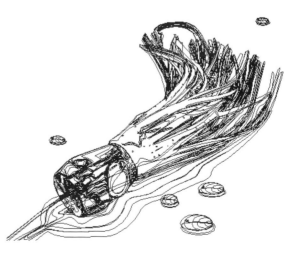

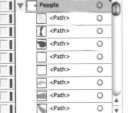

Scott Crouse

Scott Crouse created this photorealistic scene using layers of meticulously drawn and colored shapes (panel shown above). After drawing paths with the Pen tool to define an area, he colored the shapes with similar values (detail above right). In select areas such as the blue car trunk, he created a gradient. Crouse worked in a scale larger than what the final output required, so that after he reduced the image, the viewer would see smooth color transitions, not separate shapes. His technique created an illustration as lifelike as the photo from which Crouse drew inspiration (shown above the Layers panel at left).

LAMANTIA

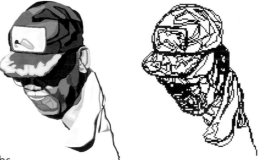

Marc LaMantia

Marc LaMantia scanned one of his photographs to create this illustration of a subway exit, in which he used the techniques described on the opposite page. In this piece, LaMantia depicts the beauty of a single moment of an ordinary day in New York City. Transparency effects were used throughout the entire illustration (see the *Transparency* chapter). Many of the shadow areas (such as within the steps) are actually made of transparent pink, red, and magenta shapes, layered above black. Rarely is a color used at full opacity. The layering of numerous transparent layers (all in Normal mode) brings enormous depth and interest to the posterized style. When viewing the image in Outline mode (above right), the level of detail becomes apparent.

Chris Nielsen

Chris Nielsen has trained his artistic eye
to recognize subtle shifts of color within
a photograph and translate them into
a striking image using layers of filled
paths. Nielsen first placed an original
photograph in a bottom layer to trace
upon. He worked on one small section
at a time, such as the eye in the detail
to the right. With the Pen tool he made
paths (no fill, with a black stroke) and
traced the areas of primary color he saw
in the photograph. He chose the darkest
value first (dark blue or black), then on
another layer, he drew the objects with
progressively lighter values (a lighter
blue, red, gray, etc.). He continued building layers of paths until the area was
completely covered. He moved throughout the image this way until the portrait
was finished. When all of the paths
were drawn he began to fill them with
color. Nielsen chose the Eyedropper tool,
pressed and held the ⌘/Ctrl key to switch
to the Direct Selection tool, and selected
an object to color. Then he toggled back
to the Eyedropper tool by releasing the
⌘/Ctrl key and sampled a color from the
photograph. He toggled between the
Direct Selection tool and the Eyedropper tool until the paths were filled. Most
of the time, Nielsen liked the sampled
colors, but if not, he would tweak the
color using the sliders in the Color panel.
Once all of the paths were filled with

NIELSEN

Copyright © 2006 Chris Nielsen

color, Nielsen hid the template layer. He saw
gaps of white in his drawing where the paths
didn't quite meet or overlap. To fill these gaps,
he made a large object that covered the area,
filled it with a dark color and placed it on the
bottom-most layer.

Web & Animation

This chapter will help you use Illustrator to prepare artwork for on-screen display. Although everything in this chapter relies heavily on Illustrator, some of the techniques also involve working with other applications. Artists produced the animations and Web graphics in this chapter using a number of programs in concert with Illustrator, including Adobe Flash, Dreamweaver, Premiere Pro, and After Effects.

Adobe has added lots of features to Illustrator dedicated to Flash interoperability (logical, since Adobe now owns Flash). They've also revamped Flash to work more fluidly with Illustrator. Users can now more easily copy and paste and drag and drop when moving from Illustrator to Flash, as well as import a native Illustrator document (.ai). What's more, Flash has significantly improved preservation of object fidelity when importing from Illustrator. You can expect better results when working with symbols, text, blends, masks, transparency, and more.

Web designers will find that Illustrator supports a wealth of file formats and a streamlined work flow for creating Web graphics. Also, content created for the Web is often times destined for portable devices such as cell phones and PDAs. Save for Web & Devices, in the File menu, makes it easy to quickly optimize graphics for the Web and, now, portable devices as well. You can visually compare examples of different quality settings, file compression options, and more in a multi-view dialog. And Pixel Preview allows you to view precise antialiasing right in Illustrator.

WORKING WITH RGB IN ILLUSTRATOR

If you're working for Web, mobile devices, or video, you should always be working in RGB as it's what the final viewing medium will be displayed on. Even though some Web formats, such as JPG, can embed a color profile, SWF and others can not contain this information. You will get

CMYK and RGB

If you're creating artwork for both print and the Web, your best bet is to work first in CMYK (with its narrower color gamut) and then create the final Web output by exporting to an RGB format and adjusting colors to approximate the original CMYK colors.

Use .ai for Flash

Using .ai files in Adobe Flash (instead of .swf files exported from Illustrator) will have many benefits, including retaining the position of the original paths, exact path shape, number of anchor points in paths, grouping of symbols, symbol names, and more.
—*Andrew Dashwood*

Choosing color models from the Color panel's pop-up menu. Cycle through color models by Shift-clicking on the Color Spectrum. Selecting a different color model to mix colors does not change the Document Color Mode.

Photoshop...

See the *Illustrator & Other Programs* chapter for working with Illustrator and Photoshop.

more consistent results if you work with sRGB color profiles, as everyone can view this information (Edit > Color Settings, then select, North America Web/Internet).

Working with RGB Document Profiles

To create artwork in RGB, select File > New, and then from the New Document Profiles, select Web, Mobile and Devices, Video or Basic RGB. All of these profiles behave slightly differently. After you have created a document using any of the profiles, you will be able to change the settings to match one of the other profiles, so you won't need to copy and paste your images to different document profiles to optimize them for other media.

- **Web document profiles.** Have their size defined by a crop area instead of the Artboard size, as CMYK and Basic RGB document profiles do. To change the size of a Web document after it has been created, you can select the Crop Area tool, and then change the width and height in the Control panel.

- **Mobile and Devices document profiles.** Have their size defined by a crop area (the same as Web profiles), but also have the transparency grid switched on (View > Show Transparency Grid).

- **Video document profiles.** Also have their size defined by crop areas, have the transparency grid enabled, and will include Center Mark, Cross Hairs, Video Safe Areas, Screen Edge, and also Crop Area Ruler (double-click the Crop Area tool and then access the Crop Area tool Options dialog in order to disable or enable these). Crop Area Rulers rulers are displayed outside of the work area and function independently of document rulers (View > Show Rulers) and start from the top left of the **X** and **Y** axis (horizontal and vertical). Crop Area Rulers will show pixel aspect ratio for anamorphic (non-square) pixel document presets, such as NTSC DV Widescreen.

- **Basic RGB document profiles.** Will work the same as legacy versions of Illustrator and the current CMYK document profiles, where the Artboard defines the document bounds and not the Crop Area.

Converting CMYK to RGB

If you already have artwork prepared in CMYK and you need to change the color mode for on-screen RGB viewing, make sure you first save a copy of your file, then choose File > Document Color Mode > RGB Colors. Remember, try not to convert your artwork back and forth between color spaces, because your colors can become muddy or muted (see the following section for details).

Rasterizing art for the screen

The process of turning vector art into a pixel-based image is called *rasterizing*. Anyone creating artwork for the Web or for multimedia applications might, at some point, need to rasterize vector art, with the exception of SWF and SVG. There are two options for rasterizing art in Illustrator. If you want to permanently rasterize an object, select it and choose Object > Rasterize. However, you can keep your artwork editable by using the option found in the Effect menu (Effect > Rasterize). This way, your art takes on the appearance of rasterization, but its underlying vector structure is maintained and can still be edited. Each Rasterize dialog provides options that make it easy to control how your artwork is rasterized.

When deciding whether to save your image as a GIF or JPEG, experiment with different optimizations in the File > Save for Web & Devices dialog to see which format looks best at the smallest file size. In general, you'll want to save your art as a GIF if it has large areas of solid color and/or is made up of vector graphics. On the other hand, save it as a JPEG if your art includes raster images (photos) with a wide range of colors or grays, or if your image contains vector gradients or gradient meshes.

Batch optimizations

You can combine File > Save for Web & Devices with the Actions panel to batch optimize GIF files that share a custom palette of colors. Make a new file, then copy into it the group of Illustrator files that need to share the same colors. Use Save for Web to find the optimum combination and number of colors, then choose Save Color Table from the bottom pop-up menu. Close this file, and open one of the individual Illustrator files. Start recording a new Action, then choose Save for Web, load the color table, and save the file. Now you can run this custom action to automatically process the rest of your GIF files.

—*Cynthia Baron*

A FEW THOUGHTS ON RGB AND CMYK COLOR

- **If you're going to use your artwork for both print and on-screen viewing, create in CMYK and then export the art to RGB.** Since the CMYK color space has a smaller color gamut than RGB and is able to produce predictable color output for print, it makes sense to create your artwork in CMYK *before* exporting it to RGB for display on a monitor. RGB has a wider gamut, so it won't clip or compress the colors of your CMYK document when you convert it to RGB.

- **Don't convert the same artwork repeatedly between RGB and CMYK.** Converting RGB to CMYK forces one range of colors (a gamut) into a smaller range of colors. This process involves either clipping or compressing certain colors, and can make the colors in your file appear muddy or muted. To experiment with clipping or compressing colors between gamuts, see *Illustrator Help* on choosing the appropriate rendering intent in the Color Settings dialog.

The Web Swatches library

Sticking to the Web safe colors—which consist of the 216 colors that are most reliable for creating artwork for the Web—is no longer considered as important in Web design as it once was. Graphics cards have developed to the point where most users can now display thousands or millions of colors. Still, if you want to be very cautious and make sure that even those using very old equipment will see your colors exactly as you've specified them, the Web safe colors remains available for use.

ASSIGNING URLS AND SLICING

Illustrator's Attributes panel lets you create interactive image maps based on selected objects or rectangular selections. You can then assign a URL (Uniform Resource Locator) to them, which can be viewed in a Web browser and link to other Web pages or e-mail addresses. When creating image maps from selected objects with rounded edges, they can either follow the contour of the image using its Polygonal image map links, or they can be straight edge links parallel to the outermost edges of the shape using its Rectangular option.

Slices created from selections will automatically change size and position when they are changed on the Artboard. When you export your document as HTML and Images, Illustrator will create a single image of the whole page in whichever format you've chosen (GIF, JPG, PNG, etc.) and will write the HTML code into a page containing the hotspots and URLs.

Note: *Image maps can be exported as SWF, which will work in the Flash player or Web browser that has the Flash plug-in installed, but if you import the SWF or AI file to Adobe Flash Professional, the interactivity will be discarded and you will need to re-create this. See the Flash help files for details on creating Image Maps in Flash using ActionScript.*

To assign a URL to a selection, open the Attributes panel (Window > Attributes), select the type of image map from the Image Map pop-up, and type the URL into the URL text field (see the Gulf Shores Web page Gallery in this chapter for more on making image maps). If you need to verify whether your URL is valid or not, simply click the Browser button in the Attributes panel. This will launch your default Web browser and automatically open the link if it is valid. You can export the file by using Save for Web & Devices, and choosing Save as Type: HTML and Images (*.html).

Slices are fixed sizes and seen as rectangular items positioned above your artwork. They will not automatically adjust their size as images change. You can resize them manually by dragging their centers or edges with the Slice Select tool. Creating slices of your pages can be useful when working with buttons; you can define a larger clickable area than the size of the button, which enables easier Web site navigation. When you export your document as HTML and Images, your entire page will be seamlessly divided into a series of images and HTML code that now contains URLs.

Save for Web & Devices

Save for Web provides many options for optimizing Web graphics:

- **Tools:** A limited set of tools lets you zoom, pan, select slices, and sample colors in the artwork.

- **Views:** Multiple views are available for you to compare compression settings against the final image quality.

- **Settings:** Preset compression settings are easily accessed from the Preset pop-up menu. If you are new to Web graphics, start with one of these settings. You'll notice that as you select different presets, the options for the specific file type are updated under the Settings grouping. Save your own settings by choosing Save Settings from the pop-up menu to the right of the Settings menu.

- **Color Table:** The color table updates the number of colors in the image for GIF and PNG-8 file formats. You can lock colors or shift to a Web safe color by clicking on the icons at the bottom of the panel.

- **Image Size:** To change the dimensions of the final optimized file, but not the original artwork, click on the Image Size tab and enter a new size.

- **Browser button:** To preview the optimized image in a browser, click on the browser button at the bottom of the dialog.

- **Color Table:** 8-bit images have a maximum of 256 colors. The Perceptual table is more sensitive to colors than the human eye can differentiate. Selective gives more emphasis to the integrity of the colors and is the default setting.

- **Colors:** You can have up to 256 colors in a color table. However, the image might not need that many. Select a smaller number of colors when you optimize by adjusting the number of colors in the color table—the fewer colors, the smaller the file.

- **Dither:** Blends colors in a limited color palette. Diffusion dither is usually best. Vary the amount of dither to reduce banding of solid-color areas by adjusting the Dither slider. Leave it off for clean-edged vector graphics.

- **Transparency:** Choose this for non-rectangular artwork that you want to put over multicolored backgrounds. To reduce edge artifacts, choose a color to blend with the transparent edges from the Matte pop-up.

- **Interlacing:** Allows viewers to see a low-resolution version of the image as it downloads, which continues to build until the image is at full resolution. A non-interlaced image draws one line at a time.

If you want to create a slice whose position remains unchanged when you update the artwork from which the slice was originally generated, choose Object > Slice > Create from Selection, or draw the slice using Illustrator's Slice tool. (In Photoshop, this kind of slice is called a *user slice*.) Slices applied as attributes are exported as layer-based slices when you choose File > Export > Photoshop (*.PSD). If you edit the exported layers in Photoshop, the corresponding slices will reshape themselves just as they would have done in Illustrator. This PSD export option only works on slices attached to elements that are not contained inside any groups or sublayers. All other slices are exported as user slices.

RELEASE TO LAYERS

Illustrator gives you the ability to take each one of your multiple objects or blended objects to distribute onto its own layer. For example, having the objects on separate layers makes it easier to develop animations. (See the "Adobe Flash (SWF) export" section later in this chapter. It explains how to move Illustrator art into Adobe Flash for animation work.)

Highlight a layer, group, or live blend in the Layers panel by clicking on it—merely selecting the artwork won't work. Next, choose Release to Layers (Sequence) from the panel menu. This creates each new layer within the current layer or group and consists of a single object. Use this option when you want each element to be separately manipulated in another program, or you want the animation to be sequential (one, then the next).

To perform an additive effect, choose Release to Layers (Build). Instead of containing a single object, each new layer is generated with one more object. You end up with the same number of layers, but what appears on those layers is very different. Use this option when you want to create a "building animation" that contains the previous elements.

Note: *If you save and import an AI file to Flash, you will need to have top-level layers, and not sub-layers that are* *automatically created by Illustrator's Release to Layers ability. Manually select all of the sub-layers in Illustrator and drag them up to become top-level layers.*

EXPORT FILE FORMATS
Save for Web & Devices

Although you might think you need to export your files from Illustrator in order to work with them in other programs, please be aware that if you plan on bringing your Illustrator image into Adobe Flash, you'll get the best results by *not* exporting your file, but instead saving in Illustrator format (.ai) and then importing it into Flash. An important feature for Web designers is the ability to export optimized files from the Save for Web & Devices dialog. GIF and JPEG are the Web's two most common image formats (see the Tip "GIF or JPEG?" in this chapter). The GIF format's compression works well with vector-based images or files that have large areas of solid color. GIF files support 1-bit transparency; JPEGs don't.

JPEG provides variable levels of compression and works best for continuous-tone images (such as photos or gradients). Although JPEG is a "lossy" format (when you optimize the file size you lose image detail), this trade-off still tends to result in good-quality images, making JPEG a particularly useful format for Web designers.

PNG-24 is a lossless format, that has 8-bit transparency (256 levels of transparency) and is well suited to both continuous-tone and solid color images. It will not be compatible with very old browsers, if they don't have a plug-in installed. As a rule of thumb, if your target audience needs their images in 216 colors, they will not be able to view PNG files.

To save a version of your artwork for use on the Web, choose File > Save for Web & Devices and adjust the various optimization settings (see the Tip "Save for Web & Devices" in this chapter). If you've defined slices in your file, use the Slice Select tool to click on and select the slice you want to optimize, then select a file type from the Optimized file format pop-up.

Selectively exporting artwork

When exporting artwork that has been created in legacy versions of Illustrator, the Basic RGB profile, or any CMYK profiles, Illustrator includes every object within the document, even if it exists outside the Artboard. If you enable the Clip to Artboard option in the Image Size tab, only the objects that exist within the Artboard will be exported. To export just a portion of your artwork, first create a rectangle around the art you wish to export and choose Object > Crop Area > Make, then open Save for Web or use the Crop tool to define the area to crop.
—*Jean-Claude Tremblay*

Change ruler to pixel units

Control-click (Mac) or Right-click on the ruler (View > Show Rulers) and select Pixels to display the units as pixels.

Transparency and Web colors

Even if you've been working in RGB mode with Web safe colors, if you've used Illustrator's transparency in your file, you will end up with out-of-gamut shades when the artwork is rasterized or flattened. Files with extensive transparency use should be saved as JPEG, not as GIF, to avoid excessive dithering.

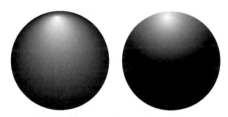

Non-centered radial gradients exported to SWF
Left: SWF exported with Preserve Appearance
Right: SWF exported with Preserve Editability

If you want to compare the compression of two or more settings, click on one of the other views, either 2-Up or 4-Up. The final file format, size, download time, and compression specifics are listed under each preview panel.

Finally, if you want to export your artwork, click the Save button to specify how you want to save files. If you have slices, you can choose to export the images and the HTML as well. If you opened Save for Web & Devices only to define the optimization settings for your slices, click the Done button to get back to your file; Illustrator remembers all the settings you just applied. See *Illustrator Help* for a complete description of format options.

Adobe Flash (SWF) export

Although saving as Illustrator (.ai) format and opening in Adobe Flash will give you the best results, exporting SWF files can be useful if you are working with a legacy version of Macromedia Flash, or if you will be producing the final animated file directly in Illustrator. If you own Adobe Flash, you can also copy and paste or drag and drop between Illustrator and Flash. Be aware that exporting as SWF may break your artwork into many simple objects. even if you have created Flash Movie Clips of them.

Here are some strategies for maximizing the quality and usefulness of your Illustrator files in Flash:

• **Use Illustrator symbols for repeating objects.** Illustrator lets you convert both raster and vector artwork into *symbols* that you can *place* multiple times, instead of using multiple copies of the original art (see the *Brushes & Symbols* chapter for more about symbols). Each time you place an instance of a symbol, you are creating a *link* to the symbol stored in the panel, rather than duplicating the artwork. This reduces the size of your Illustrator file, and can also reduce the size of any SWF files you export from Illustrator—as long as you haven't used the Stainer, Screener, or Styler on your symbols. Using those tools can actually increase the size of your exported SWF file, because what were instances in the AI file will become unique symbols in the SWF file.

- **Choosing Export Layers to SWF frames turns each Illustrator layer into a separate Flash frame.** This is a method for exporting Illustrator layers as individual elements for animation.
- **Paths that are only partly contained within the work area will be exported in their entirety,** when creating a SWF file. To reduce file size as much as possible, you can permanently remove the excess paths by selecting all of your artwork and then dragging over the unnecessary area, using the Erase tool while holding down Option/Alt to delete paths in rectangular sections.
- **When exporting SWF files,** switch between Preserve Appearance and Preserve Editability and check the Optimized view in case anything has changed.
- **Dashed strokes will be rastered when exported to SWF.** Select dashed strokes and choose Object > Expand, so the strokes remain vectors in your SWF files.

PNG-24 export for video

PNG-24 is particularly useful when working with non-square pixel (anamorphic) video projects that require bitmap files instead of vector files. Choose PNG-24 format when you Save for Web & Devices to optimally preserve the image resolution. Unfortunately, choosing PSD for anamorphic images will result in your image either being distorted when you place it in a video editing application, or reduced in quality if you have to resize it.

To export a bitmap from a document created with the NTSC DV Widescreen Document Profile, you can use File > Save For Web & Devices, and then select PNG-24 as the format. In the Image Size tab, change the size from a width of 864 pixels and height of 480 pixels by disabling the Constrain Proportions checkbox, and then entering 720 pixels width and leaving 480 pixels height (the anamorphic pixel dimensions are displayed outside of the document work area with the Crop Area Rulers). When you open the PNG file in Photoshop, choose Image > Pixel Aspect Ratio > D1/DV NTSC Widescreen (1.2), and then the image will display with the correct proportions.

Go, Go Dynamic!

You can take dynamic graphics a step further if you're using Adobe GoLive 6.0 or higher, which understands Illustrator's variable content. Simply save your file in SVG format and import it into GoLive as an Illustrator Smart Object. You can change the variables you defined in Illustrator in GoLive.

CSS layers

Illustrator allows you to export CSS (Cascading Style Sheets) layers. Modern browsers take advantage of DHTML, which allows you to overlap artwork layers. Top level layers can be converted to CSS layers on export from the Save for Web dialog, and you can specify which layers to export from the Layers tab there.

SVG Browser Plug-in

Illustrator ships standard with (and installs by default) the SVG 3.0 browser plug-in. If you're creating SVG graphics, make sure that whoever is viewing them also downloads the free SVG 3.0 viewer that's available from the www.adobe.com/svg Web page. Adobe will stop support for the SVG Viewer as of January 1, 2008, so you may need to use a different browser plug-in after that time, if security risks develop.

Garden Slicing

Designing a Web Page in Illustrator

Overview: *Set up a document for Web page design; use layers to structure artwork for pages; create guides for artwork positioning; save an image of a page; slice artwork to save an HTML file or sliced image files.*

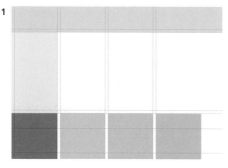

1

Gordon started the Web site by creating a 700 by 500 pixel file; he then created color-filled rectangles to represent areas of the home page and subsequent pages that would be filled with images and text.

To use Clip to Artboard...

The default Web document profile uses Crop Areas within a huge Artboard (14400 **x** 14400 pixels) to define slicing areas. To use Clip to Artboard with expected results, constrain your slice range by using File >Document Setup and reduce the Artboard to match your Crop Area. Note that Clip to Artboard still works with files created using the Basic RGB profile; these are created in the same way as legacy documents that use page size (not Crop Areas) to define slicing.
—*Jean-Claude Tremblay*

If you're comfortable designing and drawing in Illustrator, why go elsewhere to design your Web pages? Steven Gordon used Illustrator to design and preview Web pages, create comps for client approval, and slice and optimize artwork for use in his Web software.

1 Choosing document settings. To start designing your website, create a new document (File >New). In the New Document dialog, select Web from the New Document Profile menu and then chose one of the default sizes from the Size menu or key in your own custom size. Because your artwork will be exported in a bitmap format like GIF or JPEG, consider turning on pixel preview (View > Pixel Preview). With pixel preview you can see the anti-aliasing of your artwork as if it were rasterized, and can therefore make any adjustments if necessary.

2 Structuring pages with layers and adding artwork. Let the Layers panel help you design the layout and organize the content of the pages in your website. (See the *Layers & Appearances* chapter for more on layers.) Gordon made a master layer for each of the website's five pages he planned, creating sublayers within each layer for the type, artwork and images of that particular page.

Once you've set up the layer structure of your document, create a grid (Preferences >Guides & Grid) to help

you align and constrain artwork. Or, create a set of guides
by choosing View>Show Rulers (⌘-R/Ctrl-R), dragging
guides into the page from the rulers, and positioning
them precisely using the Control or Transform panels (be
sure View>Guides>Lock Guides is not enabled). Now
you're ready to create the content of each web page.

3 Saving an image and slices. Once your pages are complete, you can save an image of each page to serve as a
template for your Web software. Simply hide all layers
except the master layer and its sublayers represent a web
page. Then select File>Export and choose a file format
compatible with your Web software. Another option is
to export the text, artwork and images as image slices
so that you can use them in your Web software to build
the finished pages. Use artwork selections, guides, or the
Slice tool to divide a layer's artwork into slices. You can
use non-contiguous objects for slicing: Illustrator will
add empty slices to fill in any gaps between objects. To
begin, select an object (if the slice will be a masked image,
click on the clipping mask, not the image, with the Group
Selection tool). Then choose Object > Slice > Create from
Selection. Repeat these steps until you've created all of the
slices you need. If you want to remove a slice, select and
delete it; or in the Layers panel, drag its name (<Slice>) to
the panel's trash icon.

When you've finished slicing your artwork, you can
save the slices as text and images. Choose File>Save
for Web and Devices; in the dialog, click on the Slice
Select tool and click one of the slices. Pick the settings
that you want to use for saving that selected slice. For
the flower images, Gordon chose JPEG as the file format
and enabled Optimized to make the file sizes smaller.
After clicking on Save, he then entered a file name for the
HTML file (which automatically became the root name of
each of the sliced image files), and made sure that HTML
and Images were selected in the Format pop-up menu.
Gordon continued the website development by opening
the HTML file in his Web software.

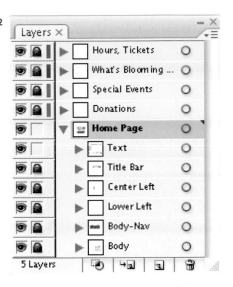

The layer structure for the Web page design,
showing the various pages as master layers and
the sublayers as elements within the Home Page

The numbered slices created after using the Object > Slices > Create from Selection command

216 colors, or millions?

The palette of 216 non-dithered,
Web safe colors was designed for
text and graphics displaying on
8-bit monitors. But how many
people are restricted to 8-bit
color anymore? Not many. Most
computers are now equipped with
24- or 32-bit video boards, rendering Web safe colors unnecessary,
so you can choose from millions of
colors, not just 216.

Layering Frames

Turning Layered Artwork into Key Frames

○

Overview: *Draw artwork for print; design animation sequences using artwork; create layers and lay out art and text in positions for animation key frames; export layers as Shockwave Flash frames.*

1

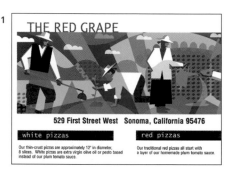

Artwork originally created for The Red Grape's printed restaurant menu

Planning an animation sequence by positioning objects and text at beginning and end of the sequence

After designing the brand identity, menu artwork, and a wall mural in Illustrator for The Red Grape, a Sonoma, California restaurant, Hugh Whyte of Lehner and Whyte faced one more task. He needed to turn his artwork into Flash animations for the restaurant's Web site (www. theredgrape.com). The key to recycling the artwork was to develop a productive workflow between Illustrator and Adobe Flash that would allow Whyte and Mark Murphy of DigitalKick to work within the software each designer knew best.

1 Drawing artwork and planning objects and type for key frames. While his drawings of people and food were originally designed for the printed menus, Whyte returned to the artwork and prepared it for the Web as a Flash animation.

Starting in Illustrator you can use artwork that you've already created. It will help if you to think ahead as to how your artwork will move in the animation sequences. Identify the starting and ending locations of each object in an animation sequence. Also note where objects will change direction as they move during the sequence.

2 Arranging artwork on layers. To facilitate their collaboration, Whyte and Murphy devised a workflow in which Whyte created in Illustrator what Murphy would use as keyframes in Flash. You can do the same, and even produce the final animation yourself in Flash, using Illustrator to build the foundation of your animation.

Begin with File >New and select Web as your New Document Profile. Copy and paste a vector image or vector logo into your new file and then turn this into a symbol. To do this, select all your paths and click on the New Symbol button at the bottom of the Symbols panel (F8), then choose Movie Clip in Symbol Options. You'll now have a new symbol in the Symbols panel and the paths on your artboard will have been converted to an instance of it. Flash will be able to convert Illustrator's layers to keyframes for animation. If you're using symbols that have been rotated, scaled, or have transparency changes from one layer to the next, Flash can automatically create all of the frames in between the keyframes.

If you're only animating one symbol at time, you can arrange your content in a single Illustrator layer and then release your symbols to layers before importing to Flash. Keep the number of keyframes that you create in Illustrator to a minimum, as Flash's Motion Tween ability creates evenly distributed, in-between frames that are easier to control, and are more easily synchronized to music.

To create an animation in which a symbol enters from beyond the "stage" (of the viewable screen), passes through in the center of stage and then moves off stage, start by positioning the first instance of your symbol outside of your page frame. Now Option-drag/Alt-drag the first instance of the symbol onto the artboard, which will later become the second keyframe. Rotate, scale, or change the transparency of the symbol, then repeat this process for however many changes are required until the symbol leaves the artboard again. To convert your artwork to keyframes that Flash will recognize, create a new blank layer for each symbol on the artboard, then select each symbol individually and drag the selection highlight indicator in the layers panel up to the next layer. Repeat this until all of the symbols are on their own layers. Save as a native AI file, then import directly to the Stage of Adobe Flash choosing Convert Layers to Keyframes.

2

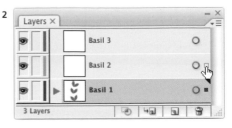

Selecting symbols on the artboard, then dragging the selection highlight indicator to move your sysmbols to different layers

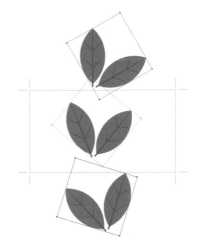

Symbol instances for the final animation sequence arranged on three layers which will become frames when brought into Flash

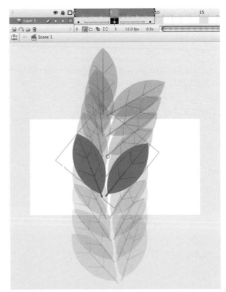

The Illustrator symbols viewed on the Flash stage after a Shape Tween has been applied with Onion Skin preview on the Timeline

Off in a Flash

Making Artwork for a Flash Animation

ATTEBERRY

Overview: *Sketch character artwork; create brushes and blend objects for moving parts in the animation; save the artwork as a static AI file and a SWF animation; preview animations in Illustrator; Import and Tween in Flash.*

Character parts sketched with a custom calligraphic brush (see the Brushes & Symbols *chapter for help with brushes)*

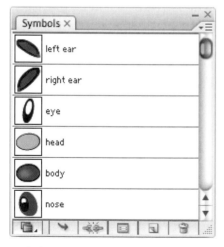

Symbols panel displayed in Large List View

Seattle artist and animator Kevan Atteberry knows how to get the most from Illustrator when preparing artwork for animation in Flash. Besides making his Illustrator file a sketchpad filled with the eyes, ears, arms, and legs of the character he will animate later in Flash, Atteberry uses the Layers panel to preview parts of the animation. He also exports a Flash animation as he works in Illustrator to view a draft version of the final animation.

1 Sketching characters, drawing body parts. Atteberry began with a custom calligraphic brush, sketching a series of facial expressions and figure poses, honing the visual character of a lemur until he was satisfied with the characterization and ready to construct the lemur's body parts. Once you're done drawing your character's parts, you can keep your artwork as Illustrator objects or turn the artwork into symbol instances. It takes fewer steps to convert your artwork to symbol instances in Illustrator than to bring your artwork into Flash and make symbols there. Also, if you plan to export a Flash movie from Illustrator, turning your character parts into symbol instances results in a smaller and faster-loading Flash file.

To make symbol instances, select and drag each part of the body you drew into the Symbols panel (or use F8). After you release the mouse button, Illustrator adds the artwork as a symbol in the Symbols panel and replaces the selected artwork in your file with an instance of the symbol you just made. (See the *Brushes & Symbols* chapter for more on symbols and instances.)

2 Making brushes, creating blends for objects, expanding blends, and creating symbols. For any part you animate, you'll need to create a sequence of that part's movements—for example, a leg that moves from straight to bent. Atteberry created art brushes for the lemur's moving parts, so he could paint each part in the motion sequence with the brush. (This saved the effort of creating separate art for each part in the sequence.) First, draw a straight version of the part. When you have the look you want, drag-and-drop it on the open Brushes panel. In the New Brush dialog, choose New Art Brush.

Next, you'll create artwork for the two extremes in the motion sequence. Draw the straight part, and a few inches away draw the bent part. Select both paths and apply the art brush to both. Now, to make other parts in the movement sequence, make sure both paths are selected and choose Object > Blend > Make; then choose Object > Blend > Blend Options and key in the number of steps in the Spacing: Specified Steps field. Consider using a small number of blend steps—Atteberry uses three or four—so that if used as frames in a Flash animation, your SWF file will have a smaller number of frames and a smaller file size. Finally, expand the blend (Object > Blend > Expand) and ungroup it so you have separate objects to use in constructing poses for the motion sequence.

3 Previewing your animation and exporting as SWF. To prepare your file for animation, first add as many layers as frames needed to show the motion sequence. Treating each layer as an animation frame, assemble the artwork for a particular pose or step in the motion sequence on

2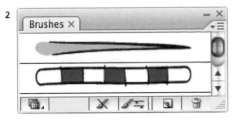

Two of the brushes Atteberry created for the moving parts

The straight and bent lemur legs representing the extremes of a motion sequence that Atteberry used to create a Blend

A blend using three steps created between the straight and bent lemur legs

From Illustrator to Flash

If you're using Adobe Flash, save your Illustrator file and import it into Flash. If you are using a legacy version of Macromedia Flash, you'll likely get better results if you use File > Save for Web & Devices or File > Export and choose SWF. It's important to note that for paths to look the same in Flash as they do in Illustrator, you must increase the Curve Quality to 10 in the SWF export dialog, otherwise the paths and Bézier curves will be simplified and altered slightly.

Previewing a motion sequence using Illustrator's Layers panel as a crude film projector

Pasting into Flash

You can copy Illustrator artwork and paste into Flash. Be careful, though: some Illustrator artwork with complex styles and bitmap effects will be rasterized and can lose their transparency settings when pasted in Flash.

each layer. Move from layer to layer, creating renditions of the character on each layer until the character has performed all of the poses or movements you want to preview. When you have completed all the layers, you can preview your animation in a browser or Flash player by exporting it as an SWF. To do so, select File > Save for Web. From the Format pop-up, select SWF (just below the word Preset) and, from the pop-up below that, choose AI Layers to SWF Frames. If your animation doesn't require any advanced techniques that need further work inside of Flash, you can export the final animation from Illustrator.

There is another animation technique you can use to preview motion—from within Illustrator itself. Atteberry constructed a draft version of part of the animation to preview the look of objects and their motion sequence. To do this, you can construct a preview by first following the steps described above for positioning poses on successive layers. After you've filled all your layers with artwork, select Panel Options from the Layers panel menu. To display large thumbnails, enable the Show Layers Only checkbox and enter 100 pixels in the Other field. To preview the animation, position the cursor over a Layers panel scrolling arrow and press the mouse button to cause the layer thumbnails to scroll like frames in a projector.

4 Saving your file to import into Flash. To create complex animations inside of Flash with interactivity or audio using your artwork, instead of exporting a .SWF with Save for Web & Devices, save a native AI file. When you are in Flash, import your AI file directly to the Stage and choose 'Convert Layers to : Frames' and your entire animation will be correctly ordered in the Timeline. Also all your Symbols will be referenced to the Library for reuse and quicker download times. To make your animation play back more smoothly, you can increase the frame rate of your Timeline and then Tween between scaled and rotated symbols, or use Shape Hinting on your expanded brushes to fine tune their movement.

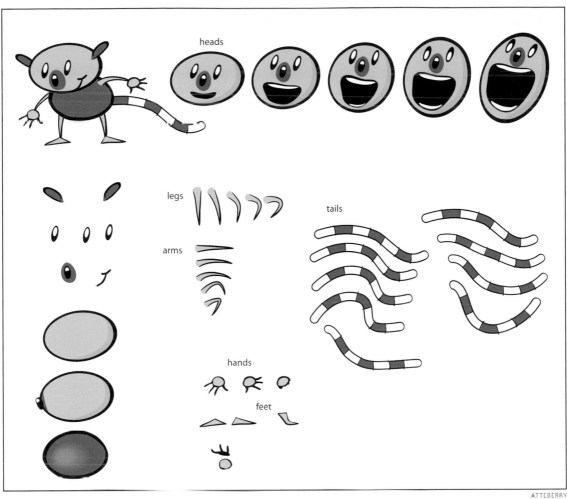

heads

legs

arms

tails

hands

feet

ATTEBERRY

Kevan Atteberry

To assist in constructing his animation "Millard and the Pear," described in the previous lesson, artist Kevan Atteberry developed a file of recyclable parts—a cartoon "morgue"—from which he copied parts and then pasted them into the animation file he created. To trim the file size of the animation, Atteberry converted the artwork for parts into symbol instances by dragging them to the Symbols panel. When he needed to edit a symbol in a file, Atteberry double-clicked the symbol either in the Symbols panel or on his artboard to enter the symbol editing isolation mode. He then edited the symbol however he wished, and when he was done, he just double-clicked on the artboard to exit isolation mode. The edited symbol automatically updated in the panel, and instances of the symbol update as well!

Animating Pieces
Preparing Files for Creating Animations

Illustrator with After Effects

Overview: *Make basic elements; cut elements using the Knife tool; order the <Path> elements and separate them into layers; export the file to create the actual animation.*

1

After drawing the huge letter forms using the Pen tool, Lush created "records" and ™ with the Text tool, then converted the text to outlines so he could modify the forms with the Direct Selection tool (final objects shown above in Outline and below in Preview modes)

2

The art shown after Lush cut the objects, in Outline mode above, and Preview mode below (the preview pieces have been moved so that you can see the cuts)

Terry Lush created the Illustrator portion of this animation for an ongoing "latest record release banner" on the hugerecords.com website.

1 Creating the basic elements. Use any tools to create your basic elements. For his animation, Lush drew the "huge" outlines with the Pen tool, based on the typeface Bauhaus. He then created the "records" and ™ text with the Type tool, and converted the text to outlines (Type > Create Outlines, or ⌘-Shift-O/Ctrl-Shift-O) so he could slightly modify the letterform paths with the Direct Selection tool. Lush saved his files in stages as he worked.

2 Cutting lines. To visualize where to cut elements, draw lines to use as guides (⌘-5/Ctrl-5 turns objects into guides). Lush used the Knife tool (under the Scissors tool) to cut the letters into pieces. To make straight cuts, he held Option/Alt while click-dragging with the Knife (adding Shift for straight lines). Objects are shown at left first in Outline then Preview mode (the pieces shown in Preview have been moved apart so you can see the cuts).

3 Ordering the animation and distributing elements into layers. To figure out the order in which the pieces should appear in the animation, Lush expanded the layer containing the separate (cut) <Path> elements. First, while hiding all the paths, he experimented with showing paths one at a time until he determined the order in which he wanted the paths to appear. He then reordered the <Path> elements to match that viewing sequence.

Once you've rearranged the paths in the correct order within a layer, you'll need to distribute each <Path> onto its own layer. To do this, click the name of the enclosing layer and, from the Layers panel pop-up, choose Release to Layers (Build). Now select these sublayers (click the top one and Shift-click the bottom one) and drag them above the enclosing layer so they are no longer sublayers.

4 Making the animation and creating variations. Lush imported the layered Illustrator file into After Effects (you should be able to download a tryout version of AE from www.adobe.com/products/aftereffects/). In After Effects, he selected all layers and trimmed the length of the layers to 7 frames. Choosing Animation > Keyframe Assistant > Sequence Layers, he set the parameters for the sequence so that each layer would be held for seven frames and then Cross Dissolve for two frames to the next layer. Keyframe Assistant automatically sequenced the layers (in order), and created the cross dissolves by generating keyframes with the correct opacity for each transition. With the file saved, Lush exported the After Effects movie in QuickTime format. Bringing this animation into his 3D program, Cinema 4D, he mapped the animation to the front surface of 3D-rendered, Times Square–like billboard. To create variations (such as the 30° rotation at right), Lush worked once more in Illustrator with a copy of the file. He selected all elements (without grouping them), double-clicked the Rotate tool, entered a 30° angle and clicked OK. He then saved this version and imported it into After Effects where he created a variation of the animation using the same procedures described above.

After cutting the objects, then after rearranging the pieces in the order of the desired animation

Release to Layers (Sequence)
Release to Layers (Build)
Reverse Order

With the containing layer selected, choosing Release to Layers (Build), then moving the sublayers out of the containing layer

Selecting all of the objects in Illustrator to rotate the entire cut group of objects 30° for a variant of the animation

Flash Animation

Creating Flash Character Animations

DASHWOOD

Illustrator with Flash

Overview: *Prepare your workspace; draw animated cels; optimize file size; import in Flash; animate in Flash.*

Andrew Dashwood created this eight cel animated figure as a background element to a larger interactive page. He used techniques requiring minimal programming in Flash so that the animation's looping playback was web-ready.

The final screen from Dashwood's website

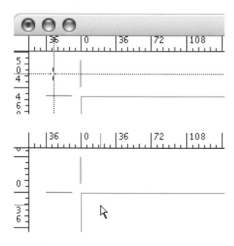

Drag the intersection point of the rulers to change the starting point of the artboard

1 Setting the stage. The Illustrator artboard is the Flash stage, so it's worth spending time planning the animation carefully before you draw anything. Make sure you visualize your final presentation and set everything up appropriately ahead of time. Flash recognizes Illustrator's document size and can change the dimensions of its stage size accordingly. Flash will also import your paths in the exact location at which they were drawn inside of Illustrator. Dashwood started by creating a new document from an RGB Web document preset. All the default presets are designed for 4:3 monitors, so he adjusted the document's dimensions to fit in a web browser on a 16:10 widescreen monitor. Dashwood chose File >New, selected Web from the New Document Profile drop down menu, and then set the width to 739 pixels and the height to 496 pixels.

By default, Illustrator's rulers and guides start in the lower left corner of the artboard; in contrast, Flash rulers and guides start in the top left. To avoid confusion, change the **X** (horizontal) ruler origin point of Illustrator to the top left: go to View >Show Rulers and drag the intersection point of **X** and **Y** (horizontal and vertical) rulers to the top left corner of the artboard.

2 Building your basic animation objects. To create the framing for his animation, Dashwood began by drawing two rectangular objects on the artboard in the shape of a TV screen. He then selected both of the closed paths, and used the Live Paint Bucket to fill the outer frame shape with a color. Next he highlighted the fill of the inner rectangle with the Live Paint Selection tool and then deleted it so that the artboard could be seen through the screen. Once your frame is created, open the Layers panel and double click the title of the layer you have been working on. When you are in the Layer Options dialog, change the name from the default title of "Layer 1" to "Foreground." Now create a new layer in the Layers panel, by ⌘-Option-clicking/Ctrl-Alt-clicking the New Layer icon, which will bring up the Layer Options dialog. Name this "Cel 1," click OK, and your layer will automatically be placed below the previous layer. Then lock the "Background" layer by clicking on the Lock toggle next to its name. Using any of the basic tools, draw the first cel of your animation so that it fills the screen of the television. As the anchor points in the paths on this layer will be moved in each of the subsequent cels, try to keep your paths simple, with a minimum number of anchor points.

3 Developing your animation. You can begin the process of animating, by creating the second version of your character. Select "Cel 1" in the Layers panel and then drag and drop it onto the New Layer button to duplicate it. Double click the layer that you have just created ("Cel 1 copy") and rename it to "Cel 2". Then drag that layer below "Cel 1" in the Layers panel and lock the layer by clicking the Lock toggle button next to its name. To use "Cel 1" as a guide for animating "Cel 2", ⌘-click/Ctrl-click the eye icon next to the "Cel 1" name so that only this layer appears in outline mode while everything else remains in preview mode. Use the Direct Selection or Reshape tools to move the paths and anchor points of "Cel 2" to create the illusion of movement between the cels. Repeat these steps for the subsequent frames in your animation.

2

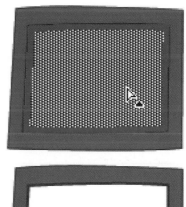

Select the inside of the screen with the Live Paint Selection tool and delete to reveal the artboard beneath.

3

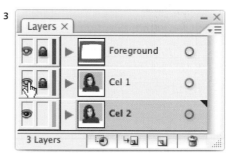

⌘-Click/Ctrl-Click the eye icon to toggle a single layer between Outline and Preview viewing modes

Move the anchor points and Bézier handles on the second layer to create movement

4

When creating symbols, you can choose between a Flash Graphic or Movie Clip

The Symbols panel containing Movie Clips

The Import to Stage dialog will alow you to choose which Symbols to import

Change the frame rate of your movie inside of the Properties panel

4 Preparing your file for importing to Flash. To reduce the file size and download time of the final animation, you can use the Symbols panel to create Flash Movie Clips of each animation cel. Instances of symbols can be used repeatedly in Flash without significantly increasing file size. Create Movie Clips of each layer in your animation by selecting all the paths on the "Cel 1" layer, then click the New Symbol button in the Symbols panel or use the F8 key, and name it "Cel 1." Next, enable the Movie Clip check box and repeat this for all of the subsequent cels. When you have finished creating your animation, save the document as a native .AI file so it can be imported directly into the Adobe Flash library.

Note: *Be careful when naming your symbols in Illustrator. Names such as 'frame,' or others that are reserved words for ActionScript, can conflict when imported to Flash. See the Flash help files or www.adobe.com for a full list of these reserved names.*

5 Importing the .AI file in Flash. The next part of the lesson requires Adobe Flash to be installed on your system. If you don't own a copy, you can download a fully functional 30-day trial version from www.adobe.com. Launch Flash and select File > New. Then inside of the General tab, choose to create a new Flash file with either ActionScript 2.0 or ActionScript 3.0. By default the Stage in Flash will be 550 pixels wide by 400 pixels high and will be set to playback at 12 frames per second (fps). All of these details will be visible inside of the Properties panel. To import the animation that you created in Illustrator, go to File > Import > Import to Stage. The Import dialog window will contain a scrollable pane of all the layers and symbols you created. Make sure the radio buttons for all of the "Cel" Symbols have been checked, but that the "Foreground" and "Background" are disabled. From the Convert Layers To drop down list, choose Keyframes and then check Place Objects in Original Position while you also Set Stage Size to same size as Illustrator Artboard. Click OK to return to the Stage and notice that it has resized to your original Illustrator document and "Cel 1" Symbol is visible on the Stage in the same position that it was in Illustrator. Also, make sure all of the other "Cel" Symbols have been placed in chronological order on the Timeline and are listed in the Library. To quickly test what your movie looks like in a separate window, go to Control > Test Movie, or press ⌘-Return/Ctrl-Enter on your keyboard. If the animation plays too quickly, reduce the frame rate in the Properties panel.

6 Looping and exporting your animation. To create an animation loop, select your frames (inside the timeline, click the first frame of the animation "Cel 1", hold Shift, and click the final frame). Duplicate the frames by Option-dragging/Alt-dragging them onto a blank frame to the right. With the duplicated frames still highlighted, go to Modify > Timeline > Reverse Frames. Test your movie again and you'll see that your animation will now loop back and forth indefinitely. Keep your animation organized by double-clicking "Layer 1" in the Timeline panel and naming it "Cels." To import the "Foreground" and "Background" that you drew in Illustrator, go back to File > Import > Import to Stage, locate your AI file, and then enable their Symbol names while disabling the ones for the "Cels." In the Convert To drop down list, choose Layers and leave Original Position enabled, and click OK to return to the stage again. The New Symbols will appear in labeled Layers in the Timeline above the "Cels" layer. You'll need to reorder the layers as they were in Illustrator. Drag the name for "Background" to the bottom of the layer stacking order and leave "Foreground" at the top.

When you've finished your animation, you'll be ready to export it for publishing on the web. Go to File > Publish Settings and, in the Formats tab, make sure you have enabled Flash and HTML. If your target audience is not likely to have updated their Flash Player recently, go to the Flash tab and choose Flash Player 8 or Flash Player 7 from the list of legacy versions. Click Publish at the bottom of the screen to complete the export.

6

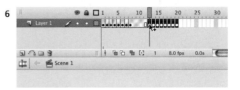

Duplicate frames by Option-drag/Alt-drag inside of the Timeline

Rename Layers by double clicking their names

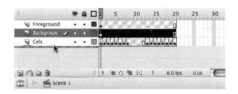

Keep Illustrator layers as named Flash layers

Reorder Layers by dragging their names

The Flash interface with the final animation

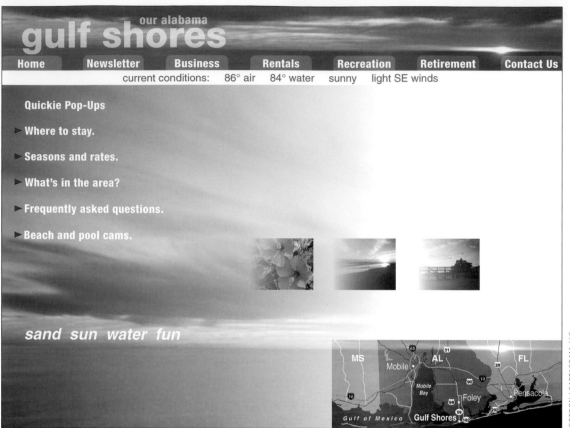

Steven Gordon / Cartagram, LLC

To build image-mapped buttons at the top of a travel Web page, Steven Gordon first placed a TIFF image in Illustrator to serve as a background image. Next, he drew a button shape with rounded corners and gave it a white Fill and a 25% Opacity using the Transparency panel. He copied the button six times and arranged the buttons in a row above the background image. To space the buttons evenly, Gordon positioned the left and right buttons, selected all buttons, and then clicked the Horizontal Distribute Space icon in the Align panel. To map the buttons to URLs, he selected each button shape and in

the Attributes panel chose Rectangle from the Image Map pop-up menu. He then keyed in the button's URL link in the URL field. In the Save for Web dialog, Gordon selected JPEG as the output file format, clicked Save, and then chose HTML and Images from the Format pop-up menu. He entered a file name in the Name field and clicked Save.

VAN DOOREN

Corné van Dooren

For one of his local clients, Dutch multimedia designer Corné van Dooren drew the basic elements of this Christmas card in Illustrator and then imported the frames into Flash where he added interactivity. Van Dooren began by taking a still photograph of a box with ribbon tied in a bow on top of it. He hand-traced his photograph with the Pen tool, creating separate elements for each of the sides of the box and bow. He moved the paths incrementally using a combination of the Free Transform, Direct Selection, and Convert Anchor Point tools to create the illusion of the bow untying itself and the box opening. After he drew each frame, van Dooren saved the file with a new version number. He was then able to preview the animation without needing to launch Flash by cycling through open documents using ⌘-~/ Ctrl-Tab. (Windows users also have the exclusive feature of tiling documents using Window > Tile). To speed up production time of the artwork, van Dooren imported the sequence of images into Flash and colored the frames there, using Shape Tweens between the frames for the shading on the box, which he would otherwise have had to create manually in Illustrator.

Illustrator & Other Programs

This chapter showcases some of the ways you can use Illustrator together with other programs. Although the range of work you can create using Illustrator is virtually limitless, combining other programs with Illustrator increases your creative opportunities, and in many instances can save you significant time in creating your final work.

Following is a discussion about how you can place artwork in Illustrator, and then we'll provide a general look at how Illustrator works with other programs. Next we'll examine how Illustrator works with specific programs, including Photoshop, InDesign, Acrobat, and 3D programs. (For details about working with Web and animation programs, see the *Web & Animation* chapter.)

PLACING ARTWORK IN ILLUSTRATOR

Illustrator can place more than two dozen different file formats. The major choice you'll need to make is whether to link or embed the placed file. When you link a file, you don't actually include the artwork in the Illustrator file; instead a copy of the artwork acts as a placeholder, while the actual image remains separate from the Illustrator file. This can help reduce file size, but keep in mind that linking is supported only for certain formats (see Tip at right). On the other hand, when you embed artwork, you're actually including it in the file. The Links panel keeps track of all the raster images used in your document, regardless of whether they were created within Illustrator, opened, or introduced via the Place command.

In general, you should embed artwork only when:
- The image is small in file size and you won't want to edit the original later so that the new edit updates the file.
- You want more than just a placeholder with a preview (e.g., you want editable objects and transparency).
- Your printer/service bureau requires embedded links.

If you're a FreeHand User...
Find "Moving from FreeHand to Illustrator" on the *Wow! CD*—a PDF Excerpt from Mordy Golding's *Real World Adobe Illustrator CS3*.

Open sesame
If you're working in an application that doesn't allow you to save in a format that Illustrator imports (such as PSD, EPS, or PDF), but does print to PostScript, you may be able to get the vector data by printing to File and then opening the PostScript file in Illustrator.

Resolution of placed images
Ensure optimal image reproduction by properly setting the pixels per inch (ppi) resolution of raster images before placing them into Illustrator. The ppi of images should be 1.5 to 2 times the size of the line screen at which the final image will print. For example, if your illustration will be printed in a 150 dpi (dots per inch) line screen, then the resolution of your raster images would typically be 300 ppi. Get print resolution specifications and recommendations from your printer *before* you begin your project!

And you should link (rather than embed) when:

- Your illustration uses several copies of the same image.
- The image is large in file size.
- You want to be able to edit the placed image using its original application.
- You can make changes to a linked file and resend only the linked file to your service bureau or client. As long as it has exactly the same name, it will auto-update without further editing of the Illustrator document itself.

ILLUSTRATOR & OTHER PROGRAMS

The first consideration when moving artwork between Illustrator and other programs is to decide which objects in your artwork you want to remain as vectors, if possible, and which you can allow to become rasterized. Next is whether you want to move the artwork between two open programs on your desktop (e.g., by using Copy and Paste or Drag and Drop), or if you will be moving your artwork via a file format. Finally, consider whether you want to move only a few objects or the whole file. Techniques for the above vary depending on the program, and are described in the corresponding program sections below.

Depending on the application, when you drag or paste objects between Illustrator and another open program, your objects will either drag or paste as vectors or as raster objects. In general, any program that supports PostScript drag and drop behavior will accept Illustrator objects via Drag and Drop (or Copy and Paste). In order for this to work, before copying and pasting, make certain that the AICB (Adobe Illustrator Clipboard) is enabled in the File Handling & Clipboard panel of the Preferences dialog. Then you can copy the objects between AI and the other application.

When you copy and paste, or drag-and-drop Illustrator art into a raster-based program (other than Photoshop), it's likely that your art will be automatically rasterized at the same physical size, or pixels-per-inch ratio, that you have specified in that raster-based program. (See the section "Illustrator & Adobe Photoshop,"

Need Photoshop Layers?

In Illustrator, if you use File > Place, with Link enabled, a layered PSD file comes in flattened (no layers). If Link is not enabled, you'll get the Photoshop Import Options dialog which allows you to Convert Photoshop layers to objects, retaining layers. Using File > Open always gives you that dialog. — *Cristen Gillespie*

So you think it's linked?

Flattening transparency of a linked image automatically embeds the image. In addition to increasing the file size, you can no longer update the link.

Which formats can you link?

Any BMP, EPS, GIF, JPEG, PICT, PCX, PDF, PNG, Photoshop, Pixar, Targa, or TIFF file can be placed as linked (rather than embedded).

When EPS is *not* recommended

If your application, such as InDesign, can place or open native AI, native PSD, or PDF 1.4 or later formats, it's better to use those than EPS, which cannot preserve layers, transparency and other features.

Illustrator File Handling and Clipboard Preferences dialog; to copy and paste vectors set the Clipboard preferences as shown here

What about MS Office?

If you're one of the many people wondering which format to choose when you want to place Illustrator artwork into a Microsoft application, there's File > Save for Microsoft Office just for you!
—Jean-Claude Tremblay

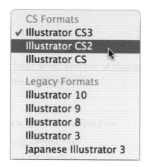

After choosing Adobe Illustrator Document, the Version pop-up choices give you access to Illustrator CS and later, and Legacy Formats

Where are my linked files?

When you use the Save As > Format: Adobe Illustrator Document (.ai) with Create PDF Compatible File enabled, any linked files are included in the PDF portion of the file—even if Include Linked Files is not enabled. The linked images can be seen if you open the AI file in Acrobat—even if the original linked files have been deleted. However, if Include Linked Files was not enabled when the Illustrator document was saved, the linked files will not be included in the Illustrator portion of the file. When you reopen it in Illustrator and the original linked files have been deleted, it will ask you to find them.

following, for details about Illustrator's special working relationship with Photoshop.)

You can Save, or Export, your Illustrator artwork to many formats. From the File menu you can Save, Save for Web & Devices, Save for Microsoft Office, and Save As Template. From Save As you can choose vector formats and PDF. In order to save in legacy Illustrator AI formats when you need compatibility, choose Adobe Illustrator Document from the Save As > Format pop-up. From the Version pop-up menu, you can choose Illustrator Creative Suite Formats or earlier Legacy Formats.

From Export, you can access additional formats including raster and Flash. Know which file formats your other application supports (i.e., Flash prefers you save in .ai format!) and the type of information (vector, raster, layers, paths) you want to bring from Illustrator into the other program to determine which format to choose.

ILLUSTRATOR & ADOBE PHOTOSHOP

Moving artwork between Illustrator and Photoshop via a file format is fairly straightforward, since Photoshop can open or place Illustrator files, and Illustrator can open and export Photoshop PSD files.

Fortunately, rasterizing isn't the one-way street it used to be, thanks to a marvelous feature called *Smart Objects*, introduced in Photoshop CS2, which greatly improves the process of bringing Illustrator art into Photoshop.

Smart Objects in Photoshop can be scaled, rotated, or warped without loss of data, and when you edit one instance of a Smart Object, Photoshop will automatically update all of your associated Smart Objects.

But the best news for Illustrator users is that you can create Photoshop Smart Objects from Illustrator data just by using the Clipboard (copying and pasting, dragging and dropping), or by inserting an Illustrator file using File > Place. You'll then have your choice of editing the placed Illustrator data either within Photoshop as rasters, or externally in Illustrator as vectors. When you double-click an Illustrator Smart Object in Photoshop's

Layers panel, Photoshop will automatically launch Illustrator and open a working copy of your artwork. You can then edit the artwork in Illustrator and save the file, at which point Photoshop will re-rasterize it in place of the original Smart Object. With Adjustment layers and new Smart Filters, you can modify an Illustrator Smart Object in Photoshop with "live" raster effects, or rasterize the Smart Object for other raster techniques if you no longer need editable objects. For more info about Photoshop's Smart Objects and how they work, see the Photoshop CS3's *Photoshop Help*.

The rules governing how Illustrator layers get translated into Photoshop layers are complex. You can find a few examples of how to move Illustrator objects (such as simple paths, text, compound paths, and compound shapes) between Illustrator and Photoshop in lessons following in this chapter.

ILLUSTRATOR & ADOBE INDESIGN

When you Copy and Paste artwork from Illustrator into InDesign, you should decide before you copy if you want transparent objects to remain transparent when placed over other elements in InDesign, or if you instead need to be able to edit the objects in InDesign, and then set your preferences accordingly. In Illustrator, your File Handling and Clipboard preferences can, as a rule, leave both PDF and AICB enabled. In InDesign, however, choosing to enable Prefer PDF when pasting creates a non-editable file that preserves any transparency from the PDF portion of the Illustrator file. Disabling Prefer PDF will paste an editable, but flattened, vector file. The object(s) will be broken up, much as if you had used the Divide Pathfinder command, but you will be able to select and modify them. Transparent objects will not, however, exhibit transparency if placed on top of other elements in InDesign.

To Place artwork, you must have saved your Illustrator CS3 file with the Create PDF Compatible File option enabled. InDesign, as well as other programs, only recognizes and previews the PDF portion of the file.

Recovering missing linked files

If you no longer have (or never had) the original linked files for an .ai file, there is a way to get the images from the PDF side of the file—if you remembered to save with Create PDF Compatible File enabled. Just drag and drop the .ai file on your Photoshop application icon. Next, in Photoshop's Import PDF dialog, choose Images. This makes it possible to open any images from the PDF portion of the illustrator file. Then, you can save the images locally and relink them in Illustrator.

Why is it a "smart" object?

Smart Objects "remember" where they came from. When you place an Illustrator file as a Smart Object in Photoshop, the original is embedded in the file and only an "instance" is transformed or duplicated, much like using a symbol in Illustrator. When you want to edit the Smart Object, and not the instance of it, the Smart Object "knows" to launch the originating program—in this case Illustrator.

```
┌ Options ─────────────────────
  ☑ Create PDF Compatible File ▸
```

Where are the *other* programs?

See the *Web & Animation* chapter for info about the Save for Web & Devices options, as well as working with animation programs.

ILLUSTRATOR, PDF, & ADOBE ACROBAT

Acrobat's Portable Document Format (PDF) is platform and application independent—this means you can transfer files between different operating systems, as well as between different applications. It is also the PDF portion of an .ai file created in newer versions that older versions of Illustrator can open. There are a number of ways to specify how PDFs are created in Illustrator. By default, the Adobe Illustrator Document CS3 format includes a PDF compatible file option that allows others to open your .ai file directly in Acrobat. If you're not sure if this default is active, choose Save As and, with Adobe Illustrator Document format chosen, click Save; in the resulting dialog make certain that the "Create PDF Compatible File" option is enabled, and Save your Illustrator file.

For full control over PDF options previously available only from Acrobat Distiller, from Save As choose Adobe PDF (pdf) from the pop-up and click Save. In the Adobe PDF Options dialog, you can set many features, including enabling the "Create Acrobat Layers From Top-Level Layers" option to save your layered Illustrator files as layered Acrobat 6, 7, or 8 files. Illustrator PDF files can also preserve Illustrator editability and native transparency support, as well as conform to a widespread standard like PDF/X1a.

PDF files created by other programs (or newer versions of Illustrator itself) can be edited in Illustrator, but you can only open and save one page at a time, and text in the PDF may be broken up into multiple text lines when opened in Illustrator.

ILLUSTRATOR & 3D PROGRAMS

In addition to Illustrator's 3D effects (see the *Live 3D Effects* chapter) you can also import Illustrator paths into 3D programs to use as outlines and extrusion paths. Once you import a path, you can transform it into a 3D object. Strata's 3D StudioPro, SketchUp!, and LightWave 3D are just a few of the many 3D programs that you can use in combination with Illustrator.

Chris Spollen
(Photoshop)

Chris Spollen often creates his collage-like illustrations by weaving back and forth between Illustrator and Photoshop. He always starts with thumbnail pencil sketches (below right), which he scans and places as a template in Illustrator (see "Digitizing a Logo" in the *Layers & Appearances* chapter). He then creates his basic shapes and elements in Illustrator. While some of his illustrations do end up being assembled in Illustrator, this piece, "Hot Rod Rocket," was finalized in Photoshop, with many of the objects becoming "Illustrator/Photoshop hybrids" (such as his white clouds on an angle, which began as simple Illustrator shapes). In order to control his layers in Photoshop, Spollen moved one or more selected Illustrator objects at a time into a single layer in Photoshop using drag-and-drop. Spollen then reworked the shapes in Photoshop using the Paintbrush and Airbrush tools. He also adjusted the opacity. The 3D-looking rocket originated as a scanned toy "rocket gun," while the moon began as a scanned photo. "Hot Rod Rocket" received an Award of Merit in the Society of Illustrators Show.

SPOLLEN

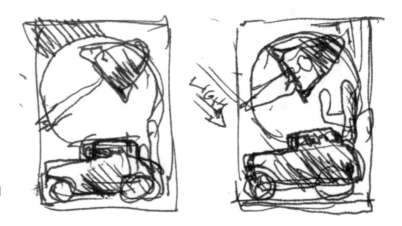

Software Relay

An Illustrator-Photoshop Workflow

Illustrator with Photoshop Overview: *Create paths in Illustrator; build a registration rectangle; organize layers for Photoshop masking; export as a PSD file; copy Illustrator paths and paste in Photoshop for masking.*

MAGIERA

1

Two stages in the construction of the image in Illustrator: left, the shapes as drawn; right, the shapes with fills

Why crop area?

Creating a crop area will automatically set the canvas size of a PSD file you export from Illustrator. Also, by making the crop area the same size as the Artboard, you can easily register the image after you've modified it in Photoshop. Just choose File>Place, select the image file, click OK, and then drag a corner until it snaps to a corner of the Artboard.

To illustrate mascots for Salt Lake City's 2002 Olympic Winter Games, Utah artist Rob Magiera drew shapes in Illustrator. He then exported the artwork as a Photoshop (PSD) file so he could airbrush highlights and shadows in Photoshop. While working in Photoshop, Magiera sometimes copied an Illustrator object and pasted it in Photoshop to serve as a selection or to modify a Quick Mask. (See the "Shape Shifting" lesson in this chapter to learn another way to move artwork between Illustrator and Photoshop.)

Although Magiera's illustration would be completed in Photoshop, his client needed the original Illustrator artwork for other uses.

1 Placing a sketch in Illustrator, drawing shapes, and making a registration box. Magiera began by scanning pencil sketches and saving them in TIFF format. He created a new Illustrator file with dimensions that were larger than the drawings he would make and then created

a crop area the size of the document by choosing Object >
Crop Area > Make (this will help when you place the Photoshop image back into Illustrator). Next, he placed the
scanned image on a template layer in Illustrator (see the
Layers & Appearances chapter for more on templates) and
drew the mascot shapes with the Pen and Pencil tools. He
filled the shapes with color, leaving the outlines unstroked.

In order to more easily modify rasterized shapes once
you get them into Photoshop, make sure you organize
your major artwork elements onto separate layers (for
help see the "Organizing Layers" lesson in the *Layers*
chapter). (On export to PSD, Illustrator preserves as much
of your layer structure as possible without sacrificing
appearance.) For objects that overlapped other objects
(like the bear's arm or the coyote's leg), Magiera created
new layers and moved the overlapping objects onto separate layers so he could easily mask them in Photoshop
when he began airbrushing them.

Knowing that he would bring some of the paths he
had drawn into Photoshop to help with masking, Magiera
devised a way to keep paths registered to other pasted
paths and to the raster artwork he would export from
Illustrator. You can accomplish this by making a "registration" rectangle in Illustrator that will keep your artwork in the same position relative to the rectangle (and
the Photoshop canvas) each time you copy and paste. To
make this rectangle, first create a new layer in the Layers
panel, and then drag it below your artwork layers. Next,
draw a rectangle with no stroke or fill that is the same size
as the Artboard. Center the rectangle on the Artboard.
With the rectangle matching the size and position of the
Artboard, copies of the rectangle will be pasted in Photoshop automatically aligned with the canvas.

Now you're ready to export your Illustrator artwork.
Select File > Export, and from the Export dialog choose
Photoshop (PSD) from the Format pop-up.

2 Working with Illustrator paths in Photoshop. After
opening the exported PSD file in Photoshop, Magiera

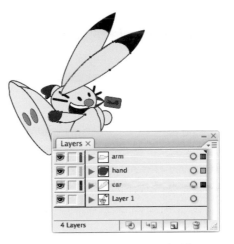

*The Illustrator Layers panel organized with
separate layers for shapes (shown as selected
objects) to be masked in Photoshop*

Illustrator's Export: Photoshop Options dialog

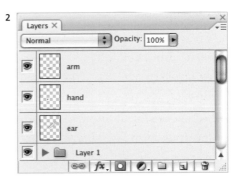

*The Photoshop Layers panel showing the layer
structure of the Illustrator-exported PSD file*

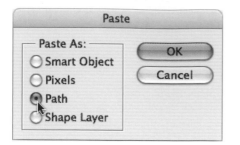

Photoshop's Paste dialog for pasting paths

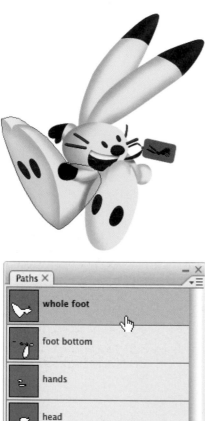

At top, the bunny figure with the "whole foot" saved path selected; bottom, Photoshop's Paths panel showing the selected path

used different masking techniques as he airbrushed highlights and shadows. To mask within a shape, Magiera usually enabled Lock Transparent Pixels for the layer on which the shape was located. If you use the Quick Mask working mode, you can create new masks from objects copied in Illustrator and pasted in Photoshop. To do this, in Illustrator, select both an object *and* the registration rectangle and then choose Edit > Copy. Next, in Photoshop, choose Edit > Paste and in the Paste dialog, choose Paste as Pixels. Notice that the artwork is in the same position on the Photoshop canvas as it was relative to the registration rectangle in Illustrator. With each pasted path, you can generate a selection and either add to or subtract from your working Quick Mask.

As Magiera worked in Photoshop, he occasionally modified a raster shape and then needed to update the Illustrator path that he originally used to generate the shape. To do this, first make a copy of the Illustrator path and the registration rectangle. Then, in Photoshop, choose Edit > Paste and, from the Paste dialog, choose Paste as Path. Now you can modify the shape's path with Photoshop's drawing tools. When you finish, Shift-select the modified path and the registration rectangle path (click close to an edge of the canvas to select the rectangle) and choose Edit > Copy. Return to Illustrator, select the original registration rectangle, choose Edit > Paste, and drag a corner of the pasted registration rectangle until it snaps to the corresponding corner of the existing registration rectangle. Now you can delete the original path that you are replacing with the modified path.

When Magiera finished airbrushing in Photoshop, he saved the file (which was still in PSD format).

3 Bringing the Photoshop image into Illustrator. For some of the changes to raster shapes he made in Photoshop, Magiera chose to edit the original path in Illustrator. He selected File > Place and imported the image into the Illustrator file, snapping it to the registration rectangle. He edited the paths using the Pen and Pencil tools.

HULSEY

Kevin Hulsey
(Photoshop)

Kevin Hulsey uses the Pen tool to draw his complex technical illustrations in Illustrator. He creates all the perspective grids he requires on separate layers (see the "Establishing Perspective" lesson in the *Layers & Appearances* chapter). He then draws all the line art for the elements, again using Illustrator's layers to keep elements organized.Hulsey's illustrations tend to be so large (often 45 inches at 300 ppi), that in recent versions of Illustrator he has been unable to export his Illustrator layers to Photoshop without saving to the legacy Illustrator 9 format. He then exports from AI 9 as a grayscale PSD file with a resolution of 350 ppi and his layers preserved. Next he opens the layered file in Photoshop and converts it to a custom CMYK with Black Generation set to Maximum in order to force the lines into just the Black (K) channel. Hulsey sets each line art layer to Multiply as the blending mode, and creates new layers below the line art layers to hold his painting. He uses the Magic Wand to select the area of the object

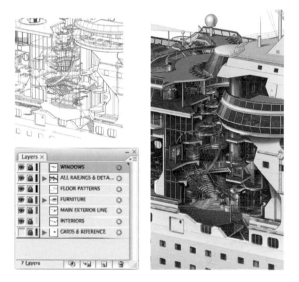

he intends to paint; then, with the selection still active, he uses a very soft, low-opacity brush to paint within the selection on the new layer. He builds up color gradually and smoothly in the same manner as he would with a traditional airbrush. For a detailed tutorial of Hulsey's digital airbrush technique using Photoshop, visit his website: http://www.khulsey.com/photoshop_tutorial_basic.html.

Shape Shifting

Exporting Paths to Shapes in Photoshop

Illustrator with Photoshop Advanced Technique

Overview: *Draw paths in Illustrator; convert paths to compound shapes; export in PSD format; apply effects in Photoshop.*

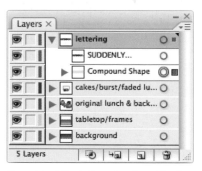

The original Illustrator artwork and the Layers panel shown before the frame, the yellow burst, and the yellow background (behind the type) were turned into compound shapes

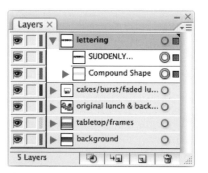

The panel showing objects in a compound shape

Artist Brad Hamann prepared this colorful illustration in Illustrator before exporting it as a PSD file and opening it in Photoshop, where he applied live effects that he could not have created in Illustrator. The key to bringing editable paths into Photoshop is to turn the objects you want to keep as paths into compound shapes. Then, after you export your document as a layered PSD and open it in Photoshop, you will see that your compound shapes have become editable shape layers while the rest of your artwork has been rasterized.

1 Drawing and layering artwork. Hamann used the Pen tool to draw objects and relied on the Blend, Reflect, and Rotate tools to create repeating elements (such as the slanting lines on the side of the milk box). For two of the objects he drew (the yellow burst and the yellow background behind the title), Hamann decided to leave each with a simple fill color in Illustrator and use Photoshop's layer styles and lighting effects to "paint" the objects. Moreover, in order to keep the outer frame looking neat in Photoshop, he had to export it as a single vector object. To do all this, Hamann converted these objects to compound shapes so they would be exported as Photoshop shape layers when he created a PSD file.

Once you've identified the objects you will bring into Photoshop as paths, select each object. From the Pathfinder panel pop-up menu, choose Make Compound Shape. (Choose Release Compound Shape from the Pathfinder panel pop-up menu if you need to turn compound shapes back into regular objects.) Hamann's compound shape frame had two components: a copy of the burst object in Subtract mode, and a rectangular frame. See the *Beyond the Basics* chapter introduction for details about working with compound shapes and shape modes.

If a compound shape is to remain an editable path when exported from Illustrator, make sure that it's not inside a group or on a sublayer. If it is, use the Layers panel to drag it out from all groups and sublayers (see the *Layers & Appearances* chapter for help with layers).

2 Exporting a Photoshop (PSD) file. Export your Illustrator file by choosing File > Export, then choose Photoshop (PSD) format and click OK. In the Photoshop Options dialog, pick a resolution setting that matches the requirements of your printing or display medium and make sure that within the Options section, all available options are selected.

Note: *See the introduction to this chapter for information on more ways to move artwork between Illustrator and Photoshop.*

3 Applying effects to shape layers in Photoshop.
When Hamann opened the exported PSD file in Photoshop, each Illustrator compound shape appeared as a shape layer in Photoshop's Layers panel. To add a layer effect to a shape layer, Hamann double-clicked the shape layer in the Layers panel. He applied Bevel and Emboss effects to his yellow rectangle and starburst shape layers, and even reshaped the shape paths using Photoshop's Direct Selection tool. Finally, he added some Photoshop effects (such as Strokes) to duplicates of some of the shape layers, and applied the Add Noise filter (Gaussian) to a duplicate of the background.

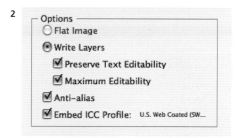

You can Paste shapes too!
To bring in just a single layer of Illustrator objects as a single Shape Layer in Photoshop: in Illustrator select and Copy, then Paste in Photoshop, and choose the Shape Layer option.

A portion of the Photoshop Export Options (PSD) dialog (File > Export > Photoshop)

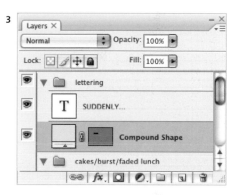

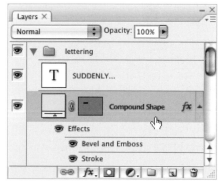

Top shows the Photoshop Layers panel as the PSD is first opened; bottom shows layer effects applied to some of the shape layers

YIP

Filip Yip
(Photoshop)

Filip Yip began by drawing Illustrator objects and organizing them on many separate layers (so each object would remain on its own layer when he later exported them to Photoshop). He decided on the overall color scheme, colored the shapes, and added blends. Yip then exported his Illustrator objects into Photoshop in order to add transparency, feathering, and lighting effects. The artwork (shown above right) was exported as a Photoshop PSD file. In Photoshop, Yip was able to easily manipulate the Illustrator objects, since they were on separate layers. He enhanced the blends with the

Airbrush tool, adjusted the transparency, and applied the Add Noise filter. Blurring effects (such as Gaussian Blur) were used to highlight details of the image. To further soften the blends, Yip also applied the Fade Brush Tool (Edit > Fade Brush Tool > Fade > Dissolve) in the Dissolve mode.

JACKSON

Lance Jackson
(Photoshop)

Lance Jackson applied Distort & Transform effects to create this illustration for an annual music festival. Jackson began by typing a list of band names in a paragraph using one font with the Type Tool. He then drew paths to outline the shape of a head with specific features such as the cheeks, lips and nose. With the Type on a Path tool Jackson applied type to the paths that defined the face. Using groups of text from the original paragraph, Jackson filled in other areas of the face. Jackson selected the type, chose Object > Expand, and colored the text. He selected a group of type and applied

Effect > Distort & Transform > Pucker & Bloat to abstract the text. He repeated this process to develop the head. Jackson placed the file into Photoshop to add more text and blocks of color to the background. In Photoshop he selected groups of type with the Magic Wand tool. He adjusted the opacity on layers of text to create depth. Jackson altered the text even further by choosing Edit > Transform to skew, scale or rotate. Finally, Jackson opened the Photoshop file in Illustrator to fill out the head with more distorted text.

Ron Chan
(Photoshop)

Ron Chan, illustrator and co-author of *How to Wow with Illustrator*, used Illustrator's drawing tools and Pathfinder commands (Effect > Pathfinder) to draw over a scanned template to create his initial composition. Illustrator is his primary drawing tool because it allows him to make color and compositional changes easily (middle detail). With the composition finalized (bottom detail), he chose File > Export and selected PSD. In the Photoshop Export Options dialog, he selected the Color Model CMYK, chose Write Layers, and specified a high resolution. In Photoshop he assembled his image in layers within his CMYK document. To give a more organic and less hard-edged feel to some of the objects (now rasterized as layers) Chan applied the Glass filter (Filter > Distort Glass). The Glass filter can only be applied to an RGB image, and Chan wanted to keep the layered file in CMYK; in order to selectively apply the effects to individual layers, he used a complex procedure that included dragging each layer he wanted filtered back and forth to an identically-sized RGB file, where he applied the filter. Then he dragged the filtered version back to the CMYK layered file (in registration).

GREIMAN

April Greiman
(Photoshop)

April Greiman, of April Greiman Made in Space, took advantage of Illustrator's ability to produce resolution-independent vector graphics when creating this large wall mural for the Cafe & Fitness Center at Amgen. Greiman began with source photos and original images. In Photoshop, she combined the images, adjusted the hue, saturation, and opacity and made adjustments with levels and curves. A variety of filters were applied to the images, such as Gaussian Blur, Motion Blur, Ripple, and Noise. Greiman knew that when the image was enlarged, the pixelated effect would enhance the image, just as she wanted. When Greiman was satisfied with the Photoshop image, she saved it as a PSD file. The PSD file was imported into Illustrator and text was added. The text was created on several layers with varying opacities. The size of the Illustrator image was 21 inches x 5 inches, and the final mural measured 36 feet by 11.3 feet. The pixels in the Photoshop image were greatly distorted when enlarged to the final mural size. This desired pixelated effect was combined with crisp text that Illustrator can produce at any magnification. The final image was output from Illustrator and printed directly on vinyl.

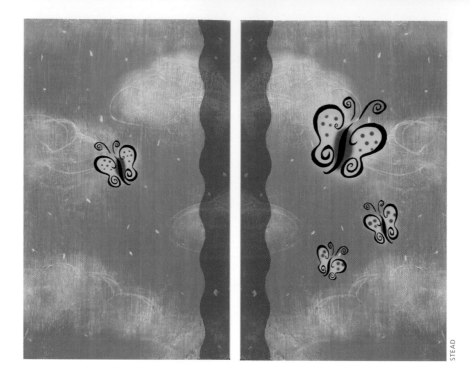

STEAD

Judy Stead
(Photoshop)

Judy Stead combined Photoshop, Illustrator, and traditional painting techniques to design the cover of this Scholastic Book Fairs journal. (Shown above are the back and front covers.) Stead alternated among the three approaches throughout her entire creative process. She first painted the blue clouds on a gesso-textured board with acrylic paint, pastels, and a white pencil (see image inset at right). The image was scanned into Photoshop and the color was adjusted from aqua blue to orange (Image > Adjustments > Hue/Saturation). Stead drew the butterfly in Illustrator, using one of the default Calligraphic brushes and a Wacom drawing tablet, which allowed

her to create a line that varied in width (see the *Brushes & Symbols* chapter). She then exported the file to Photoshop as a PSD file and made several copies of the butterfly, varying rotation, orientation, and size. Stead drew the wavy book spine in Illustrator. In Photoshop, the clouds, spine, and butterflies were combined into a layered Photoshop file. Stead set the blending mode of the cloud layer to Multiply, so the cloud texture was visible through the individual elements. She then added airbrushed detail to the butterfly and continued to adjust the color of the element using Hue/Saturation until she was satisfied with the overall effect.

STEAD

Judy Stead
(Photoshop)

Judy Stead often begins her illustrations by making traditionally painted backgrounds that are manipulated in Photoshop. With one painted background, (shown above right) Stead can create several others varying in color by using the Image menu. Stead scanned the background into Photoshop and chose Image > Adjustments > Hue/Saturation. To enhance a specific color, she chose Image > Adjustments > Selective Color. Further adjustments were made on a duplicated layer where Stead applied Blending Modes such as Multiply and Hue. The background image was saved in TIFF format. To import the background into

Illustrator, Stead chose File > Place. She then drew with the Charcoal brush imported from the Artistic_ChalkCharcoalPencil Brush Library. In the Transparency panel, Stead applied various Blending Modes to enhance specific areas. After drawing a shape, such as a leaf, she opened the Transparency panel and selected the Blending Mode, Overlay. The colored circles underneath the word "think" have the Blending Modes of Overlay, Hue and Multiply (top to bottom). The colored circles also have either a Gaussian Blur (Effect > Blur > Gaussian Blur) or a brush applied to the stroke.

David Pounds
(Photoshop)

David Pounds' highly detailed artwork began with photographing models, combining them into a single composition as neeeded, and paying careful attention to the lighting as he worked. He used Photoshop to bring out detail and then, with Convert Photoshop layers to objects enabled, he opened the image in Illustrator. Next Pounds began to draw each item on its own layer to keep all the detail organized. He found very complex subjects, such as the goggles, easier to handle by breaking them down into smaller sections, so he placed each one on a layer of its own. To achieve a high level of realism, he created blends for modeling smooth shadows and highlights. Blend modes added depth and sparkle, while he simulated metallics with gradients. For the propellors, he

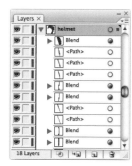

duplicated and transformed a simple propellor blade numerous times, altering the Opacity for a motion blur. Finally, using Live Trace on a photograph of clouds added contrasting texture to the smoothness of the main image.

Jason Taylor

CROUSE

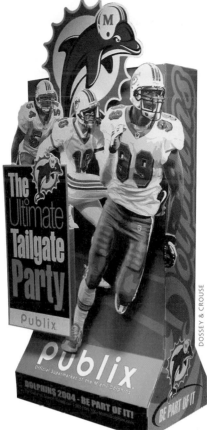

DOSSEY & CROUSE

A. J. Feeley

Scott Crouse and Warren Dossey (Photoshop)

Scott Crouse drew these illustrations for a promotion by Publix Super Markets and the National Football League's Miami Dolphins. Artist Warren Dossey used some of Crouse's drawings for a seven-foot-tall retail standee (center) created in Illustrator. Crouse hand-traced source images in Illustrator after first applying a process he developed to simplify source images for hand-tracing. In Photoshop, he lowered the number of colors by applying a Posterize adjustment layer set to about 3 levels, depending on the image. Crouse also applied the Noise: Median filter (typically with a Radius of 2 pixels) to the image's background layer to shift stray bits of color to a solid area, defining color edges more clearly. He then converted the image to Indexed Color with a Local Adaptive palette using 10 to 20 colors, again depending on the image. Crouse then placed the processed images in Illustrator as templates. He hand-traced the images using the Pen tool, following the clean color edges (detail, bottom right) resulting from his pre-processing method. (For variations on this method, see the "Trace Techniques" lesson in the *Beyond the Basics* chapter).

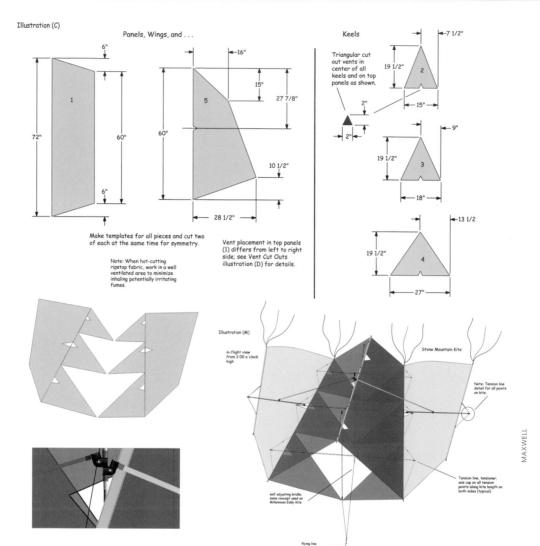

Illustration (C)

Panels, Wings, and . . .

Keels

Triangular cut out vents in center of all keels and on top panels as shown.

Make templates for all pieces and cut two of each at the same time for symmetry.

Note: When hot-cutting ripstop fabric, work in a well ventilated area to minimize inhaling potentially irritating fumes.

Vent placement in top panels (1) differs from left to right side; see Vent Cut Outs illustration (D) for details.

Illustration (M)

in-flight view from 2:00 o'clock high

Stone Mountain Kite

Note: Tension line detail for all points on kite.

self adjusting bridle; same concept used on Millennium Eddy Kite

Tension line, tensioner, and cap on all tension points along kite length on both sides (typical).

flying line

MAXWELL

Eden Maxwell
(Hot Door CADTools)

For his Stone Mountain Kite illustration (bottom right), Eden Maxwell started from part drawings (top) that he earlier drew to scale using a Wacom tablet and Hot Door CADTools (a third-party plug-in for Illustrator). To draw the kite with "in-flight" perspective, Maxwell manually adjusted the CADTools drawings by eye until they were oriented in the perspective he visualized. For example, he used the Rotate tool and the Direct Selection tool to edit wing and keel angles to achieve the desired perspective (middle left). After major components were in place, Maxwell drew smaller parts like eye loops, connectors, end caps, and tension lines (bottom left), right down to the stitching along the top sail. To simulate air under the wings during flight, Maxwell created a slight curve in the aft section of the wings for the final illustration.

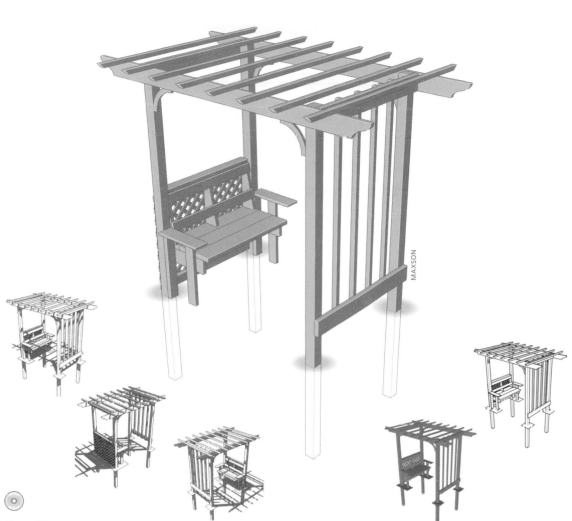

MAXSON

Greg Maxson
(SketchUp)

To draw this arbor in perspective, Greg Maxson imported files he created in the SketchUp 3D modeling application (demo at sketchup.com) and combined the files in Illustrator. First, the client provided Maxson with 2D drawings. In SketchUp, Maxson used the drawings to create a 3D model of the arbor. From the set of viewing angles Maxson provided (bottom left), the client approved the final view (top). Maxson exported two 2D EPS files from the 3D model:

one filled and one outlined (bottom right). He used the outlined version to represent underground post segments. Maxson placed the two versions in Illustrator, aligned them, and applied the project's final stroke and fill specifications. To expedite editing, he used commands on the Select > Same button in the Control panel to select objects with a common attribute. He could then change that attribute for all selected objects at once.

Chapter 15 *Illustrator & Other Programs*   **419**

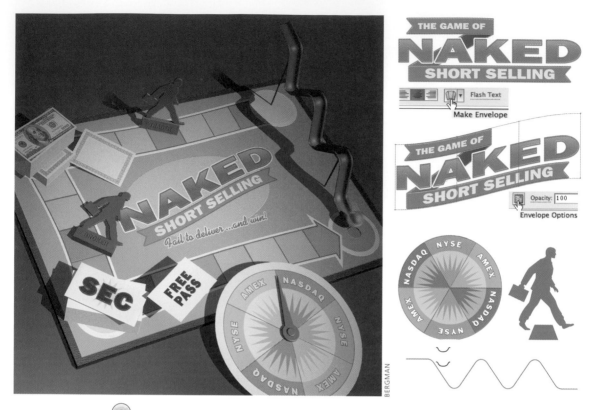

Eliot Bergman
(Photoshop and Maya)

Bergman began the creation of this convincingly three-dimensional gameboard, done for *Bloomberg Markets* magazine, by drawing all of the basic elements—the cards, the game pieces, the path for the slide and most of the bump and image maps in Illustrator. Bergman appreciates the ease and accuracy with which he can control color and create typography in Illustrator. In this example, he first laid out the logo using Franklin Gothic Heavy. Bergman then chose New Fill from the Options menu of the Appearance panel and added a gradient fill to the characters making up the word "Naked." He also chose New Stroke from the menu to add white and blue strokes behind the characters. Bergman then clicked on the Make Envelope button on the Control panel and chose Rise for Style. He set it to a 25% horizontal bend (use Envelope Options on the Control panel if you want to change it later). He then imported the vector objects into Autodesk Maya, a 3D modeling program within which the objects can be extruded, viewed from any angle, and then have precise custom lighting effects applied to them. After the 3D image is rendered, Bergman does additional retouching of the file in Photoshop as needed, such as adding motion blur to the pinball and additional texture to the blue edges of the gameboard. The result is a realistic gameboard that a reader might be tempted to reach out and touch.

CHRISTIE

Bryan Christie
(Photoshop, MetaTools Infini-D)

Bryan Christie assembled this mechanical bug with Illustrator and later integrated Photoshop and Infini-D, a 3D modeling program. The 3D shapes, such as the leg joints and circuit boards, were first drawn in Illustrator as an outline without detail or color, and then imported into Infini-D and extruded into 3D shapes. To map the color and the details of the circuit boards, Christie drew and colored the circuitry in Illustrator. He then exported the artwork as a PICT and mapped it onto the 3D shapes in Infini-D. Christie created the transparency of the wing by mapping a grayscale image that was origi-

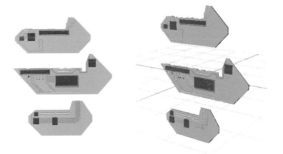

nally drawn in Illustrator onto the wing shape in Infini-D. To complete the mechanical bug, he rendered the artwork in Infini-D, opened it in Photoshop to make minor touchups (such as color correction and compositing separately rendered elements), and finally converted the entire image into CMYK.

MONROY

Bert Monroy
(Photoshop)

Famous for his urban landscapes, author and master digital artist Bert Monroy relies upon Illustrator tools to deal with constructing the man-made, repeating elements that so often fill his urban environment. A case in point is the trashcan at the Damon station. Monroy was able to quickly construct this complex-looking object by taking advantage of the Blend tool's ability to morph from one object to another. He drew a straight rectangle to represent the face-on view of the center slat. He then drew the curved slat of the trashcan's edge and selected both objects. He double-clicked on the Blend tool, chose Specified Steps, and then typed in the number needed to complete half the trashcan. To ensure the objects morphed correctly, Monroy used the Blend tool (rather than the Blend >Make command) to select an anchor point on one object, then clicked on the same relative anchor point on the other object. This told Illustrator exactly what the relationship was between the objects so it knew how to create the in-between objects. Next he expanded the blend (Object >Expand, or Object >Blend >Expand) in order to create

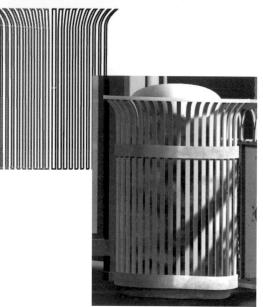

individual objects that he could manipulate separately. He selected all of the slats except the center slat and choose the Reflect tool. Monroy set the anchor point in the middle of the center slat, chose Vertical as the axis, and Copy to create the other half of the trashcan. He finished drawing the rest of the trashcan in Illustrator, then exported it to Photoshop where he added the colors, textures, shadows, and highlights that would complete his amazingly realistic painting of the trashcan.

Marcel Morin
(ArcScene and Photoshop)

Marcel Morin likes to use ArcScene, an ArcGIS plug-in for viewing and exporting 3D GIS data as images. He also uses Photoshop to composite those images. But he uses Illustrator's superb vector object handling to construct projects that rely on resolution-independent elements for high-quality output. For this two-sided waterproof map, he generated a large base image of the mountain range in ArcScene, over which he "draped" an image of the glaciers. He placed the image in Illustrator. There he traced the glaciers in order to create a clipping mask for later use in Photoshop. Back in ArcScene, he generated a grayscale version for the glaciers and exported an image of just the 3D wireframe model. In Photoshop, Morin layered the images, duplicating the base image in order to select areas representing the far distance, middle ground and foreground. He deleted portions of the images that he wouldn't need. He created the illusion of depth by applying Gaussian Blur to the far distant mountains, and again a lesser amount of Gaussian Blur to the middle ground, after which he sharpened the foreground. Morin added the grayscale layer with the clipping mask to reveal the glaciers on the mountains, and added the wireframe model in Multiply mode, masking it to show only in the foreground. Finally, Morin cropped the assembled image and placed it in an Illustrator document that would hold the entire map. There he added vector design elements used with the Summit Series maps and logos sized to suit this particular project. He set the text and got the complete map ready for the printer.

kuler

Adobe took a part of Illustrator's Live Color technology and made it available online, via kuler, the freely available online community built around color (http://kuler.adobe.com). You can also access colors from kuler using the kuler panel from within Illustrator, from the Mac OS X kuler Widget, and from the cross-platform kuler desktop which runs on Adobe AIR (Adobe's Integrated Runtime framework).

STEP 1. CHOOSE A COLOR HARMONY RULE
CHOOSE FROM SIX DIFFERENT HARMONY RULES, OR CREATE YOUR OWN. (SEE REAL WORLD ADOBE ILLUSTRATOR CS3 COLOR INSERT, PAGE C-4, FOR DETAILS ON THESE RULES.)

STEP 2. SPIN THE COLOR WHEEL
DRAG THE COLOR CIRCLES THAT APPEAR ON THE COLOR WHEEL TO EXPLORE DIFFERENT COLOR VARIATIONS BASED ON THE BASE COLOR. TO CHANGE A BASE COLOR, DOUBLE-CLICK ONE OF THE SWATCHES BELOW THE WHEEL.

STEP 3. GIVE YOUR COLOR THEME A NAME
ADD A TITLE AND ASSIGN AS MANY TAGS AS YOU CAN. THE MORE TAGS YOU ADD, THE EASIER IT WILL BE TO FIND.

STEP 4. SAVE OR PUBLISH YOUR COLOR THEME
CHOOSE SAVE TO STORE YOUR THEME ON YOUR PRIVATE MYKULER PAGE. CHOOSE PUBLISH TO MAKE YOUR THEME AVAILABLE TO ALL OTHER USERS IN THE KULER COMMUNITY.

BRIGHTNESS
ADJUST THE BRIGHTNESS OF THE COLOR WHEEL USING THIS SLIDER.

BASE COLOR
COLORS THAT ARE GENERATED BY KULER ARE BASED ON THE COLOR HARMONY RULE THAT YOU CHOOSE AND ON THE BASE COLOR.

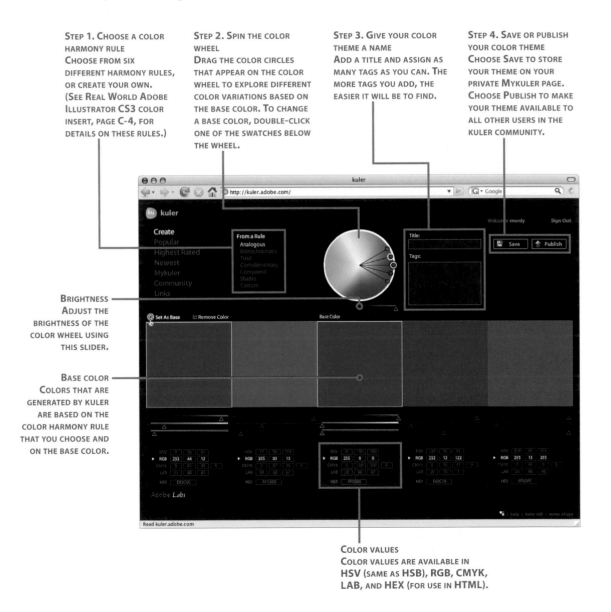

COLOR VALUES
COLOR VALUES ARE AVAILABLE IN HSV (SAME AS HSB), RGB, CMYK, LAB, AND HEX (FOR USE IN HTML).

DOWNLOAD A COLOR THEME
CLICK HERE TO DOWNLOAD A COLOR
THEME AS AN **ASE** (ADOBE SWATCH
EXCHANGE) FILE, WHICH YOU CAN LOAD INTO
ILLUSTRATOR, PHOTOSHOP, OR INDESIGN.

EDIT A COLOR THEME
CLICK HERE TO LOAD
A THEME INTO THE
CREATE PAGE, WHERE
YOU CAN TWEAK IT.

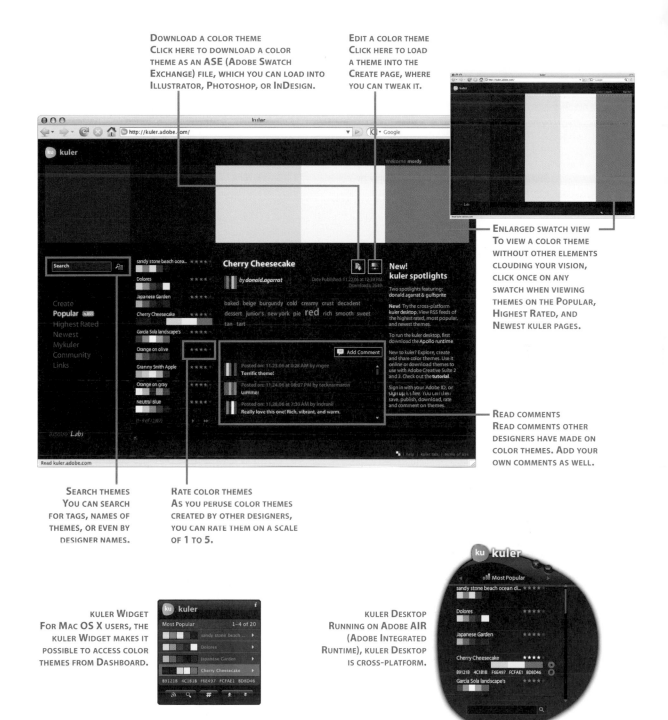

ENLARGED SWATCH VIEW
TO VIEW A COLOR THEME
WITHOUT OTHER ELEMENTS
CLOUDING YOUR VISION,
CLICK ONCE ON ANY
SWATCH WHEN VIEWING
THEMES ON THE POPULAR,
HIGHEST RATED, AND
NEWEST KULER PAGES.

READ COMMENTS
READ COMMENTS OTHER
DESIGNERS HAVE MADE ON
COLOR THEMES. ADD YOUR
OWN COMMENTS AS WELL.

SEARCH THEMES
YOU CAN SEARCH
FOR TAGS, NAMES OF
THEMES, OR EVEN BY
DESIGNER NAMES.

RATE COLOR THEMES
AS YOU PERUSE COLOR THEMES
CREATED BY OTHER DESIGNERS,
YOU CAN RATE THEM ON A SCALE
OF 1 TO 5.

KULER WIDGET
FOR MAC OS X USERS, THE
KULER WIDGET MAKES IT
POSSIBLE TO ACCESS COLOR
THEMES FROM DASHBOARD.

KULER DESKTOP
RUNNING ON ADOBE AIR
(ADOBE INTEGRATED
RUNTIME), KULER DESKTOP
IS CROSS-PLATFORM.

The Executive Summary of Graphic Design News

Get 3 Free Issues:
www.design-tools.com/ilcs3wow/

Wow! technical editor Jean-Claude Tremblay and *Design Tools Monthly's* Jay Nelson teamed up to collect and summarize for you their favorite Illustrator-related plug-ins and utilities. We encourage you to explore them on the *Wow! CD*.

Andrew's Vector Plug-ins: affordable gems

GraphicXtras has many creative plug-ins for Illustrator, affordably priced at just $15 each. We recommend:
Andrew's Vector Plug-ins vol 1 to 25 (Mac)
Andrew's Vector Plug-ins vol 1, 3, 6, 7, 13, 18, 23 (Win)
www.graphicxtras.com

ArtOptimizer: optimizes images

Zevrix's ArtOptimizer ($75) reduces the size of linked images that were resized in Illustrator. If the effective resolution of any image is higher than a target resolution you define, ArtOptimizer backs up the image, opens the copy in Photoshop, changes its dimensions and reimports it into the Illustrator document at 100% size. It can optionally also convert the image's color mode to CMYK, RGB or Grayscale, apply sharpening filters and flatten the image. (Mac)
www.zevrix.com

BetterHandles: powerful point editing

Nineblock Software's BetterHandles ($29) vastly improves your efficiency in manipulating anchor points and handles.

For example, you can:

- Select multiple handles, and collectively move, extend, rotate, or retract them.
- Extend or retract handles without changing their angles.
- Edit handles and anchor points numerically.
- And much more. (Mac/Win)
www.nineblock.com

CADTools

Hot Door CADTools ($279) is a creative CAD solution for designers who need both artistic flexibility and precision drawing power. Draw in any scale, dimension artwork with a mouse click, and numerically control size and location of objects. CADtools is even more valuable with the addition of new DXF/DWG import and export filters inside Adobe Illustrator CS3, closing the gap between traditional CAD environments and vector illustration. It can add interactive dimensional text and arrows to any line or angle; measure and change angles, the areas of shapes, and radii of circles and curves. The Trim tool automatically trims excess from overlapping segments. The Fill and Chamfer tools let you automatically round or bevel a shape's corners. The Wall tool creates two-sided wall shapes, and the amazing Wall Healer tool cleans up the intersection of Wall shapes. (Mac/Win)
www.hotdoor.com

Concatenate: auto-connect paths

Rick Johnson's Concatenate ($20) lets you connect two or more paths into one continuous path. You tell it how close the endpoints should be to combine the paths, and whether to average the endpoints together. It's especially useful for cleaning up CAD drawings or connecting and filling borders in maps. (Mac/Win)
www.rj-graffix.com

Cutting Tools

Rick Johnson's Cutting Tools ($5) adds new ways to cut paths: Hatchet cuts through all paths, not just the top path; Saber Saw cuts through all paths as you drag over them; Table Saw cuts a straight line through all paths; Vector Vac deletes all paths you drag it across. (Mac/Win)
www.rj-graffix.com

EZConstrain: change constrain angle

Nineblock Software's EZConstrain (free) creates a floating palette that lets you easily change the constrain angle, without having to go to the Preferences dialog. (Mac)
www.nineblock.com

JLG•Dimension: auto-dimensioning

Jean-Louis Garrivet's JLG•Dimension ($25 euro) adds dimensioning tools. To use it, you select a segment, angle, circle, or other path, and the dimensions of that selection are added to the outside edge of the selection. (Mac)
http://perso.orange.fr/jlg.outils/Pages/ManuelCotationsUS.html

MultiPage: multiple pages

Hot Door MultiPage ($99) fills a long-standing need in Adobe Illustrator: multiple pages. It lets you create as many pages as you'd like, using Master Pages if desired, and even export multiple-page PDF files. You can even flow text from page to page and auto-number pages. (Mac/Win)
www.hotdoor.com

Nudge Palette: nudges patterns

Rick Johnson's Nudge Palette ($15) lets you adjust the position of a patterned fill within an object or a dash pattern along a path. It also features an "Untransform" button to reset a dash or pattern to its previous position, also removing any previous transformations such as scaling, rotating, etc. (Mac/Win) (not on the CD)
www.rj-graffix.com

Path Styler Pro: much sharper bevels

Illustrator's Bevel feature can be too smooth. That's why Shinycore's Path Styler Pro is valuable. This plug-in for Photoshop or Illustrator ($99 each or $129 for both) creates sharp, clean bevels, accurate reflections, and has multiple lighting options. You can apply multiple bevels, and each bevel can have its own material, contour, textures, and procedural maps such as wood, metal, plastic, glass and others. Lights can be directional, omni, or tube. More than 100 presets are included. (Mac/Win)   www.shinycore.com

Perspective: powerful isometric tools

Hot Door's Perspective ($179) saves lots of time when doing geometric perspective drawing. It adds isometric, oblique, and perspective drawing tools to draw lines, planes, cubes and cylinders over an adjustable background grid. Your flat artwork can project instantly to front, side or top faces. (Mac/Win) (not on the CD)   www.hotdoor.com

Phantasm CS: amazing color adjustments

Astute Graphics' Phantasm CS ($37.50) adds color controls similar to Photoshop's: brightness, contrast, hue, saturation, levels and curves—but you can use them on native Illustrator shapes and imported images. All controls are available as both a Filter and a Live Effect, so you can later edit or remove your changes. (Mac/Win)   www.phantasmcs.com

Point Control: a palette to control points

Worker72a's Point Control ($10) puts Illustrator's most useful commands for manipulating anchor points and paths into one handy palette. For example:

Adjust stroke weight   Lengthen/Retract curve handles
Smooth/Close path   Align/Delete/Convert selected points
(Mac)   www.worker72a.com

QuickCarton

Worker72a's QuickCarton ($47) helps you build a complete corrugated carton layout in less than a minute. It supports different thicknesses, panels, inside or outside glue, and other details. It also adds registration marks and graphics safe area guides. (Mac)   www.worker72a.com

Scoop & Art Files: collect for output

Adobe Illustrator—even version CS3—doesn't have a "collect for output" feature. (Its Collect for Output script only collects linked images, not fonts.) Here are two options to collect everything:

Worker72a's Scoop ($47) collects placed graphics and fonts and can also extract embedded raster images. (Mac)
          www.worker72a.com

Code Line's Art Files ($50) is a utility that collects and packages placed graphics and fonts used in an Illustrator document. Several Illustrator documents can be packaged at the same time, and any images or fonts that are shared among the documents are collected only once, saving disk space. (Mac)   www.code-line.com

Select: select all similar items at once

Rick Johnson's Select (free) adds a "Select" item to Illustrator's Filter menu to select 15 additional things: guides, paths, open paths, closed paths, filled paths, unfilled paths, stroked paths, unstroked paths, dashed paths, undashed paths, compound paths, groups, live object groups, gradient meshes, envelopes, symbols, embedded raster art, and placed art. (Mac/Win)   www.rj-graffix.com

Select Effects: shows paths that use effects

Worker72a's Select Effects ($25) highlights any paths that use Transparency, Effects and Blend modes, which may cause problems when printing or flattening. (Mac)
          www.worker72a.com

SepPreview: preview separations

Worker72a's SepPreview ($47) lets you view color separations, in color. Spot and process colors can be viewed and printed individually or in any combination. (Mac)
          www.worker72a.com

SnapMeasure: a better measurement tool

Nineblock Software's SnapMeasure ($24) is a better measuring tool. It lets you scroll and zoom while measuring, and can snap to objects or Smart Guides. It can measure the radius of curvature and the angle of tangent. Measurement values display directly next to your cursor, and you can instantly change the constrain angle and keyboard nudging increment. (Mac/Win)   www.nineblock.com

SymmetryWorks: instant patterns

Artlandia SymmetryWorks 4 ($229) lets you easily create seamless patterns. You draw a simple shape, and SymmetryWorks rotates, reflects and spaces it to create a seamless pattern. As you edit the shape, the pattern updates in real time. (Mac/Win)   www.artlandia.com

White Overprint Detector

Worker72a's White Overprint Detector (free) scans each file as you open it, and tells you whether there are any paths or text that have been filled or stroked with a white overprint. An optional $25 version can reset all white text and path object overprints to knockout. (Mac)
          www.worker72a.com

Zoom to Selection

Worker72a's Zoom to Selection ($7) adds commands to the view menu to zoom into a selection or fit the selection in the window. (Mac)
          www.worker72a.com

Free Catalog of Plug-ins

ThePowerXChange has a free downloadable catalog/database of plug-ins for Illustrator, InDesign, Photoshop, Acrobat and QuarkXPress. Download it at:
          http://www.thepowerxchange.com/catalogue_download.html

The Executive Summary of Graphic Design News

Get 3 Free Issues:
www.design-tools.com/ilcs3wow/

Design Tools Monthly brings you this selection of Illustrator tips from recent issues. Read these tips and dozens more in the printable PDF of Tips on the *Wow! CD*.

Quick-Select Fields

In most Adobe applications, you can quickly select the entire content of a text-entry field in a dialog box or panel, including the Control panel, by clicking on the label (name) of the field. So, instead of clicking and dragging across the current content of a field to select it, just click the text label next to the field to select its entire contents.

Crop Areas to Export or Print

Illustrator CS3's new Crop Area tool (Shift-O) comes in handy when you want to define a specific area of your artwork to:

• File> Export
• Use it in Photoshop
• File> Save for Web & Devices
• File> Print

To use the Crop Area tool, drag it across an area. This defines a new Crop Area, complete with printer's marks. When you export or Save for Web, only that area will be used. (In previous versions, you would use the Rectangle tool to draw a rectangle around the area, then choose Object> Crop Area> Make.)

Text Updating Tip

Illustrator CS and above has a different text engine from previous versions (it's the same one that's in InDesign CS and above).

So, when you open documents created by earlier versions of Illustrator, it asks you if you want to convert your text using the new engine. If you click Update, much of your text will rewrap, and if you click OK, you won't be able to edit your text. Yikes.

Here's a way to control the process: go ahead and click OK. After that, you can convert just one text block at a time by selecting the block of type (use the Direct Select tool), and then choose Type> Legacy Text> Update Selected Legacy Text.

Or, you can be even more clever by using the Type tool, clicking on the text, then choosing Copy Text Object from the dialog that appears. This will put an editable copy of the text on top of the original text, which changes to gray. This way you can see how the new text engine has affected your text.

Three Reasons to Save Illustrator Files as PDF

By saving your Illustrator documents in Adobe PDF format (File> Save As…), you get these benefits:

1. You can include bleed and/or crop marks for importing into InDesign.
2. You can enable/disable the layers in the Illustrator file from within InDesign.
3. You can import the file into a picture box in QuarkXPress.

The PDF file is really the Illustrator file inside a PDF wrapper. It's still completely editable within Illustrator, but you can't double-click the PDF to open it in Illustrator—you must open it from within Illustrator (File> Open).

Illustrator knowhow

There's a fairly hidden, experimental feature in Adobe Illustrator CS3 that gives you tips on how to use the current tool. To open it, choose Window> Adobe Labs> knowhow.

When you click on a tool in the Tools panel, the knowhow window provides tips and options for that tool. If you click the icon that looks like binoculars, it will search Adobe's Help system and website for topics related to that tool. To return to the local tips, click the Command key icon.

Select Similar Objects

You can use the Magic Wand tool to select objects that have attributes similar to the object you click with it. Another way to accomplish this is to choose Select> Same> object attribute.

But these two approaches have different options: the Magic Wand has a Tolerance setting, letting it select objects with slightly different attributes; and the Select> Same… menu item contains attributes not available to the Magic Wand.

Surprises in Illustrator's Dock Icon

If you Control-click or right-click on the Mac OS X Dock icon of Illustrator while it's running, some surprising items appear:

• Recent Files lists the files most recently opened by that application.
• Scripts provides a list of automated actions you can apply to the open document, such as export to Flash, SVG or PDF, or use Live Trace.
• Quick Links lets you launch or switch to any Creative Suite application.

Use Adobe Dialogs to Rename & Delete Files

In Adobe's Creative Suite applications, the Open, Save and Export dialog boxes have two versions: the version provided by the operating system and the Adobe version.

When you click the Use Adobe dialog button in the dialog box, a different dialog box appears that lets you rename and delete files from any mounted volume. To rename a file, simply type over it. To delete a file, click the trash can icon.

The Adobe Dialog also lets you browse Creative Suite documents in thumbnail, icon, tile or list views; read detailed file information in any view; and see at a glance which documents are already open for editing.

Quickly Reset Adobe Preferences

One standard technique for troubleshooting the source of a problem in an application is to move or delete the application's preferences files. The application then rebuilds those files on its next launch. However, the location of those files isn't always obvious.

Adobe makes it easy to reset its applications' preferences to their defaults: just hold down all the modifier keys when launching an Adobe application (Mac: Control-Command-Option-Shift or Win: Ctrl-Alt-Shift).

This will reset any preferences you may have customized, so be sure you know which ones to change back.

Easier Circles

In Illustrator, if you know where a circle should begin, you can press the Command/Ctrl key while using the Ellipse tool. This lets you begin the circle's arc exactly where you click, instead of at a virtual "corner" of an imaginary enclosing box. Use this tip when tracing a template that has rounded corners.

Reset the Star Tool

The Star tool maintains your most recent settings, so you can easily draw more stars of the same shape. Unfortunately, to reset the Star tool to its default settings, you must quit and then relaunch Illustrator. (To reset it manually, the defaults are: Radius 1=25, Radius 2=50, Points=5.)

Disable Anti-aliasing for One Object

If you need to keep text from looking blurry on-screen or when rasterized, you can disable its anti-aliasing. First, select the text object, then choose Effect> Rasterize and set anti-aliasing to None in the Rasterize dialog. Because this is a live effect, the text remains fully editable, but is no longer anti-aliased.

Tips to Control Patterns Inside Shapes

In Illustrator, moving an object doesn't necessarily move its pattern fill. To lock them together, choose Transform Both from the side menu of the Transform panel. You can move the pattern inside the shape (without moving the shape itself) by holding down the tilde key (~).

More Patterns

Illustrator CS2 and CS3 have fewer Pattern choices than previous versions of Illustrator did. (In CS2 and CS3 there are 11 sets, versus 26 in CS.) If you have an older copy of Illustrator, you can borrow the patterns from the Illustrator/Presets/Patterns folder and then load them using the side menu on the Swatches panel: choose Open Swatch Library> Other Library.

The Hidden Flip Command

The two places that Illustrator hides the Flip command (to flip an object either horizontally vertically) are: in the side menu of the Transform panel; and in the side menu of the little palette that appears when you click on the blue X, Y, W or H in the Control panel.

If you can remember that Flip means the same thing as Reflect in Adobe-speak, you can also use the Reflect tool, which is hidden under the Rotate tool. You can also choose Object> Transform> Reflect, or invoke the Contextual menu (Control-click or right-click) and then choose Reflect from the Contextual menu.

Use Illustrator Layers & Text in Photoshop

To copy the layers and text from an Illustrator file into Photoshop, choose File> Export in Illustrator and select Photoshop format. Be sure to enable Write Layers and Preserve Text Editability. Then, when you open the file in Photoshop, the text objects from Illustrator will appear as Type layers in Photoshop.

Smaller PDFs from Illustrator

By default, Illustrator embeds a copy of the native Illustrator document inside the PDFs you save from it, making the file size of the PDF much larger than it needs to be. To reduce file size when saving the document in PDF format from Illustrator, disable the checkbox named Preserve Illustrator Editing Capabilities. Be sure to keep a copy of the original Illustrator document, though, for future editing.

Live Trace & Live Paint at Once

Often, after you use the Live Trace feature to convert a bitmapped image into a vector object, you'll want to use the Live Paint feature to color it in. You can save a step by choosing Object> Live Trace> Make and Convert to Live Paint. Illustrator will use your current settings for Live Trace and then convert the tracing to a Live Paint group.

Choose a Complementary Color

In Illustrator, you can choose the complementary color of the current fill or stroke of a selected object by Command-Shift-clicking (Mac) or Ctrl-Shift-clicking (Win) in the color ramp at the bottom of the Color panel. You can also choose Complement from the side menu in the Color panel.

These tips and dozens more are in the printable PDF DesignToolsMonthly_AI-Tips.pdf on the *Wow! CD*.

Artists

Ted Alspach
ted@bezier.com
www.bezier.com

Kevan Atteberry
P.O. Box 40188
Bellevue, WA 98015-4188
206-550-6353
kevan@oddisgood.com
www.oddisgood.com

Jean Aubé
785 Versailles #302
Montréal Québec Canada
H3C 1Z5
jeanaube01@videotron.ca

Kenneth Batelman
128 Birch Leaf Drive
Milford, PA 18337
888-532-0612
Kenneth@batelman.com
www.batelman.com

Christiane Beauregard
514-935-6794
c.beauregard@videotron.ca
www.christianebeauregard.com

Russell Benfanti
www.benfanti.com
represented by
www.mendolaart.com
212.986.5680

Eliot Bergman
212-693-2300
eliot@ebergman.com
www.ebergman.com

Peter Cassell
1185 Design
411 High Street
Palo Alto, CA 94301
650-325-4804
peterc@1185design.com
www.1185design.com

David Cater
510-232-9420
adcater@aol.com

Ron Chan
24 Nelson Ave.
Mill Valley, CA 94941
415-389-6549
ronchan@ronchan.com

Conrad Chavez
design@conradchavez.com
www.conradchavez.com

Bryan Christie
www.bryanchristiedesign.com/

Sandee Cohen
33 Fifth Avenue, #10B
New York, NY 10003
212-677-7763
sandee@vectorbabe.com
www.vectorbabe.com

Michael Cronan
mpc@cronan.com
www.michaelcronan.com

Scott B. Crouse
Lake Alfred, FL
scott@scottcrouse.com
scottcrouse.com

Andrew Dashwood
info@adashwood.com
www.adashwood.com

Rob Day & Virginia Evans
10 State Street, Suite 214
Newburyport, MA 01950
508-465-1386

Design Action Collective
369 15th Street
Oakland, CA 94612
510-452-1912
info@designaction.org
www.designaction.org

Virginia Evans, *see* Day & Evans

Gary Ferster
10 Karen Drive
Tinton Falls, NJ 07753
732-922-8903
Fax: 732-922-8970
gferster@comcast.net
www.garyferster.com/

Louis Fishauf
47 Lorne Ave.
Kettleby, Ontario
Canada L0G1J0
905-726-1597
fishauf@reactor.ca
www.fishauf.com

Mark Fox
415-258-9663
mfox@blackdogma.com

Ian Giblin
408-448-2614
n.giblin@comcast.net

Reggie Gilbert
Tech Vector
1454 Ashland St PMB#141
Ashland OR 97520
www.techvector.com

Mordy Golding
Design Responsibly LLC
320 Leroy Avenue
Cedarhurst, NY 11516
info@designresponsibly.com
www.designresponsibly.com

Steven H. Gordon
Cartagram, LLC
136 Mill Creek Crossing
Madison, AL 35758
wow@cartagram.com
www.cartagram.com

Caryl Gorska
1277 8th Avenue 105
San francisco, CA 94122
415-664-7721
408-910-6545
gorska@gorska.com
www.gorska.com

Laurie Grace
860-659-0748
lgrace@aol.com

Cheryl Graham
cherylgraham@earthlink.net
www.cherylgraham.net

April Greiman
620 MoultonAve. No. 211
Los Angeles, CA 90031
323-227-1222
info@madeinspace.la
ww.madeinspace.la

Brad Hamann
Brad Hamann Illustration &
Design
28 Aspinwall Road
Red Hook, NY 12571
845-758-6186 studio
bhamann@hvc.rr.com
www.bradhamann.com

Michael Hamm
13555 Breton Ridge St. #426
Houston, TX 77070
281-451-6841
michael@pointsandpaths.com
www.pointsandpaths.com

Scott Hansen
scott@iso50.com
www.iso50.com

Pattie Belle Hastings
Ice House Press & Design
Pattie Belle Hastings
266 West Rock Ave.
New Haven, CT 06515
203-389-7334

Rick Henkel,
rhenkel@thoughtformdesign
see also ThoughtForm Design

Kurt Hess,
dashesshaus@comcast.net
see also ThoughtForm Design

Kaoru Hollin
kaoruhollin@attbi.com

Gerard Huerta
Gerard Huerta Design, Inc.
54 Old Post Road
Southport, CT 06890
203-256-1625
gerard.huerta@sbcglobal.net
www.gerardhuerta.com

Kevin Hulsey
www.khulsey.com

IAN Symbols (Integration and
Application Network)
University of Maryland Center
for Environmental Science
2020 Horns Point Rd
(PO Box 775)
Cambridge, MD 21613
410-228-9250 ext 254
ian@ca.umes.edu
http://ian.umces.edu/symbols

Lisa Jackmore
13603 Bluestone Court
Clifton, VA 20124
703-830-0985
ljackmore@cox.net

Lance Jackson
lance@lancejackson.net
lancejjackson@earthlink.net
www.lancejackson.net

David Jennings
7 Castleton Avenue
Romanby
Northallerton
North Yorkshire
DL78SU
UK
+44(0)1609 770795
+44(0)7754 796831
david@davidjennings.co.uk
www.davidjennings.co.uk

Mohammed Jogie
PO Box 44007, Linden
Gauteng Province 2104
South Africa
+27 (0) 82 655 2999

Dave Joly
15 King St.
Putnam, CT 06260
860-928-1042

Frank Jonen
Haupstrasse 15
65510 Idstein
Germany
49-6126 9581 81
Fax 49-6126 9581 83
getinfo@frankjonen.com
www.frankjonen.com

Andrea Kelley
Andrea Kelley Design
530 Menlo Oaks Drive
Menlo Park, CA 94025
650-326-1083
andrea@jevans.com

Marc LaMantia
64 Macdougal Street Apt 5
New York, NY 10012
212-677-6907
lamantia2003@yahoo.com

Tiffany Larsen
tiffany@uberpop.com
uberpop.com

Adam Z Lein
3 Woodlands Ave
Elmsford, NY 10523
914-347-1710
adamz@lein.com
www.adamlein.com

Joe Lertola
TIME / Editorial Art Dept
1271 Sixth Avenue / Rm 2442
New York, NY 10020
212-522-3721
www.joelertola.com

Randy Livingston
Assistant Professor, Media
Design
School of Journalism,
Box 0064
College of Mass Communica-
tion
Middle Tennessee State Uni-
versity
Murfreesboro, TN 37132
615 / 898.2335
rlivings@mtsu.edu

Vicki Loader
Sandhurst, Berkshire
Gu47 8Ja, United Kingdom
+447834783218
+441252874190
vickiloader@btinternet.com
www.purepixels.co.uk
www.vickiloader.com

Terrance (Terry) Lush
PO Box 185143
Hamden, CT 06518
t.lush@tlush.net
www.tlush.net

Todd Macadangdang
348 Arco St.
San Jose, CA 95123
408-536-6373
toddm@adobe.com
toddm@illustratorworld.com

Rob Magiera
Noumena Digital
9636 Ruskin Circle
Salt Lake City, UT 84092
801-943-3650

Pete Maric
520 Terrace Plaza
Willowick, OH 44095
440-487-4205
contact@petemaric.com
www.petemaric.com

Greg Maxson
116 W. Florida Ave
Urbana, IL 61801
217-337-6069
gmaxti@sbcglobal.net
gregmaxson.com
gregmaxson.com

Eden Maxwell
artist@edensart.com
www.edensart.com

Nobuko Miyamoto
3-8 Matuba-cho
Tokorozawa-shi
Saitama-ken Japan/359-0044
04-2998-6631
venus@gol.com
http://venus.orracchi.com

Yukio Miyamoto
Matubacho 3-8
Tokorozawasi
Saitamaken Japan/359-0044
+81-42-998-6631
yukio-m@ppp.bekkoame.ne.jp
www.bekkoame.ne.jp/~yukio-m

Bert Monroy
www.bertmonroy.com

Marcel Morin
Lost Art Cartography
Box 66, Grand Pré
Nova Scotia
B0P 1MO
902-542-2934
cybermapper@gmail.com

Gary J. Moss
Moss Martin Graphic Design
319 Peck Street Box I-5
New Haven, CT 06513
203-785-8464
gm@mossmartin.net
mossmartin.net

Innosanto Nagara
see Design Action Collective

Brad Neal
Thomas • Bradley Illustration
& Design
411 Center St. / P.O. Box 249
Gridley, IL 61744
309-747-3266
bradneal@thomas-bradley.com
www.thomasbradley.com

David Nelson
Mapping Services
721 Grape St.
Denver, CO 80220
303-333-1060

Gary Newman Design
2447 Burnside Rd
Sebastopol, CA 95472
gary@newmango.com
www.newmango.com

Chris D. Nielsen
714-323-1602
carartwork@ca.rr.com
chris@pentoolart.com
www.pentoolart.com

Richard Ng, photographer
www.istockphoto/richard_ng

Ann Paidrick
314-762-1431
annpaid@attglobal.net
www.ebypaidrick.com

Ellen Papciak-Rose
Johannesburg, South Africa
inthestudio@mac.com
www.homepage.mac.com/
inthestudio

Tom Patterson
National Park Service
Media Development
Harpers Ferry Center
Harpers Ferry, WV 25425-0050
304-535-6020
t.patterson@nps.gov
www.nacis.org/cp/cp28/
resources.html

Daniel Pelavin
212-941-7418
daniel@pelavin.com
www.pelavin.com

Laurent Pinabel
laurent@pinabel.com
pinabel.com

John Pirman
johnpirman@aol.com
represented by
Gerald & Cullen Rapp
212-889-3337

Federico Platon
Jose Mtnez. Velasco 8
Madrid 28007
Tel. 91-573 2467
grafintek@gmail.com
www.federicoplaton.com

David S. Pounds
1810 Staimford Circle
Wellington, FL 33414
561-803-2414
david_pounds@pba.edu

Gary Powell
2417 SW Olson
Pendleton, OR 97801
541-276-6330
oil_artist@comcast.net

Jolynne Roorda
jroorda@folktheory.com
www.folktheory.com

Zosia Rostomian
zosia_rostomian@yahoo.com
www.ztrdesign.com

Tracey Saxby, *see* IAN Symbols

Mike Schwabauer
5605 W. 58th #113
Mission, KS 66202
913-710-1345
kcmikey@mac.com
http://webmac.com/kcmikey/
iweb/mikeschwabauerdesign

Robert Sharif
2791 Lexford Ave.
San Jose, CA 95124
rsharif@earthlink.net
sharifr@adobe.com

Rick Simonson
RLSimonson Studios
4010 Ave. R #G8
Kearney, NE 68847
rlsimonson@mac.com
www.RickLSimonson.com

Joe Shoulak
joe@joeshoulak.com
joeshoulak.com

Christopher Spollen
Moonlightpress Studio
362 Cromwell Ave.
Staten Island, NY 10305
718-979-9695
cjspollen@aol.com
spollen.com

Nancy Stahl
nancy@nancystahl.com
www.nancystahl.com

Steven Stankiewicz
artfromsteve@aol.com
www.porfolios.com/
stevenstankiewicz

Judy Stead
407-310-0051
judy@judystead.com
judystead.com

Sharon Steuer
c/o Peachpit Press
1249 Eighth St.
Berkeley, CA 94710
www.ssteuer.com

Barbara Sudick
California State University
Dept. of Communication
Design
Chico, CA 95929
530-898-5028

Brenda Sutherland
345 Park Avenue
San Jose, CA 95124

ThoughtForm
3700 South Water Street
Suite 300
Pittsburgh, PA 15203.2366
412-488-8600
www.thoughtformdesign.com

Kathleen Tinkel
MacPrePress
12 Burr Road
Westport, CT 06880
203-227-2357

Jack Tom
www.jacktom.com

Ivan Torres
12933 Ternberry Ct.
Tustin, CA 92782
714-734-4356
ivanjessica@sbcglobal.net
ivanjessica2002@yahoo.com
www.meshsmith.com

Jean-Claude Tremblay
Illustrator Instructor & Prepress
Technician
135 Boul. Champlain
Candiac (Quebec)
Canada J3R 3T1
Tel.: 450-993-0949

Judy Valenzuela
judy valenzuela14@mac.com
www.judyvalenzuela.com

Trina Wai
5027 Silver Reef Dr.
Fremont, CA 94538

Timothy Webb
Tim Webb Illustration
305 W. Maywood
Wichita, KS 67217
316-524-3881
tim@timwebb.com
www.timwebb.com

Alan James Weimer
67 Bliss Street
Rehoboth, MA 0276-1932
508-252-9236
illustrator51@comcast.net

Ari M. Weinstein
ari@ariw.com
ariw.com

Hugh Whyte
Lehner & Whyte
8-10 South Fullerton Ave.
Montclair, NJ 07402
201-746-1335

Filip Yip
877-463-4547
filip@yippe.com
www.yippe.com

General Index

E

edges
  beveled, 321
  finding, 263
  hiding/showing, 25, 30, 312
Edit tab (Live Color dialog), 281
editing
  Area Type object, 263
  art with 3D effects, 327
  brushes, 128
  Envelopes, 303
  image paths in Photoshop,
    405–406
  Live Paint objects and paths,
    101, 104
  meshes, 237
  Opacity Masks, 247
  symbol instances, 131
  unified gradients, 223
  vignettes, 269
Effect menu, 300
effects, *see also* Live Paint; Live
    Trace; 3D effects; *and*
    specific effects
  applying, 301
  benefit banner using, 314
  distorting text, 411
  Envelope, 302–304, 310
  filters vs., 68, 300
  Gaussian Blur, 202, 253, 316
  mixing brushes with, 319
  Outer Glow, 358
  Pathfinder, 304–305
  Raster, 300–301
  saving as Graphic Styles, 300
  scaling, 21, 304
  shading with mesh, 310–311
  transformations applied as, 300
  using Graphic Styles with, 315
  using on Photoshop shape
    layers, 409
  Warp, 302–304, 308–309
electric guitar in 3D, 343
Ellipse tool, 12–13
ellipses, 82
embedding images, 398–399
Empress tarot card, 113
end of lines, 67–68
Envelopes
  applying, 303–304, 310
  distort options for, 304
  editing, 303

  expanding compound shapes
    for, 91
  Fidelity settings for, 310
  using with type, 204–205
  Warps vs., 302
EPS files, 35, 98, 399
Eraser tool, 12, 70, 129
Eraser Tool Options dialog, 70
errors
  joining anchor points, 16
  message for Clipping Mask, 347
  preventing by watching
    cursors, 55
  using bevels, 321
"Establishing Perspective" lesson,
    176–177
European cityscape, 259
Evans, Virginia, 196–197, 430
evergreen tree, 312–313
Every-line Composer, 186
exchanging swatches, 64–65
Expand dialog, 237
expandable text buttons, 163
expanding
  blends, 217
  compound shapes, 91
  Live Paint groups, 103–104
  objects before erasing stroke, 70
exporting
  animation, 395
  compatible file formats for, 400
  compound shapes to .PSD files,
    408–409
  CSS layers, 381
  Illustrator type, 192
  image maps, 377
  legacy artwork selectively, 379
  paths to shapes in Photoshop,
    408–409
  PNG-24 files for video, 381
  slices as .PSD files, 378
  .SWF files, 380–381
  transparencies, 245
  type as outlines, 188
extruding objects, 320–321,
    332–333
Eyedropper Options dialog, 66, 189
Eyedropper tool
  color matching with, 360
  sampling object attributes
    with, 66
  text formatting with, 189–190
  using, 66–67

F

fading, 350–351, 352
Fall illustration, 230
Farrow, Patricia, 294–295
"Fashionable Colors" lesson,
    286–287
feather symbols, 145
Ferster, Gary, 224–225, 430
Fidelity settings (Envelope Options
    dialog), 310
files, *see also* legacy files; PDF files;
    saving; *and specific file*
    formats
  .ai, 3, 374, 378–379, 387, 388,
    394–395
  .ait, 3–4
  compatibility of, 32–33, 400
  controlling size of, 36
  EPS, 35, 98, 399
  GIF, 376, 378, 379
  HTML, 377
  Illustrator-supported formats,
    34, 399
  importing to Flash, 378–379,
    380–381, 387
  JPEG, 376, 379
  linked, 400
  multiple layer versions in, 158
  opening incompatible, 398
  PDF versions supporting
    transparency, 252
  PNG-24, 379, 381
  preparing for printing, 301
  preparing to import animation
    to Flash, 394
  .PSD, 378, 408–409, 413
  scaling complex, 21
  .SWF, 374, 377, 380–381
  testing Live Trace on, 97
  viewing effects or features
    of, 163
fills, *see also* gradient fills
  adding to appearance, 162–163
  color for, 62–63
  compound paths with, 92
  copying, 17
  covering pattern with offset,
    208–209
  defined, 60
  masks with, 345
  objects with, 20, 60–61

controlling file size, 36
earlier versions of, 34
embedding and linking images
in, 398–399
file formats supported, 34,
399, 402
help for, 28
importing sketch into, 114,
134–135
layout capabilities of, 178, 196,
197
moving art between Photoshop
and, 400–401
opening incompatible files, 398
PDF support for transparency,
252
Photoshop images opened
in, 115
placing images in other Adobe
applications, 29
plug-ins for, 426–427
status line, 23
system requirements for, 2
undo in, 25–26
using art with other programs,
399–400
Illustrator CS3 Wow! Course Outline
(Steuer and Jackmore), xvii
image maps
assigning URLs to, 376–377
exporting, 377
image-mapped buttons, 396
images, *see also* raster images;
saving; vector images
adding color to grayscale,
268–269
assigning URLs to image maps,
376–377
converting raster to vector
graphics, 94–95, 296–299
creating faded, textured
appearance for, 138
cropped when placed in other
Adobe applications, 29
cutting elements of, 390
deleting traced, 97
detecting gaps in artwork, 102–
103, 115–116
displaying using New Window
command, 27
embedding and linking,
398–399

enhancing contrast for
tracing, 122
grayscale conversion of, 294–295
Illustrator-supported formats
for, 34
importing, 268
location of linked, 400
making template from
scanned, 164
masking with letter forms, 198
moving between applications,
399–400
placing on layer as drawing
reference, 167
recovering missing linked, 401
replacing placed art on
layers, 168
rotating from centerpoint of, 210
saving, 25, 376
scaling proxies of, 22
simulating on mobile
devices, 380
slicing, 377–378, 383
importing
Illustrator file into Flash,
378–379, 387
images, 268
.PSD files to Illustrator, 413
sketch into Illustrator, 114,
134–135
in port/out port type objects, 180
InDesign
exchanging swatches with, 31,
64–65
pasting text into, 402
using Illustrator with, 401
Info panel, 223
information sharing illustration, 89
instances, 129, 130, 131
Intensity option for Symbolism
tools, 132
interrupting Preview
redrawings, 25
Intersect Pathfinder command,
107–108
"Intricate Patterns" lesson,
84–85, 356
Isolation Mode, 90–91, 130–131
"Isometric Systems" lesson, 82–83

J

Jackmore, Lisa
about, v
contact information, 431
bird bath image, 138
*Illustrator CS3 Wow! Course
Outline*, xvii
Loafers image by, 139
sketchbook page of, 357
Jackson, Lance
blended brush strokes of cover
art, 238
contact information, 431
Long Strange Trip type, 212
sketches by, 117
working with distorted text
in Illustrator and
Photoshop, 411
Jacoby, Frank, 257
Japanese Tea Garden poster, 140
Jenkins, George, 120
Jennings, David, 270–271, 431
Jerusalem map, 170
Jogie, Mohammed, 342, 431
Join command, 17–18
join types, 68
joining
endpoints, 16, 17–18
objects, 44
Joly, Dave, 114–116, 222–223, 431
Jonen, Frank, 350–353, 431
JPEG files, 376, 379

K

Kelley, Andrea, 72–74, 264–265,
431
kerning, 195
key frames, 384–385
keyboard shortcuts
adding layers with, 154
adjusting Symbolism tool
with, 132
changing, 6
conventions for citing, xviii
custom, 5–6
duplicating artwork with, 286
skipping Symbol Options dialog
with, 129
Swatches panel, 62
turning on/off Smart Guides, 304

polygons
  adding anchor points in three-sided, 43
  creating geometric shapes with, 12–13
  making six-sided, 46
  useful key combinations for, 12
portrait of Suzy Parker, 275
"Ports illustrated" tip, 180
positioning overlapping paths, 110
PostScript printing, 34–35
Pounds, David, 416, 432
Powell, Gary, 149, 169, 306–307
power-key mastery, 54–58
Preferences dialog, 200
prepress production
  converting spot to process color, 67
  converting type to outlines, 189
  drawing of 2D art for 3D package, 334
  preparing PDF files for, 32, 36
Preserve options with Harmony Rules, 298–299
Preset menu (Adobe PDF Options dialog), 32
presets
  Live Color, 281–282
  Scribble effect, 312–313
pressure settings
  drawing brush strokes with, 134
  used by Calligraphic and Scatter Brushes, 128–129
previewing, see also Flattener Preview panel
  animation, 387–388
  artwork in pixels, 380
  Live Paint Bucket swatches, 100
  screen redraw in Preview mode, 25, 26
Print dialog
  about, 4–5
  Advanced section of, 249, 251
  illustrated, 5
  interactive Print Preview features, 4
  interrupting preview, 25
  setting up options for Mac computers in, 5
printing
  correcting and avoiding problems, 35–36
  flattening process with, 34, 248

layers, 156
PostScript, 34–35
preparing files for, 301
using Print dialog, 4–5
process colors
  converting spot to, 67
  global, 63, 214
productivity, see performance
Projecting cap, 67
.PSD files
  converting objects for export to, 408–409
  exporting slices as, 378
  importing images to Illustrator as, 413
Publix Market scene, 371

Q
"Quick & Easy 3D" lesson, 326–327
"Quick Box Art" lesson, 334–335
QuickBooks logo, 224

R
radial gradients, 79, 253, 354
radials
  coloring with gradient, 79
  squashing and recoloring, 226–227
  using Gaussian Blur with gradient, 253
rainbows of color, 351–353
raster effects, 300–301
raster images
  defined, 375
  dimming, 156
  hand-tracing template as, 122
  Raster/Vector Balance setting for, 251–252
  rasterizing vector images to start fresh, 112
Rasterize dialog, 122
Read me first!, xvi
Recolor Artwork button (Live Color dialog), 80, 279, 288
Recolor Options dialog, 282, 288–289
recoloring artwork
  Color Groups for, 284–285
  preparing swatch groups before, 287

selecting single color for recoloring, 288–289
  using Live Color, 279–283
  working with complex composition, 290–292
"Recoloring Black" lesson, 288–289
recording actions, 37
recovering missing linked images, 401
Rectangle dialog, 48, 49
Rectangle tool, 42, 46
Rectangular Grid tool, 13, 49
Rectangular Grid Tool Options dialog, 200–201
Red Tip boxes, xix
reducing color, 281–282, 287, 294–295
"Reducing Color" lesson, 294–295
Reflect tool, using, 45, 137
reflecting
  Pen profiles, 45
  photos, 137
reflections
  adding lighter, 353
  bottle, 367
  simulating glass and chrome, 264–265
releasing
  blends, 217
  groups in Live Paint, 103–104
  mesh from flag artwork, 310–311
  objects onto own layer, 378–379
  single Clipping Mask, 346
  traced images, 97
removing white background when tracing images, 96
repeating patterns, 84–85
Replace control (Control panel), 130
replacing
  Graphic Styles, 305
  placed art on layers, 168
Reset Envelope Mesh dialog, 311
Reshape tool, 24
resizing
  line weight and, 6
  symbols, 147
  type and reflowing, 188

resolution
    placed image, 398
    reapplying when flattening live
        effects, 251
    setting for raster effects,
        300–301
Reverse Front to Back
    command, 216
reversing
    blends, 216–217
    brush stroke, 127
revolving objects, 321–322, 330
RGB color model
    CMYK vs., 376
    converting CMYK to, 30, 375,
        376
    Web graphics using, 374–375
Rivers for Life logo, 210–211
robot character, 114–116
Rogalin, Elizabeth, v
"Rolling Mesh" lesson, 236–237
Roorda, Jolynne, 112, 432
Rostomian, Zosia, 75, 228,
    229, 432
Rotate tool, 49, 52, 364–365
rotating
    exercises for, 52
    objects in 3D space, 322–323,
        327
    paths to create rose, 78–79
    setting image's centerpoint
        for, 210
    square, 42, 47
    symbols, 148
Roughen effect
    applying, 206–207
    type with, 209
    using with masked ovals, 349
Roughen filter, 80
Round cap, 67
Round Corners dialog, 332
Round join, 68
Rounded Rectangle dialog, 72
Rounded Rectangle tool,
    12–13, 332
rows, 186, 218
rulers, 28–29, 320

S

Santa Claus, 253
Save Adobe PDF dialog, 32
"Save for Web & Devices" tip,
    377, 379
Save Swatch Library as ASE
    command, 64
Save Swatches for Exchange
    feature, 31
Save Transparency Flatterner Preset
    dialog, 251
saving
    .ai files for Flash import,
        378–379, 388
    Color Groups as swatches, 87,
        294–295
    custom workspaces, 21
    dock set-ups, 19
    effects as Graphic Style, 300,
        308–309
    Illustrator type, 192
    images as GIF or JPEG, 376
    linked files, 400
    PDFs, 32–33
    regularly, 25
    sliced images, 383
    swatch libraries, 64–65
    transparency flattener
        presets, 251
    transparent objects, 246
    Web graphic images, 377,
        379–380
    Web page image as template, 383
Saxby, Tracey, 150–151, 432
Scale dialog, 78
Scale tool, 50–51, 180
scaling
    brushes, 127
    complex files, 21
    enabling Scale Strokes & Effects
        option before, 22
    exercises for, 50–51
    objects to exact size, 22
    objects to squash radial fill,
        226–227
    text frames and content, 180
    unavailable for Photoshop
        effects, 304

scanned images
    converting pencil drawing to
        template layer, 328
    creating template from, 164
    using textiles for, 198, 199
    working from, 176
Scatter Brushes
    about, 126
    creating, 127
    distributing artwork to
        layers, 128
    making and using, 153
    pressure settings for, 128–129
    symbols vs., 132
Schwabauer, Mike
    benefit performance banner, 314
    blood drive announcement, 331
    contact information, 432
    crosshatching using Scribble, 302
Scissors tool, 12, 109
"Scratchboard Art" lesson, 306–307
"Scribble Basics" lesson, 312–313
Scribble effect, 207–208
    about, 301–302
    antiquing type with, 206–207
    crosshatching using, 302, 318
    filling type with, 208–209
    hiding edges of, 312
    preset styles for, 312–313
Scribble Options dialog, 207, 208,
    302, 313
Select All Instances command, 130
selecting, *see also* selecting objects
    Area type, 179–181
    color for recoloring, 288–289
    color matching systems, 31–32
    container before applying
        clipping mask, 345
    fonts, 187
    Harmony Rules, 280, 281
    selection techniques for Layers
        panel, 160–161
    targeting vs., 160
    text, 179
    type by path only, 178
    unified gradients, 223
selecting objects
    about, 13, 179
    after unlocking layers, 158
    before making changes, 19–20
    in groups, 14–15, 305
    from layers, 155, 158

sublayers
  adding art on, 168
  appearance of, 90–91
  deleting, 168
  hierarchical layer structure and, 158
  locating objects on, 157
  organizing, 166–168
  working with, 154, 155
subtracting shapes, 211
subway exit, 372
Sudick, Barbara, 187, 433
Sutherland, Brenda
  Appearance panel options, 162
  contact information, 433
  Eraser's effect on brushed paths, 129
  example of stroke effects by, 70
  mapping tips by, 324
  modifying logo with Live Color, 293
  moving from photo to illustration, 296–299
  selecting 3D effects, 321
SVG 3.0 browser plug-in, 381
swatch libraries
  creating and saving, 64–65
  developing Web, 376
  using with traced images, 97, 98
Swatch Options dialog, 62
Swatch panel, 63
swatches, *see also* swatch libraries
  coloring tracing layers with global, 297–298
  creating Graphic Styles, 307
  deleting, 64
  exchanging, 31–32, 64–65
  Live Color, 278
  preparations before recoloring artwork, 287
  saving, 87, 208, 294–295
  selecting, 31–32
  spot and global process color, 63
Swatches panel
  effect of deleting swatches, 280
  keyboard shortcuts for, 62
  sorting swatches on, xviii
.SWF files, 374, 377, 380–381
"Symbol Basics" lesson, 146–148
symbol instance sets, 131
"Symbol Libraries" lesson, 150–151
Symbol Options dialog, 129, 132
Symbol Options dialog box, 394

Symbolism tools, 131, 132, 147–148
symbols
  animating, 385
  blending between, 215
  creating, 129
  custom, 149
  defined, 129
  developing libraries of, 150–151
  editing, 130–131
  feather creation using, 145
  Flash animation with, 130
  icons used in Instance Name field for, 130
  mapping, 324, 329, 335
  rearranging order of, 151
  Scatter Brushes vs., 132
  stacking order for, 148
  Symbol Basics lesson, 146–148
  Tropical Card, 146–147
  types of, 132
  using in exported .SWF files, 380
  working with Symbolism tools, 131
Symbols panel
  about, 129–130
  illustrated, 129, 386
  rearranging symbol order on, 151
system requirements, 2

T

tab leaders, 180–181
target icon, 160
targeting
  all elements, 162
  locked objects and, 159
  selecting vs., 160
tear off panels, 7, 19
techniques in book, xx
template layers
  about, 155–156
  creating sketch as, 106
  deriving image shape and color from, 360
  non-printing, 155, 156, 170
  organizing complex map using, 171
  placing scanned image on, 164–165
  scanning pencil drawing as, 328
  templates vs., 156
  using, 164–165

templates
  hand-tracing, 164–165
  importing existing art as, 134–135
  product photo use for, 229
  rasterizing hand-tracing, 122
  resolution, 37
  saving Web page image as, 383
  template layers vs., 156
  using, 3–4
Templates folder, 4
testing
  intricate patterns, 85
  Live Trace on small file, 97
text, *see also* type
  changing case of, 187
  composers for, 186
  distortion effects for, 411
  entering into panel fields, 20
  expandable text buttons, 163
  greeking, 188
  joining blocks of, 190
  legacy, 184
  masking images with letter forms, 198
  overflow, 180
  pasting into InDesign, 402
  threaded, 180, 181, 182–183
  transparency with, 244
  wrapping around objects, 183
texture of sketchbook page, 357
ThoughtForm Design, 214, 433
threaded text, 180, 181, 182–183
3D Bevels Shapes, 321
3D effects
  about, 320
  adding arrowheads to map with, 338
  applying multiple, 301
  applying surface shading to objects, 323–324
  book cover with, 342
  building 3D objects from multiple paths, 332–333
  concept design for PDA, 341
  converting 2D art to 3D package, 334–335
  designing logo with, 330
  electric guitar rendered with, 343
  extruding objects, 320–321, 333
  map symbols using, 326–327
  mapping art onto objects, 324, 337

loading Graphic Styles, 305
minimizing 3D profile's
    points, 323
multiple layer versions, 158
preparing files for printing, 301
preserving spot color, 301
protecting layer's appearance
    attributes, 160–161
quick symbol creation, 129
recoloring single color, 288–289
scaling text frames and
    content, 180
tracing EPS format images, 98
using Clip to Artboard, 382
working with 3D Bevels
    Shapes, 321
Tropical Card, 146–148
troubleshooting
    lost appearance attributes,
        160–161
    options when unable to group
        objects, 14
    printing, 35–36
Tupperware containers, 325,
    332–333
tweening in Flash, 388
2D effects, *see* effects
type
    adding strokes to, 190
    Appearance panel features for,
        190–192
    applying brushes to letterforms,
        202–203
    changing case, 187
    character and paragraph styles
        for, 183–184
    creating typeface from grid,
        200–201
    filling with scribble pattern,
        208–209
    finding fonts, 186–187
    fitting headlines, 187
    fitting to curved paths, 192,
        194–195
    flow of vertical Area, 192
    font selection, 187
    formatting with Eyedropper,
        189–190
    giving letters hand-rendered
        look, 319
    glyphs, 185
    greeking text, 188

improved Illustrator
    features, 178
joining text blocks, 190
kerning manually, 195
legacy text, 184
Long Strange Trip, 212
masking images with letter
    forms, 198
multinational font support
    for, 188
Opacity Mask used with,
    206–207
OpenType fonts, 184–185
outline, 187–189, 195
panels for, 178–179
Point, Area, and Path, 179–181
resizing and reflowing, 188
saving and exporting Illustrator,
    192
scaling text frames and
    content, 180
selecting, 178, 179
setting tab leaders, 180–181
simulating sunburst in, 193
Single-line and Every-line
    Composers, 186
transforming with Warps and
    Envelopes, 204–205
transparency and effects with,
    262–263
transparency backgrounds
    for, 191
unable to copy stroke and fill
    of, 17
using as Clipping Mask, 347
working with, 190–191
wrapping, 183
type objects, 180, 190–191
Type on a Path Options dialog, 182
Type on a Path tool, 179, 181–182
"Type Subtraction" lesson, 210–211
Type tool
    changing case of text, 187
    converting Selection tool to, 192
    cursors for, 183
    kerning with, 195
    selecting text with, 179
    vertical/horizontal mode
        toggling in, 183
"Type tool juggling" tip, 183
typefaces, *see* fonts

U

underlined text, 7, 179
undoing operations, 25–26, 54–55
ungrouping objects, 14
"Unified Gradients" lesson,
    222–223
units of measurement
    displaying as pixels, 379
    selecting and typing in, 16
    setting, 7
updating legacy text, 184
urban landscape, 422
URLs assigned to image maps,
    376–377
Use Preview Bounds option, 15, 16

V

Valentine's Day card, 272–274
Valenzuela, Judy, 113, 433
van Dooren, Corné, 397
vanishing points, 176–177
variation on animations, 391
Variation Options dialog, 65
vector images
    Raster/Vector Balance setting
        for, 251–252
    rasterizing, 112, 375
    using multiple images with
        Opacity Masks, 252
Version pop-up menu, 400
Vertical Area Type tool, 182
vertical type, 183, 187
video
    document profiles for, 375
    exporting PNG 24 files for, 381
    turning layered images into key
        frames, 384–385
views
    limiting to Artboard, 26
    New, 26–27
    using Preview and Outline
        modes, 26
vignettes, 269

W

Wai, Trina, 336, 433
wall mural, 413
Warp Options dialog, 308, 309
Warps
  applying, 302–303
  Envelopes vs., 302
  using with type, 204–205
"Warps & Envelopes" lesson,
    308–311
washes, 136
water
  simulating colored, 240–241
  wave shapes for, 210–211
Web Color Warning, 61–62
Web document profiles, 375
Web graphics
  GIF options for, 378
  using RGB color mode for,
    374–375
  using Web swatch libraries
    for, 376
Web pages
  banner for, 390–391
  designing, 382–383
  image-mapped buttons for, 396
Web safe color
  about, 383
  developing swatch libraries
    of, 376
  limiting Color Picker to, 380
Webb, Tim, 219, 433
Weimer, Alan James, 84–85,
    356, 433
Weinstein, Ari
  contact information, 433
  recoloring artwork, 284–285
  using Opacity Mask with type,
    206–207, 302
Welcome screen, 3, 4
Whyte, Hugh
  contact information, 433
  Day at the Circus poster, 86–88
  layering frames, 384–385
Window menu, xviii
windows, 26, 27
wine glass, 238
wine label, 324, 337
woodcut illustration look, 219
wooden pallet, 83

workspaces
  preparing animation, 392–393
  setting up Live Color, 278–279
  working with Mac and
    Windows, 21
Wow! CD
  additional *Zen Lessons* on,
    xvii, xx
  automating isometric's
    formulas, 83
  Bézier curves lessons on, 8–9
  Brenda Sutherland's art on,
    70, 129
  Design Tools Monthly tips on,
    428–429
  "Moving from FreeHand to
    Illustrator", 398
  Y. Miyamoto's Graphic Styles
    on, 315
  Zen of the Pen lesson, xvii, 9
wrapping text around objects, 183

Y

Yip, Filip, 410, 433

Z

Zen lessons, xx, 38–58
"Zen of the Pen" lesson, xvii, 9
"Zen Rotation" lesson, 52
"Zen Scaling" lesson, 50–51
Zion National Park label design,
    193
zippers, 142–143
zooming in/out
  disabled for Live Trace, 98
  options for, 27–28
  shortcuts for, 27
Zorro poster and flyer, 288–289

WOW! BOOK PRODUCTION NOTES:
Interior Book Design and Production

This book was produced in InDesign CS2 using primarily Adobe's Minion Pro and Frutiger OpenType fonts. Barbara Sudick is the artist behind the original *Illustrator Wow!* design and typography; using Jill Davis's layout of *The Photoshop Wow! Book* as a starting point, she designed the first edition in QuarkXPress.

Hardware and Software

With the exception of some of the testers and consulants, all of the *Wow!* team uses Macintosh computers. We used Adobe Illlustrator CS3, Photoshop CS2, and Ambrosia Software's Snapz Pro X for the screenshots. We used Adobe Acrobat 6, 7, and 8 for distribution of the book pages to testers, the indexer, Peachpit and the proofreaders. Adam Z Lein created an online *Wow!* database for us so the team could track the details of the book production. Many of the team members use Dantz Retrospect for backups of our computers. CDS Documentation Services printed this book.

How to contact the author

If you've created artwork using the newer features of Illustrator that you'd like to submit for consideration in future *Wow!* books, please send printed samples to: Sharon Steuer, c/o Peachpit Press, 1249 Eighth Street, Berkeley, CA 94710.

Windows Finger Dance Summary *from "The Zen of Illustrator"*

Object Creation — *Hold down keys until AFTER mouse button is released.*

⇧ Shift	Constrains objects horizontally, vertically or proportionally.
Alt	Objects will be drawn from centers.
Alt click	Opens dialog boxes with transformation tools.
[ ]	Spacebar turns into the grabber Hand.
Ctrl [ ]	Turns cursor into the Zoom-in tool. Click or marquee around an area to Zoom in.
Ctrl **Alt** [ ]	Turns cursor into the Zoom-out tool. Click to Zoom out.
Caps lock	Turns your cursor into a cross-hair.

Object Selection — *Watch your cursor to see that you've pressed the correct keys.*

Ctrl	The current tool becomes the last chosen Selection tool.
Ctrl **Alt**	Current tool becomes Group Selection to select entire object. Click again to select next level of grouping. To move selection release Alt key, then Grab.
Ctrl **Tab**	Toggles whether Direct Selection or regular Selection tool is accessed by the Ctrl key.
⇧ Shift click	Toggles whether an object, path or point is selected or deselected.
⇧ Shift click ▷	With Direct Selection tool, click on or marquee around an object, path or point to toggle selection/deselection. **Note:** *Clicking inside a filled object may select the entire object.*
⇧ Shift click ▶ ▶₊	Clicking on, or marqueeing over objects with Selection tool or Group Selection tool, toggles selection/deselection (Group Selection tool chooses objects within a group).

Object Transformation — *Hold down keys until AFTER mouse button is released.*

⇧ Shift	Constrains transformation proportionally, vertically and horizontally.
Alt	Leaves the original object and transforms a copy.
Ctrl **Z**	Undo. Use Shift-Ctrl-Z for Redo.
	To move or transform a selection predictably from within dialog boxes, use this diagram to determine if you need a positive or negative number and which angle is required. (*Diagram from Kurt Hess / Agnew Moyer Smith*)

Windows Wow! Glossary of Terms

Ctrl **Alt**	**Ctrl** will always refer to the Ctrl (Control) key. **Alt** will always refer to the Alt key, and is used to modify many of the tools.
←↑→↓	The keyboard Arrow keys: Left, Up, Right, Down.
Toggle	Menu selection acts as a switch: choosing once turns on, again turns it off.
Marquee	With any Selection tool, click-drag from your page over object(s) to select.
Hinged curve	A Bézier curve that meets a line or another curve at a corner.
Direct Selection tool **Group Selection tool** **Selection tool**	Direct Selection tool selects points and paths. Group Selection tool. The first click always selects the entire object, subsequent clicks select "next group-up" in the grouping order. Selection tool (selects the biggest grouping which includes that object— if an object is ungrouped, then only that object is selected). **Note:** *See the* Basics *chapter for more on selection tools.*
Select object(s)	Click on or marquee with Group Selection tool to select entire object. Click on or marquee with the regular Selection tool to select grouped objects.
Deselect object(s)	To Deselect *one* object, Shift-click (or Shift-marquee) with Group Selection tool. To Deselect *all* selected objects, with any selection tool, click outside of all objects (but within your document), or press Shift-Ctrl-A.
Select a path	Click on a path with the Direct Selection tool to select it. **Note:** *If objects are selected, Deselect first,* then *click with Direct Selection tool.*
Select anchor points	Click on path with Direct Selection tool to see anchor points. Then, Direct-select marquee around the points you want selected. Or, with Direct Selection tool, Shift-click on points you want selected. **Note:** *Clicking on a selected point with Shift key down deselects that point.*
Grab an object or point	After selecting objects or points, use Direct Selection tool to click and hold down mouse button and drag to transform entire selection. **Note:** *If you click by mistake (instead of click-and-hold), Undo and try again.*
Delete an object	Group-Select the object and press the Delete (or Backspace) key. To delete grouped objects, use the Selection tool, then Delete.
Delete a path	Direct-Select a path and press the Delete (or Backspace) key. If you delete an anchor point, both paths attached to that anchor point will be deleted. **Note:** *After deleting part of an object the entire remaining object will become selected; therefore, deleting twice will always delete the entire object!*
Copy or Cut a path	Click on a path with Direct Selection tool, then Copy (Ctrl-C) or Cut (Ctrl-X). **Note:** *See the "Windows Finger Dance Summary" for more ways to copy paths.*
Copy or Cut an object	Click on an object with Group Selection tool, then Copy (Ctrl-C) or Cut (Ctrl-X). For grouped objects, Click on one of the objects with the Selection tool, then Copy (Ctrl-C) or Cut (Ctrl-X).